Dying for the nation

Manchester University Press

Cultural History of Modern War
Series editors

Ana Carden-Coyne, Peter Gatrell, Max Jones, Penny Summerfield and Bertrand Taithe

Already published

Carol Acton and Jane Potter *Working in a world of hurt: trauma and resilience in the narratives of medical personnel in warzones*

Julie Anderson *War, disability and rehabilitation in Britain: soul of a nation*

Michael Brown, Anna Maria Barry and Joanne Begiato (eds) *Martial masculinities: Experiencing and imagining the military in the long nineteenth century*

Quintin Colville and James Davey (eds) *A new naval history*

James E. Connolly *The experience of occupation in the Nord, 1914–18: Living with the enemy in First-World-War France*

Lindsey Dodd *French children under the Allied bombs, 1940–45: an oral history*

Rachel Duffett *The stomach for fighting: food and the soldiers of the First World War*

Peter Gatrell and Lyubov Zhvanko (eds) *Europe on the move: Refugees in the era of the Great War*

Christine E. Hallett *Containing trauma: nursing work in the First World War*

Grace Huxford *The Korean War in Britain: Citizenship, selfhood and forgetting*

Jo Laycock *Imagining Armenia: orientalism, ambiguity and intervention*

Chris Millington *From victory to Vichy: veterans in inter-war France*

Duy Lap Nguyen *The unimagined community: imperialism and culture in South Vietnam*

Juliette Pattinson *Behind enemy lines: gender, passing and the Special Operations Executive in the Second World War*

Chris Pearson *Mobilizing nature: the environmental history of war and militarization in Modern France*

Jeffrey S. Reznick *Healing the nation: soldiers and the culture of caregiving in Britain during the Great War*

Jeffrey S. Reznick *John Galsworthy and disabled soldiers of the Great War: with an illustrated selection of his writings*

Michael Roper *The secret battle: emotional survival in the Great War*

Penny Summerfield and Corinna Peniston-Bird *Contesting home defence: men, women and the Home Guard in the Second World War*

Trudi Tate and Kate Kennedy (eds) *The silent morning: culture and memory after the Armistice*

Spiros Tsoutsoumpis *The People's Armies: a history of the Greek resistance*

Laura Ugolini *Civvies: middle-class men on the English Home Front, 1914–18*

Wendy Ugolini *Experiencing war as the 'enemy other': Italian Scottish experience in World War II*

Colette Wilson *Paris and the Commune, 1871–78: the politics of forgetting*

https://www.alc.manchester.ac.uk/history/research/centres/cultural-history-of-war//

Dying for the nation

Death, grief and bereavement in Second World War Britain

LUCY NOAKES

Manchester University Press

Copyright © Lucy Noakes 2020

The right of Lucy Noakes to be identified as the author of this work has been asserted by her in accordance with the Copyright, Designs and Patents Act 1988.

Published by Manchester University Press
Oxford Road, Manchester M13 9PL
www.manchesteruniversitypress.co.uk

British Library Cataloguing-in-Publication Data
A catalogue record for this book is available from the British Library

ISBN 978 0 7190 8759 2 hardback
ISBN 978 1 5261 6391 2 paperback

First published 2020
Paperback published 2022

The publisher has no responsibility for the persistence or accuracy of URLs for any external or third-party internet websites referred to in this book, and does not guarantee that any content on such websites is, or will remain, accurate or appropriate.

Typeset by Deanta Global Publishing Services

Contents

	Acknowledgements	vi
	Introduction: death, grief and bereavement in wartime Britain	1
1	Shadowing: death, grief and mourning before the Second World War	21
2	Feeling: the emotional economy of interwar Britain	45
3	Planning: imagining and planning for death in wartime	73
4	Coping: belief and agency in wartime	101
5	Dying: death and destruction of the body in war	125
6	Burying: the disposal of the war's dead	155
7	Grieving: bereavement, grief and the emotional labour of wartime	193
8	Remembering: remembering and commemorating the dead of war	229
	Conclusion: the personal and the political	265
	Bibliography	271
	Index	291

Acknowledgements

This book has been a long time in the making. While I have worked, in various ways, on the Second World War for over twenty years, I have always circled cautiously around what war does to human beings, both emotionally and physically. This book is an attempt to get to grips with death, which is at the heart of war – its management, and what it leaves behind. The impact of war on the human body, and the emotional, political and cultural responses to this, are the focus of this study.

I have been the beneficiary of research support and funding that has made visits to British national and local history archives possible. Thanks to the University of Brighton, and especially to Paddy Maguire, head of the School of Humanities, and to the History Department at the University of Essex. Thanks also to the archivists and librarians who have made this research easier and often, despite the subject matter, pleasurable. The staff of Bristol City Archives; the British Library; Clydebank Local History Centre; the Commonwealth War Graves Commission; Coventry City Archives; Glamorgan County Archives; Hackney Archives; Hull History Centre; the Imperial War Museum; London Metropolitan Archives; the Mass Observation Archive in the Keep, Brighton; the Mitchell Library, Glasgow; Newham Local History Centre; the National Archives in London and the National Records of Scotland in Edinburgh; the Public Record Office of Northern Ireland; Plymouth City Archives; and the Wolfson Centre, Library of Birmingham all provided invaluable help with the research for this book, often directing me to sources that I wouldn't otherwise have discovered. Particular thanks go to Max Dutton at the Commonwealth War Graves Commission, for sharing his research on headstone inscriptions. I wish to thank the trustees of Mass Observation for permission to quote from the archive. My editor at Manchester University

Acknowledgements

Press, Emma Brennan, has been both supportive and extremely patient, as deadlines were passed time and time again.

Colleagues and students at the universities of Brighton and Essex provided wonderful environments within which this research developed and, I hope, matured. The often unacknowledged work that scholars around the world put into organising research seminars, workshops, colloquia and conferences is recognised, and thanked, here. The opportunity to share my 'work in progress' at research seminars and symposia at the universities of Cambridge, Edinburgh, Essex, Hanyang, Seoul, Lancaster, Kent, King's College London, Madison-Wisconsin, Manchester, Mississippi, Oldenburg, Oxford, Sussex and Warwick and invitations and opportunities to speak at the British Academy; the Library of Congress in Washington, DC; the North American Conference on British Studies; the Arts and Humanities Research Council 'Passions of War' International Research Network led by Philip Shaw at the University of Leicester; and the Social History Society Annual Conference, provided rich and valuable feedback from colleagues and helped to shape this work in numerous ways. For thought-provoking conversations, for hospitality and especially for their generosity in sharing their own ideas and research, I would particularly like to thank Afxentis Afxentiou, Alan Allport, Stephen Brooke, Joanna Bourke, Ian Cantoni, Mark Connelly, Alison Fell, Matthew Grant, Garitoitz Gomez Afaro, Rae Frances, Yasmin Khan, Senia Paseta, Bruce Scates, Kasia Tomasiewicz and Dan Todman. All errors are, of course, my own.

I am lucky to be surrounded by a generation of wonderful female historians, many of whom have become friends as well as inspiring colleagues. Sue Grayzel, Claire Langhamer, Tracey Loughran, Kate Newby, Helen Parr, Gill Plain and Penny Summerfield all read parts of this book, and were ready with wit, kindness and good coffee or wine whenever it was needed. Dorothy Sheridan has been, as ever, an inspiration and a role model of how to conduct thoughtful and ethical research.

I am also lucky in my family and in the times that I live in: my children, Hannah, Calum and Skye, have been able to grow up unscathed by the horrors of war, but with compassion for the many whose lives are still destroyed and thrown into chaos by this most terrible of human actions. I recognise my luck in being a woman living at this point in history. Growing up at the tail end of the welfare state, I benefited from a stable household income and a fantastic comprehensive school education, where I was taught by committed teachers who had the time

Acknowledgements

to help us imagine other worlds and opportunities. I attended university on a full state grant. Thanks to my family and to feminism I never doubted that the world was as much mine as it was that of men, or of the wealthy and powerful. I have been able to combine a rewarding career with an equally rewarding family life; I hope that my children and my students have the same opportunities.

Finally, I am lucky in my partner, Martin Evans, whose appalling and endless jokes provided a welcome distraction from the grim nature of much of the research that informed this book. With his own deadlines, he still found time to listen to me talk endlessly about this project, and to read the manuscript with the care and tact that a partner needs to show when asked to be a critical friend. It's a thankless task, and I promise to do the same for him some day.

Lucy Noakes
Brighton, 2019

Introduction
Death, grief and bereavement in wartime Britain

Mrs Lane's loss

By the end of the Second World War, approximately 369,405 British nationals, both combatant and civilian, had been killed.[1] Among these were the four sons of Mrs Lane, a middle-aged woman from North London. Mrs Lane's sons had all been members of the Royal Air Force (RAF): Donald had been killed during the retreat to Dunkirk in June 1940, Desmond in September 1942, John in March 1943 and Patrick, her oldest son, in a flying accident in January 1945. Only her daughter, Sheila, had survived the war. The loss of four of her five children must have been devastating, yet, according to an interview in the *News Chronicle* soon after Patrick's death, she 'felt no bitterness'. Instead, she claimed, 'it is a glorious thing to have brought up and educated four sons who never gave me a moment's trouble and who have now so willingly given their lives for their country'. In her pride in her sons and their sacrifice, Mrs Lane gave voice to a form of maternal, wartime bereavement which chimed with the mood of a nation that had endured over five years of war, with all its losses and heartaches. Like so many others, her sons had died for the nation. Now her grief had to work for the national war effort.

Yet a closer reading of Mrs Lane's interview in the *News Chronicle* does tell us more of the impact of wartime loss. While her sons may have been dead, their presence was still visible in her home. The interview took place in her Hampstead flat, next to 'a sideboard covered with photographs and snapshots of "the boys"'. The ongoing emotional labour of grief, and Mrs Lane's daily struggle with her loss, also became clear in her remark, 'in a voice little more than a whisper', that 'the future seems so frighteningly empty, but I try not to think about it. If

I give way to my feelings I feel that I should be letting the boys down.'[2] Surrounded by material reminders of her sons' lives, Mrs Lane faced a daily struggle not to yield to her feelings of loss, fear and grief, as such a capitulation risked not only undermining her efforts to make pride in their sacrifice her foremost emotion, but also 'letting down' their memory. If she surrendered to her grief, she felt, she would be undermining both the victory that her sons had died for and the imagined collective of the wartime nation. Grief, particularly in wartime, has a political value, and the grief of bereaved mothers – when it can be put to work for the nation, mobilised to support ideas of willing sacrifice and parental pride – is of especially high value.

Mrs Lane's bereavement, and her grief, occurred in a particular time and place and, as such, have a history. The outbreak of war in 1939 meant that the violent death of loved ones in conflict once again became a reality for many, just twenty-one years after the end of the First World War. The emotional economy in which these deaths were anticipated, experienced and mourned shaped the ways in which people gave voice to grief, bereavement was experienced and loss was felt. Like Mrs Lane, many laboured to control their feelings, worried that by 'giving way' to grief they would be both letting down the memories of those they had lost and undermining the stoicism and determination to 'carry on' that was articulated again and again during the war years. This book tells something of their struggle, writing the history of death, grief and bereavement into the wider history of Britain's Second World War.

Death and the 'people's war'

This book places death, and the grief that so often accompanied it, at the heart of our understanding of Britain's Second World War. The dominant cultural memory of the British experience of this war that circulates in Britain in the second decade of the twenty-first century has little space for representations of death, of grief or of bereavement. It is, as all memories must be, a partial story of the war years – one that centres around stories of national unity, decency, stoicism and good humour that work to illustrate how the vast majority of the British people united across divisions of class and political affiliation to fight the common enemy of fascism. At the war's end they were rewarded for their steadfastness by the creation of the welfare state promised by economist William Beveridge in the *Social Insurance and Allied Services Report* of 1942. While the cultural memory of the Great War at

Introduction

its centenary between 2014 and 2018 continued to be shaped by stories of death, sacrifice and suffering, there is little space for such stories in British imaginings of the Second World War.

The reasons for this are complex. In Britain, despite the ubiquity of war memorials in shared public spaces and civic sites, there is no national memorial to victims of the Blitz. Furthermore, although there were earlier regional sites of remembrance, including the Air Forces Memorial at Runnymede, a central London memorial to the dead of Bomber Command was only erected in 2012, the decision to do so shedding light on the ongoing debate about the legitimacy of the 'bombing war' and the targeting of German and other civilians by Bomber Command between 1942 and 1945.[3] The war's military dead are largely remembered in public culture in the lists of names added to the memorials erected following the Great War. The decision taken in the years following the war's end to officially commemorate the dead of both wars on Remembrance Sunday, the Sunday closest to Armistice Day on 11 November, and to maintain the rituals of remembrance developed for Armistice Day in the 1920s, meant that it has usually been the dead of the First World War, outnumbering the military dead of the Second by almost half a million, who are at the centre of this shared ritual. More broadly, while the end of the Cold War saw the unravelling of many 'official' memories of the war in Europe and the destabilisation of some foundational myths of national unity and resistance, British cultural memory remained largely unchallenged, able to maintain the affectionate, nostalgic and congratulatory tone that had shaped many popular and influential cultural texts since the 1950s.[4] While the growth of public interest in the Holocaust, and the centrality of this genocide to understandings of the Second World War in Europe and North America, worked to open up space for other memories of trauma, death, fear and grief on the public stage, these have remained marginal to the cultural memory of the war, at least in Britain.[5]

In part, this is because there was little space for images of death or narratives of grief during the war itself, or in its immediate aftermath. To maintain morale, and to avoid providing information to the Luftwaffe on the success or otherwise of bombing raids, numbers of casualties and names of towns and cities targeted by the bombers were often withheld, leading some in heavily bombed cities like Liverpool and towns like Clydebank to feel that their suffering was secondary to that of London. When the aftermath of air raids was reported, as it was in Coventry in November 1940, coverage included the dead but emphasised the determination and steadfastness of the survivors. In contrast, the experience of Bristol, described by Mass Observation in the social survey organisation's report for the Ministry of Information as showing 'quite open defeatism' and 'wishful thinking about the war soon being over' after repeated bombing raids, received little coverage in the national media.[6] However, descriptions of death and injury were not entirely absent from the war years. While letters from friends and relatives in the military were censored to avoid the accidental disclosure of battle and strategic plans, many of the sources drawn upon in this study show that letters home and memoirs written during the war, such as that of the soldier poet Keith Douglas, often contained graphic descriptions of the impact of weaponry on the human body, and reflections on the death of comrades and friends.[7] As Mary Lou Roberts and Alan Allport have both shown, the physical and sensory presence of the human corpse on the battlefield both fascinated and repelled combatants, reminding them not only of what war had done to the bodies of others, but what it could, potentially, do to their own.[8] It is testament to the powers of the dominant emotional economy and of wartime popular culture, in which death was usually marginal, often unseen, and news of which almost always received with stoicism, that personal reflections like these have made little impact on the dominant cultural memory of the war.

The emotional economy of wartime, which valued stoicism and self-control over emotional expressiveness, shaped both these cultural representations and the ways in which individuals and families discussed death and grief. In the war's aftermath, the dead had little presence on the public stage. Unlike the dead of the Great War, they were not remembered through new national rituals of shared mourning and remembrance, and few new war memorials were erected, names instead usually being added to the existing memorials to the dead of the Great War. The prevailing mood favoured what were termed 'living memorials' over stone edifices whose only function was to memorialise; the dead of the Second World War were to be remembered through the work of the living to build a better world, more prosaically through the creation of new recreation and sports grounds, the building of homes and hospital wings, and the opening up of tracts of land for public leisure through the establishment of the Land Fund in 1946. While this desire to remember the dead through improvements in the lives of those they fought and died for tells us something of the meanings of the 'people's war' for those who lived through it, it also meant

Introduction

that, as the dead being commemorated slipped from living memory, the lack of memorials 'visibly and permanently' associated with the dead meant that they also, often, slipped out of public consciousness.[9] With so little public and cultural space for remembrance of the war's dead, personal memories of those killed only rarely found a larger audience. Sometimes the war's dead were not even spoken of in their own families, the lack of a language of grief, or a formal architecture of remembrance, acting to silence memories and make the articulation of loss impossible.[10] The emotional culture of restraint and the concurrent lack of public space for expressions of wartime grief and postwar loss have combined to marginalise the war's dead, and the grief of the bereaved, in the dominant British cultural memory of the war.

Counting the dead

As a 'total' war, using new weaponry and involving entire populations of nation-states around the world, the costs of the war were almost unimaginably high. In Britain alone, the first two years of the war saw government expenditure as a percentage of the gross domestic product leap from 19.6 per cent in 1939 to 47.2 per cent by 1941. In the same period, spending on defence grew from £626 million in 1939 to £4,085 million by 1941.[11] In 1941, 75.1 thousand tons of raw materials were lost at sea, most of it to the U-boats prowling the ocean during the Battle of the Atlantic.[12] The rural landscape was changed irrevocably, with large areas of southern grassland being lost to the plough and hundreds of acres in the east of England requisitioned for use as bases by the RAF and the US Army Air Force.[13] By the war's end, the Lend-Lease programme, in operation since 1941, meant the British Empire was in debt to the United States to the tune of $30,073 million.[14] Other costs, and costs outside Britain, were even greater. The American air force lost 6,571 of its aircraft in the bombing war over Europe; in the most deadly air raid of the war, on Tokyo in March 1945, 16 square miles of the city were burnt to the ground, and more than 100,000 people were killed in one night.[15] Japan itself lost approximately 12,000 aircraft during the war, and over 5 million tons of shipping.[16] Over 30 million people lost years of their lives as prisoners of war.[17] The costs of war were multiple, complex and vast.

The most important cost was in lives lost. The war came at a time of falling mortality rates in Britain, when rising standards of living together with the introduction of mass vaccination programmes had, for example, brought about a fall in the annual number of deaths in infants under one year old from 89,380 in 1915 to 34,092 in 1935. The year 1940 saw 581,000 deaths registered in the United Kingdom, excluding military deaths overseas, the highest figure since 1918 – when the Spanish influenza epidemic contributed to the 611,000 deaths registered – and an increase of 103,000 on the last full year of peace in 1938.[18] While the majority of these deaths were not directly attributable to the war, the rise in mortality was nonetheless an aberration in a long-term trend of declining death rates. Though the 1945 tally of all the British war dead was substantially lower than that in 1918, it encompassed civilian as well as military victims: 63,635 civilians died as a result of 'operations of war', some lost at sea but the majority killed in air raids. The majority of these were killed in the wave of air raids known as the Blitz between September 1940 and May 1941, but others died in the 1942 Baedeker raids on small provincial towns and cities; the 'little Blitz' of 1944, which targeted London and its environs; and the V1 and V2 rocket attacks of 1944 and 1945.[19] The majority of those who died, however, were combatants. Bomber Command, with its multinational crews – made up of men from Britain, Canada, Australia and other Commonwealth countries, Poland and Czechoslovakia – had the highest fatality rate of any of the armed services. Over 55,000 of the 125,000 men who served with Bomber Command were killed, some in accidents but most shot down while flying on the bombing missions that devastated towns and cities in Germany and Occupied Europe, killing hundreds of thousands of civilians on the ground.[20] In total, 264,443 members of the armed forces, the women's auxiliary services and the merchant navy were killed during the war. Most of the military dead, 144,079, were killed while serving in the army, and the majority of these, 121,484, died in Europe, in the war against Germany.[21] Of the soldiers who died as a direct result of enemy action, 68,401 were infantry, at the front line of most battles.[22]

Large though these figures are, they are small in comparison to the numbers of dead in many other combatant countries. The chaos of war, and the sheer scale of the numbers involved, means that accuracy in the counting of the dead has often proven impossible. Between 10 million and 20 million are estimated to have perished in China between 1937 and 1945, and 27 million to 28 million of the war's dead were citizens of the Soviet Union.[23] Many millions were murdered in Nazi death camps or by units of the SS, the *Einsatzgruppen* and local collaborators. The Bengal famine of 1943 led to the deaths of 2.1 million to 3 million.[24] It is estimated that the total number of war dead by 1945 was in excess of 60 million.[25] More, of course, would die as a consequence of the war's multiple legacies: of cold and hunger in Europe, of disease and war wounds, and while trying to travel home at the war's end. The Second World War caused the deaths of more people than any other war in recorded history.

The figures pale in comparison to the numbers anticipated in the interwar years. The imagined 'war to come' was envisaged as killing hundreds of thousands in Britain alone. The experience of death and loss in the Great War combined with the fear of aerial warfare to produce a potent and apocalyptic vision of any future war. Memories of poison gas and explosives on the Western Front, the legacies of which were still visible in the bodies and minds of many veterans, together with the rise of the bomber, framed expectations of deaths that would be both numerous and horrible. In the 1930s, wars in China, Abyssinia and Spain demonstrated that in the age of the aeroplane, nobody would be safe. In the future, front lines would run through homes, schools and factories rather than trenches.

Those tasked with the counting of the war dead would have to include civilians alongside combatants, themselves only really deemed worthy of counting and naming by the British state since the Great War.[26] The responsibility assumed by the state during this war, for naming, burying (where possible) and commemorating the war's dead, was driven by the impact on Britain of total war. In a newly democratic age, when the vast majority of British men and women were able to vote, the sense that the state would protect them to the best of its abilities, and that it would honour their sacrifice if they should die, was crucial to the successful prosecution of war. Newly central to war, civilians would lie with combatants among the dead at the war's end. As the world moved inexorably towards a second total war, the political importance of the dead to the state was matched only by the strength of their emotional significance for the living.

Managing the dead

The ongoing impact of death and loss in the Great War, together with changing technologies of warfare and the increasingly apocalyptic imaginings of war in the 1930s combined to ensure that both the state and people recognised that the coming war would have a high cost in lives lost, and that the management of this would be key to morale.[27]

Total war threatened the very notions of liberty and freedom that Britain and its allies claimed to be fighting for; individual agency was curtailed by the multiple demands of war which included, crucially, that the individual citizen be ready to give up their life, and the lives of loved ones, for the wider, collective war effort. Wartime thus demanded enormous sacrifice from its citizens, but for these sacrifices to be borne, the state's obligations to its citizens had to not only *be* practised, but be *seen* to be practised.

One of these obligations was the management of the war dead. The best ways to prevent and manage the mass death of combatants and civilians in the war that was to come were widely debated across government departments in the late 1930s. However, while civil defence was widely publicised, through the establishment of the Air Raids Protection Department of the Home Office in 1937, planning for the management of the war's civilian dead was highly secret. Fears about morale, the undermining of which was understood as central to the practise of modern warfare, meant that while mass death was widely anticipated, official preparations for war focused on its prevention. The evacuation of civilians, mainly young children, from towns and cities; the provision of gas masks and air raid shelters; and the establishment of civil defence bodies all helped to protect civilians from harm. Civilians who joined the armed services, recruited under the National Service Acts, had to rely on their training and the training of those around them to protect them, while the Imperial War Graves Commission's management of the dead of the Great War was widely understood as evidencing the state's care for, and honouring of, those who died as combatants. If badly managed, death was bad for morale; if managed well, the dead could continue to work for the war effort.

Morale was important because the lives, thoughts, feelings and actions of the people were important. This was especially true in a democracy facing total war. While authoritarian states like Nazi Germany and the Soviet Union could rely to an extent on coercion to ensure the participation of their citizenry in the war, democracies relied to a greater degree on consent, seen as both more appropriate, and more effective, than coercion alone.[28] If people felt unprotected by the state, then they also felt undervalued and were thus less likely to be willing participants when asked by the state to take on the burdens of warfare. If they felt that their death or the deaths of loved ones in war was a likelihood, and if they felt that these deaths were not properly valued by the state, consent was again less likely to be forthcoming. The state thus had

Introduction

to convince people both that it would do its utmost to protect them and that, if they died, it would honour this sacrifice.

The state could thus plan for the management of death in war and attempt to convince people that it would try to protect them and that the sacrifice of the dead was both worthwhile and valued by the nation. But this planning, and the management of death, could only go so far. The management of grief – itself central to the war effort – could not be legislated for. Instead, the feelings of the people at war were to be self-managed within an emotional economy that valued restraint, stoicism and self-control.

Feelings in wartime

By the middle of the twentieth century, the management of feeling was important. And it was even more important in a war that drew on the participation and sacrifice of a democratic citizenry. The social survey organisation Mass Observation, which was employed by the Ministry of Information during the war to collect and assess information on morale, certainly saw people's feelings as central to the war effort. In its first publication, *Mass Observation*, the organisation was described as a 'weather map of popular feeling'.[29] By 1940 Mass Observation was promoting itself as having observers who were 'in close touch with the feelings, rumours, behaviour in ordinary homes', and a national panel of directive respondents and diarists whose value lay in their position as 'subjective reporters' whose responses to and feelings about the conduct of the war provided valuasble access to shared attitudes and thus to morale.[30] The work of Mass Observation, drawn upon throughout this book, both tells us of the interest in feeling, in emotion, during the war and allows us to explore not only the ways in which people experienced war but how they *felt* about this experience.

Emotions are at the heart of war. Their mobilisation and management can enable members of collectives like the nation-state, the military battalion and the munitions factory to feel a sense of shared identity, aims and purpose; if they are not mobilised or managed effectively, they can undermine morale, and lead to a lack of support for war aims and operations. Pride, fear, anger, love, hope and grief have all proven to be effective drivers of individual and shared war enthusiasm. Equally, these emotions can act to challenge and weaken support for war.

Historical interest in emotions in war can be traced back to the work of the Annales historians Marc Bloch and Lucien Febvre. Bloch and

Febvre both understood that not only did emotions have a history but they could help to *shape* history. Their own experiences of total war, and of the success that the demagogues of the mid-twentieth century had in mobilising emotions, undoubtedly shaped these early historical studies of the role of emotions in wartime. Bloch's 1921 essay on the power of rumour in war linked this to the feelings of villagers in France living close to the front line, scared and exhausted by years of war.[31] The linguist Albert Dauzat, writing in 1919, had made a similar argument, suggesting that a popular belief in France that the deadly Spanish Flu of 1918 was, in fact, cholera gained purchase through a combination of grief and a lack of trust in authority after four long years of war.[32] Febvre, writing at the outbreak of the Second World War and observing the popular appeal of fascism and Nazism, urged contemporaries to analyse feelings and sensibilities in their historical research.[33] It was not until the emergence of social, and then cultural, history, however, in the second half of the twentieth century that historians began to take up this challenge. Social and cultural history provided the tools to examine the history of warfare beyond the parameters of military strategy and high politics. Gender and feminist history, and oral history, with their interrogation of experience, subjectivity and memory, enabled a wave of writing on the ways in which individuals experience, imagine and remember wars and on the impact this can have on their sense of self. From this work emerged a body of writing that has explicitly set out to explore a wartime history of emotions.

This research has taken many different avenues. Some scholars have examined the history of what psychologists term 'primary' or 'basic' emotions in wartime: Jan Plamper, for example, traces the evolution of a language of fear among Russian soldiers, showing how fear was absent from soldiers' descriptions of battle in 1812 but central to their stories of the First World War. Richard Bessel has shown how hatred, as a powerful legacy of war, can motivate individual action and be mobilised by the nation-state seeking to build new alliances and loyalties in the aftermath of conflict. But war can also provide the conditions for other forms of emotional experience and expression. Holly Furneaux and Claire Langhamer have explored, respectively, the emotional, empathetic impulse towards care-giving expressed by participants in the Crimean War, and the centrality of the social, cultural, political and economic shifts of the Second World War to changing experiences and expectations of romantic love in Britain. Others have studied the ways in which individuals experiencing the often violent disruptions of wartime, and finding ways to live with its multiple legacies, have sought emotional support or have communicated their experiences in an emotional language, or through an emotional performance, that is historically situated within, and shaped by, these very disruptions. As this growing body of scholarship shows, not only do emotions have a history and a politics, but this history and politics shape the ways in which historical actors are able to comprehend, and express, their experiences.[34]

Studies of emotions in wartime have drawn upon a rich body of research that has worked to conceptualise and explore the wider history of emotions. Peter and Carol Stearns' ground-breaking work on the social meaning of emotions, William Reddy's *The Navigation of Emotion* and Barbara Rosenwein's concept of emotional communities have all shaped the field of the history of emotions.[35] These texts, and others that followed them, have provided tools with which to explore the historically specific meaning of terms like 'fear' and 'love', and the multiple ways in which historical actors have used a language of emotion to try and articulate the subjective impact of experience, both to themselves and to others.[36] The feminist theorist Sara Ahmed has urged work on the emotions to explore the kinds of work that emotions themselves can do. Ahmed argues that the pertinent question for a study of emotions should not be 'What are emotions?', but rather 'What do emotions do?'[37]

Ahmed's assertion has been particularly useful to this study of death, grief and bereavement in wartime, as it foregrounds the labour that emotions can undertake. Emotions can be put to work by the state, as seen, for example, in the creation of official rituals of remembrance and in the organisation of the mass burials of victims of air raids. People can be encouraged to work on their own emotional self-knowledge and self-management, enabling many in wartime to exhibit stoicism and self-control when faced with the multiple and often terrible effects of war. And emotions can be a form of work in themselves, as individuals work hard to communicate their feelings in a manner that is acceptable not only to others but also to themselves as they labour to control, endure and survive the impact of disruptive emotions like grief. These emotions are felt, and expressed, in the world, shaped by environment and by cultural process. As Laura Kounine has argued, 'we need to understand emotions not just as inchoate feelings but as bodily practices that are culturally and historically situated'.[38] Emotions are historically specific, and as such they have historically specific meanings and value.

This study uses the term 'emotional economy' to discuss the meaning and value of emotions in wartime Britain, as it provides a means of thinking about the worth and importance of emotions when they were expressed and performed in particular ways, the ways in which emotions and emotional guidance circulated and the emotional labour that often underpinned this. For example, Mrs Lane's expression of pride in her sons' wartime deaths was obviously of high value in a nation at war: her claim to find consolation in the belief that their deaths had been for a shared cause acted as a model for the many other bereaved. But this consolation was hard won, the emotional labour that underpinned it clearly shown in the description of her surroundings and her voice.[39] If the interviewer for the *News Chronicle* had found her tearing her hair and rending her clothes, both in themselves means of communicating grief deemed appropriate in different times and places, then her grief would have been of little value to the emotional economy of wartime.[40] Its value lay in the ways in which her performance of bereavement followed a model that, as this study will show, was to be found in many wartime texts: control, restraint and the claim to find consolation in sacrifice. In wartime, the ways in which the British people expressed emotion were experienced within, valued and shaped by the demands of a nation at war. One of these demands was that grief should be borne in a manner that worked to support the collective war effort.

Death, grief and bereavement in wartime

This book traces the history of death, grief and bereavement in Britain in the Second World War, and in the years preceding and immediately following the war's end. This period is a time when British practices around bereavement, and ways of expressing and communicating grief, underwent profound shifts. Broadly, as shown by the historian Pat Jalland, British attitudes to death, grief and bereavement have been understood as moving from the expressive grieving, elaborate bereavement practices and familiarity with death of the mid-nineteenth century to the virtual disappearance of death and its surrounding rituals from everyday life by the 1960s.[41] Falling mortality rates and the increased medicalisation of death saw the deaths of many move from the home to the hospital, with medical staff and undertakers increasingly more likely than family members to care for the dead body and to prepare it for disposal. The anthropologist Geoffrey Gorer argued in the 1960s that this shift, together with increasing secularisation and an emotional economy that valued stoicism and restraint, had led to a silence around death and an embarrassment at grief that caused misery and isolation for the bereaved, not only unable to communicate their sorrow to others but denying its impact on themselves.[42] At the heart of these shifts was the experience of the Second World War.

Three arguments are developed in this book, interwoven throughout the chapters and interlinked with one another. The first argument is that in a democracy at war, death matters. It always matters, of course, to individuals faced with the chance of their own death as a result of conflict, and to the bereaved and those threatened with bereavement. But it matters in wartime more to a democracy than to other political formations, as the thoughts, feelings and commitment of the people to the war effort are crucial. When states at war rely on consent as well as coercion, they have to work hard to ensure this consent. And in times of total war, with its multiple and often unrelenting demands, they have to work still harder. The Britain that fought the Second World War was a mass democracy, but this was a democracy that was new, and whose coherence and stability could not be taken for granted.[43] While war helped to unify the nation against external enemies, it also tested this cohesion. The ways in which the British state managed the death of its civilians killed during the war, in the military and in civilian life, was crucial to the maintenance of consent.

The second argument developed in this book is that the dead can continue to work for the nation in wartime. The dead bodies of kings, queens and other political leaders have long done this work, interred in cathedrals and mausoleums and functioning as symbolic sites of national history and identity, as well as tourist attractions. Such bodies, however, can also be disruptive and divisive. The Spanish government's plans to remove the remains of the dictator General Franco from the Valley of the Fallen outside Madrid, and the angry and emotional responses to these plans, for example, demonstrate the political power that can be imbued in a body and the ways in which these bodies can still divide people and societies, long after their death. In the two total wars of the twentieth century, the bodies of 'ordinary' people were also put to work. While the burial of the body of the Unknown Warrior in Westminster Abbey in 1920 is probably the best-known instance of a body being put to work by the British state, functioning as a symbol of sacrifice, of shared loss and of imperial gratitude, the Second World

War saw multiple bodies working for the nation, the 'ordinary' dead serving to represent steadfastness, dedication and a shared determination to win the war. This work, however, was by no means assured; at times the dead were understood as representing the failures of the state, most notably its failure to care for and protect the bodies of its citizens.

The final argument is that war, and especially the Second World War, is central to the development of an emotional economy that valued stoicism and restraint over a more expressive emotional culture. In this, it built on the changes brought about by the experience of the Great War. It may seem strange that a book focusing on the period between 1939 and 1945 begins some twenty-five years earlier, with the war of 1914–1918. However, British people in the Second World War experienced the conflict within an emotional economy that did not emerge fully formed in 1939, but which itself had a history, one that was profoundly shaped by the need to manage grief and bereavement during and after the First World War. The emotional economy of mid-century Britain, this book argues, was one that not only placed a high value on stoicism in the face of death, and restraint in the articulation of grief, but asked its citizens to manage this through careful work on the self. The bereaved of the Second World War experienced and felt their bereavement in an emotional economy that emphasised the desirability of controlling individual grief as a means of both overcoming individual sorrow and contributing to the war effort.

The structure of the book is broadly chronological, and it has three themes: emotional responses to death in wartime, and the management of these responses by individuals, by an emotional culture and by the British state; the management of death and the corpse in wartime, and attempts to ensure that the dead continued to work, symbolically, for the nation; and the commemoration and memorialisation of the dead in the immediate postwar period. Chapter 1 examines the multiple legacies of the Great War for the emotional economy of the following decades, but also traces the history of death, grief and bereavement in Britain back to the nineteenth century, considering the ways in which the Great War furthered pre-existing shifts in understandings of bereavement and expectations of grief. Chapters 2 and 3 look at the interwar period. Chapter 2 explores the management of feeling in this period and the growth of an emotional economy that encouraged individuals to be self-reflective to cope with the multiple demands of modern life, while Chapter 3 examines the ways in which a growing awareness of the need to manage mass death in wartime shaped

Introduction

plans for war in the 1930s. Chapters 4, 5, 6 and 7 focus on death, grief and bereavement during the war years. Chapter 4 considers the extent to which people facing another total war drew on ritual, superstition and religion for emotional support, and outlines contemporary beliefs about death, life after death and the ongoing presence of the dead in the world. In Chapter 5, the multiple ways in which modern warfare could injure and kill the human body are outlined, together with the ways in which the state attempted to use these bodies and to protect them from harm. Chapter 6 focuses on wartime burial practice, considering the ways in which the state tried to ensure the symbolic stability of the dead, and how the bereaved responded both to violent wartime death and to the state's treatment of the bodies of their loved ones. In Chapter 7 attention turns to grief, the emotional response to bereavement, the emotional economy within which grief was experienced and articulated and the individual experiences of some of those bereaved by war. Chapter 8 examines the immediate postwar period, assessing the emotional and memorial afterlife of the war and considering the multiple ways in which the war's dead were remembered, grieved for and memorialised.

Outside the historical arguments of this book, its central purpose is to remind us that war destroys lives. In this it is not alone. Thomas Laqueur's wide-ranging exploration of the cultural work of mortal remains details the necessity of remembering the dead, and the drive to inscribe the names of war's dead on to the tombstones and monuments of the twentieth century's total wars.[44] Jay Winter's work on mourning and the aftermath of war reminds us of the impact of this destruction long after peace treaties have been signed.[45] Thomas Dixon has traced the history of tears in Britain, showing the influence of the two World Wars on the spread and gradual decline of a 'death taboo', and a culture of isolation in bereavement, in the second half of the twentieth century.[46] Drew Gilpin Faust's *This Republic of Suffering* placed death and grief at the heart of the experience of the US Civil War.[47] Pat Jalland's history of death and bereavement in England highlights the ways in which mass death in wartime shaped both bereavement practices and individual lives.[48] Other historical studies have examined wounding in war, both wounds of the body and wounds of the mind, and have worked to remind us that the central purpose of military training is to enable men to kill or maim the enemy.[49] This book looks at what happens when wounds are not healed, and when the aim of killing becomes a reality.

Notes

1. Central Statistical Office, *Fighting with Figures: A Statistical Digest of the Second World War* (London: HMSO, 1995), p. vi.
2. 'Mother of 4 dead sons feels no bitterness', *News Chronicle*, 16 January 1945, p. 2.
3. R. Overy, *The Bombing War: Europe 1939–1945* (London: Allen Lane, 2013).
4. For discussion of the cultural memory of the war in Britain, see M. Connelly, *We Can Take It! Britain and the Memory of the Second World War* (Harlow: Pearson, 2004); G. Eley, 'Finding the "people's war": film, British collective memories and World War II', *The American Historical Review*, 103:3 (2001), pp. 818–38; P. Gilroy, *Postcolonial Melancholia* (London: Routledge, 2004); L. Noakes and J. Pattinson (eds), *British Cultural Memory and the Second World War* (London: Bloomsbury, 2014); P. Summerfield, 'War, film, memory: some reflections on war films and the social configuration of memory in Britain in the 1940s and 1950s', *Journal of War and Culture Studies*, 1:1 (2008), pp. 15–23.
5. For an overview of the shifts in European memory, see D. Stone, 'Memory wars in the "new Europe"', in D. Stone (ed.), *The Oxford Handbook of Postwar European History* (Oxford: Oxford University Press, 2012).
6. Mass Observation (MO), File Report (FR) 529, *Report on the Aftermath of Town Blitzes* (19 December 1940), p. 2.
7. K. Douglas, *Alamein to Zem Zem* (London: Editions Poetry, 1946).
8. A. Allport, *Browned Off and Bloody Minded: The British Soldier Goes to War, 1939–1945* (New Haven, CT: Yale University Press, 2015); M. L. Roberts, 'Five ways to look at a corpse: the military dead in Normandy, 1944', *The Male Body of War* (forthcoming, 2020).
9. *Hansard*, House of Lords Debate (HoL), 5:134, 'War memorials', Archbishop Lang, col. 1038 (14 February 1945).
10. Some examples of this silence are discussed in Chapter 8, but probably the best known is the belief among many of the survivors, and the bereaved, of the disaster at Bethnal Green Underground station in 1943 that it was never to be spoken of.
11. D. Todman, *Britain's War: Into Battle 1937–1941* (London: Penguin, 2016), pp. 588–89.
12. Central Statistical Office, *Fighting with Figures*, Table 6.23, 'Losses of raw materials at sea', p. 147.
13. For a history of agriculture during the war, see A. Howkins, *The Death of Rural England: A Social History of the Countryside Since 1900* (London: Routledge, 2003), pp. 115–41.
14. Central Statistical Office, *Fighting with Figures*, Table 10.9, 'United States lend-lease aid to the British Empire', p. 225.

Introduction

15 T. Davis Biddle, 'Anglo-American strategic bombing, 1940–1945', in J. Ferris and E. Mawdsley (eds), *The Cambridge History of the Second World War. Volume 1, Fighting the War* (Cambridge: Cambridge University Press, 2015), pp. 485–526, here 509, 521.

16 A. Patalano, 'Feigning grand strategy: Japan, 1937–1945', in Ferris and Mawdsley (eds), *The Cambridge History of the Second World War. Vol. 1*, pp. 159–88, here 182, 185.

17 B. Moore, 'Prisoners of war', in Ferris and Mawdsley (eds), *The Cambridge History of the Second World War. Vol. 1*, pp. 664–89, here 664.

18 Office for National Statistics, *Causes of Death over 100 Years* (18 September 2017), https://www.ons.gov.uk/peoplepopulationandcommunity/births deathsandmarriages/deaths/articles/causesofdeathover100years/2017-09-18 (accessed 11 March 2019).

19 Central Statistical Office, *Fighting with Figures*, Table 2.3, 'Civilian deaths registered: analysis by age and cause. Males', p. 15; Table 2.4, 'Civilian deaths registered: analysis by age and cause. Females', p. 18.

20 The memorial to Bomber Command, erected in Green Park, London, in 2012, gives the figure for those killed as 55,573. It also commemorates the victims of the air raids.

21 Central Statistical Office, *Fighting with Figures*, Table 3.8, 'Casualties suffered during the war by the armed forces, auxiliary services and merchant navy'. A footnote to this table notes that 'These figures include men from overseas fighting in the United Kingdom forces, in particular from Newfoundland and Southern Rhodesia', p. 43.

22 Allport, *Browned Off*, p. 208.

23 R. Bessel, 'Death and survival in the Second World War', in M. Geyer and A. Tooze (eds), *The Cambridge History of the Second World War. Volume 3, Total War: Economy, Society and Culture* (Cambridge: Cambridge University Press, 2015), pp. 252–76, here 254, 258.

24 S. Devereux, 'Famine in the 20th Century', *I.D.S. Working Paper 105* (Brighton: Institute of Development Studies, 2000), p. 5.

25 Bessel, 'Death and survival in the Second World War', in Geyer and Tooze (eds), *The Cambridge History of the Second World War. Vol. 3*, p. 252.

26 T. Laqueur, *The Work of the Dead: A Cultural History of Mortal Remains* (Princeton, NJ: Princeton University Press, 2015), p. 458. As Laqueur shows, moves towards the naming of the military dead by the British state had begun, tentatively, in the nineteenth century.

27 Morale is a slippery and complex term. For a useful discussion, see D. Ussishkin, *Morale: A Modern British History* (Oxford: Oxford University Press, 2017).

28 Ussishkin, *Morale*, p. 5.

29 C. Madge and T. Harrisson, *Mass Observation* (London: Frederick Muller, 1937), p. 30.

30 C. Madge and T. Harrisson, *War Begins at Home* (London: Chatto and Windus, 1940), p. 17, 20.
31 M. Bloch, 'Reflections of a historian on the false news of the war' (1921), trans. J. P. Holoka, *Michigan War Studies Review*, 51 (2013), pp. 1–11.
32 Cited in A. Rasmussen, 'The Spanish Flu', in J. Winter (ed.), *The Cambridge History of the First World War. Volume 3, Civil Society* (Cambridge: Cambridge University Press, 2012), pp. 334–57, here 343.
33 L. Febvre, 'Sensibility and history: how to reconstitute the emotional life of the past' (1941), in P. Burke (ed.), *A New Kind of History: From the Writings of Febvre* (London: Harper & Row, 1973).
34 See, for example, R. Bessel, 'Hatred after war: emotion and the postwar history of East Germany', *History and Memory*, 17 (2005), pp. 195–216; S. Das, 'Indian sepoy experience in Europe, 1914–18: archive, language, and feeling', *Twentieth Century British History*, 25:3 (2014), pp. 391–417; H. Furneaux, *Military Men of Feeling: Emotion, Touch and Masculinity in the Crimean War* (Oxford: Oxford University Press, 2016); C. Langhamer, *The English in Love: The Intimate Story of an Emotional Revolution* (Oxford: Oxford University Press, 2013); A. Loez, 'Tears in the trenches: a history of emotions and the experience of war', in J. Macleod and P. Purseigle (eds), *Uncovered Fields: Perspectives in First World War Studies* (Leiden: Brill, 2004), pp. 211–26; J. Plamper, 'Soldiers and emotion in early twentieth-century Russian military psychology', in Plamper and B. Lazier (eds), *Fear: Across the Disciplines* (Pittsburgh, PA: University of Pittsburgh Press, 2012), pp. 78–98; M. Roper, *The Secret Battle: Emotional Survival in the Great War* (Manchester: Manchester University Press, 2010); A. Twells, '"Went into raptures": reading emotion in the ordinary wartime diary, 1941–1946', *Women's History Review*, 25:1 (2016), pp. 143–60.
35 W. Reddy, *The Navigation of Feeling: A Framework for the History of Emotions* (New York: Cambridge University Press, 2001); B. H. Rosenwein, *Generations of Feeling: A History of Emotions, 600–1700* (Cambridge: Cambridge University Press, 2016); P. N. and C. Z. Stearns, 'Emotionology: clarifying the history of emotions and emotional standards', *The American Historical Review*, 90:4 (1985), pp. 813–36. A particularly useful collection of work on approaches to the history of emotions can be found in *History and Theory*, 51 (2012).
36 J. Bourke, *Fear: A Cultural History* (London: Virago, 2005); Bourke, 'Foreword', in C. Langhamer, L. Noakes and C. Siebrecht (eds), *Total War: An Emotional History* (Oxford: Oxford University Press, 2019); Langhamer, *The English in Love*.
37 S. Ahmed, *The Cultural Politics of Emotion* (London: Routledge, 2012; first published Edinburgh: Edinburgh University Press, 2004), p. 4.
38 L. Kounine, 'Emotions, mind and body on trial: a cross-cultural perspective', *Journal of Social History*, 51:3 (2017), pp. 219–30, here 221.

Introduction

39 *News Chronicle*, 16 January 1945.
40 The tearing of clothes in response to grief is an ancient practice, described in the Old Testament.
41 For key studies of British cultures of death in this period, see P. Jalland, *Death in War and Peace: A History of Loss and Grief in England, 1914–1970* (Oxford: Oxford University Press, 2010); T. Walter, *On Bereavement: The Culture of Grief* (Maidenhead: Open University Press, 1999).
42 G. Gorer, *Death, Grief and Mourning in Contemporary Britain* (London: Cresset Press, 1965).
43 The nature of British democracy, and political culture, between the wars is widely debated. The key text remains R. McKibbin, *Classes and Cultures: England, 1918–1951* (Oxford: Oxford University Press, 2001); for an overview of debates and interventions, see H. McCarthy, 'Whose democracy? Histories of British political culture between the wars', *The Historical Journal*, 55:1 (2012), pp. 221–38.
44 Laqueur, *The Work of the Dead*.
45 J. Winter, *Sites of Memory. Sites of Mourning: The Great War in European Cultural History* (Cambridge: Cambridge University Press, 1995).
46 T. Dixon, *Weeping Britannia: Portrait of a Nation in Tears* (Oxford: Oxford University Press, 2015).
47 D. Gilpin Faust, *This Republic of Suffering: Death and the American Civil War* (New York: Alfred A. Knopf, 2008).
48 Jalland, *Death in War and Peace*.
49 See, for example, J. Anderson, *War, Disability and Rehabilitation in Britain: Soul of a Nation* (Manchester: Manchester University Press, 2011); J. Bourke, *An Intimate History of Killing: Face to Face Killing in Twentieth-Century Warfare* (London: Granta, 1999); A Carden-Coyne, *The Politics of Wounds: Military Patients and Medical Power in the First World War* (Oxford: Oxford University Press, 2015); J. Damousi, *The Labour of Loss: Mourning, Memory and Wartime Bereavement in Australia* (Cambridge: Cambridge University Press, 1999); T. Loughran, *Shell Shock and Medical Culture in First World War Britain* (Cambridge: Cambridge University Press, 2017); E. Mayhew, *Wounded: The Long Journey Home from the Great War* (London: The Bodley Head, 2013); B. Shephard, *A War of Nerves: Soldiers and Psychiatrists, 1914–1994* (London: Jonathan .Cape, 2000).

1

Shadowing

Death, grief and mourning before the Second World War

Introduction: five graves at Nijmegen

As Allied troops moved north and east towards Germany in September 1944, a strange funeral was held in the small Netherlands town of Nijmegen. Fierce fighting took place in the town and its surrounding area as the Allies and the retreating German forces fought to control vital river crossings. The eight days of fighting that followed the airborne and ground assaults by the Allies that constituted Operation Market Garden left at least 22,000 dead. Five of these dead, members of the Guards Armoured Division, were buried during the fighting at Nijmegen. Burial of the military dead close to the site where they fell was normal; what was unusual about this funeral was its coverage by Eric Baume, the Australian journalist reporting on the war in northwest Europe for the *Daily Mirror*. Trapped under fire at Nijmegen, Baume described the importance of the graves for the comrades of the dead, themselves aware that they too could meet the same fate. Again and again, men gathered close to the graves to pay their respects and to reflect on their own chances of surviving battle. Prayers were read over the burial site by a Franciscan friar, by American Jewish paratroopers, by local civilians and by an Anglican padre. As Baume wrote, the graves represented more than the final resting place of the five men:

> It occurred to me then, suddenly, as the planes roared overhead that none of the five guardsmen had done anything more valiant or outstanding or unusual than to die. But that in being thus dead, almost on an island around which their contemporary world now moved, they had become the very epicentre of quiet, unemotional, unsentimental, thought, and had been a lodestone to those who, praying for peace, thought seriously, rightly or wrongly, that they could obtain it hard by this hallowed ground, within these sacred portals.[1]

The graves were a locus between past and present, standing not only for the individuals buried there and the multiple losses of war, but for the hopes of those still fighting, and the aims and future that they were fighting for.

Baume's description of these graves, and their meaning, illustrates the multiple ways in which, as Thomas Laqueur has argued, the dead 'work'.[2] This work can be intimate and personal, as individuals, families and communities construct an image of those that they have lost; it can be social, as communities unite around, or are sometimes divided by, memories of the dead; and it can be political, as nations and other collectives create narratives around the dead that are useful in the present. The dead guardsmen of Nijmegen were doing both social and political work: acting as a unifying force for those trapped in the town, military and civilian, and prompting them to reflect on shared war aims. But they were also working as a reminder for Baume's audience, reading his account towards the end of the war in Europe, of both the sacrifice entailed in victory and of the work of the living, who now had to honour those who died by building a lasting peace.

The five men buried in these graves at Nijmegen would have been mourned as individuals, as loved sons, husbands, comrades, friends, brothers and lovers. Those who mourned also had work to do. This work was both emotional – the hard work of grief – and social, undertaking the behaviours and rituals expected of the bereaved. By 1945, as Baume's reflection on these graves shows, the language of death was largely expected to be 'unemotional, unsentimental'. At the end of almost six years of war, British culture had little space for voluble expressions of grief or for elaborate bereavement or funerary practices. Emotional and cultural restraint shaped both the rituals of bereavement and the articulation of grief. The work of the dead, and of the living who mourn them and grieve for them, is thus situated in time and place. Death is a biological event, the point at which life leaves the body, but it is also a social and cultural process. The ways in which these men died and were buried, grieved for and mourned were all specific to a time and a place: death in battle in mid-twentieth-century Europe, burial as British or imperial combatants and being grieved for and mourned over by members of both the Allied nations, and local inhabitants. Causes of death, the 'disposal of the dead', the expression of grief and the rituals of bereavement in Second World War Britain were all shaped both by a long history, and by the specific conditions of wartime. This chapter begins by exploring this longer history of death, grief and bereavement

Shadowing: death, grief and mourning before the Second World War

in Britain, and then examines the particular legacies of death in the Great War for those experiencing the Second.

Death, grief and bereavement in modern Britain

First published in France in 1977, and translated into English in 1981, Phillipe Ariès' influential *The Hour of Our Death* argued that modern, Western societies had made death invisible. Tracing changing attitudes towards death in Western culture from the early Christian period to the contemporary, Ariès explored a shift over the *'longue durée'* which saw concerns move from ensuring the wellbeing of the soul to the wellbeing of the bereaved. For Ariès, the twentieth century suffered from the cumulative effects of the critique of religious beliefs rooted in the Enlightenment and modern medical practice, bringing about a definitive break with past traditions and rituals of death. Arguing, together with the British sociologist Geoffrey Gorer, that death had been hidden in hospitals, medicalised and bureaucratised, Ariès claimed that death had become taboo, rarely seen and rarely spoken of, a condition that he argued was unhealthy, even pathological.[3] Critics of Ariès have been numerous: Laqueur argues that far from disappearing, 'the dead have never been more prominent' as they 'continue to enchant our disenchanted world', while Jonathan Dollimore and Joachim Whaley have both critiqued his linkage of the decline of religious belief with a pathologising of death.[4] As this book will show, in wartime at least, death was rarely invisible or hidden away. Instead, as with the combatants and civilians of Nijmegen, the living often existed alongside the dead, who were buried close to where they fell or whose bodies were putrefying in the rubble of bombed buildings or the detritus of battle. Public remembrance of the war dead was important, *In Memoriam* notices in newspapers and the rituals of Armistice Day reminding the living of their sacrifice while their names were inscribed on military memorials and in books of the dead, placed for public consultation in local authority buildings in Britain.

However, although both combatants and civilians lived with death during the war years, and with loss and grief in war's aftermath, there was little public display of grief, or of the opulent mourning rituals associated with the Victorian era in Britain. To some extent, this was a feature of total war: nations involved in long wars of attrition, with heavy casualties and enormous demands made on both civilians and combatants, could ill afford the luxury of lengthy mourning periods, elaborate mourning dress or lavish funerals. Equally, public expressions of the anguish of grief were seen as unhelpful, even unpatriotic, at a time when all were being asked to make sacrifices, and to put the common good above individual happiness. But for the people of Second World War Britain, the experience of death was also shaped by an existing emotional economy which privileged stoicism and restraint over expressiveness, and sense over sensibility. The growth of this widely shared emotional economy in the early twentieth century is discussed in Chapter 2, but this chapter considers the longer relationship between attitudes to death, mourning practice and the articulation of grief as they shifted from the expressive early Victorian period to the more restrained twentieth century.

As Pat Jalland has argued, the history of death and bereavement in Britain after the Great War can be understood, in part, as a reaction against the Victorian 'way of death', widely perceived in twentieth-century Britain as overly ornate, sentimental and indulgent.[5] The Victorians were believed to celebrate death, to indulge in extravagant funerals that they could often ill afford, and to see such funerals as indicators of social status rather than an expression of loss and an opportunity to support the bereaved and bid farewell to the newly dead. Some of this was probably justified: the Duke of Wellington's funeral in 1852, admittedly an elaborate and expensive affair even by the standards of the aristocracy, was several months in the planning and believed to have cost over £90,000.[6] While Wellington's funeral was exceptional, extravagance in mourning etiquette was well established in the first half of the nineteenth century. The funerary expenses listed by Jalland in *Death in the Victorian Family* include £803 for a funeral in 1826 that featured, among other things, 'a rich plume of best black ostrich feathers' and twelve pages with wands, each wearing a black hatband and silk gloves. By 1843, when Edwin Chadwick published his influential *Report on the Practice of Interment in Towns*, an aristocratic funeral could cost £500 to £1,500, while the average middle-class household would spend between £50 and £70 on funerary costs.[7] Condemning both the extravagance of the Duke of Wellington's funeral and the wider fashion for costly funerary practice, Charles Dickens argued that 'the most solemn of human occasions' was being undermined by 'unmeaning mummeries, dishonest debt, profuse waste, and bad example in an utter oblivion of responsibility'.[8] Dickens was also concerned by the duke's bodily remains, relating the three months that passed between his death and his interment in St Paul's Cathedral to the threat to public health that, with reformers like Chadwick, he associated with the overcrowding of churchyards, especially in large and growing cities like London. Together with the growth of the nonconformist churches, this fear of contagion in an age of epidemics and high mortality rates drove major changes in burial reform in the first half of the nineteenth century.

The new commercial 'joint-stock' cemeteries which opened were independent of the parish church, and thus broke the near monopoly of the Anglican church over burial rites. The 'garden cemeteries', including the seven that opened between 1832 and 1841 in London, and the Glasgow Necropolis in 1833, provided burial sites for nonconformists and others in semi-rural settings, far from the overcrowding and poor interment associated with many urban churchyards. Shaped by the romantic sensibility that underpinned the idea of the rural idyll, these cemeteries provided burial spaces among grassy lawns, often shaded by trees, that could be visited by strolling along winding paths. Individual burial in these new cemeteries was, however, beyond the reach of most people, the working class especially continuing to rely on the local church for interment.

The year 1832, when the Cemeteries Act enabled the building of the new, commercial cemeteries, also saw legislation that was to shape the experience of death and burial for many of the poor. The Anatomy Act allowed for the unclaimed corpses of paupers to be used by medical schools for dissection, a much-feared bodily fate previously reserved for criminals executed by the state. Two years later, the New Poor Law introduced the parsimonious burial by the local parish of those who could not afford to pay for a funeral, a practice which, as Julie-Marie Strange has shown, was closely linked to the intended humiliation of recipients of the New Poor Law itself, as 'stripped of all mourning paraphernalia, the pauper coffin bore little or no indication of the personality of the corpse or those who mourned it'.[9] These mourners had little or no control over the place of interment, Laqueur describing burial plots where the poor were buried in graves three coffins wide and twelve deep.[10] Given this anonymity, it is not surprising that the most common addition to the pauper funeral paid for by mourners was a brass name plate, screwed onto the plain coffin in an attempt to ensure some semblance of individuality for these otherwise nameless dead.[11] The gradual diminution of the churches' authority over burial, seen for example in the refusal to bury suicides or unbaptised infants in consecrated ground, may have enabled the wealthier to choose interment in a garden cemetery rather than an overcrowded churchyard, but for the poorest the disposal of the dead simply transferred to the state, a change that was to have profound implications for the burial of the civilian dead in the Second World War.

Strange discusses the importance of the working-class 'respectable' funeral, critiquing the conflation of respect for the dead with the idea of 'respectability' which led contemporary observers and some historians of Victorian funerary practice and bereavement to focus almost entirely on its opulence.[12] Such an approach has tended to position the working-class funeral as an opportunity to display 'respectability' and status – an approach that concurrently ignores the potential for funeral rites to have multiple meanings, and for them to function as important rituals for the communication and recognition of grief, and for the social transition of the dead to some form of afterlife, spiritual or in memory only. Funerals provided an opportunity for neighbours, friends and the local community to support the bereaved: undertaking rituals like helping to prepare and 'lay out' the corpse for burial, closing curtains as the coffin and mourners left for the funeral, standing in silence as the funeral cortege passed on the street and attending the funeral, burial and funeral tea all provided ways for the local community to show sympathy for the bereaved. All too often a culture of silence around grief has been read as an emotional detachment: both the working class of the nineteenth century, whose lives were shaped by high mortality rates and repeated losses, and the people of the Second World War, who experienced the multiple losses of wartime, were understood to be accepting of death because they lived within cultures that emphasised restraint rather than emotional expression in the articulation and performance of grief, and because they lived at a time when high mortality rates were to touch many.

The burial reform movement of the second half of the nineteenth century valorised restraint over emotional expression in its campaign for rational reform of funeral practice. Edwin Chadwick's 1842 report into burial practice in towns rapidly became a bestseller, reinforcing fears of contamination and epidemic emanating from the overcrowded burial sites of cities and providing the motor for the reform movement that would go on to reshape funerary practice and bereavement rituals. The Metropolitan Interments Act of 1850 (extended to the rest of England and Wales in 1853) closed old burial grounds, prohibited burial within a church or other building and established local Boards of Health as fixed-charge funeral providers. The Burial Grounds (Scotland) Act of 1855 similarly gave the Parochial Boards of local parishes the power to close old and open new burial grounds, to fix payments for interments and to arrange, when necessary, for the transport of bodies to the cemetery and a place where corpses could be stored prior to burial. This rationalisation of burial practice also entailed a critique of the elaborate funerary practices of the period, such as Dickens' criticism of the Duke of Wellington's funeral in 1852. By the 1870s, elaborate mourning traditions were being replaced by more modest practices, as 'good taste' became associated with simplicity and restraint. Pat Jalland records that by this time, simple funerals had become '*de rigueur*' for the elite classes, Gladstone's funeral in 1898 described by an attendee as 'simple, impressive, dignified, grand, real emotion displayed'.[13] As funerals and burials were reformed, simplicity and restraint became indicators of 'real' emotion, symbols of a deeply felt yet private grief, all the more admirable for being controlled.

Mourning rituals were gendered, classed and shaped by region. While, by the late nineteenth century, the upper class could employ nurses to wash the body, and undertakers to store it before the funeral, for the majority the corpse remained a member of the household until their burial. Customs grew up that both established a divide between the living and the recently dead with whom they shared their homes, and reinforced the affective bonds between them. In the Scottish Highlands and the fishing villages of the east coast, milk was poured on to the ground, and onions and butter were thrown away.[14] In both Scotland and Ireland, as well as English cities with large Irish populations, the funeral was usually preceded by a wake, in which neighbours, friends and family would share the duty of ensuring the body was not left alone before burial and share stories, food and drink with the bereaved. Keeners were sometimes hired to wail and lament at burials in rural Ireland and the Presbyterian communities of the Scottish Highlands, where only men traditionally attended funerals. Outside the Highlands, women undertook the majority of these rituals, the upper classes following an elaborate code for mourning dress and mourners across all social classes wearing black, both as a mark of respect for the deceased but also as an indicator of loss, and the need for solace. While the customs associated with mourning dress were simplified in the latter half of the century, the wearing of black, especially by women for some time after the funeral, was maintained and, as the second part of this chapter will discuss, remained common practice until the Great War. Working-class women also undertook the greater part of caring for the sick and the dying, often laying out the corpse for viewing in the home prior to burial, a final act of intimacy and care. The corpse, usually resting in the home for several days before burial, would be washed and have its orifices packed with herbs to mask the odour of decomposition, pennies placed on eyelids and mouth bound shut by a bandage under the chin. Hair was brushed, fingernails were cleaned and men were shaved. The corpse was usually dressed for burial in a nightgown or a shroud, 'best' clothing being too valuable to bury the body in. Local women often assisted with the cleaning and laying out of the dead, usually for a small fee, but also as an act of condolence and support for the bereaved, and of respect for the dead.[15] Such acts were an integral part of a wider, largely feminine, culture of care-giving and support, with the affective relationships at the heart of this culture encompassing care for the dead, as well as for the living.

Women also took most responsibility for remembering the dead. While the organisation of the funerals was a largely male affair, women both signified bereavement in their mourning dress, and kept mementoes of the dead at home, including locks of hair, mourning jewellery and photographs. Post-mortem photographs, especially of children, were popular with the late Victorian upper classes, staged so as to provide comfort to the bereaved through a visual reminder of the peaceful nature of death. Speaking about the dead by reminiscing with family, friends and neighbours was the most economical means of remembering them, especially for the poorest who could not always afford the luxury of keeping mementoes, instead pawning or selling personal items like jewellery after a family member had died, and passing on clothing to surviving family members.

By the late nineteenth century, speaking to the dead had become a means of managing grief and continuing intimate relationships after death. Spiritualism grew rapidly in the late nineteenth century, popularised by celebrity adherents like Arthur Conan Doyle and driven by a combination of dominant Christian belief, which imagined the dead as embodied, and a growing confidence that science would eventually 'prove' the existence of an afterlife, and enable the living and the dead to communicate between the two worlds. For some, the Christian promise of reunion in the afterlife was not enough. Jennifer Hazelgrove argues that spiritualism had its greatest adherents among the more radically minded, the 'Owenites, herbalists and Methodists of the North of England', individuals and groups who already dissented from mainstream belief in important ways.[16] Speaking with the dead could help to ameliorate grief and to maintain affective relationships after death.

Shadowing: death, grief and mourning before the Second World War

Such conversations did not have to take place within the séance room or at the Ouija board. The socialist and feminist Hannah Mitchell, recalling her early life in a poor Derbyshire family, remembered her grandmother 'talking to her husband who had died many years before and would seem surprised if I said I couldn't see him'.[17] A desire to maintain some sort of relationship with the dead was not the preserve alone of spiritualists and believers in the power of mediums and others to converse with the spirit world. Many lived with the dead, not just in the days after death when the corpse remained in the household, but in their everyday emotional and social lives.

Grief could manifest itself in multiple ways, but its expression took place within specific historical conditions, and was shaped by emotional economies, social expectations and material circumstances. By the Edwardian era, the extravagant funerary customs and complex mourning traditions that had been seen in the first half of the nineteenth century were in decline, widely seen as inappropriate in an age of rational reform. Britain was a largely Christian nation, one in which earlier visions of hell had been largely replaced in the Anglican imagination by a heaven in which the living would be reunited with the embodied dead – a vision of the afterlife that provided comfort to the bereaved and perhaps contributed to the decline of the extravagant early Victorian funeral. Of course, such funerals had ever only been the preserve of the upper classes; death, grief and bereavement, like all other aspects of life, were shaped by material and local conditions. When the poor spent precious money on funerary goods and entertainment, they were seen as extravagant spendthrifts, driven by the notion of respectability rather than respect for the dead. When they could not afford a funeral, or showed little overt emotion, they were seen as fatalistic or apathetic, existing as they did in a world where early and multiple deaths were often a part of life.[18] Like funerals and bereavement practice, customs of consolation, and forms for the articulation and performance of grief were shaped by gender, by class and by locality; grief could be expressed in multiple ways. The shared experience of the Great War was to shape both the forms that death took, bereavement practices and the articulation of grief across the nation.

The impact of the Great War

The Great War cast a long shadow. For Britain, it shaped both international and domestic politics, and the emotional economy of the interwar years. Many individuals had their lives moulded by the losses of war, and the economic, social and cultural repercussions of the conflict were widely felt, as households struggled to survive without a breadwinner, and thousands learnt to live with the anguish of grief. The physical and cultural space of towns, cities and villages was shaped by the erection of war memorials, and the national and imperial calendar encompassed Armistice Day as a means of honouring the dead and remembering the loss of so many. In response to the losses of war, the British did not return to the elaborate funerals and complex mourning rituals of the earlier period. Instead, the shifts in cultures of bereavement and grief in Britain before the Great War were strengthened by the demands of the war years, and acted to shape the British 'way of death' in the interwar years. Thus, as Britain embarked on another devastating war in 1939, a culture of containment and self-control shaped both the prevailing emotional economy, and in particular, expectations of how bereavement would be experienced, and grief expressed.

What remained of elaborate Victorian funerary customs and mourning rituals was fragmented by the Great War, as the move towards rationalisation and simplification was hastened by the need to cope with death and grief on the scale brought about by modern, industrialised total war. Total war, the mobilisation of all the resources of the state for the purpose of victory, touched every aspect of life, including mourning practice and the means by which people could express their grief. As early as August 1914, an editorial in the *Times* suggested that there was an urgent need to

> Come to some common decision as to what the common tokens of our grief should be. The letters which reach us show a strong and widespread feeling that they should not be the customary mourning we use for our dead who have died in the course of nature. The anguish caused by the death in action of our dearest and our best, in the flower of their manhood and the full vigour of life, is perhaps the most poignant of all, but it is mingled with feelings which no other death can bring. They have fallen in a sacred cause ... they have died for freedom and for right.

The *Times* Editorial went on to suggest that the bereaved should abjure from traditional mourning dress and instead wear a token 'of such a kind that all may wear it whose nearest have died upon the field'.[19] Obituaries began to appear that stipulated 'no mourning' or more commonly, 'no flowers', and letters were printed attacking the opportunistic activities of businesses selling funerary wares and portraiture, who approached bereaved families once the death of men in service had been announced in the local press.[20] Notions of patriotic and appropriate behaviour in wartime had started to shape the culture of mourning and bereavement. Grief itself was to be mobilised for the war effort.

At first, established mourning rituals and bereavement practices were maintained. When Geoffrey Gorer's father was drowned, a victim of the sinking of RMS Lusitania in May 1915, he was given black ties to wear and had 'bands of crepe sewn into the sleeves of my suits' while his mother wore mourning dress for fifteen months.[21] In this, she was not alone: a November 1915 article in the *Fortnightly Review* reflecting on fashion trends noted that 'mourning has grown very decorative in detail'.[22] Nor were all wartime funerals notable for their patriotic simplicity: when the eighty-two-year-old Field Marshal Roberts died while visiting troops in November 1914, a 'very large, silent and respectful crowd' gathered to view the procession of his funeral cortege from Charing Cross Station to his lying in state and funeral at St Paul's Cathedral. The coffin was transported on a gun carriage and accompanied by several battalions from Britain and the empire, cavalry and a band of the Scots Guards and of the London Scottish regiments. The Hampshire Artillery fired a nineteen-gun field marshal's salute from nearby St James' Park as the cortege left the station, and an orchestra played Chopin's 'Marche Funebre'. It should be noted that this was the third funeral procession for Roberts, whose body had already processed through Boulogne and his home town of Ascot.[23]

However, a careful reading of Roberts' funeral illustrates the extent to which funerary and mourning practice was already combining the movement towards rationality and plainness that had typified such practices in the decades before the war, with a sense that simplicity and, crucially, silence, in the face of wartime death, were patriotic. The bands of the London battalions that accompanied the cortege were silent, and the soldiers all wore khaki – 'with just one splash of dull red' in the turbans of the men from the Indian Mountain Batteries. Silence was a key motif in the *Times'* coverage of the funeral. An 'orderly, respectful crowd' was 'very still and silent', and the descriptions of the size of the cortege were contained by a final coda: 'When the gun carriage had reached St Paul's those unending horsemen must still have been riding silently along the Embankment with silent people watching them, in the rain.' While the crowds watching the funeral procession on a cold, wet autumn day may have been drawn by the promise of spectacle as much as by a desire to pay their respects to Roberts, their solemnity was accentuated by the censorious description of 'the hawkers, who proclaimed their memorials and programmes with raucous cries, and continued to do so even as the procession was passing'.[24] The London hawkers, like the voracious undertakers of the Victorian era and the unscrupulous funerary businesses of the war years, were seen to be profiting from death, an unpatriotic as well as opportunistic activity in the midst of war. The crowds symbolised the nation, being composed of civilians and servicemen, including the wounded, who watched from a hotel balcony. Roberts' funeral, impressive in scale and dignity, was presented as a simple, unifying affair, dignified and solemn, and thus entirely suited to a nation united not only in the war effort, but also in sorrow.

By the middle years of the war, the advocacy of simplicity in bereavement and funerary practices was widespread. Rudyard Kipling's 1915 story 'Mary Postgate' has his protagonist ask her employer, 'shall we wear black?' to mark the death of a much-loved nephew, killed while training for the Air Force. The reply was 'certainly not ... except of course at the funeral'.[25] When Field Marshal Lord Kitchener drowned in June 1916, the very 'lack of pomp' at his memorial service was commented on favourably, the *Daily Express* noting the 'studiously simple' service and the 'dead silence' as the congregation filled St Paul's Cathedral. This silence extended to the crowds who waited outside, who 'showed their sympathy in a remarkable way. As the King and Queen drove past ... hats were raised but not a word was spoken.'[26] Ostentatious mourning was increasingly seen as unpatriotic. A letter to the *Saturday Review* published soon after the calamitous losses of 1 July 1916 claimed,

> There is still too great an outlay on funerals and mourning ... money which might reasonably be saved is thrown away on flowers. Surely it ought to suffice in every case if one or two wreaths were provided by the actual mourners, and then there could be more flowers – to say nothing of real comforts – for the sick and wounded in numerous hospitals ... why need there be any 'in memoriam' notices in the daily papers? ... Are not these the days for self-restraint and for the curbing of sentimental display?[27]

Two months later, an article in the *Fortnightly Review* argued, 'the morale of a nation demands that its signs of external bereavement should be as few as possible'.[28] Black crepe, the staple of Victorian mourning dress, went unused, and was repurposed by some quick-thinking entrepreneurs as suitable material for homemade gas masks in the aftermath of the first large-scale use of poison gas on the Western Front in 1915.[29] As the numbers of the dead, and of the bereaved, mounted, silence and restraint were increasingly seen as the only appropriate, patriotic response; a means of both demonstrating resolve and placing the needs of the wartime community over the mediation of individual grief.

The multiple deaths of war, and the understanding that simplicity and restraint were more patriotic than a self-indulgent and sentimental expression of grief through mourning practice, undoubtedly acted to bolster the existing movement towards funerary reform. It also saw the strengthening of a secular stoicism, in which the consolations of religious belief, while still widespread and understandably popular, were accompanied by an emphasis on shared suffering and the idea of the sacrificial wartime death. Civilians were urged to maintain a 'stoical silence, no matter what befalls our army', and the Duchess of Devonshire, Lady Pembroke, Lady Castlereagh and Lady Kerry wrote to the *Times* in August 1914 to state that, if bereaved, 'we will not show our sorrow as for those who come to a less glorious end'.[30] Of course, this outward stoicism was by no means universal, and while it did provide the bereaved with a model of how to act in public, it could also act to obscure grief, and thus lessen opportunities for consolation and comfort from others. The gulf between private feeling and public expression cut across the social classes. When George Cecil, the stepson of Alfred Lord Milner and son of Violet Cecil, was declared first missing and then killed in 1914, his mother, while keeping up her public duties and maintaining the patriotic stoicism which she understood to be her duty, wrote to her sister that 'I am broken'.[31] Cecil, who was a dedicated imperialist and member of the British social and political elite, no doubt felt that it was her responsibility in wartime to appear brave and stoical in public, and to keep her distress within the private, familial sphere; at the other end of the social spectrum Jack Lawson's mother, a working-class woman from the Durham coalfield, also maintained a silence around her grief when her youngest son was killed in battle. Mining communities were experienced in the sudden death of young men; in the industry's worst disaster, 439 men and boys had been killed in 1913, when gas caused an explosion at the Universal Colliery in Senghenydd in south Wales. Funerals for miners killed at work were often accompanied by brass bands, and the coffin draped with the Union flag, normally used to signify war service.[32] As Pat Jalland has shown, the heavy casualty rates in the industry led some commentators to assume that mining communities were hardened to death, J. B. Priestley commenting of the minefields of County Durham in his 1934 *English Journey* that repeated bereavement and poverty had acted to blunt the sensibilities of the miners and their families, distancing them from the emotional impact of sudden death.[33] The reticence and stoicism with which members of these communities treated bereavement, however, could be misleading. Lawson recorded how his mother barely spoke about the death of her youngest son, but while 'tears there were none', her grief was communicated through retreating to her bedroom, and refusing food, drink and consolation.[34] Local traditions of bereavement and cultures of grief shaped the ways that it was communicated and understood; here, Lawson's mother's silence was eloquent. Grief did not have to be displayed publicly to be felt profoundly.

As the war ground on, changes in military burial practice provided further challenges for those attempting to negotiate grief and the restraints that the demands of wartime placed on bereavement practice. For most of those bereaved by the war, traditional funerary and burial rites became impossible in wartime. Familial control of the body, seen in the practice of washing and laying out the corpse, had acted as a means through which grief could be expressed and intimacy maintained through the transition from life to death. The presence of the dead body in the house could assist 'the bereaved in renegotiating the boundaries between themselves and the dead whilst framing visual memories of the deceased at peace'.[35] Visits from friends, family and neighbours provided an opportunity for communal support and comfort for the bereaved. Without a body to lay out and bury, these traditional rituals of bereavement, which provided a framework through which grief could be expressed and shared, were unavailable. The decision not to repatriate the bodies of any of the war dead to their families but to inter them close to the site of battle, taken in 1915 as an attempt to ensure that a family's ability to pay for repatriation did not act to reinforce the divide between rich and poor in wartime, and that there was equality of practice across the empire, meant that the body of the dead soldier became a de facto possession of the state. The bodies of the five guardsmen buried at Nijmegen in 1945, together with thousands of other British and imperial troops, were treated in the same manner in the Second World War. Equality in death was important in both conflicts. When the Graves Registration Commission, under the leadership of Fabian Ware, who was to become the first director

Shadowing: death, grief and mourning before the Second World War

of the Imperial War Graves Commission (IWGC) on its establishment by Royal Charter in May 1917, announced the decision not to return bodies to their families, they received numerous letters from relatives demanding that they reverse their decision. At the war's end, the commission insisted on a level of uniformity regarding headstones in the war cemeteries, replacing the wooden crosses which had often marked temporary graves during battle with white headstones when bodies were disinterred and placed in war graves cemeteries. In January 1918, the commission issued a statement of intent regarding war cemeteries:

> The Commission feels that it would be inadvisable to leave the provision of memorials to private initiative. If memorials were allowed to be erected in the War Cemeteries according to the preference, taste and means of relatives and friends, the result would be that costly monuments put up by the well-to-do over their dead would contrast unkindly with those humbler ones which would be all that poorer folk could afford … in death, all, from General to Private, of whatever race or creed, should receive equal honour under a memorial which should be the common symbol of their comradeship and of the cause for which they died.[36]

Ware was determined that the new cemeteries would both erase distinctions of social class and represent the 'union and strength of the Empire', with officers buried alongside other ranks, and soldiers from the colonies and dominions buried next to those from Britain.[37] While next of kin would be allowed to choose the inscription on the headstone, they were limited to sixty-six characters, and charged three-and-a-half pence per character, a decision that raised concerns regarding the ability of some families to pay for the inscription they desired. Lady Florence Cecil, who had lost three sons in the war, coordinated a petition in 1919 which gathered 8,000 signatories, requesting that stone crosses should be considered as an alternative to the white headstones which marked combatants' graves.[38] The request was turned down, although the commission did agree to ship home the temporary wooden crosses if families so wished. While the uniformity of sacrifice symbolised by the decision not to repatriate bodies, and to create cemeteries where distinctions of rank, of class and of religion were disguised, may have provided a measure of consolation to some, for others it provoked further heartache.

For many of course, the burial of their loved one's body was an impossibility, as no body existed to be interred. Over 200,000 British and imperial troops were listed as missing, their bodies destroyed by industrial warfare. Some of those who were buried in named plots were lost after death, as shellfire destroyed cemeteries and splintered the temporary wooden crosses erected above graves. Their names were inscribed on the great battlefield memorials to the missing at Ypres, Belgium, and Thiepval, France, and on memorial walls at the cemeteries, while unidentified bodies were interred in IWGC war cemeteries, their headstones marked with Kipling's epitaph, 'A soldier of the Great War known unto God'. The absence of a body to be cared for and interred, and the accompanying lack of funerary rites and burial rituals, for so long central to the management of grief, could be disruptive of the very process of grieving, as hope that the missing would be found alive could persist long after official notification that they were missing. Rudyard and Carrie Kipling continued to search for their son John long after he was lost at the Battle of Loos in September 1915, their despair hidden behind 'a stoical facade of acceptance'.[39] Their story, no less harrowing for being well known, is only one of many thousands: the Red Cross alone received over 342,000 enquiries from relatives of those declared missing during the war.[40] The need to bring the dead home, to have a body to inter and a burial place to visit, was widely felt. In 1920, the ceremonial funeral and interment of the Unknown Warrior at Westminster Abbey functioned both as a symbolic return of the war dead and an attempt to ameliorate the terrible grief of those whose loved ones were still 'missing'.

The return of the Unknown Warrior was carefully choreographed to ensure that he stood for the British Empire's need to honour its almost 1 million military dead in the aftermath of four years of industrial warfare.[41] That the funeral procession bore much in common with the 1914 funeral of Field Marshal Roberts was not accidental: the coffin was carried by gun carriage from Victoria Station to Westminster Abbey, receiving a nineteen-gun field marshal's salute, and the funeral was attended by the royal family and ministers of state, as well as women whose grief had manifested itself through repeated dreams that the body being buried was that of their lost son or husband.[42] Total war in an age of mass democracy demanded that the state take note of the feelings of the ordinary people. Just twenty-one years before the state funeral of the Unknown Warrior, Thomas Hardy had written 'Drummer Hodge', marking the anonymous burial of a young soldier in South Africa during the Boer War:

> They throw in Drummer Hodge, to rest
> Uncoffined, as is found[43]

Shadowing: death, grief and mourning before the Second World War

Buried without a coffin, thrown into an unmarked grave, Hardy's Drummer Hodge was a child of his time, mourned by those who knew him but not by the state, his final resting place fated to be unmarked. Although the Boer War signals the beginning of a change in official attitudes towards the war dead, with 6,000 small iron crosses eventually being provided to signify the graves of those who would otherwise have no marker, it was not until the Great War that naming the dead became symbolic of both shared and individual sacrifice.[44] Before the Great War, death, burial, bereavement and grief were understood to be private, the concern only of the immediately bereaved unless the dead were deserving of a state funeral, or so destitute that the state had to take responsibility for their interment. The multiple demands of the Great War changed this. Grief had a politics as never before. In the Second World War, this politics was to be extended to encompass the civilian dead, alongside the military.

The shifting politics of grief shaped the way that civilian casualties, as well as military, were to be grieved for and remembered. On 13 June, 1917, German Gotha airplanes carried out the first daylight raid on Britain, with bombs largely falling on east London, killing 145 and injuring another 382. Among the dead were eighteen young children, pupils in the Infant Department of Upper North Street School in Poplar.[45] At the inquest, the Coroner stated that 'these boys and girls have died for their country as … any of our men at the front or on the high seas', a sentiment echoed by the mayor of Poplar at the joint funeral of fifteen of the children a week later, when he claimed that 'they have died for England'.[46] In a manner that prefigured responses to similar tragedies in the Second World War, parental and others' grief was thus subsumed into the notion of shared sacrifice. Children, alongside combatants, could die for the nation in an age of total war.

In the aftermath of the Great War, the physical, temporal and emotional landscapes of Britain were changed. Every city and town, and the great majority of villages, erected communal memorials to the dead, accompanied by workplace and school memorials and memorials to groups and individuals in churches and other places of worship. The shared calendar of Britain and the empire now encompassed Armistice Day, 11 November, which became a solemn occasion for marking the multiple deaths of war across the empire at the ceremony held by the Cenotaph in central London each year, and more local losses at war memorials across the nation. The ceremonies performed at these memorials reinforced the emotional economy that had developed in wartime, and shaped both mourning practice and the expression of grief. The dead were commemorated, first, through silence.[47] The two-minute silence held at 11 a.m. marked the moment the war ended, but also echoed the injunctions to a silenced grief during the war. The ceremonies functioned to both demonstrate national and imperial cohesion; to remind the community of who had been bereaved, and may thus need support; and to direct these bereaved to remember but *not* to grieve for their dead. The 'Ode of Remembrance', a stanza from Laurence Binyon's 1914 poem 'For the Fallen', was regularly recited:

> They shall not grow old as we that are left grow old
> Age shall not weary them, nor the years condemn
> At the going down of the sun, and in the morning
> We will remember them.[48]

The stanza combines a collective determination to remember the dead with a secular denial of death, a reframing of the Christian verse 'Oh death, where is thy sting?' from Corinthians in which commemoration by the state replaces eternity in heaven as solace for the bereaved. However, as Jay Winter has shown, this does not mean that religious imagery, motifs or beliefs were displaced by the impact of war or in the post-war mediation of mourning. Rather, these traditional forms of remembrance and consolation became embedded in the emotional economy of the period together with the understanding that stoicism in the face of grief was the most appropriate response.[49]

This emotional economy, which valued stoicism and restraint over emotional expression, and thus over elaborate mourning rituals or expressive grief, shaped the often overlooked wave of death and bereavement which arrived towards the end of the war in the form of the influenza pandemic. The pandemic, nicknamed the 'Spanish Lady' in Britain, was, on a global scale, more deadly than the war, killing between 40 million and 50 million worldwide, including around 200,000 in England and Wales.[50] The victims could in many ways make a claim to be war victims themselves. Possibly originating in outbreaks of 'purulent bronchitis' seen in 1916 and 1917, the virus may have mutated in the chaotic conditions of the Western Front, where it was known as 'Flanders Grippe' to British soldiers and 'BlitzKattarh' to German troops. Mark Honigsbaum suggests that it originated in the huge complex of army camps in Étaples, northern France, where livestock lived in close contact with troops and workers from around the world, and where medical staff recorded the appearance of 'a strange new respiratory infection' in 1916.[51] Other historians have identified the army camps of Kansas or the port of Canton in China as the seat of the infection.[52] Wherever it originated, the virus found easy pickings across the world among populations that were often weakened by four years of warfare and its accompanying privations. The young were particularly vulnerable; as Niall Johnson has argued, '1918 was not a good year to be a young adult in Britain', with approximately 45 per cent of fatalities occurring in those aged between fifteen and thirty-five.[53] Stoicism seems to have been at the heart of official advice. Sir Arthur Newsholme, chief medical officer of the Local Government Board and the leading public health official of his day, wrote in 1919 that 'there are circumstances in which the major duty is to "carry on" even when risk to life and health is involved'.[54] Writing in the *Times* in December 1918, the newspaper's medical correspondent claimed that '[n]ever since the Black Death has such a plague swept over the face of the world; never perhaps has a plague been more stoically accepted'.[55] The discourse of stoicism, seen so widely during the war in public codes of mourning and advice on bereavement, carried over into much of the representation of, and official reaction to, influenza. Civilians were encouraged to follow the example of the wartime combatants and the wartime bereaved, stoically bearing their suffering for the greater good of the nation.

In claims that were to be echoed in concerns about the civilian population's ability to cope with aerial bombardment in the Second World War, some communities were perceived to be less than stoical in their response to the pandemic. The *Times* reported that outbreaks of influenza had provoked alarm in working-class districts of Ireland, and the densely populated industrial cities of Glasgow and Sheffield, both badly hit by the illness, reported bodies piling up at local morgues and chemists running out of quinine, which was believed to provide some relief from influenza's symptoms.[56] Riots were reported in West Belfast during the deadly second wave of infections, and newspapers recounted a spate of suicides among both the ill and the bereaved, including that of a gardener from North Wales, who attempted, unsuccessfully, to murder his wife and six children, but succeeded in killing himself.[57] The *Daily Mirror* reported that 'doctors in London are unable to cope' and the *Daily Mail* that the disease was 'sweeping big towns' and 'seriously interfering with work all over the country'.[58] Large cities and port towns saw some of the highest rates of infection as the mobile wartime populations carried the disease with them on their travels. In one week in October 1918, the Registrar General recorded the death rate in London as 20.1 per thousand; in the port city of Liverpool it reached 41.9 per thousand in the same week.[59] By the following week, that death rate had doubled.[60]

Although the memory and history of the pandemic has been largely subsumed into that of the war, it nonetheless marked British society in the interwar period. Many of the victims were quickly buried in mass graves, and in London council workers were employed as temporary gravediggers amid rumours that the city was about to run out of coffins. In Birmingham, the city drew on additional labour supplied by the military to take bodies from homes to temporary mortuaries before burial.[61] Obituaries in local newspapers across the country provide clues to the tragedies being played out in homes, streets and communities. The *Brighton Herald*, for example, reported the deaths of Grace Mills, who died just ten days after her wedding, and of Ada Wright, whose husband and daughters, also struck down with the illness, were too unwell to attend her funeral.[62] An editorial in the *Times* of 2 February 1921 described the pandemic as 'the great death', reflecting that it had been 'a hurricane across the green fields of life, sweeping away our youth in hundreds of thousands and leaving behind it a toll of sickness and infirmity which will not be reclaimed in this generation'.[63] The victims of the influenza pandemic, however, their names never inscribed on public memorials, their remembrance taking place largely in private, unmarked by public ceremonies of commemoration, were gradually overshadowed by the memory of the war dead – the 'lost generation' of the early twentieth century.

Conclusion

As David Cannadine has argued, interwar Britain was 'probably more obsessed with death than any other period in modern history'.[64] Silence, whether stoical or shocked, in response to great loss, or the two-minute silence that stood for communal remembrance of the dead each year, was not the same as absence. War memorials, ceremonies of remembrance, *In Memoriam* notices and battlefield pilgrimages all shaped collective and individual mourning and remembrance in interwar Britain, acting as a means both for the bereaved to give voice to their loss, and to remind others of the vast loss of life that total, industrial warfare brought in its wake. It was a watershed for changes in mourning and bereavement rituals that were already in place, as well as a model for

Shadowing: death, grief and mourning before the Second World War

the ways that death would be managed, and grief could be mobilised for the nation, in any future wars. Attitudes to death in the interwar period were shaped by both the memory of the Great War and, as the 1930s came to an end, foreboding of a war to come. The next chapter examines the dominant emotional economy of interwar Britain, considering how the emotional lives of the British people were shaped by the experience of the Great War, and by preparations for the next war.

Notes

1 E. Baume, *Five Graves at Nijmegen* (London: The Westminster Press, 1945), p. 27.
2 T. Laqueur, *The Work of the Dead: A Cultural History of Mortal Remains* (Princeton, NJ: Princeton University Press, 2015).
3 P. Ariès, *The Hour of Our Death*, trans. H. Weaver (New York: Alfred A. Knopf, 1981); G. Gorer, *Death, Grief and Mourning in Contemporary Britain* (London: Cresset Press, 1965).
4 Laqueur, *The Work of the Dead*, p. 14; J. Dollimore, *Death, Desire and Loss in Western Culture* (New York: Routledge, 1998), p. 121; J. Whaley, 'Introduction', in J. Whaley (ed.), *Mirrors of Mortality: Studies in the Social History of Death* (London: Europa, 1981), p. 5.
5 P. Jalland, *Death in War and Peace: A History of Loss and Death in England, 1914–1918* (Oxford: Oxford University Press, 2010), p. 2.
6 P. Jalland, *Death in the Victorian Family* (Oxford: Oxford University Press, 1996), p. 197.
7 Jalland, *Death in the Victorian Family*, p. 195.
8 C. Dickens, 'Trading in death', *Household Words* (27 November 1852), cited in C. Pearsall, 'Burying the Duke: Victorian mourning and the funeral of the Duke of Wellington', *Victorian Literature and Culture*, 27:2 (1999), p. 367.
9 J. M. Strange, 'Only a pauper whom nobody owns: reassessing the pauper grave circa 1880–1914', *Past and Present*, 178 (2003), p. 148.
10 T. Laqueur, 'Bodies, death and pauper funerals', *Representations*, 1 (1983), p. 116.
11 Laqueur, 'Bodies, death and pauper funerals', p. 114.
12 J. M. Strange, *Death, Grief and Poverty in Britain 1870–1914* (Cambridge: Cambridge University Press, 2009).
13 Jalland, *Death in the Victorian Family*, pp. 202, 203.
14 W. Gregor, *Notes on the Folklore of the North-east of Scotland* (London: The Folklore Society, 1881), p. 206.
15 Strange, *Death, Grief and Poverty*, pp. 74–5.
16 J. Hazelgrove, 'Spiritualism after the Great War', *Twentieth Century British History*, 10:4 (1999), pp. 405–6.

17 Strange, *Death, Grief and Poverty*, p. 221.
18 Strange, *Death, Grief and Poverty*, p. 221.
19 'Editorial', the *Times* (31 August 1914), p. 9.
20 See, for example, obituaries and letters published in the *Times*, 11 November 1914, p. 1; 9 February 1915, p. 9; 23 February 1915, p. 1.
21 Gorer, *Death, Grief and Mourning*, pp. 3–4.
22 E. Ana, 'Fashion, its survivals and revivals', the *Fortnightly Review*, 98:587 (November 1915), p. 937.
23 'Funeral of Lord Roberts of Kandahar', the *Times*, 20 November, 1914, p. 9.
24 The *Times* (20 November 1914), p. 9.
25 R. Kipling, 'Mary Postgate', *Nash's Pall Mall Magazine* (January 1915), p. 5.
26 'In memory of Kitchener', *Daily Express*, 14 June 1916, p. 1.
27 The *Saturday Review*, 122:3170 (29 July 1916), p. 113.
28 M. Bateman, 'War and pain', *Fortnightly Review*, 100:597 (September 1916), p. 471.
29 Thanks to Susan Grayzel for this point.
30 The *Times*, 20 August 1914, p. 4; 29 August 1914, p. 6.
31 Jalland, *Death in War and Peace*, p. 41.
32 Jalland, *Death in War and Peace*, p. 85.
33 Jalland, *Death in War and Peace*, p. 85; J. B. Priestley, *English Journey* (London: Victor Gollancz, 1934), pp. 321–50.
34 Jack Lawson, *A Man's Life* (1932), cited in Strange, *Death, Grief and Poverty*, p. 271.
35 Strange, *Death, Grief and Poverty*, p. 66.
36 P. Longworth, *The Unending Vigil: The History of the Commonwealth War Graves Commission* (Barnsley: Pen & Sword Books, this ed. 2010, first published 1967), p. 33.
37 A. Prost, 'The dead', in J. Winter (ed.), *The Cambridge History of the First World War. Volume Three, Civil Society* (Cambridge: Cambridge University Press, 2014), pp. 561–91, here 574.
38 A. Gregory, *The Last Great War: British Society and the First World War* (Cambridge: Cambridge University Press, 2008), p. 255.
39 Jalland, *Death in War and Peace*, p. 51.
40 J. Bourke, *Dismembering the Male: Men's Bodies, Britain and the Great War* (London: Reaktion Books, 1996), p. 235.
41 For an estimate of those whose lives were lost during, or because of the Great War, and the difficulties involved in estimating these figures, see Probst, 'The dead', especially Appendix, 'Table 22:1. Estimate by army of total number of soldiers who died during the First World War', p. 587.
42 S. R. Grayzel, *Women's Identities at War: Gender, Motherhood and Politics in Britain and France during the First World War* (Chapel Hill, NC: University of North Carolina Press, 1999), p. 230.

43 T. Hardy, 'Drummer Hodge' (1899), in J. Gibson (ed.) *The Complete Poems of Thomas Hardy* (London: Macmillan, 1976), p. 90.
44 Laqueur, *The Work of the Dead*, p. 458.
45 J. White, *Zeppelin Nights: London in the First World War* (London: The Bodley Head, 2014), p. 212.
46 S. R. Grayzel, *At Home and Under Fire: Air Raids and Culture in Britain from the Great War to the Blitz* (Cambridge: Cambridge University Press, 2012), p. 68.
47 For an excellent analysis and history of the ceremony, see A. Gregory, *The Silence of Memory: Armistice Day, 1914–1946* (Oxford: Berg, 1994).
48 'For the fallen', the *Times*, 21 September 1914, p. 9.
49 J. Winter, *Sites of Memory, Sites of Mourning: The Great War in European Cultural History* (Cambridge: Cambridge University Press, 1995).
50 A. Tanner, 'The Spanish Lady comes to London: the influenza pandemic 1918–1919', the *London Journal*, 27:2 (2002), p. 51.
51 M. Honigsbaum, *Living with Enza: The Forgotten Story of Britain and the Great Flu Pandemic of 1918* (London: Macmillan, 2009), p. 24.
52 See A. Rasmussen, 'The Spanish Flu', in J. Winter (ed.) *The Cambridge History of the First World War. Volume Three, Civil Society* (Cambridge: Cambridge University Press, 2012), pp. 334–357.
53 N. Johnson, 'The overshadowed killer: influenza in Britain in 1918–19', in H. Phillips and D. Killingray (eds), *The Spanish Influenza Pandemic of 1918–19: New Perspectives* (London: Routledge, 2003), p. 132.
54 Tanner, 'The Spanish Lady', p. 59.
55 '6000,000 world deaths', the *Times*, 18 December 1918, p. 5.
56 Honigsbaum, *Living with Enza*, p. 61.
57 Honigsbaum, *Living with Enza*, pp. 140–41.
58 'Flu's tighter grip on the country', *Daily Mirror*, 22 October 1918, p. 2; 'Influenza sweeping big towns', *Daily Mail*, 2 July 1918, p. 4.
59 'Mainly young people', *Daily Mail*, 24 October 1918, p. 3.
60 'Last week's doubled', *Daily Mail*, 31 October 1918, p. 3.
61 *Manchester Guardian* (27 November 1918), cited in Jalland, *Death in War and Peace*, p. 33.
62 'Deaths', *Brighton Herald*, 9 November 1918, p. 12.
63 'The great death', the *Times*, 2 February 1921, p. 11.
64 D. Cannadine, 'War and death, grief and mourning in modern Britain', in Whaley (ed.) *Mirrors of Mortality*, p. 189.

Feeling

The emotional economy of interwar Britain

Introduction: Ceddy Dickens' grave

In her autobiography, published in 1978, the popular author Monica Dickens reflected on the impact of multiple wartime bereavements on British society, and on her own, upper middle-class family. Death is threaded throughout the book. Dickens' brother, Bunny, died of malaria shortly after his marriage, leaving her parents emotionally and physically diminished as, in their grief, they 'immediately became much smaller'. Employed as a nurse during the Second World War, Dickens cared for a woman who had been doubly bereaved, losing her baby shortly after her husband, a pilot, had been killed. She recounted her remorse at the death of a patient whose symptoms she felt she should have recognised, and her feelings of relief, followed by guilt, when a V1 rocket engine 'cut out' elsewhere, sentencing others to a probable death. Most strikingly, she described the effect of her Uncle Ceddy's death in the Great War on her paternal grandmother, Ceddy's mother. Cedric Dickens, the youngest of six brothers and a favourite in the family, was killed during the Battle of the Somme in 1916. While his mother maintained the stoicism demanded by society in public, in private she grieved for her son until her own death in 1940. She kept a full-size replica of the cross at the head of his grave in her bedroom, with a prayer desk in front of it. Rather than agreeing to Ceddy's body being moved to one of the 'concentrated' Imperial War Graves Commission (IWGC) cemeteries in the years immediately following the war's end, she paid to maintain the grave herself, buying the land and employing a local man to look after the small garden she had planted around the grave. She visited the grave every year. After her death and following the Second

World War, the family finally acceded to the IWGC's request to move Ceddy's remains. However,

> When the grave was dug up, there was nothing there. There never had been, no bones, nothing. When Ceddy was blown up there had been nothing left of him to bury. The old lady had been making her healing pilgrimages to a patch of empty earth.[1]

Dickens' story can stand for the wider experience of many of the bereaved in interwar Britain. As Helen Parr has argued in relation to the Falklands War, the grief of the bereaved was often more boundless, and more awful, than that witnessed in public.[2] Often shattered by the loss of children, friends, lovers, siblings and spouses, the bereaved struggled to rebuild their lives, largely maintaining the requisite 'stiff upper lip' and 'carrying on' in public while developing a range of coping rituals that were sometimes contained completely within the domestic sphere, such as placing a photograph of the dead prominently on a mantelpiece, or otherwise ensuring that memories of the deceased were passed on through family stories and through the preservation of letters and other mementos of a life cut short.[3] The personal, affective impact of wartime bereavement, however, also bled through into the public sphere. Rituals were developed around particular dates, such as placing an *In Memoriam* message in a newspaper to commemorate the anniversary of the death or a birthday, while regimental dinners and less formal gatherings were held to mark particular battles and significant wartime events, and to collectively remember dead comrades.

Public dates, most notably of course Armistice Day, provided an opportunity for loss to be recognised in the wider, national and transnational community, as well as ensuring – through the sale of British Legion poppies of remembrance – an income for the many veterans left disabled by the war, and in the 1930s, an opportunity for pacifist groups to highlight the need to work for peace. Many thousands, like Dickens' grandmother, made a pilgrimage to the war graves and cemeteries. The small Belgian city of Ypres was, arguably, transformed as much by its postwar designation as a site of imperial memory, as it was by the destruction of the war itself. Five large battles had been fought around Ypres during the war, and at its end the city and the country around was home to hundreds of military cemeteries, containing the bodies of thousands of dead. Visitors began to arrive soon after the Armistice, some there as tourists, keen to see the battlefields, but most searching for a grave, or for evidence of the survival, or burial place, of the missing. An infrastructure grew up to support these visitors, who soon became known as pilgrims, their presence demonstrating the widely felt need to have a grave to mourn beside and to care for – a last resting place to visit. For those who had no known grave the Menin Gate, inscribed with the names of 56,000 British and imperial troops missing on the Ypres Salient up until August 1917, with the remainder listed on the memorial wall at nearby Tyne Cot cemetery, was a key site of pilgrimage, its unveiling in July 1927 attracting huge crowds.[4] The largest 'pilgrimage' was that organised by the British Legion to the battlefields, cemeteries and memorials of the Western Front in August 1928, the tenth anniversary of the war's end, in which around 11,000 participated.[5] For some though, the consolation hoped for in visiting the grave was not enough, and often of course there was simply no graveside to visit, and so a more tangible form of contact with the dead was sought. The many war memorials erected in the interwar years provided focal points for individual, as well as communal grief, serving especially for those who had no grave to visit, and for those who could not, or could only rarely, afford to visit the battlefield cemeteries, as a kind of substitute grave. Some attempted to communicate with the dead via séances offered by the many mediums operating at the time, and in a more organised fashion through the teachings of the spiritualist church.[6] For others, of course, established religion provided comforting rituals and a reassurance that the dead and the bereaved would meet again.[7] The sudden losses of wartime and the influenza pandemic left many searching for both consolation and reassurance.

Grief and religious practice in interwar Britain

For some, traditional religious practice seemed an inadequate means of coping with the sudden loss of so many. The war, though, was not the only factor behind declining church membership in the interwar period. Evangelicalism, so dynamic in the early and mid-nineteenth century, had been in decline since the 1880s, as changing leisure habits combined with the growth of the labour movement and the rise of socialism to produce alternative forms of social organisation, and models for social reform. At the same time, the work of social investigators such as Charles Booth and Seebohm Rowntree uncovered the widespread nature of poverty and inequality, challenging the efficacy of the evangelical churches as vehicles for such reform.[8] Nonconformism, historically strongest in working-class industrial areas, was badly affected by the economic depression of the late 1920s and early 1930s; as workers and their families moved to southern England and the Midlands in search of work, congregations went into sharp decline. The impact of the Great War on religious practice was complex, differing across regions, between churches and, according to Gregory, between men and women.[9] Perhaps the best that can be said is that the war accelerated a move towards lower church membership that was already ongoing, informed as much by the shifts of the nineteenth and early twentieth centuries as by the war experience. Church attendance declined throughout the middle years of the twentieth century: the Church of England and the nonconformist churches could claim 20 per cent of the adult population as active members in 1901, but by 1951 this had dropped to 15 per cent.[10] Attendance, however, could be driven as much by tradition, community and habit as by a deeply felt religious belief, and religious belief could be profound without necessitating church attendance. Indeed, as J. C. D. Clark has argued, church attendance and religiosity do not necessarily map onto one another, as people seek spiritual experiences outside the formalities of established religions.[11] For a significant minority of the population of interwar Britain, spiritualism appealed in a way that the established church could not.

The war years, and the interwar period, saw a revival of spiritualism. This, of course, should not be surprising, as Desmond Shaw observed in the 1930s, an eagerness to know 'whether their loved ones survived the holocausts of the Western Front … not in this world but in the next', meant that 'thousands of people the world over became deeply and actively involved in the question of survival'.[12] The spiritualist movement that had grown in the late Victorian and Edwardian period provided a home for many of those struggling to come to terms with their bereavement, promising not only a life after death but a means of communicating with the dead. Despite a wartime campaign by the mainstream press against the 'fraudulent mediums and fortune tellers' of spiritualism, the movement's promise to break down barriers between the living and the dead gave hope to many of the bereaved, and by 1919 there were 309 registered spiritualist societies, more than double the number registered in 1914. The number of societies continued to increase between the wars, with the Spiritualists' National Union claiming 520 members by 1937.[13] Together with the growing interest in astrology, discussed in more detail in Chapter 4, spiritualism formed a part of a complex nexus of belief, superstition and faith in mid-century

Britain, both reflecting and helping to shape the emotional economy of the times.

While for some spiritualism was simply an interest, something that could provide an evening's entertainment, or a diverting newspaper story, for others it promised continued communication with the dead. Spiritualism provided a framework for the ongoing presence of the dead felt by many of the living, enabling unfinished conversations to continue and imparting some consolation to the bereaved. Spiritualists purported to mediate between the living and the dead, who were keen to reassure the grief-stricken that the afterlife was preferable to the material world, appearing as a place where friends and family were reunited and physical injury disappeared. The moment of death, according to many of these communications, was nothing like the agony that might have been imagined. Instead, it was a moment of relief, in which 'the soul leaves the body as a boy jumps out of a school door'.[14] As well as providing consolation about the experience of death for loved ones, spiritualism also urged the bereaved to countenance their loss in other ways, suggesting that the pain of grief could prevent them from communing with the dead as it 'counteracts the delicate mechanism of the waves' and 'confiscates or changes the nature of the message' allegedly passing between the worlds of the living and the dead.[15] It thus both encouraged the grieving to manage their feelings in a manner that could ensure internal comfort and outward stability, and provided an emotional refuge and a community for the bereaved in a society that, as the First World War became more distant, increasingly expected the emotional legacies of wartime loss to be contained, both by the individual bereaved, and within the national calendar.

The dead of the war were, however, present in the material and cultural landscape of the interwar years. War memorials formed part of the new, material landscape of Britain, paid for by public subscription and erected in town squares and on village greens, in churchyards and in schools, in workplaces and in railway stations. As Jay Winter argues, as well as providing a site for collective remembrance, the list of names inscribed on these memorials also acted as a very practical reminder of which households in a community had suffered bereavement, and might be in need of practical, as well as emotional, support.[16] Among these were the 225,536 women recorded as being in receipt of a war widow's pension by 1925.[17] Children grew up never having known their fathers, and many thousands of young women were viewed as 'surplus', allegedly condemned to the neurosis that many believed would be the outcome of the unmarried state. As Joel Morley has shown, family stories of the war, and remembrance of the family dead, shaped the expectations of the war to come among many of those who would have their own lives shaped, and sometimes cut short, by the Second World War.[18]

War memorials, and the ceremonies that surrounded them, were central to remembrance of the war dead. The ceremonies of Armistice Day, which had their national and imperial focus on Lutyens' Cenotaph in Whitehall, were also enacted at war memorials up and down the country. Originating in the recognition that the dead, and the bereaved, had to be acknowledged in the Peace Day Parade of July 1919, and the erection of what was planned to be a temporary cenotaph in Whitehall, the dead quickly became central to the rituals of Armistice Day. The two-minute silence at 11 a.m., described by the *Manchester Guardian* as 'a silence which was almost pain', was at the heart of Armistice Day ceremonies, while the formal language of remembrance shaped public acknowledgement of the war dead and the multiple bereaved.[19] While the meanings of Armistice Day were never secured, with veterans celebrating the war's end until the mid-1920s, and peace campaigners of the 1930s seeing the rituals of remembrance as a symbol of the need to avoid future wars, 11 November nonetheless served as a public reminder of the losses of the war, and the impact of these losses for the bereaved.

Richard Overy has described this period as 'the morbid age', a period in which cultural and intellectual activity was shaped by a pre-occupation with death, decline and crisis.[20] In part, this was driven by intellectual concerns about the impact of modernity, and, as Chapter 3 will discuss, very real fears concerning the nature of any coming war. But it was also shaped by the emotional legacy of mass death between 1914 and 1920. The numerous deaths of wartime, combined with the death of thousands in the influenza outbreak between 1918 and 1920, meant that hundreds of thousands of Britons had experienced sudden bereavement, often of the young, within a period of roughly six years. Public acts of commemoration and remembrance, an interest in spiritualism and the growth of a tourist industry centred around the battlefields and burial grounds of the war each marked shifts in the mourning practices of interwar Britain, and together demonstrate the ongoing impact of wartime bereavement on British society in the 1920s and 1930s. A combination of the decision early in the war not to repatriate the bodies of dead soldiers, but to bury them instead in special war cemeteries close to the place of death, and the impact that modern warfare had on the human body, often destroying it so completely that there were no remains to be buried, meant for many there was a lack of a body around which burial rites could be enacted. In place of pre-war mourning practices then, there grew up new rites and rituals, largely centred around the war memorials that appeared across the country and the ceremonies on and around Armistice Day on 11 November each year. These rituals were enacted and experienced by individuals within a society that had a particular emotional culture; a culture that privileged stoicism, self-control and resolve over public displays of emotion. The next section of this chapter maps some of the key aspects of the emotional economy of the interwar years, paying particular attention to the ways in which this was gendered.

The emotional economy of interwar Britain

Jon Lawrence has shown how, in the immediate postwar period, fear of the perceived brutalising effects of war, widely understood as lying behind the involvement of soldiers in the riots of 1919, the massacre of 379 unarmed protestors in Amritsar by soldiers under the leadership of Sir Reginald Dyer and the violence of the Black and Tan War in Ireland, helped to drive a reshaped sense of British national identity that emphasised reasonableness and restraint.[21] The emphasis on a militarised masculinity, so central to late Victorian and Edwardian concepts of the British national character, seemed increasingly out of place in a nation that had experienced four years of total, industrial warfare, and that was desperate to avoid the worst of the civil violence and instability that plagued much of Europe in the postwar period.[22] In its place developed a sense of Britain as a 'uniquely peaceable kingdom', inhabited by a temperate people who preferred domesticity to disorder, and restraint to revolution.[23] This demanded personal, as much as political, control and helped to shape the emotional economy of self-restraint and self-management that came to dominate in the interwar years.

Self-restraint was central to this new emotional economy. As Frank Mort has argued, the years between the wars saw the emergence of 'an emotionally centred sense of self' that expected individuals to manage their feelings through a process of self-reflection and self-control.[24] This self-reflection should not be confused with repression; people were encouraged to reflect upon and to understand their feelings, not to ignore them. A body of advice literature, popular psychology and voluntary organisations acted to energetically police the expression of emotions in public, equating self-awareness and a subsequent ability to master emotional expression in public with emotional and physical health and the performance of good citizenship. The 'experts of experience' providing this advice included newspaper and magazine agony aunts, psychologists, doctors and teachers of health and hygiene.[25] However, we should not make the mistake of reading this body of literature as an accurate guide to the multiple ways in which people controlled or expressed their feelings: the poet Ted Hughes' recollection that the Calder Valley of his interwar childhood was inhabited by melancholic, weeping women reminds us that the advice seen in public texts is not always the same as lived experience and feeling.[26] Although the emotional codes being outlined here were widespread, and no doubt informed the ways that many people experienced and expressed their emotions, for some, in particular circumstances, or in communities with strong local traditions of emotionality, or with social identities which allowed for a greater or lesser expression of these feelings, different codes could apply. Emotional codes, while being powerful social forces, are always and everywhere negotiated, mediated and contested.

Nonetheless, the dominant emotional economy of interwar Britain valued self-reflection and restraint. Seen as being 'naturally' more emotional, and less rational than men, women were subject to a wave of advice as to how to control and moderate their emotions in the public sphere, even as this was increasingly feminised. In his work on the concept of honour in post-Revolutionary France, William Reddy has described how 'the relationship between gender and emotion is … so intimate and elemental that it has shaped and continues to shape public action, though actors often have no awareness of it'.[27] Women had long been seen as driven by sentiment, while men were perceived as more able to apply reason and rationality to their actions, a gendered 'emotional topography' that, Ute Frevert suggests, acted to help naturalise the roles assigned to men and to women in modern Europe.[28] There were multiple forces bearing on gender roles in interwar Britain that acted to reshape the emotional codes than women, in particular, were largely expected to abide by. As women became full citizens, and moved into new areas of public life, a form of femininity that privileged self-awareness and control, seen in changing codes of bereavement in the Great War, began to appear more widely. Modern domesticity too, as lived by growing numbers in suburban houses replete with new household appliances, increasingly demanded emotional restraint: the ideal housewife was sensible rather than sensitive, a household manager ably juggling the multiple needs of children, husband and the modern household. The discourse of efficiency seen in the new light industries that provided employment for many young women in the Midlands and the south of England was also seen in the domestic home, where women were expected to manage their households through the knowledgeable acquisition and application of consumer goods.[29] Efficient household management, for the women who were moving to new homes in the suburbs, both on council-built estates and in the new developments of 'Metroland', and for the women learning to manage with 'daily' domestic service rather than live-in servants, was a signifier of a modern, rational femininity.[30]

Men too were expected to understand, and thus effectively manage, their feelings. Middle-class men and boys, and increasingly boys of the working class, through the growth of militaristic organisations like the Boys' Brigade and the Boy Scouts, had long been exposed to models of masculinity that emphasised restraint, bravery and stoicism. The experience of the Great War showed that no amount of training could enable most men to completely control emotional responses to conditions such as fear, and the growth of a popular interest in psychology in the 1920s, identified by Michael Roper, was driven by an awareness of the psychic impact of combat experiences on many of the surviving veterans.[31] Novels and memoirs written by many of these veterans in the late 1920s and early 1930s sought to explore the experience, and legacies, of wartime fear and violence for these men; heroic, desirable models of masculinity were those that were able to recognise and manage emotions like fear, these models replacing the earlier ideal of the man who did not feel fear. The new self-awareness that men and women were expected to demonstrate, and the tools for self-management that they were expected to use, demanded emotional labour of their subjects.

Magazines, novels, voluntary organisations and the new 'discipline' of popular psychology were ready and willing to monitor this work and to provide guidance. The growth of this code of emotional management was shaped by class, region and nation as well as by gender. It was a mode of emotional being that was particularly associated with middle-class identities and middle-class life. This large, diverse and increasingly dominant group in British social and political life were becoming ever more used to seeing themselves reflected in cultural texts. While stars like Gracie Fields and George Formby, the biggest box-office attractions of the 1930s, continued to perform a highly popular version of geographically specific working-class identities, they were largely comic characters, representatives of a slowly dying cultural form – the variety theatre – who were able to find a niche in the film industry that was replacing it.[32] Nonetheless, in their embodiment of a 'down-to-earth', cheerful and practical approach to the multiple problems their characters were presented with in their popular films, they provided a working-class, northern counterpart to the stoical middle-class and usually southern characters of much popular fiction. New magazines like *Picture Post*, with its photographic essays on British life; the new women's magazines such as *Woman* and *Woman's Own*, with their intimate knowledge of everyday middle-class domesticity; Noel Coward's popular plays, which explored the small cruelties and kindnesses of middle-class family and romantic life with such success; and popular novels such as those by Agatha Christie reflected the cultural life of the middle classes back to themselves.[33] This was also a peculiarly English emotional culture: while Scottish, Welsh and Irish inhabitants of Britain no doubt also displayed the self-control and emotional restraint that was so visible in numerous cultural texts of the period, citizens of Britain's 'Celtic fringe' were understood to have their own, historically grounded emotional cultures, separate from that of their English counterparts, made visible for example in the canny Scottish ghost outwitting wealthy Americans in the 1935 film *The Ghost Goes West*, and in the emotionally expressive mining communities of the Welsh valleys in Richard Llewelyn's 1939 novel *How Green Was My Valley*.[34]

While codes of reticence and stability were being represented as a British, and peculiarly English and middle-class, character trait, not all people could be relied on to display these characteristics. Working-class and lower middle-class women living in the new suburbs of the interwar years were identified in the pages of the medical journal the *Lancet* as being particularly likely to display neurotic characteristics. The anxieties experienced by women in the new suburban housing estates were diagnosed as a form of mental illness by Stephen Taylor, senior medical officer at the Royal Free Hospital, London. Taylor described the symptoms that he was seeing in female patients in his outpatients clinic as a 'suburban neurosis', a mental and physical response to the isolation and boredom experienced by some women living in the suburbs, who, he argued, lacked the emotional and intellectual resources to manage the 'boredom ... anxiety ... [and] false set of values' that they found there.[35] The 'false values' of the suburbs, he argued, were peculiar to lower middle-class women, who had 'made a fetish of the home' and were trying, unsuccessfully, to emulate 'the kind of life successfully led by people to whom books, theatres and things of the intellect matter'.[36] Lacking both the imagined cultural and intellectual resources of the established middle class, and this group's emotional stoicism, women suffering with 'suburban neurosis' were being referred to Taylor with a range of symptoms, including headaches, backache, digestive complaints, shortness of breath, insomnia and weight loss. Taylor understood his patients to be a social problem, the cure for which lay, largely, in social solutions. Arguing that 'we have allowed the slum which stunted the body to be replaced by a slum which stunts the mind', Taylor advocated the establishment of social clubs, libraries and sports centres on the new estates.[37] It was in the interests of the state to provide for these women, Taylor warned, as suburban neurosis was not seen in 'totalitarian states' which had 'reasserted the "leader principle"'. Without such leadership, entertainment or other diversion, the bored, un-resourceful and neurotic 'Mrs Everywoman' of the new suburban estates would provide 'a most hopeful field for the teachers of new, and possibly dangerous, political ideologies'.[38] There was no room for emotional states such as 'suburban neurosis' in the 'peaceable kingdom' of interwar Britain, by the late 1930s positioning itself as the moderate, self-controlled antithesis of continental nations where the interwar years had been marked by civil unrest, conflict, revolution and political extremism.

The apparently depressed and anxious female inhabitants of Britain's suburbs were understood here as a social and political problem because they were believed to lack the internal, emotional resources to cope with the demands of their situation. This lack of resources, it was feared, could make them vulnerable to extremist political ideologies. Reporting on the inquest of a woman who had gassed herself, the *Daily Mail* cited 'medical man' Dr J. E. Elam:

> The outpatients departments of London hospitals are full of women suffering from 'suburban neurosis'. It is a grave social problem what to do with the women.

Talking to a 'few suburban wives at random', apparently culled from the London telephone directory, the *Daily Mail* reporter found that many were, unsurprisingly, keen to distance themselves from this malady, an accountant's wife from Surbiton responding 'I cannot understand any suburban housewife being lonely these days,' while the Purley wife of a civil servant said she found her children 'absorbingly interesting, and when I am with them I never have a dull moment'.[39] If they were able to cope with the demands of suburban life, then those who failed to do so were inadequate; the problem surely lay in their failings, not in the nature of domestic suburban life. The suburban female neurotic was both a pathetic and a dangerous figure, whose failure to impose self-discipline and manage her depression and anxiety threatened her own health, her family's happiness and, ultimately, the wellbeing of the nation.

Advice as to the desirability of achieving the requisite emotional stability was widespread. Physical and emotional health were conjoined, and exercise, fresh air and moderation in food and drink were understood as underpinning individual and national health. Numerous groups, including the Sunlight League, the People's League of Health, the Legion of Health and Happiness and the Women's League of Health and Beauty, equated individual and national health with exercise, a plain diet and self-control, as did George Newman, Chief Medical Officer for Health, who recommended 'self knowledge, moderation and simplicity' as the key to a healthy life.[40] Organisations like these were part of a wider movement in the interwar period concerned with improving national health, culminating in the Chamberlain government's 1937 Physical Training and Recreation Act, which attempted to improve the 'physical well-being of the people' through group exercise, healthy diets and fresh air.[41] The Women's League of Health and Beauty, which described women as 'the makers or breakers of the race', wanted to create desirable, healthy and sensible wives and mothers by enabling its members to both 'improve their figures and develop their personalities'.[42] The collective took precedence over the individual in an emotional as well as a physical sense: advice to members taking part in the 1935 Olympia Display exhorted them to 'cut out feelings of shyness and self-consciousness. They are selfish, fundamentally, and unnecessary.'[43] Internal self-management would impact not only on the body but on society more widely, one member writing that

> One of my friends in the League tells me that she never used to think about unemployment, war and slums because she did not see what she could do about them. But when she found out there that were things in her life that caused all these problems – bad temper, selfishness and chronic untidiness – she decided that she'd got to change.[44]

Emotional, as much as physical, self-control was at the heart of the new health groups' teachings and advice. They were creating ideal citizens: physically fit, socially aware and emotionally controlled.

The gendered nature of the relationship between a disciplined mind and a disciplined body was evident both in advice on how to achieve beauty, and in beauty contests of the period. Adverts for 'Poudre Tokalon' face powder in 1925 warned women that 'no man likes a woman with a shiny nose' because 'he feels she is careless and slovenly'.[45] Irene Vanbrugh, judging a 1935 beauty competition in Westminster, told *Daily Mirror* readers that for her, 'intelligence and charm' were preferable to 'mere perfection of feature'.[46] Entrants in the *Daily Mail*'s 1928 beauty contest were described as including 'many sports loving, out of doors English girls', among them a Miss Florence Gilliland, a busy woman whose hobbies included swimming, golf, tennis, hockey, motor cycling and making her own clothes.[47] When the same newspaper announced the winners of its 1935 'Charm and Beauty Contest', it distinguished between women whose faces showed 'true loveliness and character' and those who merely displayed a 'chocolate box prettiness'. Miss Winnifred Tate, winner of the not inconsiderable £500 first prize, was described as being 'not only beautiful, but gloriously vigorous and healthy'.[48] In Lancashire, the Cotton Queen beauty pageants of the 1930s rewarded young female mill workers who possessed, in the judges' view, a 'wholesome natural vision of beauty'.[49] Feminine beauty, it appeared, did not simply depend on physical perfection but could be achieved by rigorous management of both the body and the emotions.

Rational, self-controlled behaviour was urged on the women of Britain in a range of different cultural texts, and in relation to a range of different circumstances. As Thomas Dixon has shown, weeping was increasingly seen as undesirable, women's magazines advising their readers that excessive tearfulness would not only make them unattractive, but also unemployable.[50] In 1919, the *Daily Mail* warned its female audience that 'self indulgence in the matter of undesirable emotions' would have a detrimental effect on their appearance, as 'emotions generate material poisons in the system'.[51] The 'surplus women' of the period were especially advised to maintain a close grip on their emotions: a tendency towards public displays of grief, which would make them appear 'neurotic, quarrelsome and fussy', could be suppressed by keeping busy, attending evening classes or taking up a new hobby.[52] Emotional restraint was seen as an indicator of being 'modern', particularly suited to the busy lives of young women. An article in the *Daily Mirror* approvingly contrasted the freedom of contemporary women with the formal and restrictive clothing on display at an exhibition of nineteenth-century dress, saving particular scorn for the mourning traditions which meant that a bride of the 1860s 'had never been able to wear her trousseau, as she had continually been in mourning for some relative or other'.⁵³ In contrast, a respondent to the *Daily Mail's* agony aunt, Anne Temple, concerned that she had not shown her dying husband enough affection, was reassured that an unstated mutual affection and understanding meant that there had been no need even for 'a last word between you two'.⁵⁴ This shifting emotional economy also had financial implications; in 1934, a Southwark judge reprimanded a working-class woman who had applied for £13 in funeral expenses. Awarding her £3 10s., he explained that 'people don't wear mourning nowadays; it is ridiculous … It is stupid to waste your money on mourning. It does no good for the dead either.'⁵⁵ The woman's application had been for mourning clothes for her infant son to wear to his brother's funeral.

Men, too, were expected to display self-restraint. The model of the self-possessed, stoical British man had existed long before the emergence of his female counterpart, and although Victorian and late Edwardian notions of masculinity which equated a physical and spiritual heroism, a desire for adventure and a taste for chivalric self-sacrifice with the conquest and defence of empire were in retreat following the Great War, codes of masculinity, like femininity, were complex and often ambiguous.⁵⁶ A heroic masculinity lived on in the novels of John Buchan, in Korda's epic films of men and empire such as *The Four Feathers* and in the numerous adventure books and magazines produced for boys and young men.⁵⁷ Captain W. E. Johns' numerous 'Biggles' stories, 'unashamedly patriotic and gung-ho stories of combat', were immensely popular.⁵⁸ The continued popularity of this adventure genre, deploying a language and imagery of heroic masculinity, provided one of the routes by which

> Men constantly travelled backwards and forwards across the frontier of domesticity … attracted by the responsibilities of marriage or fatherhood, but also enchanted by fantasies of the energetic life and homosocial camaraderie of the adventure hero.⁵⁹

The domestic, 'temperate' man of the interwar period, in retreat from the dreadful meeting of chivalric masculinity and industrial warfare in the Great War, nonetheless had a complex emotional life, one in which the appeal of a traditionally heroic masculinity could remain strong.

Attention to the fashioning of selfhood was expected of men as well as women, and although perhaps less visible than the advice on emotional management so readily offered to women, codes of masculine behaviour and appropriate emotional forms of expression were nonetheless woven into the fabric of interwar Britain. Michael Roper has shown how the need for soldiers experiencing anxiety and fear in the trenches of the Great War to recognise and thus control these feelings underpinned a growing expectation that men would understand, and thus successfully manage, their own feelings.[60] Stoicism was still expected of men, but it was to be built on an understanding of feeling, not on their repression. In his work on the mid-twentieth-century popular press, Adrian Bingham has shown how the development of an 'ordinary, "respectable" masculinity' was often articulated through a focus on marital companionship and domestic pursuits.[61] While these domestic roles were still gendered – the *Daily Express* running a weekly column 'Man About the House' which set out the domestic work and household repairs that the modern man was responsible for – the ideal husband had changed considerably since the Edwardian period.[62] The *Daily Mirror*'s male audience were reminded that 'fathers must take their share in the life of the home – and take it seriously', while a survey in the *Daily Express* claimed to have found that the majority of women wanted their households to be organised 'on a partnership basis, with the husband ready to sympathise and help with domestic issues'.[63] Although the wife may have been responsible for the management of day-to-day concerns, the self-reflective men of the interwar years were expected to be more involved in the life of the home, on both a practical and an emotional level.[64] More widely, men and women were expected to regulate their emotional lives and their emotional expression, not just in the home and in their intimate and familial relationships, but in the workplace and the wider public world.

A world of consumer products existed that would allegedly aid the British man or woman in the satisfactory management of their emotions, and maintenance of their daily routines. Yeast-Vite tablets appear to have had a particularly wide-ranging effect on the physical and emotional health of those who took them. According to adverts, Yeast-Vite was not only a remedy for ulcers and influenza, but also brought relief for more psychological problems, including 'nerve pains … lassitude, depression, nerves … exhaustion and sleeplessness'.[65] Women were exhorted to 'strengthen your nerves with Sanatogen' as 'nerves … are responsible for your tired feelings, they are behind our sleepless nights'.[66] Dr Cassell's Tablets promised a cure for 'nerve exhaustion' and 'nerve crisis', while the ubiquitous Bile Beans offered to support the digestive system and strengthen nerves.[67] The extent to which any of these remedies worked is debatable: in July 1938, the *Manchester*

Guardian reported a meeting of the British Medical Association during which doctors were warned that nervous states and strains were 'probably the single commonest cause of ill health'. Laymen, the article concluded, 'would do well to think about their nerves as little as possible; not to boast of "living on one's nerves" but, so far as may be, to leave them alone'.[68]

The wave of democratising processes in early and mid-twentieth-century Britain – an increasingly universal education, growing levels of literacy and the concurrent expansion of the press, extensions to the franchise – meant that both the external actions and the internal feelings of the people became a site for enquiry and concern. The rise of fascism, with its apparent ability to appeal to and manipulate feelings, meant that the thoughts, feelings and beliefs of a newly enfranchised electorate mattered more than ever before. A range of cultural texts and experts encouraged individuals to reflect on their internal lives, and counselled that both physical and emotional self-management were crucial to personal fulfilment and good citizenship. In this landscape of self-reflection and emotional management, two concurrent trends emerged: a mounting interest in the diary as a source of self-exploration and fulfilment, and the growth of advice from 'everyday experts' on techniques for managing the self.

In the first half of the twentieth century, diary keeping became a widespread activity, one that was encouraged through newspaper articles and radio broadcasts reflecting on its purpose, and demonstrated through the exponential growth in sales of diaries by their leading producer, the Charles Letts company, which saw sales rise from 1 million in 1900 to 3 million by 1936.[69] Widely read versions, like Jan Struther's fictional diary of 'Mrs Miniver' for the Court Page of the *Times* between 1937 and 1939, helped to further popularise the act of recording one's everyday life and innermost thoughts, while the recruitment by Mass Observation (MO) of diarists and panellists as part of its project of creating 'an anthropology of our own people' helped to validate diary keeping as a social, as well as a personal, act.[70] The first edition of the organisation's first book, *Mass Observation*, used extracts from Day Surveys on its dust jacket, demonstrating to readers and critics the value of collecting apparently mundane, everyday observations as a means of enabling people to speak for themselves and by so doing, to build a bridge of understanding and commonality between the social classes, and between the governed and the government.[71] In MO's third publication, *First Year's Work, 1937–38*, Charles Madge described the observers as 'the cameras with which we are trying to photograph contemporary life', but 'subjective cameras' who will 'tell us not what society is like but what it looks like to them'.[72] Nonetheless, to be effective observers, they were expected to be aware of this subjectivity. Mass Observers were encouraged to engage in self-reflection: every new panellist was asked to write a 500-word report that described their social background, and considered the impact that their identity might have on their observations.[73] By developing self-awareness in its contributors, and expecting them to reflect on this in written form, MO hoped to counter the charges of bias and unrepresentativeness that have dogged the organisation since its inception. Only self-aware, reflective observers, it believed, would be able to step back, and view and record British society 'with some extra degree of detachment'.[74]

MO aimed through its collection of the thoughts, feelings and opinions of so-called ordinary people to make these people more knowable to those who governed them: motivated by a democratic and egalitarian impulse, the organisation's insistence that people's thoughts and feelings mattered served at the same time to validate the act of writing about, and reflecting upon, the self. While the Second World War was crucial in elevating the political significance of people's feelings, the pre-war directives issued by MO demonstrate that period's burgeoning interest in subjective, emotional responses. A January 1939 directive, focusing on music and dance halls, asked the respondents to record what they 'think about', and whether they 'look forward to a dance with pleasure or fear?'[75] The August 1939 appeal for diarists to join their body of volunteer writers focused almost entirely on personal and subjective responses in its instructions to diarists to keep 'political discussion at a minimum, concentrating on the details of your everyday life, your own reactions and those of your family and others you meet'.[76] The diaries were both the raw material that MO drew on in its regular reports on daily life and popular feeling during the war, and sites for self-reflection, self-management and self-construction by their authors.

The feelings that were at the heart of the MO diary project, however, could not simply be left to the management of individuals. The growth of the 'everyday experts' in self-management helped to professionalise the existing socialisation of restraint within the emotional economy of the period. Good emotional citizens were expected not only to exercise emotional control, but increasingly to do so through rational, practical reflection on the self, and the mobilisation of this reflection as an agent of personal change. The columns of the new, popular, women's magazines and the daily newspapers the *Daily Mail* and the *Daily Mirror*, both imagined to have large female readerships, advised their female consumers on matters of emotional management as well as offering tips on household management, childcare, relationships and beauty regimes. Anne Temple's 'Human casebook' column in the *Daily Mail*, its title a reflection of the growing professionalisation of expert advice, was largely a space for advising women on how to recognise, and manage, potentially disruptive feelings. Responding to an engaged woman who described herself as 'terror stricken' at the thought of caring for 'a husband, in a town where I knew no-one', Temple advised her that it was 'doubt of yourself which is causing the trouble', encouraging her to understand that it was her upbringing as a sheltered, only child that lay at the root of her fears, rather than anxiety about life in an isolated suburb, and advising her to 'go out and do something difficult on your own every day' as a means of overcoming her fear.[77] Emotional labour, she suggested, could thus overcome deficiencies of the self that stemmed from childhood. Self-knowledge, accompanied by an engagement with the wider community and social world, were the means to self-improvement: a woman who believed she had holidayed in a haunted house, and was subsequently anxious about staying away from home, was advised that she had developed 'the habit of allowing your feelings to control your mind instead of governing by reason'. To overcome this she was told to

> practise controlling daily your emotions in small ways by your mind. For instance, if some small thing annoys you, reason it out, accept the difficulty, smile over it, set your mind at work to remove it.[78]

Emotional control could thus be learnt, and improved on, by disciplined practice. The emergence of the idea of self-help, seen in the advice given by these agony aunts, and understood as especially relevant and helpful to women negotiating the complex demands of interwar modernity, was also seen in the emergence of a literature of popular, applied psychology in the years immediately before the outbreak of war.

Mathew Thomson has identified the growth of this popular, practical psychology in the interwar years as a key site through which British men and women were encouraged to both be self-reflexive and to undertake the work of emotional self-management, increasingly seen as important to both individual happiness and to so-called national character.[79] Popular experts like Anne Temple were able to draw on ideas of childhood development impacting on the adult self in the expectation that their readers would have a sense of the theories they were drawing on, and a recognition that modernity could cause anxiety, neurosis and trauma which had to be managed if they were not to be socially disruptive. Although a detailed knowledge of psychoanalysis, and the financial and time commitments required to undergo analysis, remained the preserve of a small elite, ideas drawing on the field were rapidly popularised. Psychoanalysts' insistence that the thin veneer of civilisation covered a multitude of internal impulses and desires was used to explain a range of different actions and issues. Agatha Christie's novels often provided psychological explanations for crime, and a diagnosis of hysteria was made, variously, for the actions of crowds at football matches, lively parliamentary debates and attempted murder.[80] It does not take a great leap of the imagination to begin to understand why, in the aftermath of a war in which individual agency was removed both from those on the battlefield and from those waiting anxiously at home, psychology's promise of success and contentment through work on the self was appealing. In contrast to techniques of psychoanalysis, however, in practical psychology 'mind, memory and instinctive energies were to be harnessed, put together and enhanced, not taken apart in self-critical analysis'.[81] Alongside other popular pastimes like Pelmanism and physical fitness, practical psychology promised individuals access to a range of techniques guaranteed to ensure both mental and physical health, and success in business and personal relationships. Local branches of the British Union of Practical Psychologists, which offered visiting speakers, libraries and training in techniques of self-improvement, were popular, and numerous publications appeared which acted to popularise psychological theories and techniques.[82] *Practical Psychology*, which became the more commercial *You: The Popular Psychology Magazine* in 1938, the magazine of the Union, was a key vehicle for the diffusion of ideas about, and programmes for, emotional self-management in the later 1930s.

The editorial of the very first edition of *Practical Psychology* set out what it saw as the clear link between emotional self-management and social, personal and political ills:

> Creative thought is a very real source of dynamic energy, yet the extent of its employment in a positive and enriching direction by the people of today is trifling. On the contrary, the extent of the misery, unemployment, unhappiness, disease and sometimes death, is due to negative thinking; such conditions have actually been created and are being maintained by the same ill-nurtured and ill-directed mind processes.[83]

Self-knowledge and reflective self-control, it suggested, were the keys to individual and social happiness. Local branches of the union offered practical lessons in this project: Bradford reported well-attended lectures on 'the emotions and health', while nearby Leeds held a popular lecture on 'The Science and Art of Living for Health and Happiness'.[84] With training and effort, the magazine suggested, anyone could master their emotions, the contributor P. J. Pinnard arguing that in the relationship between the mind and the body, 'any kind of emotion can be nipped in the bud … by inhibition of the physical counterpart through mental intervention'.[85] Not just emotional expression, but the whole inner world of feeling, it was suggested, could be controlled with the right sort of effort.

Emotional life, however, is experienced and expressed within, and shaped by, specific historical conditions, and by the late 1930s the advice being offered to readers by the magazine was increasingly driven by concerns about the possibility of another war. War had been a recurrent issue in the magazine since its inception, but by 1938 articles had shifted from discussing the 'psychology of war' in fairly abstract terms, to advising readers on how to best prepare themselves psychologically for any future conflict. There were regular articles on the importance of 'Courage' and 'Hope', and in February 1939 the magazine printed a list of common fears, and how to overcome them.[86] The belief that fear and anxiety would need to be contained in the coming war by both combatants and civilians was widespread, with individuals being given responsibility for, in the first instance, managing their own anxiety and apprehension. On the eve of war, good citizenship depended in part at least on self-regulation and adherence to dominant emotional codes.

The Munich crisis and 'Gas Mask Sunday' in September 1938 gave the British people a foretaste of the anxieties to come. The Great War cast a long shadow, and as growing tensions over the Sudetenland increased fears of imminent war in Britain an 'anxious crowd' gathered outside Downing Street on 12 September, waiting for news as Hitler gave a speech on the Sudeten crisis. When the speech failed to declare war on Czechoslovakia, there were 'cheers of relief' beneath 'the Cenotaph, the Empire's memorial to the men who gave their lives in the last war – the "war to end all wars"'.[87] MO reports on public responses to the ongoing crisis showed a widespread fatalism among respondents in 'Metrop' (Hammersmith, west London): a twenty-five-year-old shop assistant stated, 'I stopped bothering about it … every day they say it's worse ... let it come, it'll be the end of everything ... who cares?', while a thirty-eight-year-old woman explained her lack of engagement with the complex negotiations in her comment that 'it's too much to cope with and we can't do anything'.[88] While a sense of powerlessness clearly underpinned these responses, fatalism was largely interpreted in the press as evidence of stoicism and self-control: lack of panic on the streets of London, according to some newspaper articles of the time, reflected the national character. The claim that self-control was a vital component of the national good was seen across the political landscape of the popular press. The leader in the centre-right *Daily Sketch* on 9 September affirmed the importance of emotional self-management in its statement that '[I]t is in this uncertain atmosphere that the calibre of the individual, as of a nation, undergoes a severe test. On the whole we are reacting to this strain upon the nerves in a very creditable way.' The following day, the leader in the *Daily Herald*, aligned with the Labour movement, reminded its readers that '[N]ot to believe, not to spread, sensational or tendentious rumour, or wild speculation, is at this time both a national duty and a really valuable contribution to the cause of peace.'[89] The fatalism and apathy that MO diagnosed during the crisis of September 1938 could equally be presented in the press as fortitude and resilience.

For some however, fear of a future war was almost unbearable. MO recorded some disturbing replies to its question 'What will you actually do if war breaks out?' from those who were old enough to remember the previous war. One woman, a forty-two-year-old mother, answered at some length:

> I have been collecting poison for some time with guile and cunning. I have sufficient to give self, husband and all the children a lethal dose. I can remember the last war. I don't want to live through another, or the children either. I shan't tell them, I shall just do it.

She was not alone. A man of forty-five said he would poison his two sons if war broke out, and a woman of fifty claimed, 'I'd rather see my girl, who is my only one, killed outright than suffer.' Younger respondents too, their expectations of a future war shaped by the apocalyptic representations of poison gas and air raids seen so widely in the culture of the 1930s, and by coverage of the decade's conflicts in Spain, China and Abyssinia, were similarly unwilling to subject themselves or their children to the expected horrors: a thirty-three-year-old woman explained that 'I want to see my children dead before I am if there is to be a war, and I'll see that they are if they bomb here', while a woman of thirty-four agreed, 'I'd sooner see kids dead than bombed like they are in some places.'[90] For these respondents, the belief that any future war would be horrific led not to stoicism or to apathy, but to a terrible, despairing, desire to assert some form of agency.

'Gas Mask Sunday' on 25 September 1938 put particular demands on the emotional resilience of the British people. Long viewed with fear and loathing, the gas mask was an object that seemed, to many, to embody all that they feared of modern war, but at the height of the Munich crisis, the government began to issue masks to the civilian population.[91] Reporting that 'Britain has shown her will to be prepared', the *Daily Mirror* reported long lines of resigned people waiting outside schools and church halls for their gas masks to be fitted.[92] The *Daily Express* reported on 'cheerful uproar' at Chelsea Town Hall as 'titled people and telephone girls' queued together for their masks. In Chelsea as elsewhere, the newspaper claimed, people greeted the distribution of gas masks with phlegm and pragmatism:

> Wondering how the average family acts in times of crisis I searched for reports of hysterics, or emotional upset to the smooth machine ... Everywhere they told me 'no excitement; we've had no fuss'.[93]

Many of the reflections on 'Gas Mask Sunday' sent by respondents to MO appeared to support this sense that masks were seen as a sensible precaution. One woman, from Laindon in Essex, described the 'cheerfulness' and 'joking and laughing' in the queue for gas masks at her local church hall on Sunday evening, where she explained, 'all was order and kindness and good temper', while an actress, in Newcastle-upon-Tyne, described a boy 'jumping up and down and rubbing his hands with excitement at getting a gas mask'.[94] Others, however, noticed an underlying tension, not always expressed verbally but present in the body: one man recorded that 'nervous fingers twiddle the saltcellar. Faces are strained and worried'.[95] A woman from Ipswich explained that 'elderly people are apparently suffering with stomach trouble owing to the anxiety of listening or reading reports of the crisis', while the respondent from Laindon reported that her sister had written that 'her boy cannot eat for fear and excitement'.[96] The British may have learnt to reflect upon and control the ways that they expressed their feelings verbally, but the bodily impact of fear, anxiety and excitement was less easy to control and contain.

Feeling: the emotional economy of interwar Britain

Conclusion

Of course, the existence of the emotional codes that have been outlined here does not mean that people abided by them. Indeed, the very plethora of advice about the importance of self-management, reflexivity and adherence to the correct forms of emotional expression could suggest the exact opposite: a concern that the men and women of interwar Britain were not demonstrating enough emotional control. Specific cultural and material spaces where grief could be expressed and communicated were a part of the national landscape; the ceremonies that took place around war memorials on Armistice Day, and the 'pilgrimages' to the battlefields and cemeteries of the Great War were just two such sites. Public expressions of grief and sorrow were extensive when ninety-nine submariners died on HMS *Thetis* when it was lost off Orme Head in 1939, with 2,000 attending a service of remembrance at St-Martin-in-the-Fields and the BBC broadcasting a memorial service from Portsmouth, during which 'the whole nation listened to a woman's sobs'.[97] Public, and highly gendered, expressions of grief continued to be seen at funerals, for example in the description of 'hundreds of weeping women' at the funeral of two victims of the Gresford Colliery disaster in 1934.[98] Obviously, not everyone had internalised the advice on self-restraint, and equally obviously, there were times and places where a public display of feeling was expected and considered appropriate.

The interwar period saw the growth of an emotional economy that validated restraint, and increasingly saw expressions of emotion, in particular feelings of sadness, anxiety and fear, as problematic, unsuitable behaviour for the modern British woman or man. The fortitude that middle-class men were expected to display before the Great War became a more widespread trait during and immediately after the war when it helped to contain the grief of so many, especially in public. Women, especially working-class women, always seen as less controlled, more expressive, were especially encouraged to practise self-management, and to control the ways in which they expressed themselves. For women, a model of femininity that emphasised the desirability of being wholesomely athletic, enthusiastic and sensible replaced earlier models of a more emotional, sensitive and frail femininity. Men too were expected to recognise the complexity of their emotional life, and to work on the management and expression of feeling. Emotional control became associated with emotional stability and strength.

Dying for the nation

As Britain moved towards war once again in the late 1930s, it was increasingly recognised that the ways people felt and acted would be central to the wartime community. Asked once again to bear mass death and bereavement, people were reminded that good citizenship included careful emotional self-management. As the Munich crisis and 'Gas Mask Sunday' made clear, however, in any coming war, the home would become a battlefield, and civilian casualties would be mourned alongside those from the military. In the coming war, the feelings of the people would be crucial. While popular psychology and everyday experts attempted to provide tools for the negotiation of everyday life, and for the management of emotions like fear and anxiety, state planning for the future war had to include measures that would both reassure people that they and their loved ones could survive the conflict, and ensure plans were in place to manage the very worst scenarios. The next chapter looks at the ways the coming war was imagined in the 1920s and 1930s, and the subsequent development of plans for the management of the mass fatalities that the British state increasingly expected.

Notes

1. M. Dickens, *An Open Book* (London: Heinemann, 1978), pp. 16, 28, 73, 82.
2. H. Parr, 'Representations of grief and the Falklands War', in L. Åhäll and T. Gregory (eds), *Emotions, Politics, War* (Abingdon: Routledge, 2015), pp. 154–66.
3. See L. Noakes, '"My husband is interested in war generally": gender, family history and the emotional legacies of total war', *Women's History Review*, 27:4 (2018), pp. 610–26.
4. For further discussion of Ypres, see M. Connelly and S. Goebel, *Ypres* (Oxford: Oxford University Press, 2018).
5. 'A noble epitaph', the *Times*, 6 August 1928, p. 11.
6. J. Hazelgrove, *Spiritualism and British Society Between the Wars* (Manchester: Manchester University Press, 2000).
7. P. Jalland, *Death in War and Peace: A History of Loss and Grief in England, 1914–1970* (Oxford: Oxford University Press, 2010), pp. 56–9.
8. C. Brown, *Religion and Society in Scotland Since 1707* (Edinburgh: Edinburgh University Press, 1997), p. 125.
9. A. Gregory, *The Last Great War: British Society and the First World War* (Cambridge: Cambridge University Press, 2010, 2008), p. 183.
10. R. McKibbin, *Classes and Cultures in England, 1918–1951* (Oxford: Oxford University Press, 2000), p. 274.

11 J. C. D. Clark, 'Secularization and modernization: the failure of a grand narrative', *The Historical Journal*, 55:1 (2012), pp. 161–94.
12 D. Shaw, 'The unknown world', *Nash's Pall Mall Magazine*, 92:488 (January 1934), p. 8.
13 Hazelgrove, *Spiritualism and British Society*, p. 14.
14 J. Bourke, *Dismembering the Male: Men's Bodies, Britain and the Great War* (London: Reaktion Books, 1996), p. 234.
15 B. King, 'The abolishing of death', *Nash's Pall Mall Magazine*, 64:321 (January 1920), p. 388.
16 J. Winter, *Sites of Memory, Sites of Mourning: The Great War in European Cultural History* (Cambridge: Cambridge University Press, 1995), p. 95.
17 J. Lomas, *War Widows in British Society, 1919–1990* (PhD dissertation, University of Staffordshire, 1997), p. 49, Appendix A, Table 8, 'Number of War Widows Pensions in payment each half decade since 1915', p. 276.
18 J. Morley, 'The memory of the Great War and morale during Britain's phoney war', *The Historical Journal* (online, Cambridge University Press, 27 March 2019).
19 'The silence: impressive moments in Manchester', *Manchester Guardian* (12 November 1919), p. 8.
20 R. Overy, *The Morbid Age: Britain and the Crisis of Civilisation, 1919–1939* (London: Allen Lane, 2009).
21 J. Lawrence, 'Forging a peaceable kingdom: war, violence and fear of brutalization in post-First World War Britain', *The Journal of Modern History*, 75:3 (2003), pp. 557–89.
22 See R. Gerwarth, 'The continuum of violence,' in J. Winter (ed.), *The Cambridge History of the First World War. Volume 2, The State* (Cambridge: Cambridge University Press, 2014), pp. 638–62.
23 Lawrence, 'Forging a peaceable kingdom', p. 559.
24 F. Mort, 'Love in a cold climate: letters, public opinion and monarchy in the 1936 abdication crisis', *Twentieth Century British History*, 25:1 (2014), p. 38.
25 N. Rose, 'Assembling the modern self', in R. Porter (ed.), *Rewriting the Self: Histories from the Renaissance to the Present* (London: Routledge, 1997), p. 224.
26 See D. Middlebrook, *Her Husband: Hughes and Plath – A Marriage* (London: Viking, 2003), p. 69. Thanks to Wendy Ugolini for drawing my attention to this example.
27 W. Reddy, *The Invisible Code* (Berkeley, CA: University of California Press, 1997), p. 6.
28 U. Frevert, *Emotions in History – Lost and Found* (Budapest: Central European University Press, 2011), pp. 87–148.
29 J. Giles, *The Parlour and the Suburb: Domestic Identities, Class, Femininity and Modernity* (Oxford: Berg, 2004).

30 'Modern', efficient household management was, of course, out of reach for those who lived in slum housing, and below the poverty line. In 1930 and 1931, between 25 per cent and 40 per cent of the families in Merseyside, Southampton, Sheffield and Plymouth (areas where social surveys of poverty were undertaken) were living in poverty. H. Glennerster, J. Hills, D. Piachaud and J. Webb, *One Hundred Years of Poverty and Policy* (York: Joseph Rowntree Foundation, 2004), Figure 4, p. 44.

31 M. Roper, 'Between manliness and masculinity: the "war generation" and the psychology of fear in Britain, 1914–1950', *Journal of British Studies*, 44:2 (2005), pp. 343–62.

32 S. Featherstone, 'The mill girl and the cheeky chappie: British popular culture and mass entertainment in the Thirties, *Critical Survey*, 15:2 (2003), pp. 3–22.

33 On this, see A. Light, *Forever England: Femininity, Literature and Conservatism Between the Wars* (London: Routledge, 1991).

34 *The Ghost Goes West* (dir. R. Clair, 1935); R. Llewelyn, *How Green Was My Valley* (London: Michael Joseph, 1939).

35 S. Taylor, 'The suburban neurosis', *Lancet* (28 March 1938), p. 760.

36 Taylor, 'The suburban neurosis', p. 760.

37 Taylor, 'The suburban neurosis', p. 761.

38 Taylor, 'The suburban neurosis', p. 761.

39 'No need to be dull in the suburbs', *Daily Mail*, 9 June 1938, p. 9.

40 I. Zweiniger-Bargielowska, *Managing the Body: Beauty, Health and Fitness in Britain, 1880–1939* (Oxford: Oxford University Press, 2010), p. 157.

41 The National Archives (TNA), Housing and Local Government (HLG) 120/1464, *Physical Training and Recreation Act, 1937* (London: HMSO, 1937), p. 1.

42 J. Julius Matthews, '"They had such a lot of fun": The Women's League of Health and Beauty between the wars', *History Workshop Journal*, 30 (Autumn 1990), p. 27.

43 Julius Matthews, 'They had such a lot of fun', p. 33.

44 Julius Matthews, 'They had such a lot of fun', p. 39.

45 'Poudre Tokalon', *Daily Mirror*, 12 July 1925, p. 8.

46 'Five points that go to make beauty', *Daily Mirror*, 22 November 1935, p. 9.

47 '£3,560 for pretty girls', *Daily Mail*, 1 August 1928, p. 16.

48 '£500 charm and beauty contest', *Daily Mail*, 8 February 1935, p. 20.

49 R. Conway 'Making the mill girl modern? Beauty, industry and the popular newspaper in 1930s England', *Twentieth Century British History*, 24:4 (2013), p. 530.

50 T. Dixon, *Weeping Britannia: Portrait of a Nation in Tears* (Oxford: Oxford University Press, 2015), pp. 222–23.

51 'Beauty and emotion', *Daily Mail*, 20 June 1919, p. 9.

52 'Lonely women', *Daily Mail*, 23 October, 1936, p. 24.

53 'Cavalcade of clothes', *Daily Mirror*, 25 May 1934, p. 15.
54 Anne Temple, 'Human casebook', *Daily Mail*, 18 August 1938, p. 18.
55 'Wearing mourning is "ridiculous"', *Daily Mirror*, 9 October 1934, p. 26.
56 For a thoughtful overview of work on masculinity in nineteenth- and twentieth-century Britain, see M. Francis, 'The domestication of the male? Recent research on nineteenth and twentieth century masculinity', *The Historical Journal*, 45:3 (2002), pp. 637–52.
57 K. Boyd, 'Knowing your place: the tension of manliness in Boys' Story Papers, 1918–1939', in M. Roper and J. Tosh (eds), *Manful Assertions* (London: Routledge, 1991); M. Paris, *Warrior Nation: Images of War in British Popular Culture, 1850–2000* (London: Reaktion Books, 2000).
58 E. Jones, 'The psychology of killing: the combat experience of British soldiers during the First World War', *Journal of Contemporary History*, 41:2 (2006), p. 234.
59 Francis, 'The domestication of the male?', p. 643.
60 Roper, 'Between manliness and masculinity'.
61 A. Bingham, *Gender, Modernity and the Popular Press in Interwar Britain* (Oxford: Clarendon Press, 2004).
62 Bingham, *Gender, Modernity and the Popular Press*, p. 241.
63 *Daily Mirror*, 16 November 1935, p. 14; *Daily Express*, 6 May 1931, p. 5. Both cited in Bingham, *Gender, Modernity and the Popular Press*, pp. 241, 218.
64 On social class, gender and the household in mid-twentieth-century Britain, see McKibbin, *Classes and Cultures*, pp. 518–21.
65 'Yeast-Vite', *Daily Mail*, 1 January 1937, p. 3.
66 'Sanatogen', *Daily Mail*, 6 January 1936, p. 12.
67 'Dr Cassell's Tablets', *Daily Mail*, 6 January 1936, p. 6; 'Bile Beans', *Daily Mirror*, 21 December 1934, p. 13; 1 January 1937, p. 12; 19 December 1939, p. 15.
68 'Nerves and their owners', *Manchester Guardian*, 22 July 1938, p. 10.
69 J. Moran, 'Private lives, public histories: the diary in twentieth-century Britain', *Journal of British Studies*, 54 (2015), p. 169.
70 J. Hinton, *The Mass Observers: A History, 1937–1949* (Oxford: Oxford University Press, 2013), p. 1.
71 C. Madge and T. Harrisson, *Mass Observation* (London: Frederick Muller, 1937).
72 Mass Observation, *First Year's Work, 1937–38* (London: Lindsay Drummond, 1938), p. 66.
73 Hinton, *The Mass Observers*, p. 65.
74 Mass Observation, *First Year's Work*, p. 66.
75 Mass Observation, Directive Questionnaire, January 1939.
76 Moran, 'Private lives, public histories', p. 147.
77 A. Temple, 'Human casebook', *Daily Mail*, 17 September 1937, p. 8.

78 A. Temple, 'Human casebook', *Daily Mail*, 1 April 1937, p. 8.
79 M. Thomson, *Psychological Subjects: Identity, Culture and Health in Twentieth-Century Britain* (Oxford: Oxford University Press, 2006).
80 Light, *Forever England* (1991), pp. 102–04; *Dundee Evening Telegraph*, 27 April 1926, p. 5; *Dundee Courier* (28 June 1923), p. 4; *Portsmouth Evening News*, 9 October 1924, p. 4.
81 Thomson, *Psychological Subjects*, p. 19.
82 Thomson, *Psychological Subjects*, p. 32.
83 *Practical Psychology*, 1:1 (February 1936), p. 2.
84 *Practical Psychology*, 1:5 (June 1936), p. 111; *Practical Psychology*, 2:2 (April 1937), p. 70.
85 *Practical Psychology*, 2:4 (June 1937), p. 112.
86 *You: The Popular Psychology Magazine*, 3:2 (April 1938), pp. 79–80; *You*, 3:11 (January 1939), pp. 660–6; *You*, 3:12 (February 1939), pp. 713–19.
87 'In the shadow of the last war', *Daily Mirror*, 13 September 1938, p. 3.
88 Mass Observation, *Britain by Mass Observation* (Harmondsworth: Penguin, 1939), p. 31.
89 Both cited in *Britain by Mass Observation*, pp. 38, 39.
90 *Britain by Mass Observation*, 1939, pp. 49, 51.
91 On the gas mask as an emotional object, see Susan R. Grayzel, '"Macabre and hilarious": the emotional life of the civilian gas mask in France during and after the First World War', in C. Langhamer, L. Noakes and C. Siebrecht (eds), *Total War: An Emotional History* (Oxford: Oxford University Press, 2019).
92 'Britain queues up in millions on Gas Mask Sunday', *Daily Mirror*, 26 September 1938, p. 14.
93 'This was "Gas Mask Sunday"', *Daily Express* (26 September 1938), p. 6.
94 Mass Observation Day Surveys, *'Munich'* (September 1938), Respondents 072, 045.
95 Mass Observation (September 1938), Respondent 293.
96 Mass Observation (September 1938), Respondents 072, 038.
97 'Ships of grief in sea of flowers', *Daily Mail*, 8 June 1939, p. 9.
98 'Pathetic scenes at funerals of pit fire victims', *Daily Mirror*, 27 September 1934, p. 1. For further discussion of the Gresford Colliery and other mining disasters of the period, see Jalland, *Death in War and Peace*, pp. 84–92.

3

Planning

Imagining and planning for death in wartime

Introduction: the age of anxiety

The 1930s were an anxious time, not just for those who feared or anticipated an apocalyptic future war, or who watched with trepidation the emergence of new ideologies and new governments willing to attack civilians. They were also a time of anxiety for the civil servants, politicians and military bureaucrats charged with planning for the prevention and management of death in any future conflict. The interwar years were a complex period for the development of theory and policy regarding warfare. The devastation of the Great War had left governments and governed fearful of another destructive conflict, and had directly informed the establishment of the League of Nations in 1920 and international pacts such as the Kellogg-Briand Pact of 1928, which saw nations agreeing not to resort to warfare in the settlement of disputes. At the same time, the development of new military technologies was ensuring that if these strategies failed, any future war would be even more damaging, with even higher casualty figures spread across military and civilian populations than past wars. The death of millions was central to the imagining of, preparation for and opposition to any future war.

This chapter traces the development of British plans to prevent, mitigate and cope with the mass death of civilians that was expected in any future conflict. It sets these within the political, social and cultural history of the decade – in particular, the growth of an emotional culture of self-management, discussed in the previous chapter; the bombing of civilians in the 1930s, most importantly for the British imagination in Spain; and the widely shared belief that any future war would be apocalyptic. These strands in British social and cultural life underpinned both political movements such as the campaigns for pacifism and for re-armament, and public policy, in particular the (often highly secret) preparation for the management of death in wartime.

The chapter begins by examining the multiple ways that death in war was imagined in the interwar years, tracing the ways in which the new technologies of warfare were envisaged as leading to terrible, multiple deaths in both fiction and in political debate. This anticipation of mass death was woven into the development of military technology and military doctrine. Often implicit within analyses of the growth of air power in this period, mass civilian death was in fact at the centre of this new form of military technology, the impact of air power becoming horribly real to both planners and the public as a result of the deteriorating international situation in the 1930s, when the bodies of civilians joined those of combatants in the new 'front lines' of towns and cities in China, Abyssinia and Spain. Tracing the emergence of both air raid precautions and secret plans for the 'disposal' of the civilian dead in the 1930s, and outlining the development of burial policies for the armed forces in the same period, the chapter argues that mass death was central to preparation for the coming war. David Cannadine's description of interwar Britain as being 'obsessed by death' can be seen not only as a comment on the impact of the Great War, but as an apt description of planning, policy and popular culture as it looked towards the future.[1]

Imagining warfare in the 1920s and 1930s

The desire to avoid another largely static war of attrition, such as that seen on the Western Front during the Great War, encouraged the rapid development of a whole range of battlefield weaponry. The US and Japanese navies designed aircraft carriers that could accompany their fleets into battle, while Britain, Germany and France invested in armoured vehicles, including tanks, and fighter planes and bombers were both honed.[2] As David Edgerton has shown, the interwar British state continued to invest in the production of new weaponry, and private arms companies found a ready market for their products in the British armed forces.[3] Key to this new military technology was the bomber. Air Vice Marshal Hugh Trenchard was keen to establish the new Royal Air Force (RAF), formed in 1918, as an independent military service, and as such, argued for investment in aeroplanes, and especially for the strategic importance of the bomber, both for 'policing' conflicts in the empire, and for success in future international conflicts.

Planning: imagining and planning for death in wartime

Of these new technologies of warfare, aerial warfare was to become the most significant, and most destructive by far of both human lives and the communities and landscapes within which these were lived.

The development of the aircraft did more than anything else to damage the long-cherished British belief that being an 'island nation' with a powerful navy provided an adequate defence against invasion and destruction. The use of bombardment from air and sea against troops and civilians during the Great War meant that Britain was newly vulnerable to what became widely known as 'the knockout blow' from the air, as the bombardment of cities, carried out with the intent of breaking civilian morale as much as causing physical devastation and economic disruption, moved to the centre of military tactics and strategy, political debate and popular representations of warfare in the interwar years.[4] This 'knockout blow' was widely imagined across all of these spheres as being an aerial attack on major cities and conurbations, launched without warning and carried out without mercy or respite, by wave after wave of bombers. These assaults would make cities uninhabitable and destroy civilian morale, leaving the government with little choice but to surrender. In his 1921 treatise on air power, the influential Italian military strategist Giulio Douhet argued that

> No longer can areas exist in which life can be lived in safety and tranquillity, nor can the battlefield any longer be limited to actual combatants. On the contrary, the battlefield will be limited only by the boundaries of the nations at war, and all of their citizens will become combatants, since all of them will be exposed to the aerial offensives of the enemy.

This, he claimed, was essentially a more humane form of warfare than the attritional conflict of the Western Front, or indeed the slow starvation of civilians in the Central Powers, as the overwhelming nature and terror of bombing would mean that wars would come to an end quickly.[5] Attacking civilians, and their morale, was not a new aspect of warfare, and the centrality of civil society – both in terms of willingness to support a lengthy war and in terms of industrial and agricultural production – to the Great War demonstrated that the civilian populations of modern, industrialised societies could never again be on the margins of conflict. The emergence of aerial warfare made these civilians, now so central to the successful execution of modern warfare, more vulnerable than ever before to attack. Far from being 'collateral damage', incidental victims of warfare, the bodies of civilians, and the morale of these same civilians and of their loved ones in the military, were to be the new targets of warfare.

The bodies of colonial subjects provided an opportunity for British military strategists to test the effectiveness of aerial bombardment. Throughout the 1920s, control of rebellious regions in Iraq, Egypt, Somaliland and northern India through the use of air power appeared to offer the seductive combination of low outlay, in both financial terms and terms of 'British' lives lost, with high success rates. Iraq in particular was seen as an especially suitable region for 'policing' by air: its size, presumed flatness and emptiness promised both little cover to insurgents and opportunities for surveillance impossible in more urban and densely populated areas.[6] Villages were attacked not only for harbouring rebel leaders but for 'general recalcitrance' or refusal to submit to British rule.[7] Arthur Harris, then an RAF squadron leader in Iraq, later to become chief of Bomber Command and to oversee the area bombing of German cities that marked the last three years of the Second World War, reported the 1924 bombing of an Iraqi village:

> [T]he Arab and Kurd ... now know what real bombing means in casualties and damage; they now know that within 45 minutes a full sized village ... can be practically wiped out and a third of its inhabitants killed or injured by four or five machines which offer them no real targets, no opportunity for glory as warriors, no effective means of escape.[8]

Iraqi civilians, together with those in northern India, the Sudan, Yemen, Somalia and Afghanistan, thus became subject to one of the beliefs dear to the strategists of twentieth-century 'total war'; namely, that all civilians contributed to the war effort by a variety of actual or potential means, and were thus legitimate targets of warfare.

In 1931, Japan invaded Manchuria, violating the Nine-Power Treaty of 1922 and giving a foretaste of the use of airpower by aggressive nations. While the British bombing of insurgent areas had largely taken place away from the gaze of journalists, the Japanese bombing raids on Manchuria in 1931 and Shanghai in 1932 were widely observed and reported. The *Daily Mail* reported on the 'havoc' caused by air raids, and the *Daily Mirror* described how 'the earth and heavens rocked with thunderous explosions' when Shanghai was attacked.[9] Fears for the impact of air raids on the human body were focused in the British press on European bodies, and particularly on those of the residents of the International Settlement in Shanghai. The centrality of civilians to this warfare, and the stoicism of British women in Shanghai was emphasised

Planning: imagining and planning for death in wartime

in the *Daily Mail*, which reported on the women 'playing their heroic part here by keeping the home fires burning while shells drop in the streets and gardens ... menacing their lives and also the lives of their children'.[10] This fortitude was contrasted in the *Daily Express* with the reaction to bombing by the Chinese refugees who sought shelter in the settlement, described as an 'insanitary and evil smelling lot' who 'constitute a real menace' as 'every time they hear a shot they stampede'.[11] If the actions of the British women epitomised calm endurance under fire, the reaction of the Chinese civilians, like that of the rebellious subjects of empire, appeared to demonstrate the chaos that could ensue when civilians became the targets of warfare.

By late 1932, the League of Nations Disarmament Conference, which had opened in February as a means of reducing armaments and thus protecting victims of warfare like those in Shanghai, had singularly failed to do so. A House of Commons debate on international affairs revealed a growing disenchantment with the league, and a parallel concern with the destructive nature of aerial warfare. The Labour Party, which had regularly called for disarmament throughout the 1920s, used the debate to call for the British government to push harder for success in Geneva. Opening the debate, Clement Attlee reminded the House that any future war would take place in a newly expanded democracy, and directly threaten the lives of large numbers. Attlee argued for the importance of the views of those who had experienced war – a category within which he famously included 'the mother of some child who had been killed by bombing' alongside 'a man who had actually been gassed' and 'an ordinary rating who had been torpedoed'.[12] In a democracy, the thoughts, feelings and opinions of the 'ordinary' man and woman mattered; in conditions of 'total war', their support, their 'morale', was of vital importance. This meant both coaxing them to believe that the state was doing its utmost to protect them, and persuading them to accept that the deaths of some, civilians as well as combatants, were both inevitable and worthwhile.

Despite, or perhaps because of, its failure, the Disarmament Conference provided a focus for discussion of aerial warfare, and politicians debated the most effective means of protecting British civilians from attacks from the air. Belief in the ability of bombing fleets to successfully attack towns and cities, thus undermining morale and leading to calls for a truce or surrender from a desperate population, underpinned these discussions. Stanley Baldwin's oft-repeated warning that 'the bomber will always get through' was a point that resonated with the press, with the public, with policy makers, politicians and military strategists.[13] Baldwin had chaired the Committee of Imperial Defence for five years, and was well acquainted with the potential impact of air raids; their place within a popular culture that increasingly fictionalised future war meant that many in his audience were able to imagine what they might mean for civilians. Using a somewhat unfortunate metaphor, the *Daily Mail* described how Baldwin's speech 'thrilled the House. Cheers, starting like the muffled echo of a single gun, swelled to a salvo which lasted for a whole minute.'[14] Described by the *Manchester Guardian* as 'a remarkable speech on the appalling menace of the air weapon', Baldwin's words resonated widely.[15] A leader in the *Times* two days later stated that it was 'frankly inconceivable that the civilised countries of today should be unable to reach some contract by which the horrors of indiscriminate destruction may be prevented'.[16] When the Liberal politician Sir Herbert Samuel criticised Baldwin's pessimistic vision at a Bolton meeting in support of the League of Nations, he provoked a furious debate in the letters column of the *Times* in which he was accused of attempting to 'misinterpret and misunderstand the most helpful pronouncement – and the most truthful one – that has been made for a long time'.[17] A veteran response came from a correspondent signing himself 'Icarus', who had served as a pilot and observer in Palestine and France, and who was now a doctor. Claiming to have 'personally dropped several tons of bombs ... nearly all' of which 'were dropped on non-combatants', Icarus stated that although he would fight again, he would 'never again drop bombs on enemy, still less on allied, towns'. Explicitly positioning himself as the veteran voice of experience, Icarus critiqued bombing as a weapon of war, both as an act of conscience, and in terms of military effectiveness.[18]

The vision of any future war as infinitely more destructive than anything that had been experienced in the past underpinned much public discussion of warfare in the 1930s, both while disarmament seemed possible in the first years of the decade, and as disarmament failed and war once again appeared on the international stage in its later years. This vision crossed political boundaries, and was articulated as much by those who advocated the necessity for re-armament, as by those who positioned themselves as pacifists. In November 1934, in the debate on national defence which followed the final collapse of the Geneva Conference in June, Winston Churchill, who as Air Minister had overseen the 'policing' of Iraq by the RAF, advocated re-armament as the best defence against attacks on British cities, arguing that 'a week or ten days intensive bombing attack upon London' would result in the death or injury of 30,000 or 40,000 people.[19] In addition to providing for the defence of the population, Churchill argued, the building up of a British air force, including long-range bombers, 'substantially stronger than that of Germany' should be a priority.[20] In March 1934, Britain had announced its first programme of air force expansion since 1923. Trenchard had stated his preference for making the enemy 'squeal before we did' as early as 1923, but international policy, combined with economic constraints and a widely shared lack of enthusiasm for attacking civilian targets in Europe, meant that it was not until Germany began to re-arm, and threaten the tenuous balance of power, that re-armament began to be seriously considered in Britain.[21]

Whether the solution was seen as disarmament or re-armament, most commentators agreed that any future war would be catastrophic in terms of civilian dead and injured. The public debate, in Parliament, in the press and in political associations and campaigning groups up and down the country, was often framed in explicitly emotional and affective terms. The potential dead of air raids were at the heart of this debate. For example, when Stanley Baldwin addressed the International Peace Society in 1935 he asked his audience to imagine war not in the abstract but in more intimate and familial terms, thinking of its impact on 'the lives of our children and grandchildren, of our friends and companions'.[22] The numbers of possible dead, and the manner in which they would die if air raids came to Britain, were described with relish by those who saw re-armament as a solution, as much as they were by those arguing for disarmament.[23] The pathetic figure of the dying child, lying alone in rubble or choking on poison gas, came to act as a powerful symbol of the horrors of modern warfare.

Images of dead, dying and injured children, torn apart by high explosive and poisoned by gas, were widespread in the 1930s, seen in both popular fictional imaginings of the next war and, increasingly, in journalistic accounts of warfare in China and especially in Spain. It was fiction and journalism, together with political debate, rather than the lengthy and specialised publications of military and 'air power' theorists, that had the greatest impact on popular perceptions of modern conflict. The ideal of a suburban domesticity, which had become so important as a means of portraying the national character and virtues of the British, was repeatedly portrayed as threatened and destroyed in fictional representations of a future war.[24] Much popular fiction that depicted a future war, while claiming to act as a warning about the perils of re-armament and particularly of aerial warfare, in fact focused on often lurid depictions of the impact of bombing on civilian populations. The best known of these fictionalised accounts of war is probably the film version of H. G. Wells' 'future history' of 1933, *The Shape of Things to Come*. Alexander Korda's 1936 film *Things to Come* replaced Wells' distanced and analytical narrative with a deeply personal representation of the impact of war on cities, families and individuals that invited an emotional reaction from its audience. The film, which achieved the ninth-highest box office takings in Britain in 1936, stuck largely to Wells' plot but for contemporary audiences, it was probably the first third of the film, which vividly depicted an air raid on 'Everytown' and ended with a 'slow and eloquent track into the body of a child buried in the rubble', that resonated.[25]

Wells' predictions of the impact of a future war on cities and their inhabitants were restrained in comparison to many of the 'next war novels' of the 1930s.[26] Driven by a combination of international crises, the failures of disarmament and internationalism, weapons development and air power theory, these novels often included lurid descriptions of the impact of both high explosive and poison gas on undefended cities. Miles' *The Gas War of 1940* was first published in 1931 but was republished several times as the crises of the 1930s drove a public fascination with aerial warfare. Like Wells' *The Shape of Things to Come*, this was a 'future history' recounting the 'war of gas and aeroplanes' of 1940 from the viewpoint of a surviving politician. Miles' description of the destruction of London and of other British towns and cities, including Southwold, Suffolk, where the narrator's family are evacuated and subsequently killed, focused on the impact of war on families, and especially children. A description of people dying 'in their homes with the familiar walls crashing about them in flames' was followed by a graphic account of the impact of poison gas on a school assembly in West Ham, where

> first one, then another and another child, its hands to its eyes, screamed and began to run round and round and round in frantic circles until deadlier gases halted them and flung them to lie, twisting and jerking convulsive limbs, tearing at the floor, until death at last suffered them.[27]

This focus on the suffering of children and the destruction of families was a common trope in much of this body of literature. *Air-Gods'*

Parade, another lurid 'future history', published in 1935, recounted a gas attack on an east London suburb:

> From the little strip of green outside, and from every house in the row, came frantic crying and confusion. By the time Mrs Prettyman had prepared a tepid bath in a bowl, the baby's body had broken out into sores and there were violent spasms of retching and coughing, followed by the vomiting of fearsome pieces of tissue ... as the child's body touched the water, the limbs stiffened. There was no life there now.[28]

Even when families survived the first wave of gas attack, the novel suggests they could still be destroyed by the strains and stresses of a new kind of warfare that attacked the home. When a Stepney family successfully follows instructions and makes their home gas-proof, they still die, victims of the father who, maddened by days of isolation and diminishing supplies of air, food and drink, smashes the windows of the home, allowing the poison gas outside to enter.[29] In these novels, the horrors of any future war lay not only in what unrestrained conflict could do to the body, but in the emotions unleashed by such warfare, and by the mass death that resulted. As *Air-Gods' Parade* attempted to show, lack of self-control in the face of the horrors of war, as much as war itself, was something to be feared.

Probably the best-known representation of the experience of actual, rather than imagined, air raids was Pablo Picasso's painting *Guernica*. Picasso's contribution to the World Fair held in Paris in May and June 1937 toured Britain in the autumn and winter of that year, attracting 15,000 visitors when it was exhibited at the Whitechapel gallery in east London. The admission charge was a pair of boots for Republican soldiers in Spain.[30] The violent and chaotic nature of Picasso's painting reflected the nature of the attack on Guernica, in which civilians fleeing the bombing were strafed from the air as they attempted to escape. The assault on the Basque city by the German Condor Legion in April 1937 came to stand, more than any other single act of the Spanish Civil War, both as a symbol of the brutality of that conflict, and for the potential annihilation of European cities and their inhabitants from the air. The *Times* correspondent George Steer was in nearby Bilbao, and was one of the first journalists to arrive in Guernica, recording for the paper's audience the 'destruction of this open town far behind the lines' where 'women and children are said to have been trapped in an air raid refuge under a mass of burning wreckage'.[31] The *Daily Express* emphasised the innocence of the victims in its coverage, commenting that 'the Basque people met in that place as devout Catholics ... They were not under arms.'[32] The attack was described in the House of Commons as 'a deliberate effort to use air power as an instrument of massacre and terrorism', while a letter to the *Times* warned 'now we know ... what to expect when the squadrons of the air are let loose to work their havoc upon the capitals of Europe'.[33] Although Guernica was not the first Spanish city to be bombed, its fate captured the world's imagination as it was not a major centre for industry like nearby Bilbao, but the historic capital of the Basque region and a local centre of population.[34] The attack on Guernica was an example of terror bombing; an attack on a city designed to break the morale of the civilian population, as expounded by air power theorists from Douhet onwards. This point was not lost on audiences for newsreel footage of the aftermath of the air raid in British Gaumont cinemas, who were reminded in the commentary that 'this was a city, and these were homes, like yours'.[35]

The journalist John Langdon-Davies, who covered the war for the *News Chronicle*, reflected on the impact of air raids on the population of Barcelona in *Air Raid: The Technique of Silent Approach High Explosive Panic*, published in 1938. Langdon-Davies astutely commented that the aim of the raids 'was not casualties, but the creation of panic'.[36] Arguing that the British government needed to plan for the evacuation of children and their mothers from cities in the event of war, Langdon-Davies described both the physical impact of high explosive on the human body, and the psychological effect on those who lived under the bombs and thus encountered the effect of high explosive on bodies, recounting one woman's story of the bombing of a tram:

> My woman janitor was on the platform. The arm and shoulder of a youth were severed by the explosion and his body fell at her feet. She pushed it away and sprang from the tram and ran away. She was caught and taken to hospital. To this day she cries whenever she hears sirens or even ... a motor horn.[37]

While the dominance of an emotional economy that valued the stoical and the phlegmatic response to trauma could have been expected by contemporary observers to mitigate against some of the panic, fear and loss of control that air raids were designed to create, the individual could not be relied on to face the horrors of war from the air alone. As battlefield trenches and bombed cities had shown by the late 1930s, no matter how much training in self-reflection and self-control the individual possessed, panic and psychological collapse under fire were

Planning: imagining and planning for death in wartime

always a real possibility. The attacks on Spanish cities like Guernica and Barcelona had brought the reality of death from the air back to Europe for the first time in almost twenty years, and both government and people had to be prepared to face air raids in any future war.

Awareness of the impact of air raids on civilians elsewhere, together with the cultural imaginings of the form a future war would take in Britain, and a growing awareness towards the end of the 1930s that another war was becoming more and more likely, combined to shape perceptions of this coming conflict. Mass Observation (MO) surveyed people's thoughts and feelings on Armistice Day in 1937 and 1938, and their findings demonstrate the ways that memories of the Great War and anxieties about a future war combined to produce a widespread belief that losses would be high, and would be spread between military and civilian victims. MO, observing reactions to Armistice Day in 'Worktown' (Bolton), found that, for many, thoughts about past and future wars were interwoven. Asked what he had been thinking about during the two-minute silence at 11 a.m., an ex-serviceman answered 'I was thinking about how soon we will be joining up again. I also thought of a couple of pals who were blown to hell at Ypres [in] 1915.' Likewise, an unemployed man, aged about thirty, responded that his 'first thoughts went back to September 2nd, 1918, when word came by first post that two cousins of mine had been killed, and I offered a short prayer in their memory. I thought of all the people who had had all the real horror of war brought home to them … and whether they believed or not war would come again.' Conversations overheard at the town's war memorials included 'discussions raging all around about war … In Doncaster they are getting the pits ready to receive the people in case of an air attack. It will all be in the air.'[38] Members of the MO national panel who responded to a directive asking them to keep a diary for Armistice Day in 1937 similarly found their thoughts shaped by remembrance of the past war, and anticipation of the war yet to come. While some avoided collective acts of remembrance, or simply paused in their activities, at home or in public, for two minutes at 11 a.m., others recorded how they reflected on 'the men who had lost their lives in vain' and 'the awful spectre of "what if it happens again" which haunts every thought'.[39] For another respondent, who noted unhappily that the smoke from a garden bonfire 'looks like poison gas this morning', memories of past weaponry shaped fears of future conflict in a specific, presumably unwelcome, manner.[40]

When MO surveyed the public for the thoughts on Armistice Day 1938, it was in the aftermath of the Munich crisis, and Gas Mask Sunday, discussed in the previous chapter. This year MO combined observation of activities at ceremonies of remembrance with interviews with members of the public in Camden and Fulham, two largely working-class areas of London. For one forty-year-old woman living in Fulham, the relationship between the Great War and the coming war was all too clear:

> My God, I lost my father and mother and three brothers ... how can I ever forget it all [cries] ... on Armistice Day I take the children and we kneel down and pray ... I tell them about what it means ... I tell them about what an air raid was like ... we can't live with the dead but we can think of them that day. When they told me there was no mask for the baby ... I told them they could have the gas masks back for all the family. See them two medals, well I always tell the children what they represent, and what they meant in deaths in our family.[41]

For others, as war edged closer, Armistice Day was understood in terms of the ongoing impact of the Great War on their families: one woman, widowed in the war, described how 'it makes me miserable all day', and another described how 'when he hears the whistle for the silence' her father 'goes off into a fit, it makes him think of the lad killed'.[42] As Michael Roper has argued, one of the lasting legacies of the Great War was its enduring impact on families; the MO survey gave some of these families a chance to express the ways the war continued to shape their lives. For others, who had not been personally bereaved, the coming war was uppermost in their minds, meaning that for some, Armistice Day simply served to highlight the failures of politicians to avoid war. One woman was forthright in her assertion that 'it's disgusting. The crisis showed that they might very well have had us fighting again by November 11', while a man claimed 'there should be capital punishment for the crime of organised hypocrisy'.[43] By November 1938, the initial euphoria that had greeted the Munich agreement was giving way to the more sombre realisation that war was, nonetheless, coming. The army, lagging behind the RAF in both funding and public esteem, and which had struggled to fill available posts during the 1930s, with just 550 of the 650 available subaltern positions filled in 1937, found it had a steady stream of volunteers for the Territorial Service in 1938–39.[44] Awareness of the nature of warfare in the middle of the twentieth century combined with memories of the Great War, and the centrality of

Planning: imagining and planning for death in wartime

the army to that conflict, as Britain prepared once again for war in the late 1930s.

Planning for death in war: official responses in the interwar years

Preparation by the state for the expected attacks on British towns and cities in what was increasingly imagined as a war against Germany took two forms. One was the range of measures introduced which would offer some form of protection against the 'knockout blow from the air'; the second was the management of the colossal number of corpses that were expected as a consequence of this 'knockout blow'. While the provision of protection was highly publicised, depending as it did for any measure of success on the voluntary involvement of large numbers of the civilian population, the plans for what was referred to as 'the disposal of the dead' were highly secret. Planning for mass death – both for its prevention, and for the management of its aftermath, was at the heart of British preparation for the coming war.

The imperial British state had begun to consider the possibility of aerial attacks on its citizens and subjects in the 1920s. In 1924, the Air Raid Precautions (ARP) Sub-Committee of the Committee of Imperial Defence was formed to consider how best to defend nation and empire in the coming age of aerial warfare. The sub-committee continued to investigate the best means of mitigating the impact of air raids over the next ten years, but it was not until 1935 that the term ARP began to enter public consciousness, when the ARP Department of the Home Office was formed under the leadership of Wing Commander E. J. Hodsoll, issuing its first public circular in the same year.[45] As the international situation deteriorated, and against the background of the well-documented bombing of civilians in Spain, and the remilitarisation of the Rhineland by Germany in 1936, more and more time and money was devoted to preparing civilians for war, and to providing some degree of protection for these civilians from poison gas and high explosive delivered from the air.

Protective measures discussed by the state and the public included public shelters, the provision of shelters for the home, evacuation, gas mask design and distribution, and the creation and management of a vast, largely voluntary, ARP organisation. All of these took up more and more of the time of civil servants in the second half of the 1930s, and all of them were problematic. Underpinning the development and discussion of what came to be known as 'civil defence' were two aims. The first was the desire to harness the popular fear of air raids, which popular fiction and journalism had done so much to encourage throughout the 1930s, to the mobilisation of the civilian population in the defence of their homes, neighbourhoods, cities and nations. The strong associational culture of the 1930s was also drawn on, as against the backdrop of a deteriorating international situation the ARP Act of 1937 was passed (1938 in Northern Ireland), which both compelled local authorities to organise for the protection of their populations through the provision of shelters, and established a range of voluntary organisations that civilians were encouraged to join to better defend themselves, their families and their neighbours.[46] Much of this planning was problematic, seen by some as a necessary means of protecting their families from the worst effects of aerial warfare, by others as making war more likely and by still more as an irrelevance. Membership of the voluntary ARP organisations remained stubbornly below the numbers projected as necessary to their successful functioning; in Belfast for example, only 3,000 volunteers had come forward to fill the 16,000 the municipality estimated that it needed by December 1938.[47] The second aim was to assuage the anxieties that had been fuelled by the growing threat of warfare in the 1930s. Bearing in mind the expected high levels of casualties, the Ministry of Health conducted a survey of hospital accommodation available in England and Wales during 1937, and in the same year the British Medical Association drew up a list of doctors who were willing to be registered as providing medical care during a 'national emergency'.[48] The emergency medical services established by the Ministry of Health in the late 1930s and launched on the outbreak of war in 1939 included first aid posts, detailed schemes for casualty transport and evacuation and the dispersal of hospital beds outside of the large cities that were expected to be the primary targets of bombardment.[49] As the democratic state moved towards war, citizens – already trained in self-reflection and self-control – had to be persuaded that they and their families could survive the coming conflict.

Critics of government policy largely focused on the perceived inadequacy of state preparation for the physical protection of civilians from aerial assault, claiming instead that people were being misled by a state more concerned with preventing the potential psychological effects of air raids, particularly panic and lowered morale. For these critics, the development of provisions like civilian respirators and air raid shelters in the home were, primarily, designed to appease fears rather than offer any real protection. The absence in particular of deep air raid shelters, as had been provided eventually in Madrid and Barcelona, meant for these critics that official ARP measures were instead offering an illusion of security and safety, one that was designed to prepare the nation psychologically for aerial warfare rather than ensure the safety of civilians in the face of this novel form of attack.[50] While most criticism of ARP policy took the form of pamphlets and articles disparaging its efficacy, in Republican areas of Belfast it took a different turn in April 1939, as 'gangs of young men' collected gas masks that had been given out to households and burnt them in public bonfires, a radio broadcast claiming that they had only been offered to the people 'to wean them over to her side if ["England"] happened to be involved in a conflict'.[51] This psychological preparation of the nation for the new forms of warfare, seen in the state's attempts to persuade the population that Anderson shelters, civilian gas masks, fire watching and voluntary enrolment in civil defence organisations, alongside the training in emotional control discussed in the previous chapter, took precedence over expensive investment in deep shelters.[52] Given that ARP and civil defence measures were largely concerned with morale, this aspect of preparing for the war to come was regularly publicised through newspaper and radio coverage, in the regular issuing of ARP leaflets to the public, in parliamentary debate and discussion and in the organisation and training of civilians in ARP measures by local authorities around the country.

The second set of measures taken by the state in preparation for aerial bombardment, however, remained highly secret. Home Office files record that in 1926 and 1931, the ARP Sub-Committee of the Imperial Defence Committee had recommended that plans for the disposal of the dead after an air raid be researched and drawn up. However, it was not until 1936 that the Home Office drew up a list of points that would need to be taken into account when planning for the expected numbers of civilian fatalities in any future war. ARP planners and statisticians, basing their estimates on casualty figures for the air raids of the First World War, argued that an average of seventeen people would be killed by each tonne of bombs dropped, and that enemy aircraft were capable, 'during the opening weeks (of any war), of dropping 150 tonnes of bombs daily'. This algorithm, slightly adjusted downwards, gave them the figure of 2,350 fatalities per day, with at least 1,000 per day predicted in Greater London, the conurbation expected to be the primary target of enemy bombardment.[53] Probable fatalities for the rest of the country were carefully calculated, using population figures from the 1931 census, and grading areas from the densely populated and vulnerable 'AA' districts, where it was estimated one tonne of bombs would fall on 60,000 people, to more sparsely populated 'Grade D' rural areas where the same tonnage would be spread among a population of 400,000. Using this formula, it was estimated that while densely populated districts like Stepney in east London would have to cope with an average of sixty-four fatalities per day, rural counties with no large centres of population, such as Westmoreland and Rutland, could, respectively, expect average daily casualties of three and one. A handwritten note, probably influenced by the bombing of Spanish cities, attached to the estimate suggested that these figures could be multiplied upwards, leading to a 'daily aggregate of, approximately, 18,000 corpses', of which 7,000 'would be in Greater London'.[54] This higher figure became the one most often cited in subsequent paperwork. With these alarming figures in mind, civil servants began to pay serious attention to the question of the disposal of the dead. Between 1936 and 1937, an interdepartmental committee, known as the Burials (Civilians) Committee, held regular, secret, meetings to plan for this.

In November 1936, the first circular to borough and district councils outside London on the matter of air raid casualties was drafted. This would later become Circular 1779, 'Management of Civilian War Dead,' which was sent out to Local Authorities around the country in February 1939. Responsibility for the disposal of the dead was to be managed at a local level, and although the circular acknowledged that the bodies of air raid victims will 'in many cases be removed for burial by relatives or friends of the deceased', local authorities were advised to begin to put plans in place to remove and bury bodies which were not claimed, either because they were unidentifiable, or because there was nobody left alive to claim them.[55] A similar letter was drafted to be sent to London County Council and to the metropolitan councils of other large cities which could expect sustained air raids, asking them to work together by offering aid and burial accommodation to neighbouring districts where necessary.[56] Densely populated inner-city areas often did not have their own burial space, and instead relied on the use of cemeteries in other areas for the disposal of their dead.

Given the predicted high number of fatalities in the air raids that were expected to open any conflict, and the limitations on burial space, especially in areas anticipated to suffer from particularly heavy raids such as East London, the Burials (Civilians) Committee had to consider other means of 'disposing' of the dead. One suggestion made in 1936, though never developed any further, was that bodies be buried at sea;

Planning: imagining and planning for death in wartime

another was that bodies be cremated, rather than buried. Seen by its opponents as both expensive – cremation in Manchester for example costing well over £5.00 at the beginning of the century, while burial could cost as little as 10s. – and unchristian, as the body should be preserved intact until the Day of Judgement, cremation did not gain widespread popularity in Britain until the 1950s.[57] In 1935, the annual number of cremations stood at 8,766, more than the 4,287 cremations recorded by the Cremation Society of Great Britain in 1930, but a fraction of the 130,060 taking place in 1955.[58] Nonetheless, the Federation of British Cremation Authorities wrote to the Ministry of Health in 1939 to argue that, in the case of large air raids, cremation would be the most efficient and hygienic method of disposing of the dead. Arguing that they could cremate an average of 10,000 bodies per week, thus avoiding possible problems of disease, wasted manpower used in grave digging and the potential for bombs to hit graveyards and disinter the recently buried bodies, and body parts, of previous victims, the federation urged the government to invest in mobile crematoria in the form of gas vans, as a means of avoiding the problems of gas and electricity supply after air raids. Drawing on the long-standing cultural association between decomposing bodies and disease by comparing the 'pit burials' that they argued would be needed following large air raids to 'London's plague pits', the organisation posited cremation as 'the most efficacious method of disposing of the bodies … from a public health point of view'.[59] Cremation, they urged, should be compulsory for the bodies of both the identified and unidentified dead in times of national emergency, and should be paid for by the state.[60] The unpopularity of cremation, its expense and the impossibility of a later identification of unidentified bodies, however, meant that large-scale cremation was never adopted as a means of disposing of the dead in wartime. Instead, local authorities were urged to co-operate and help their neighbours by providing burial space when needed, and to consider using mass graves as a means of burial following heavy air raids.

Burial in mass graves was perhaps even less popular with the British people than cremation. Long associated with the 'common grave' and the pauper's funeral, the collective burial of bodies was often seen as a source of ignominy.[61] Although the burial of combatants in the Imperial War Graves Commission (IWGC) cemeteries of the Great War had attempted to alleviate the shame associated with burial by the state and was now largely accepted for the military dead, the idea of the common grave, where bodies were usually piled one on top of the other, often with nothing to distinguish them, remained a powerful signifier of disgrace; a final reminder of the lack of public esteem and significance attributed to those buried there. While not uncommon – in 1938 around one in eleven London funerals were conducted by the Public Assistance Committee and the bodies interred in common graves – they were unpopular.[62] Nonetheless, mass burial was an integral part of the planning for civilian death in air raids; a means of disposing of large numbers of bodies quickly, avoiding both the impact on morale of repeated individual funeral corteges passing through the streets, and of the problems of manpower that the digging of thousands of individual graves would create.

Expectations of mass civilian casualties at the outbreak of war, caused by the ubiquitous 'knockout blow from the air', meant that non-traditional spaces were considered for the interment of the dead: in Edinburgh, it was estimated that up to 9,000 bodies could be buried in the city's parks if necessary.[63] Although the state recognised that many people would want to bury their own dead, it also assumed, in its early planning, that mass burial would be the most appropriate method of disposing of large numbers of corpses following air raids, a report undertaken for the Committee of Imperial Defence in 1937 recommending that 'responsibility for interments will, in general, be undertaken by the Local Sanitary Authorities'.[64] As late as 1940, the London Metropolitan Boroughs Joint Standing Committee commissioned a survey of burial space available in the city. It concluded that the best solution would be trench burial by local authority, which, it estimated, would allow approximately 'three and a half million bodies to be accommodated'.[65] Similar preparations were ongoing in Scotland, where the Department of Health for Scotland wrote to local authorities to suggest that they prepare trenches 'deep enough to take five tiers of bodies'.[66] Trench burial rather than burying corpses vertically in one plot, as was the case in pauper burials 'on the parish', appears at least in part to have been an attempt to avoid the stigma associated with this practice, building on the practice of trench burial sometimes used in the Great War cemeteries overseas.[67] As Chapter 6 will show, at times this was successful; at others it was deeply problematic.

The burial of combatants was expected to be far less problematic than the management of the civilian war dead. The death and disposal of large numbers of civilians was a new problem for the state, while the three military services had histories and traditions of managing their dead to draw on. The Royal Navy, the oldest of the services, had traditionally used 'burial' at sea to dispose of corpses. Although the Admiralty considered transporting bodies back to harbour before burial from another ship, and burial ashore, it soon fell back, for the most part, on disposing of corpses at sea, as storing and transporting corpses 'placed a great strain on the ship's company'. If military action meant that 'burial' at sea couldn't be accompanied by a religious service, memorial services were to be held on shore at a later date.[68]

Fabian Ware, still vice-chair of the IWGC, returned to the War Office in 1938 in an honorary capacity, to re-establish a Department of Graves Registration and Enquiries, first formed in the Great War, under the auspices of the Adjutant General's Office. This department would oversee the treatment of the army's dead. They were to be buried, and commemorated, in three stages. First, bodies, and body parts, were to be collected from the battlefield and buried by their comrades. Secondly, the Army Graves Service would confirm the identity of the dead, and the eventual place of burial, moving the bodies to 'concentrated IWGC cemeteries where appropriate'; and thirdly, the IWGC would manage the war cemeteries where the bodies were finally interred. Identification of casualties was especially important. When identity discs could not be found, collection and burial parties were expected to carefully note other details that could aid with later identification, such as cap badge and shoulder title, and to keep equally careful notes of the place of burial. Army chaplains were expected to both minister to the dying, and to conduct funerals. All of these details were inscribed in the 1930 Field Service Regulations, and all of them were to prove far more straightforward on paper than they were in practice.

The newest of the military services, the RAF, perhaps had the hardest task when it came to planning for the management of death. RAF policies were set out in its 1939 manual, which had remained largely unchanged since 1930. RAF personnel working under the auspices of the Casualty Branch were to be responsible for locating, identifying and burying dead aircrew. Again, however, planning proved to be inadequate to the nature of death in modern warfare, in which the causation and place of death meant that bodies were often burnt and broken beyond recognition, and that the fate of aircrew reported 'missing in action' over enemy or occupied territory often remained unknown for many years after the war.[69]

The identification of the bodies of air raid casualties was a matter that took up much of the time of the Burials (Civilians) Committee. Two doctors from the Catalan General Hospital in Barcelona, which had suffered around 350 air raids during the course of the Spanish Civil

War, were interviewed by members of the Intelligence Branch of the ARP Department at the Home Office in March 1939. Their report, discussed in more detail in Chapter 5, noted that 'there were a considerable number … of unidentifiable remains' and that when people had been trapped by falling masonry, and their bodies extricated at a later date, when identification was possible, this was 'by means of clothing, rings or merely by the fact that the persons concerned were known to have been in the building at the time the bomb fell'.[70] Spain had long acted as an example to those concerned with arrangements for the collection and identification of bodies following air raids in Britain: a 1937 meeting of the Burials (Civilians) Committee noted that 'some of the bodies might be in a shocking state, where bombs had exploded in a street or in a roomful of people. The Spanish government … have published gruesome photographs of dismembered bodies, resulting from air raids on Madrid.'[71] The committee assumed, correctly, that most of the bereaved would want to claim the bodies of their loved ones, and so identification of these bodies was of prime importance.

Identity discs were suggested but discounted, as 'unless mutilation rendered identification impossible it might normally be assumed that recognition would be secured by friends and relatives'.[72] The distribution of identity discs, previously only used to identify the combatant dead of warfare, to the civilian population could also have been an unwelcome reminder that the state could not guarantee their survival under fire. Instead, the Civilian War Dead Form was created: a detailed document on which as many details as possible of bodies found at air raid sites were to be recorded by the workers at mortuaries dealing with air raid victims as soon as the bodies arrived. In the case of bodies that were unidentified on arrival, the form included space for details such as 'height, build, dress, hair, moustache, beard, complexion, eyes, shape of nose, shape of face, and physical marks and peculiarities'.[73] There was heavy demand for these forms; the records of the Scottish Home Affairs department show that their decision to order 100,000 forms for Scotland in the summer of 1939 was delayed owing to requests for multiple forms from authorities around the country.[74] Although the numbers ordered, which reflected the extent to which the 'knockout blow from the air' had become the standard expectation for the opening days of war by 1939, were never necessary, these forms were often to prove invaluable in the identification of those killed in air raids during the war years.

By 1939, the plans for the management of the war dead had gained a new urgency. They were a vital aspect of Britain's preparation for conflict

Planning: imagining and planning for death in wartime

in the new age of aerial warfare. In January 1939, responsibility for managing the civilian war dead moved from the Home Office to the Ministry of Health, and a conference held at the ministry in the same month on the burial of civilian war victims summarised the quandary in which the state found itself: caught between the need to provide information to local authorities so that they could prepare for the predicted aftermath of air raids by stocking up on supplies of coffins and shrouds, by identifying buildings that could be used as emergency mortuaries and by preparing mass graves, they also wanted to avoid the fear and possible panic that could be engendered by such instructions becoming public.[75]

The conference decided that the time had come to contact local authorities, and so Circular 1779, 'Civilian Deaths Due to War Operations', was distributed to the town clerks of local authorities in England, Wales and Scotland. The circular stated that first aid parties were to be responsible for the collection of bodies that had not been removed by family or friends from the site of death. These should then be taken in 'suitable covered vehicles' to mortuaries, where the mortuary attendant would oversee the collection of details that would, hopefully, help with identification where needed, and pass on the name of the deceased to the registrar. Coroners would not be needed to certify death when the mortuary superintendent was certain this was 'due to war operations', and local authorities would have powers to use 'any burial ground, churchyard or cemetery not under their control' if there were a large number of casualties.[76] With some adaptations and additions over the next six years, Circular 1779 became the basis for the management of the civilian war dead across the country.

Conclusion

When Britain declared war on Sunday 3 September 1939, the expectation was that Chamberlain's announcement would immediately be followed by the much anticipated, devastating, air raids on British towns and cities. Although air raid sirens were sounded in London and southern England, and ARP workers in Belfast, reporting for duty to the Antrim Road barracks that morning, were told that London was being bombed, the first air raids were aimed at the fleet of the Royal Navy, in and around Scapa Flow in Orkney, just north of the Scottish mainland.[77] The first civilian death as a result of aerial bombardment was also in Orkney – a householder was killed when bombs, presumably aimed at the nearby airfield, fell on cottages. The first bombs to fall on England were not directed at London, or any other large centre of population. Instead, in an opening sally of what was to become the Battle of Britain during the summer, they fell on the Kentish village of Chilham on 9 May 1940. Small air raids continued throughout the summer of 1940; the industrial centre of Middlesbrough was bombed on 25 May, and nine people were killed when bombs fell on Cambridge in June.[78] While the expected 'knockout blow from the air' failed to materialise in the first year of warfare, death instead came from the sea. In October 1939, 833 men and boys died on board HMS *Royal Oak* when a German submarine found its way into Scapa Flow.[79] The 'knockout blow from the air', in the first months of war, was transformed by the German U-boat fleet in the Atlantic into a 'knockout blow from the sea'.

The anticipation, and fear, of devastating air raids that had been so prevalent in British fiction and political activism, and that had shaped policy and planning in the 1930s, was not matched by the appearance of large-scale air raids until September 1940, when the Blitz on London began. By this time, the British people had been prepared, both emotionally and in material terms, for this new type of total war. Fiction, and observation of aerial warfare against civilians in Spain, Abyssinia and China had taught that war from the air would be brutal, and that civilian 'morale' would be its primary target. Investment in civil defence was designed to develop the belief that aerial warfare could, after all, be survivable, particularly when people co-operated by drawing on the strong culture of associational and voluntary organisations, and giving up their time to train as air raid wardens, fire fighters and first aid workers. Anderson shelters had been widely distributed, trenches had been dug and public street shelters had been erected. Gas masks had been developed and distributed, and schoolchildren had been evacuated from (and often returned to) major cities. Secret, detailed plans had been drawn up to cope with the mass fatalities that air raids were expected to inflict on British towns and cities, and with the loss of life that could also be expected among service personnel. Perhaps most crucially, an emotional economy which valued stoicism was underpinned by expectations of emotional self-management, with people encouraged to recognise their state of mind and develop strategies for managing the impact of disruptive or difficult feelings brought about by war, at least in public. As Britain moved ever closer to war, both state and people worked to prepare themselves to cope with the demands of a second 'total war' in three decades.

Planning: imagining and planning for death in wartime

Notes

1. D. Cannadine, 'War and death, grief and mourning', in J. Whaley (ed.), *Mirrors of Mortality. Studies in the Social History of Death* (London: Europa, 1981).
2. W. Murray and A. R. Millet (eds), *Military Innovation in the Interwar Period* (Cambridge: Cambridge University Press, 1996).
3. D. Edgerton, *Warfare State: Britain 1920–1970* (Cambridge: Cambridge University Press, 2006).
4. For the construction and popularisation of this concept, see B. Holman, *The Next War in the Air* (Basingstoke: Ashgate, 2014), pp. 24–54.
5. G. Douhet, *The Command of the Air* (1921), trans. D. Ferrari (London: Faber & Faber, 1943), p. 315.
6. P. Satia, 'The defence of inhumanity: air control and the British idea of Arabia', *The American Historical Review*, 111:1 (2006), p. 28.
7. Satia, 'Defence of inhumanity', p. 34.
8. D. Omissi, *Air Power and Imperial Control: The Royal Air Force, 1919–1939* (Manchester: Manchester University Press, 1990), p. 154.
9. 'Japanese air raids, *Daily Mail*, 27 February 1932, p. 10; 'Furious shelling', *Daily Mirror*, 27 February 1932, p. 3.
10. 'British women under fire', *Daily Mail*, 22 February 1932, p. 11.
11. 'British armoured car in "Shanghai incident"', *Daily Express*, 2 February 1932, p. 2.
12. *Hansard*, House of Commons (HoC), 5:270, 'International Affairs', Clement Attlee, col. 532 (10 November 1932).
13. *Hansard*, HoC, 5:270, Stanley Baldwin, col. 632 (10 November 1932).
14. 'Mr Baldwin urges abolition of Air Forces', *Daily Mail*, 11 November 1932, p. 13.
15. 'Getting Germany back to Geneva', *Manchester Guardian*, 1 November 1932, p. 9.
16. 'The menace from the air', the *Times*, 12 November 1932, p. 13.
17. 'Letters to the Editor', the *Times*, 14 November 1932, p. 14.
18. 'Letters to the Editor', the *Times*, 14 November 1932, p. 14.
19. *Hansard*, HoC, 5:295, 'Debate on the Address', Winston Churchill, col. 859 (28 November 1934).
20. *Hansard*, HoC, 5:295, Churchill, col. 864 (28 November 1934).
21. The National Archives, London (TNA), AIR 2/1267, *Chief of the Air Staff Meeting* (19 July 1923).
22. Speech by Stanley Baldwin to the International Peace Society, 31 October 1935. Cited in R. Overy, *The Morbid Age: Britain and the Crisis of Civilisation, 1919–1939* (London: Allen Lane, 2009), p. 176.
23. For a taste of the language used in 'air power' theory, see the discussion of this literature in Holman, *The Next War in the Air*, especially pp. 23–54.

24 A. Light, *Forever England. Femininity, Literature and Conservatism Between the Wars* (London: Routledge, 1991); M. Francis, 'The domestication of the male? Recent research on nineteenth and twentieth century masculinity', *Historical Journal*, 45:3 (2002) pp. 637–52.
25 J. Sedgwick, *Popular Film Going in 1930s Britain: A Choice of Pleasures* (Exeter: Exeter University Press, 2000), p. 78, 272; J. Richards, *The Age of the Dream Palace: Cinema and Society in 1930s Britain* (London: I. B. Tauris, 1984), p. 282.
26 Holman, *The Next War in the Air*, p. 60.
27 Miles, *The Gas War of 1940* (London: Eric Partridge at the Scolatis Press, 1931), pp. 249–50.
28 S. Stokes, *Air-Gods' Parade* (London: Arthur Barron, 1935), pp. 137–38. Stokes was the pseudonym of the author Frank Fawcett. For more on this novel (and others of this genre), see S. R. Grayzel, *At Home and Under Fire: Air Raids and Culture in Britain from the Great War to the Blitz* (Cambridge: Cambridge University Press, 2012), p. 230. Also see M. Ceadel, 'Popular fiction and the next war, 1918–39', in F. Gloversmith (ed.), *Class, Culture and Social Change: A New View of the 1930s* (Brighton: Harvester Press, 1980).
29 Stokes, *Air-Gods' Parade*, p. 180.
30 Overy, *The Morbid Age*, p. 337.
31 'The tragedy of Guernica', the *Times*, 28 April 1937, p. 17. Steer's report was representative of the bulk of coverage of Guernica in the British press.
32 'Who bombed city of the Basques?', *Daily Express*, 28 April 1937, p. 2.
33 *Hansard*, HoC, 5:323, 'Spain', Sir A. Sinclair, col. 318 (28 April 1937); 'To the editor of the Times', the *Times*, 29 April 1937, p. 12.
34 The preceding year had seen the Italian air force bomb the Abyssinian cities of Harrar and Jijiga. Although these raids provoked criticism in the British press and a resolution asking the League of Nations to intervene to stop the 'intolerable suffering of the Ethiopian people' by the Women's Peace Crusade, coverage of Italian air raids was less widespread than that of Guernica a year later. See, for example, 'Women's appeal for Abyssinia', *Manchester Guardian*, 26 March 1936, p. 12; 'Italy's use of bombs and gas: great outrage on civilisation', *Manchester Guardian*, 31 March 1936), p. 6; 'Bombed city ablaze after Italian air raid', *Daily Mirror*, 30 March 1936, p. 4. In contrast, coverage in the pro-Mussolini *Daily Mail* focused on the 'perfect formation' used by the bombers. 'Mass attack by 30 bombers', *Daily Mail*, 26 March 1936, p. 15. Japanese air raids on Chinese cities from September 1937 also provoked widespread criticism, but their geographical distance from Britain meant they did not attract as much public interest as the bombing of Spanish cities between 1936 and 1939.
35 Cited in Overy, *The Morbid Age*, p. 335.
36 J. Langdon-Davies, *Air Raid: The Technique of Silent Approach High Explosive Panic* (London: George Routledge, 1938), p. 15.

37 Langdon-Davies, *Air Raid*, p. 94.
38 Mass Observation (MO), Worktown Collection 27/A, *Armistice Day* (1937).
39 MO, Day Surveys, *Day Diary for Armistice Day 1937*, Respondents F058, F004.
40 MO, *Armistice Day 1937*, Respondent F038.
41 MO, 1938, Special Day Report, *Armistice Day* (1938).
42 MO, *Armistice Day* (1938).
43 MO, *Armistice Day* (1938); M. Roper, *The Secret Battle: Emotional Survival in the Great War* (Manchester: Manchester University Press, 2009).
44 A. Allport, *Browned Off and Bloody Minded: The British Soldier Goes to War, 1939–1945* (New Haven, CT: Yale University Press, 2015), p. 21; G. Sheffield, 'The shadow of the Somme: the influence of the First World War on British soldiers' perceptions and behavior in the Second World War', in P. Addison and A. Calder (eds), *Time to Kill: The Soldier's Experience of War in the West, 1939–1945* (London: Pimlico, 1997), pp. 29–39, here 31.
45 For the official history of state planning and organisation of civil defence, see T. H. O'Brien, *Civil Defence: History of the Second World War* (London: HMSO, 1955).
46 On the gendered nature of ARP recruitment in the 1930s, see L. Noakes, '"Serve to Save": gender, citizenship and civil defence in Britain, 1937–41', *Journal of Contemporary History*, 47:4 (2012), pp. 734–53. On the wider history of voluntarism in 1930s Britain, see H. McCarthy, 'Parties, voluntary associations and democratic politics in interwar Britain', *The Historical Journal*, 50:4 (2007), pp. 891–912.
47 Public Record Office of Northern Ireland, Belfast (PRONI), CAB 3/A/69, *Draft Typescript of History of Civil Defence in Northern Ireland* (1945), p. 12.
48 'Doctors for air raid duty', *Daily Mail*, 6 December 1937, p. 15.
49 A. S. MacNulty and W. Franklin Mellor (eds), *Medical Services in War: The Principal Medical Lessons of the Second World War* (London: HMSO, 1968), pp. 277–90.
50 See, for example, T. Wintringham, *Air Raid Warning* (London: Communist Party of Great Britain Leaflets, 1937); Labour Party, *ARP: Labour's Policy* (London: Labour Party, 1939); J. B. S. Haldane, *ARP* (London: Victor Gollancz, 1938).
51 PRONI, CAB 3/A/69, *Draft Transcript* (1945), p. 15.
52 J. S. Meisel, 'Air raid shelter policy and its critics in Britain before the Second World War', *Twentieth Century British History*, 5:3 (1994), pp. 300–19.
53 The National Archives (TNA), Home Office (HO) 45/18142, *War. Burial of the Dead Killed in Air Raids* (1936).
54 TNA, HO 45/18142, *Burial of the Dead Killed in Air Raids* (1936).

55　TNA, HO 45/18142, *Burial of the Dead Killed in Air Raids* (1936).
56　TNA, HO 45/18142, *Burial of the Dead Killed in Air Raids* (1936). While these letters were drafted, they were never sent. Notes on the file detail an internal debate about the best time to release these letters: too soon and they would spread panic; too late and they would be useless.
57　'A brief history of cremation: the Manchester experience', *Manchester Genealogist*, 37:2 (2001), p. 6.
58　Figures cited in J. Rugg, 'Consolation, individuation and consumption: towards a theory of cyclicality in English funeral practice', *Cultural and Social History*, 15:1 (2018), pp. 61–78, here 73.
59　On the long history of this association, see T. Laqueur, *The Work of the Dead* (Princeton, NJ: Princeton University Press, 2015), pp. 215–38 and passim.
60　TNA, HO 45/18142, *Burial of the Dead Killed in Air Raids*, Federation of British Cremation Authorities, 'A plan for the disposition of the dead in a national emergency through a scheme to control and co-ordinate cremations and crematoria' (April 1939).
61　On pauper graves and burial practices in Britain, see T. Laqueur, 'Bodies, death and pauper funerals', *Representations*, 1 (1983), pp. 109–31, J. M. Strange, '"Only a pauper whom nobody owns": reassessing the pauper grave circa 1880–1914', *Past and Present*, 178 (2003), pp. 148–75.
62　J. Rugg, 'Managing "civilian deaths due to War Operations": Yorkshire experiences during World War II', *Twentieth Century British History*, 15:2 (2004), pp. 152–73, here 163.
63　National Records of Scotland, Edinburgh (NRS), HH (Department of Health for Scotland) 50/127, *Burial of the Dead in Wartime*, Letter from J. Storrar, Deputy Town Clerk of Edinburgh, to Assistant Director, Department of Health for Scotland (27 April 1939).
64　TNA, Housing and Local Government (HLG) 7/436, *Civilian Deaths Due to War Operations: Funeral Expenses of Members of Civil Defence Volunteers Killed and Civilians Dying as Result of Enemy Action*, 'Memo on Civilian Funeral Expenses' (1939).
65　TNA, HO 186/376, *Blitz: Burial of Casualties*, Letter from E. C. H. Salmon, London County Hall, to Harold Scott, London Regional Headquarters (3 January 1940).
66　Mitchell Library, Glasgow (MLG), Glasgow Corporation Civil Defence Department, D-CD4, *Memo on Emergency Mortuaries and Arrangements for Burial Issued by the Department of Health for Scotland, Edinburgh* (17 June 1940).
67　See Laqueur, 'Bodies, death and pauper funerals', *Representations*, p. 116 for a description of a 'common' or 'public' grave such as this in the nineteenth century.
68　Surgeon Captain C. H. Joynt, 'The Royal Naval Medical Services', in MacNulty and Mellor (eds), *Medical Services in War*, p. 36.

Planning: imagining and planning for death in wartime

69 For an excellent account of the management of death in the army and the RAF, see S. Spark, *The Treatment of the British Military Dead of the Second World War* (PhD dissertation, University of Edinburgh, 2010).
70 TNA, Medical Research Council, FD 1/5372, *Air Raid Precautions: Home Office*, 'Medical aspects of air raid casualties in Barcelona' (25 March 1939).
71 TNA, FD 1/5372, *Air Raid Precautions* (25 March 1939).
72 TNA, HO 45/18142, *Burial of the Dead Killed in Air Raids*, 'Interdepartmental Conference on the Burial of Those Killed in Air Raids' (29 October 1936).
73 MLG, Glasgow Corporation Civil Defence Department, D-CD4, *Form C.W.D: Death Due to War Operations*.
74 NRS, HH 50/127, *Burial of the Dead in Wartime* (1939).
75 TNA, HO 186/1225, *General File: Dead Persons, Burial Of*, 'Burial of War Victims: Conference at Ministry of Health' (24 January 1939).
76 TNA, HLG 7/761: *Civilian War Dead Bible*, 'Ministry of Health. Circular 1779: Civilian Deaths Due to War Operations' (28 February 1939).
77 PRONI, CAB 3/A/62, *Civil Defence: Miscellaneous*, 'A Short History of D District'.
78 PRONI, CAB 3/A/60. *Air Raids on Belfast. Chronological Record of Air Attacks on Great Britain and Northern Ireland 3 Sept 1939–1 June 1944*.
79 D. Taylor, *Last Dawn: The Royal Oak Tragedy at Scapa Flow* (Argyll: Argyll Publishing, 2008), p. 96.

4

Coping
Belief and agency in wartime

Introduction: belief in 'total war'

> Now may God bless you all. And may He defend the right. For it is evil things that we shall be fighting against – brute force, bad faith, injustice, oppression and persecution – and against them, I am certain that the right will prevail.[1]

Thus Neville Chamberlain concluded his radio broadcast of 3 September 1939, announcing that Britain and the empire were at war, with a religious blessing, and a claim that God would be on the side of Britain and her allies. Chamberlain was broadcasting to a country that largely understood itself as Christian. Although the numbers who counted themselves as active members of the major Christian denominations declined as a percentage of the overall population in the first half of the twentieth century, Christianity still 'infused public culture and was adopted by individuals, whether churchgoers or not, in informing their own identities'.[2] Most were still baptised in, married in and buried by one of the Christian churches, and Christian morality continued to shape public opinion on issues such as divorce, sexuality and illegitimacy. Although other religious beliefs existed alongside Christianity, most notably Judaism, the rituals of the Christian church remained the most closely entwined with everyday life, shaping both the national calendar, and individual patterns of work, education and leisure. The Christian festivals of Christmas and Easter were national holidays, the BBC broadcast a daily church service and shops and most workplaces closed on a Sunday.

However, while Christianity shaped the structures of everyday life in 1939, the British people also embraced a range of complementary and alternative belief systems. Heterodox beliefs co-existed with, and were often intermeshed with, a predominantly Christian public culture. In this 'promiscuous eclecticism', as Michael Snape and Stephen Parker have termed it, spiritualism consoled many with its promise of continued contact with the dead, and organisations like the Theosophical Society offered an alternate world view and philosophy that in many ways preceded the 'new age' movements of the 1960s.[3] Astrology had gained a new following and wider popularity with the introduction of a daily horoscope column by the *Daily Express* in 1930. Superstition and a belief in the supernatural were as much a part of the everyday lives of many as were a belief in the power of prayer, or the existence of God.

This chapter explores people's use of these everyday beliefs as they once again experienced total war, considering the ways that belief helped people to navigate war's challenges, and to face the threat of death and bereavement. As Chapter 2 showed, the people who faced war in 1939 were part of an emotional economy that valorised self-reflection as a means of enabling emotional knowledge and self-control. Self-control and emotional self-management were seen as tools that could help the individual achieve agency; a means of traversing and managing the challenges of the modern world. However, in wartime the limits to this agency were stark. While conscription, evacuation and rationing all shaped the parameters within which individual lives were lived, it was the threats of death, serious injury and bereavement that were the strongest challenge to any self-determination. Faced with the multiple dangers and constraints of wartime, many were aided by the consolation offered by a range of beliefs and coping mechanisms. Faith in the religious, the supernatural and superstition could both provide comfort and help people to endure the challenges of wartime, particularly the risk of death and bereavement faced by so many.

Ritual, superstition and belief in wartime

While the war did little to increase church attendance – a Gallup Poll of 1941 finding that only 9 per cent of respondents said they now went to church more frequently than in peacetime, while 52 per cent said they attended less frequently and 32 per cent that they never went to church – this does not mean that religious belief and ritual offered no comfort.[4] For some, religious faith appeared to offer a level of protection that the state could not. A sixty-year-old woman interviewed by Mass

Coping: belief and agency in wartime

Observation (MO) at the height of the London Blitz in January 1941 was dismissive of those who took shelter in London's underground stations, combining fatalism with faith in her claim:

> I always stay in bed. The Lord'll look after me, that I know. I've got more faith than ever when I see them down the tube – cowards! If they had more faith in the Lord they would stay in bed like me.[5]

This woman's faith gave her both a sense of security and a sense of individual superiority to the wartime collective, who in her eyes lacked the religious belief that would either ensure physical survival, or the promise of eternal life after death. Her religious belief, she claimed, meant that air raids held no fear for her. Religious faith, and the rituals associated with it, were interwoven into the personal survival strategies of many, just as much as the journey to the shelter, or the checking of aircraft controls before take-off. Charles Cane, who experienced the bombing of Kingston-Upon-Hull as a child, remembered a woman in his shelter 'counting the rosary, and getting faster as the bombs dropped nearer'.[6] A Roman Catholic artillery officer recalled a chaplain giving out cardinals' crosses and rosaries to all who attended a midnight mass in 1941, and belief in the protective powers of the Bible was widespread among military prisoners of war in Singapore.[7] Others turned to religious ritual for the first time in many years: a Lincolnshire vicar, stationed close to the airfields in the county, described a woman who 'asked me to go into her house and say a prayer for her son, who is an airman'. Her husband commented that 'it was the first prayer that he had heard, apart from the wireless, since he was in the Navy in the last war'.[8] For this couple, the rituals of religion provided a comfort specific to the conditions of wartime, and perhaps a sense of hope or protection when faced with the high casualty figures for airmen. Prayers of intercession like this were a notable feature of wartime life. In Bristol, outdoor prayers led by a local vicar, in which 'names of absent husbands and sons are handed in for special remembrance' were described in a letter to the *Times* in June 1940, while letters from relatives of the missing of Bomber Command to the Reverend G. H. Martin again and again asked him to pray for their safe return, or described their own prayers for divine intervention.[9] Back in London, the Reverend Maurice Wood, curate of St Paul's Church, Portman Square, held a well-attended evening prayer meeting in the church's crypt shelter, which doubled as an air raid shelter during the Blitz.[10] Religious faith could thus offer individual consolation, reassuring the believer that they were particularly worthy of survival or of a place in heaven should they be killed, but could also bring people together in a collective emotional community.

At times, the formal adherence of the British state to Christianity was mobilised to both provide a source of comfort, and to unite people in a collective emotional community. The evacuation of troops from the beaches of Dunkirk in 1940 was attributed by some to divine intervention, the answer to a widely shared national day of prayer held on 26 May 1940, which spread beyond the Christian nation to encompass Muslim worshippers at the London Mosque in Southfields, and the Jewish congregation of Hampstead Synagogue.[11] One man, describing a mist that had sheltered his regiment as they retreated to Dunkirk, recalled that when he told his mother of this on his safe return, she responded that the prayers of the nation lay behind his survival.[12] The archbishop of Canterbury agreed, describing the evacuation of some of the British army from Dunkirk as a 'miracle' in response to the nation's prayers.[13] The evacuation of Dunkirk was by no means the only time when direct divine intervention in the progress of the war was requested. This was the first of eleven national days of prayer called during the war. British Pathé newsreel of the days of prayer held in May 1940 and September 1942 showed these as moments of national and imperial unity, in which Britain and its empire 'show the world that we still believe in divine guidance', and Royal Air Force (RAF) personnel were described as 'modern crusaders who are not ashamed to pray'.[14] Newspapers published prayers for readers to use, and the archbishop of Canterbury suggested that all Anglican services include the prayer 'Peace and Deliverance from our Enemies', while Catholic churches performed a Solemn Mass of Remembrance and a High Mass of Thanksgiving, and prayers of thanks were offered at Free Churches after the Dunkirk evacuation.[15] The discursive Christianity of mid-century Britain meant that rituals like these were widely recognised and acknowledged, and church attendance on these special days was higher than average, MO finding that in a heavily bombed area of London, church attendance was higher at the national day of prayer held in March 1941 than on Easter Sunday.[16] For believers and non-believers alike, the national days of prayer were designed to act as unifying events, bringing together the nation as a consolatory, emotional community, united in the belief that the war was just, and that victory would eventually be achieved.

At times, religious faith was intertwined with the supernatural in the popular imagination of wartime. In May 1944, many reported seeing a vision of the crucifixion in the sky over Ipswich in Suffolk, during an air raid over the town. Reporting on the phenomenon, the *Daily Mail* said that those who saw the vision agreed that 'it appeared to them for a quarter of an hour, gradually becoming bolder in outline before finally fading away'. A Mrs H. M. Day gave more detail, describing 'a perfect cross, and on looking at it, the form of Christ crucified took form'.[17] The Reverend Harold Green, of St Nicholas Church, Ipswich, claimed that hundreds had seen it, and preaching to a 'record congregation', he stated that he had 'completely satisfied himself of the authenticity of the vision of the crucifixion seen in the sky recently'. Interpreting it as a good omen for Britain, Green announced that 'if only a dozen people had seen it instead of hundreds, I should still say it was God's call to this nation'.[18] Like the legend of the Angel of Mons, which originated in a short story by Arthur Machen of Agincourt bowmen appearing to support hard-pressed British soldiers during the Great War, the vision was appropriate to the form of warfare being experienced in Britain in 1944, speaking of both sacrifice and of protection, and appearing in the sky, now understood as a site of both danger and protection.

While the vision of the crucifixion appealed to many, with hundreds reported to have attended Green's sermon, for others it was both irrational and archaic.[19] MO asked respondents to its directive of May 1944 to tell them their thoughts on the '"vision" of Christ on the Cross which is alleged to have appeared over Ipswich recently'.[20] Many of the replies agreed that there would be a rational, natural or scientific cause of the image that so many believed they had seen in the sky. Explanations offered included 'cloud formations' and 'the moon shining through a rift in the clouds', while elsewhere one man wrote to the *Daily Mail* to explain that the vision was probably 'due to the searchlights, or the light from a building on fire throwing the reflection of an outdoor Calvary onto the sky'.[21] Others, however, were not so sure that the 'vision' was entirely understandable through rational inquiry. Although some simply responded by describing it as 'bunk', 'tripe' and 'mass deception', others thought that the conditions of war could account for the popularity of the phenomenon.[22] The comfort that such a vision might offer was widely recognised, one respondent noting that 'it is easy to believe one has seen things if one wants to badly enough', while others compared it to the earlier stories of the Angel of Mons, reflecting on the consolation such beliefs could provide.[23] For these respondents, the meaning of the vision lay in the emotional comfort that it brought to those who believed they had seen it. A significant minority of the respondents, however, expressed either a belief that the vision was real, or a desire that they could believe this. One respondent linked the phenomenon to her own experience, recounting how she had

> experienced 'vision' myself once. Cross in sky at evening of cremation of very dear and very pious friend. Gave me help and comfort, but sure it wasn't there for that purpose.

For this respondent, the appearance of a cross in the sky might be real enough; what she objected to was the assumption that this had the specific meaning that was attached to it in wartime – that of protection and reassurance of eventual victory – asserting instead that this interpretation risked harming 'real religion, which is robust and forceful'.[24] The yearning to believe, to be able to draw comfort from the meanings of the vision, criticised by this respondent, was clear in responses from others. One described what he felt as the contradictory pull of faith and the rational, explaining that while 'I am quite sure that I would have accepted it as a natural thing', he nonetheless 'shouldn't be surprised to see Christ walk down a searchlight beam'.[25] The particular conditions of modern warfare, its threats and dangers, combined here to make the appearance of Christ in the world an appropriate and understandable response to the suffering of war. For those who believed they saw a crucifixion in the sky over Ipswich, and for those who were willing to accept the reality of this vision, it both offered comfort and reassurance, and helped to bind them together in an emotional community of belief.

Belief in the protective powers of the supernatural, in ritual, totems and folklore, helped many to navigate the multiple challenges and threats of wartime. Alongside, or sometimes intertwined with, religious faith, this wide range of beliefs provided some with a sense of agency and control over their destiny that war had undermined. A supposedly pre-modern belief in miracles, visions and symbols continued during this most modern of wars. Given the often random nature of death in wartime, it is not surprising that many sought such reassurance. Geoffrey Gorer's *Exploring the English Character* found that 14 per cent of people used a lucky mascot for personal protection during the war, and many had individual rituals that they felt offered them a sense of protection in times of heightened danger.[26] One man from Greenock gave his younger brother, conscripted into the army in 1939, the shilling coin that he had carried throughout the Great War as a lucky charm, while Charles Embury, a petty officer in the Royal Navy, became convinced that he had a 'guardian angel' after an injury meant he was not drafted to HMS *Royal Oak*, sunk in Scapa Flow in 1939 with the loss of 833 lives.[27] One man, writing for MO in 1942, recounted his ritual while fire watching, and reflected on the amusement that it caused his neighbours:

> But I did it partly for the sake of their safety. I felt impelled to turn around several times while I walked along because I felt that if I had fought against the impulse the German airmen would have dropped many a bomb on mine, and their, property. So the neighbours benefitted.[28]

The same MO report listed numerous, widespread superstitions that were commonly observed in wartime, including throwing spilt salt over a shoulder, not wearing green and avoiding walking under ladders, all of which were hoped to avert bad luck. Others devised their own, personal rituals, including the man who avoided reading the *News Review* during an air raid because 'I did this consistently last winter and each time I did a bomb dropped' and the Auxiliary Fire Services member who became 'superstitious about cleaning my rubber boots. After cleaning my boots we generally suffer a blitz and I am out all night fighting fires.'[29] Shops in west London (and presumably elsewhere) sold a range of lucky charms and totems, including hat pins in the shape of black cats, rabbits' feet mounted in silver and a 'thin metal plate for soldiers to wear as a heart protector'.[30] While beliefs, rituals and superstitions like these were not new, the conditions of wartime meant that they had a particular appeal, and were perhaps invested with an emotional importance, that was shared across, and sometimes shaped by, social class, gender and region.

Recruits and conscripts to the army, navy and air force, no less than the civilian population from which they were drawn, made use of rituals, beliefs and totems as they faced the threat of violent death. While the Royal Navy, the oldest service, was suffused with superstition, and army regiments often had their own complex nexus of tradition and belief, the RAF, the newest branch of the armed forces, that prided itself on its rational and meritocratic structure and its expertise in the new science of aeronautics, was nonetheless riven with superstitious belief.[31] Fighting men, whose survival was bound up with their mastery of technology, found as much comfort as civilians in superstition when faced with the threat of death in wartime. They could also find consolation in a surrender to fate. Writing for MO in 1941, a member of Bomber Command described the 'sort of mystical fatalism' that he observed on his air base. He defined this mystical fatalism as the belief that (with regard to air raids on the base) 'if there is a bomb that has your name on it you're for it whatever you do, and if not you're OK'. For these men, a fatalistic renunciation of agency provided them with a form of comfort: if they died, it was not because of anything they had done. In contrast, he found that while aircrews flying over Germany and occupied Europe professed a belief in luck, fatalism was less widespread, as 'an air battle is recognised as a matter of skill, and the quality of aircraft and weapons'.[32] Unlike the ground crew, who felt passive and unable to defend themselves under the bombs, the aircrew were able to retain a sense of agency, and to put their faith in technology and training, as much as in luck or providence. For both flying crew and ground crew, shared sets of beliefs in fate and luck helped to bind them together in emotional communities with their own, highly specific, set of beliefs and rituals.

Martin Francis's cultural history of the RAF during the war demonstrates how a scientific rationalism was interwoven with superstition in the cultural life of the service. Francis finds little evidence of a religious sensibility amongst airmen, but instead a belief in the supernatural, in particular the ability of particular items to bestow luck on an aircraft and its inhabitants, was widespread. Men flew with childhood teddy bears, medallions, dolls, badges and female underwear, all of which served as a link with their life on the ground. Cecil Beaton noted that aircrew avoided the word 'goodbye,' and the crews of Lancaster bombers in 50 Squadron had a shared ritual of listening to an Andrews Sisters song in the mess before a mission.[33] One man always urinated on the wheels of his plane before take-off.[34] Members of the most self-consciously 'modern' of the military services, reliant on technology, skill and training for their survival, the men of the air force nonetheless drew comfort from the presence of totems and the enactment of collective as well as individual rituals which served to unite them as a group as well as to reassure them as individuals as they faced the dangers of combat.

The collapsing of distinctions between the modern and the pre-modern seen here also informed the popular practice of astrology. Like folklore and superstition, an interest in astrology preceded the war, but the particular conditions of wartime furthered its appeal. According to an MO report of 1941, interest in astrology was widespread in wartime, as people sought interpretative frameworks to help them understand, and to guide them through, the complex and sometimes unknowable challenges of war:

> People want to believe in something that at least *appears* to interpret events and trends in the dangerous and complex civilisation in which

uneducated people find themselves confused, worried, many of their certainties weakened.[35]

As well as attributing this interest in astrology to wartime, MO also argued that social class, gender and education made people more or less likely to consult their horoscopes for guidance. According to MO, the circumstances of wartime created the ideal conditions for astrology to extend its reach, as

> The ordinary person ... who is particularly at sea in these days of constant crisis and change can find in astrology a crude means of integrating all sorts of happenings, and of persuading himself (or more often herself) that she is born under a lucky star and that in times of harm less harm can come to her.[36]

Of these 'ordinary people', women were twice as likely as men to have some belief in astrology, and many women's magazines included weekly horoscope columns. MO found that astrology was more popular among women and among the working class, patterns that were also seen before the war, but the dangers of wartime created ideal conditions for a further interest in the predictive abilities of the stars.

One of the reasons for astrology's popularity was that it could be incorporated into everyday life. As well as predicting the course of the war, the popular astrologers who wrote for newspapers provided tips and guidance for their readers as to the course of their coming day or week. In a time of uncertainty, the attraction of such advice is clear: the 'everyday experts' of the astrology columns offered a focus on the self combined with the erasure of blame for poor decision making. In addition, the decision to follow (or not) the advice of astrologers provided individuals, somewhat counter-intuitively, with a degree of agency that was otherwise limited by the demands and constraints of total war. The individual exercised this agency in two ways. First, by selecting which astrologer to read, and perhaps follow, and second through the interpretation and active application of their advice to their individual circumstance. Astrology thus both returned a sense of agency to its followers, and allowed for an assertion of the significance of the individual amidst the collective of wartime.

For every person who thought that astrology was 'piffle', another pointed out that popular astrologers had predicted key events, such as the sinking of ships in the Battle of the Atlantic.[37] Some used their daily horoscopes as a means of planning their days, one woman telling MO that if Lyndoe, the astrologer writing for the *People*, predicted an accident for those born under her star sign, 'I would never leave the house, not even to go into the garden'.[38] While this respondent may have been unusual in the strength of her belief, and her willingness to apply astrological predictions to her daily life, many others were regular readers of both their own horoscopes and of the forecasts popular astrologers made about the progress of the war. Wartime conditions provided fertile ground for the popularisation of astrology: as a second MO report of 1941 concluded, astrology's followers were 'ordinary human beings, average civilised citizens, reacting in a normal way to this time when spiritual and moral satisfactions and goals are inadequate to the human need'.[39]

Astrology, religion and superstition were often intertwined in wartime, helping to provide people with reassurance and guidance among the disruptions and upheavals of conflict. To borrow from the historian of early modern France, Olwen Hufton, we might understand the coping strategies of the people of wartime Britain as an economy of makeshift belief: a temporary solution, patched together from a range of sources, to a particular set of historical conditions.[40] While all the beliefs and coping strategies discussed here existed before the war, the demands of wartime gave them a particular importance, as people sought comfort and encouragement from sources other than one another, politicians and other public figures. Unlike politicians, these coping strategies could offer the promise of individual survival as well as collective victory. Many looked for evidence that both divine and supernatural forces were firmly on the side of the Allied cause, and hoped that the following of rituals, the possession of totems, the protective power of prayer or the predictive power of astrologers would ensure individual safety. Attending church, reading horoscopes, praying, seeing visions and following rituals, the British drew on a wide range of beliefs, both religious and superstitious, during the war years. These both gave comfort and gave some sense of control over largely uncontrollable events. And no event was more uncontrollable than death.

Beliefs about death and the dead

War, for so many, meant separation. Through conscription, evacuation, overseas service and the destruction of housing, many were separated from their loved ones for all, or part, of the war. And for some, this separation was to be permanent. Death sundered the lived bonds between individuals, but an emotional bond, linking the living to the dead, continued. The emotional power of grief, and of love for those who had died, meant that while the dead were no longer physically present, an emotional connection remained. While Chapter 7 explores wartime grief in more detail, this grief was experienced, felt and performed within a wide-ranging set of beliefs about death, some driven by the conditions of wartime, others extending over the entirety of mid-twentieth-century Britain. These beliefs, and the emotional landscapes they existed within, sometimes helped people to navigate the harsh terrain of grief and bereavement.

Religion, which for the majority of the British people meant Christianity, and most commonly Anglicanism, provided believers with a picture of a life after death in which friends and family would meet once again, and spiritual progress, begun on earth, could be continued. Even for the faithful, however, this consolatory promise was sometimes not enough to assuage their terrible grief: Geoffrey Bickerstaff, whose son was killed in Greece, wrote to his mother that the promise of eventual reunion was of little comfort as 'Julian in paradise might just as well be non-existent'.[41] The mass experience of death, grief and bereavement in wartime did little to strengthen the Christian belief in an afterlife. In its 1947 book *Puzzled People*, MO found that of churchgoers surveyed in west London 'nearly half the women and nearly two thirds of the men incline to think there is no afterlife, or are undecided about it', although belief in life after death among the organisation's national panel increased from 35 per cent in 1940 to 45 per cent by 1942.[42] A wider Gallup poll found that 48 per cent of respondents in 1939 believed in an afterlife, and 49 per cent did so in 1947.[43] Spiritualism, while it reached its popular peak in the 1930s, offered its followers the possibility of ongoing communication with the dead, rather than the delayed reunion of the Christian church.

In the autumn of 1940, MO conducted an investigation into spiritualism, concluding that the Blitz had increased the numbers of those interested in its beliefs. It cited a forty-five-year-old woman who thought that 'the blitz has made people a lot more questioning than they were' and that 'the spiritualists are asking the questions you want answered', whereas 'with so many clergymen you feel that it is no use asking – everything is known and yet it doesn't answer your questions'.[44] For this woman, the belief systems of the established church were too rigid, inadequate to the often violent disruptions of wartime, but spiritualism, with its tradition of questioning established mores and beliefs, provided a space in which the challenges of war could be explored. The promise of continued contact with the dead was central to spiritualism. In the spring of 1940, the weekly newspaper the *Sunday Pictorial* ran a short investigation into spiritualism, one story appearing to confirm not only that the living and the dead could continue to communicate, but that such contact could provide solace for the dead, as well as the living. The story was of a séance which made contact with a young naval cadet who had been killed when the MV *Domala* was attacked on 2 March 1940 with the loss of at least 100 of those on board, most of whom were Indian merchant seamen who were being repatriated from Germany. Speaking through a medium, the cadet recounted the attack, emphasising the barbarity of the enemy ('I saw the swine come back and machine gun us, just as they were putting a boat off') and his subsequent confusion, and unawareness of his own death. His anxiety to 'make port' and bewilderment were alleviated by the séance, which ended with the medium, who had been giving voice to the boy's spirit, resting 'in the attitude of one who finds sudden peace after strife'. Spiritualism, as represented here, both re-affirmed the rightness of fighting a vicious enemy, and through the promise of communication between the living and the dead, offered solace and consolation to both.[45]

Hugh (later Baron) Dowding, the commanding officer of RAF Fighter Command during the Battle of Britain, became increasingly interested in spiritualism and the wider world of mysticism and supernatural beliefs following his retirement in 1942. Dowding published several books detailing his beliefs, including his many conversations with combatants who had been killed during the war. These 'conversations', with their assertions of a painless death and a continued life after death, must have been of comfort to some of the bereaved. In *Many Mansions*, first published in 1943, Dowding recounted messages received though a Mrs Gascoigne, a widow whose husband, Captain Gascoigne, was himself busy in the afterlife, organising contacts between the living and the military dead. One of these messages, from a sailor, echoed the stories of the moment of death and the afterlife recorded in Oliver Lodge's 1916 book *Raymond*, which itself offered consolation to Lodge himself and to the bereaved of the Great War with its stories of dead comrades gathering to play cricket and drink whiskey:

> I was in an oil tanker and we were all drowned when she was hit, it was very quick and I did not suffer any pain but tremendous surprise at finding myself possessed of the most wonderful strength and able to heave

away all kinds of wreckage ... I got free and so did some of my friends and we moved away without quite knowing what we were doing. We found a stranger who had joined us, his clothes were quite dry and he walked through the water without it seeming to touch him ... Then very slowly, we all knew that we were what we used to call 'dead', but it was so different that I couldn't believe it ... It's grand, just GRAND. I wish my mother could know about it. We are in a far better land than the one we left.[46]

This vision of death and its aftermath both referenced Christian imagery in the presence of the stranger who could walk through water, and offered reassurance to the bereaved that not only were their loved ones still in existence, they were happy and had, crucially, suffered no pain at the moment of dying. In its combination of traditional religious symbolism with an insistence on a knowable, recognisable afterlife, whose inhabitants could communicate with the living, Dowding's writings demonstrate the ways that religious faith could intermesh with other beliefs to provide consolation.

Dowding's visions may have functioned to comfort the bereaved, but they also performed political work in wartime. Other messages that he reported reassured his readership that, even in death, British forces continued to fight for the Allied cause. One such message was from a dead tank commander, recounting how he and his crew intended to 'go on fighting, hampering the enemy, throwing sand in their eyes, putting ideas into our leaders and playing an invisible hand', while a soldier killed in Libya told how he and his commanding officer continued to load and fire guns, aided by 'lots of shadowy people [who] came round us and worked with us'.[47] In *Lychgate*, published towards the end of the war in 1945, Dowding explicitly sought to manage and ameliorate the grief of the bereaved, claiming that he had been 'overwhelmed by grateful messages from the boys themselves' who were pleased when 'the black and hopeless grief of their dear ones is dissipated'.[48] Grief, he told his readers, not only had no place in a united wartime nation, but it could actively dismay the dead. It was the duty of the bereaved not only to restrain expressions of sorrow in public, but to manage their feelings, actively working to control and master the emotional impact of grief. The much vaunted unity of the people's war continued after death, linking the living with one another around the world, and with the dead in a shared set of war aims: a munitions worker, killed in the Blitz, recounted how he and a female colleague were looking after two children, also victims of air raids, while Dowding himself claimed to use astral projection to travel to Asia and comfort prisoners of war.[49]

For Dowding, the war's dead were ever-present, and were thus not to be grieved. Indeed, death did not put an end to either their war work, or their unity with the living. Instead, living and dead were united in their desire to win the war, the justness of the Allied cause demonstrated by the ability of the war dead to aid those still fighting. Dowding's dead truly did continue to work for the living.

Not all of the dead were as benign as Dowding's spirits. Elizabeth Bowen returned again and again to the continued presence of the victims of war, particularly those killed suddenly and violently. The dead of the Blitz appeared in her postwar novel *The Heat of the Day* as a resentful presence, who 'continue to move in shoals through the city day … drawing on this tomorrow they had expected'.[50] Bowen's dead were rarely helpful or benevolent. In what is probably her best-known short story, 'The Demon Lover', a woman is haunted by the malevolent ghost of her fiancé, killed in the Great War, but making use of the disturbances of the Second World War to reappear in blitzed London, reminding her, and by implication the wartime nation, that 'nothing has changed. I shall rely on you to keep your promise.'[51] The ghosts of Bowen's fiction are resentful of the living, at once envying their survival, and working to ensure that their (unwilling) sacrifice is not forgotten. In Bowen's fiction as elsewhere, the disruptions of wartime create an uncanny landscape in which the boundaries between the living and dead were often porous and unreliable.

The threat and experience of loss in wartime meant that the dead, and the possibility of an afterlife that enabled communication with them, were in the thoughts of many. Ghosts were not confined to fiction: they appeared in a small number of newspaper stories following the air raids of 1940–1941, indicating something of the ways that this assault on towns and cities transformed the previously safe space of the domestic home and the everyday spaces of peacetime into unstable and uncanny sites of danger, dread and destruction.[52] In contrast, when MO asked its panellists about ghosts in 1942, replies emphasised that when these had been encountered they were almost always friendly and familiar, providing comfort rather than provoking dread. MO reported that 'ghosts or human apparitions are told of in profusion', and 'in a number of cases special mention is made of the fact that the person seeing the ghost is not afraid'.[53] Indeed, the dead that appeared to the living were often recently dead family and friends; a familiar and comforting presence in the midst of wartime upheaval and insecurity.

Coping: belief and agency in wartime

While the presence of the wartime dead was often experienced as comforting to the living, the thought of their own deaths as a result of war was usually distressing. As ever concerned about emotions and their shaping of wartime morale, in 1942 MO asked its panellists to 'describe your present feelings about death and dying'.[54] The majority of respondents replied that while they were not afraid of death itself, they were fearful of the process of dying. The war had, unsurprisingly, made thoughts of death more common, with 30 per cent replying that they now thought of death more frequently. Specific wartime conditions often drove these thoughts. In its analysis of the replies, MO highlighted a widespread fear of suffocation, linked, it argued, to anxieties about being trapped beneath a building hit during an air raid. The mother of a young child wrote that 'all through the blitz the thought of death itself did not bother me. The thought I hated was being buried and not dead' (original emphasis). Another woman, who had been an air raid warden in a small town that had suffered a Baedecker raid, wrote that 'thoughts of being drowned or burnt are quite appalling', while a male respondent avoided air raid shelters altogether because he did not want 'to be buried alive during an air raid'.[55] For others, close brushes with death had alleviated their fears, and allowed them to face death stoically. One woman recalled that when she had thought she was about to die during an air raid, her 'only feeling was a strong wave of sorrow that I should have to be there just when the thing happened. Had I been killed it would have all been over in a flash.' A man felt that the actions of others had enabled him to face his own death with equanimity, citing the example of occupied France, where 'hundreds of people without pretending to be brave face the firing squads dauntless and unafraid'.[56] War, with its multiple uncertainties and its threat of sudden, violent and often random death, forced many to contemplate their own deaths, and the deaths of others.

As Judith Butler has written, death is destructive not just of the individual and the individual body, but also of the relationships and identities that are destabilised by the demise of that individual. Butler suggests that mourning, the socially constituted response to bereavement, involves 'agreeing to undergo a transformation ... the full result of which one cannot know in advance'.[57] Death disrupted both intimate and social relationships, and many of those responding to the MO directive were concerned about the impact their death would have on those around them. Female respondents in particular worried about the effect their deaths might have on their families:

> I am really worried about the effect my death might have on my younger children.
> I have hoped several times lately that I do not die until my children are grown up.
> I have made arrangements for my children in case I am killed and so feel easier about it now.[58]

MO diagnosed these concerns as being about the 'economic responsibilities they may leave behind them when they die', and indeed the responses are phrased in the restrained register so valued within the emotional economy of wartime Britain. However, the frequency with which concerns for those left behind were voiced, and the recurrent mentions of the impact of loss on children illustrate an underlying anxiety of wartime, and the usually strong emotional bond between mothers and young children. The strength of this tie, and the anxiety that thoughts of its rupture through death produced, were of course not specific to wartime, but were felt as a response to the increased dangers that were central to the conflict. One woman recalled the ways that the daily threat of air raids had shaped her feelings about her family:

> My feelings then were that should death strike us when we were together, i.e. my husband, my son and myself, it would be the best way of dying. I have realised since that this was a selfish thought. I didn't mind the thought of dying myself so much as the fear of being left without my loved ones.[59]

The strength of this woman's emotional relationships with – her love for – her husband and child made the thought of living without them unbearable; she was unwilling to undertake the process of transformation described by Butler. Once the crisis of the Blitz had passed, however, she reverted to the more stoic narrative, describing her thoughts as 'selfish' in their emphasis on her own needs and desires, rather than those of others. Her fear of death and loss was real, even if she subsequently renounced her immediate emotional response to this fear. War disrupted at the intimate, as well as the public level, pulling apart families and friends as it destroyed nation-states and brought down governments.

The emotional labour of wartime that we can read through this woman's response was identified more widely by MO in what they described as the war's tendency to 'harden people to the idea of death and to make them in some cases almost indifferent to it'.[60] MO argued that women

Coping: belief and agency in wartime

were more distressed by thoughts of mass death, and by pity for those affected by it, and were also more likely than men to recognise and reflect on the 'creation of a self-protective crust of indifference'. One woman wrote,

> The war at the outset and during the blitz affected my thought of death by compelling me to think of it more often, and by making me regard natural death almost as a fortunate escape from some more horrible form. The thought of thousands of people being killed [in] the most horrible manner day after day was almost too much to bear and remain sane. I think I have now grown a sort of protective shell of insensitiveness to all the horror – unless it comes near enough to threaten me or my friends personally.[61]

The empathy with, and sympathy for, those suffering in war that this woman described, and her efforts to overcome her own fears, show the emotional work demanded by the valued stoical response to the challenges of wartime. While the necessity for such emotional labour may have been shaped by the need to maintain wartime morale, this respondent experienced it as an internalised necessity, something required less because society demanded it, than for her own ability to cope with the horrors of war.

Male respondents more often used an impersonal and determinedly unemotional language to describe the ways that war had reshaped their thoughts about their own death. A young man waiting to join the RAF wrote that 'reading of thousands killed and fully realising that I may join the RAF soon and may soon be dead … I regard death in a much more matter of fact way'. An older man explained that

> I have thought about death a good deal since Munich. I have wondered whether there are any last minute sensations when HE is dropped in close proximity; whether there is time to feel one's body violently disintegrating in the explosion before unconsciousness. I don't dread death as such but it annoys me to think I would not be missed.[62]

Contemplating their own dying in responses notable for their lack of attention to the idea of an afterlife, these men were able to present themselves as dispassionate, brave and self-sacrificing, key attributes of the 'temperate man' of mid-century Britain, and able to display the 'unflappability' that Francis has identified as a dominant code within masculine emotional culture of the time.[63] It appears that for many the proximity of death meant that they had to find a means of distancing themselves from contemplation of their own or others' death in order to meet social expectations of stoicism. At the same time such distancing may have helped them to cope, and to maintain a stable sense of self amidst the turmoil of war.

This emotional management was shaped by and articulated within an emotional economy that valued individual stoicism while disparaging excessive emotional expression, widely understood as a form of weakness that could impact negatively on group morale. As Chapter 7 shows, much wartime popular culture endeavoured to represent stoical responses to the multiple emotional demands of wartime as ideal, as evidence of the individual placing the needs of the national community over their own. Film was a particularly popular form of entertainment in wartime, 'far and away the most popular', according to Angus Calder, with average weekly attendance increasing from 19 million in 1939 to 30 million by 1945.[64] Many successful war films, such as *In Which We Serve* (1942) and *Millions Like Us* (1943), represented bereaved characters as sad, but as working successfully to overcome their personal sorrow to re-join the national community and shared war effort; a process which offered them comfort as well as contributing to eventual victory. Combatants as well as civilians were reminded of correct attitudes towards their own death through film. Carol Reed's *The Way Ahead*, released in 1944, and originating as a training film for new recruits, urged a war-weary nation on to victory in its depiction of the creation of a British army battalion. The recruits, from all corners of the British Isles and from all social classes, are shown as they develop from resentful civilian recruits to become an effective and united fighting force, detailed with defending a small North African town against an overwhelming German counter-attack. Low on ammunition, they are invited to surrender by the surrounding forces, who warn them that if they continue to fight they will be 'destroyed completely', to which they reply 'go to hell'. The last that the audience sees of the battalion is their advance against these German forces as they disappear into the smoke of battle. The final credits read 'The Beginning' rather than 'The End'; a statement that would have resonated with audiences on the film's release, just days after D-Day in June 1944.[65]

The scene of soldiers disappearing on the battlefield, walking to meet their probable deaths, was similar to the preferred narrative conclusions of readers to the *Sunday Dispatch* who entered a competition to find their favourite film 'fade outs' in 1940. As MO noted when it analysed the results, the top five 'fade outs' all represented or suggested the death of a lead character. The most popular ending was that of the 1938 Hollywood production of Erich Maria Remarque's 1936 novel *Three Comrades*, which told the story of three young war veterans and one woman in interwar Germany. The final scene shows the two surviving comrades walking away from both the camera and a Germany riven with political strife, heading towards a new life in South America, accompanied, unseen, on either side by their dead friends.[66] This image of the dead as constant companions reflected many of the beliefs circulating in wartime Britain: the dead may have been gone, but in many ways they were still present, living on in the emotional connections that were maintained by the living.

Conclusion

The emotional economy of wartime Britain emphasised the individual's duty to the collective: to allow grief or indeed any other potentially disruptive emotion, such as fear, to shape one's actions, was counter to the war effort, undermining of both collective morale and wartime efficiency. However, war made many unique and difficult demands on the individual, and sometimes the internalisation of emotional management seen in the cultural emphasis on self-control and self-discipline, was not enough. The coping mechanisms, and the complex combination of religious and heterodox belief systems that people lived with and drew on helped many to withstand the stresses, strains and struggles of wartime. Religious faith, superstition, spiritualism and astrology together provided tools that people could use when attempting to cope with wartime's multiple demands. In an age of scientific, rational warfare, it should not be surprising that the supernatural, the occult and the irrational continued to appeal. This belief in the unseen and the unknowable offered a means by which people could hold on to a sense that they had some power in a world where individual autonomy was severely limited.

Beliefs about death, too, existed within this nexus of belief, superstition and faith. Contemplating the possibility of their own death as a result of enemy action, some found comfort in reflecting on the ways that others had faced death, while some used totems and rituals as a way to try and convince themselves that they would be lucky. Sometimes they drew on established religious practice – taking rosary beads to an air raid shelter, or a Bible into battle – and at other times folk religion and superstition offered comfort, as airmen carried mascots with them on flying missions, and civilians enacted particular rituals during air raids. This range of rituals and beliefs functioned to provide both consolation, reassuring the individual that they or their loved ones would survive, and a sense of agency, some control over the violence that was at the heart of warfare. Ritual and belief thus provided individuals facing impersonal, violent death with the hope that they could cheat the odds, reclaiming some autonomy in a conflict determined to remove this.

The war's dead remained members of the national community, their sacrifice standing for both the brutality of the enemy and for collective war aims. While some turned to spiritualism as a way of trying to continue contact with the dead, for most the dead lived on in the emotional relationships with loved ones that continue long after death. The dead thus continued to work for the nation, not only in the practical manner envisaged by Dowding, but symbolically and emotionally, functioning both as emblems of collective sacrifice and as figures whose memory could offer emotional solace and act as a spur to a continued war effort. The dead were present in numerous and complex ways in wartime Britain, and this presence often helped the living to cope with the demands of war.

Notes

1. BBC Archive, 'Written Document', 1939, *The Transcript of Neville Chamberlain's Declaration of War*, www.bbc.co.uk/archive/ww2outbreak/7957.shtml?page=txt (accessed 12 September 2017).
2. C. Brown, *The Death of Christian Britain: Understanding Secularism 1800–2000* (London: Routledge, 2001), p. 8.
3. M. Snape and S. Parker, 'Keeping faith and coping: belief, popular religiosity and the British people', in J. Bourne, P. Liddle and I. Whitehead (eds), *The Great World War: 1914–45. Volume Two: The People's Experience* (London: Harper Collins, 2001), pp. 397–420, here 410.
4. J. Gardner, *The Blitz: The British Under Attack* (London: Harper Press, 2010), pp. 264–65.
5. Mass Observation (MO) Topic Collection, *Religion*, Box 1, 1940–1941, p. 4.
6. C. Cane, *Peace, War and Wigging In* (York: Courtney Publishers, 2013), p. 223.
7. M. Snape, *God and the British Soldier: Religion and the British Army in the First and Second World Wars* (Abingdon: Routledge, 2005), pp. 35, 33.
8. MO, Diarist 5110 (13 February 1943).
9. The *Times*, 10 June 1940, p. 7; Imperial War Museum (IWM), *Papers of Squadron Leader Reverend G .H. Martin*, Documents 93/48/1.

Coping: belief and agency in wartime

10 P. Zeigler, *London at War, 1939–1945* (London: Pimlico, 2002), p. 203.
11 'The people's day of prayer', the *Times*, 27 May 1940, p. 7; 'Forward. With God's help we shall not fail', *Daily Mirror*, 27 June 1940, p. 8. For claims of divine intervention see letters, the *Times*, 10 June 1940, p. 4. For a history of days of prayer in the twentieth century, see P. Williamson, 'National days of prayer: the churches, the state and public worship in Britain, 1899–1957', *English Historical Review*, CXXVIII:351 (2013), pp. 323–65.
12 Newcastle CSV, 'Mist over Dunkirk', BBC People's War website, www.bbc.co.uk/history/ww2peopleswar/stories/20/a5198420.shtml (accessed 12 September 2017).
13 See Williamson, 'National days of prayer', p. 353.
14 *National Day of Prayer*, British Pathé (May 1940), https://www.britishpathe.com/video/national-day-of-prayer (accessed 12 September 2017); *RAF on National Day of Prayer*, British Pathé (September 1942) https://www.britishpathe.com/video/raf-on-national-day-of-prayer (accessed 12 September 2017).
15 'In time of war', *Daily Mirror*, 27 May 1940, p. 9; 'Wartime prayer', *Daily Mirror*, 6 June 1940, p. 12.
16 MO, File Report (FR) 693, *Paddington Church Count* (May 1941). MO counted attendance at twenty-four churches in Paddington, west London, and found that there were 419 worshippers on the national day of prayer, 300 on Easter Sunday and 260 on a random Sunday two months later.
17 'Multitude hears of "vision"', *Daily Mail*, 8 May 1944), p. 3.
18 'Crucifixion vision seen in raid was real, says vicar', the *Eastern Daily Press*, cited in D. Mayman, *Led Soldiers: The Second World War Diaries of a Royal Hussar* (Authors Online: Bedfordshire, 2008), p. 86. No further reference given.
19 '1000 queue to hear vision sermon', the *Daily Mirror*, 15 May 1944, p. 5.
20 MO Directive, Questionnaire (May 1944).
21 MO Directive (May 1944), Respondents 1016 and 1146; 'The Vision', *Daily Mail*, 11 May 1944, p. 2.
22 MO Directive (May 1944), Respondents 1980, 1635 and 1688.
23 MO Directive (May 1944) Respondents 1651 and 1362.
24 MO Directive (May 1944), Respondent 1046.
25 MO Directive (May 1944), Respondent 2254.
26 G. Gorer, *Exploring English Character* (1955), cited in S. Parker, *Faith on the Home Front: Aspects of Church Life and Popular Religion in Birmingham, 1939–1945* (Oxford: Peter Lang, 2006), p. 87.
27 T. Robertson, 'The Second World War as seen through the eyes of a Greenock schoolboy', BBC People's War website, www.bbc.co.uk/history/ww2peopleswar/stories/10/a3939410.shtml; C. Embury, 'Biographical Notes', *HMS Dunedin Society*, www.hmsdunedin.co.uk/pre-1941/embury-c/ (both accessed 8 September 2017).
28 MO File Report (FR) 975, *Report on Superstition* (November 1941), p. 22.

29 MO FR975, *Superstition* (November 1941), p. 9.
30 MO FR44, *Astrology* (March 1940), p. 18.
31 On the traditions and culture of the Royal Navy as a means of creating a cohesive group identity, see G. Prysor, *Citizen Sailors: The Royal Navy in the Second World War* (London: Viking, 2011), pp. 126–41. On the culture of the British army in the Second World War, see J. Crang, *The British Army and the People's War, 1939–1945* (Manchester: Manchester University Press, 2000).
32 MO FR569, *Airmen* (February 1941) pp. 1, 9.
33 M. Francis, *The Flyer: British Culture and the Royal Air Force, 1939–1945* (Oxford: Oxford University Press, 2008), p. 124.
34 Snape and Parker, 'Keeping faith and coping', p. 415.
35 MO FR769, *Mass Astrology* (July 1941), p. 3.
36 MO FR769, *Mass Astrology* (July 1941), p. 35.
37 MO FR769, *Mass Astrology* (July 1941), p. 21.
38 MO FR812, *Mass Astrology* (August 1941), p. 4.
39 MO FR812, *Mass Astrology* (August 1941), p. 6.
40 O. Hufton, *The Poor of Eighteenth Century France, 1750–1789* (Oxford: The Clarendon Press, 1974).
41 Cited in P. Jalland, *Death in War and Peace: A History of Loss and Grief in England, 1914–1970* (Oxford: Oxford University Press, 2010), p. 170.
42 MO, *Puzzled People: A Study in Popular Attitudes to Religion, Ethics, Progress and Politics in a London Borough* (London: Victor Gollancz, 1947), p. 28; S. Field, '*Puzzled People* revisited: religious believing and belonging in wartime Britain, 1939–45', *Twentieth Century British History*, 19:4 (2008), p. 455.
43 Field, '*Puzzled People* revisited', p. 454.
44 MO, Topic Collection (TC), *Religion*, Box One, January 1941, p. 20.
45 'I speak – to a boy who was killed two weeks ago', *Sunday Pictorial*, 17 March 1940, p. 25.
46 H. Dowding, *Many Mansions* (London: Rider & Co., 1943), p. 29; O. Lodge, *Raymond, or Life and Death* (London: Methuen & Co., 1916).
47 Dowding, *Many Mansions*, pp. 35, 37.
48 H. Dowding, *Lychgate* (London, Rider, 1945), foreword, n.p.
49 Dowding, *Lychgate*, pp. 76, 62.
50 E. Bowen, *The Heat of the Day* (London: Jonathan Cape, 1949), p. 91.
51 E. Bowen, *The Demon Lover and Other Stories* (London: Jonathan Cape, 1945), p. 82.
52 See, for example, 'Ghosts in hostel', *Aberdeen Press and Journal*, 27 October 1941, p. 3; 'Ghosts', *Daily Mirror*, 6 December 1940, p. 4.
53 MO, TC *Religion*, Box Three (1942), p. 3.
54 MO FR1315, *Death and the Supernatural* (1942).
55 MO FR1315, *Death and the Supernatural* (1942), p. 8.

56 MO FR1315, *Death and the Supernatural* (1942), p. 9.
57 J. Butler, *Precarious Life: The Powers of Mourning and Violence* (London: Verso, 2004), p. 21.
58 MO FR1315, *Death and the Supernatural* (1942), p. 18.
59 MO FR1315, *Death and the Supernatural* (1942), p. 18.
60 MO FR1315, *Death and the Supernatural* (1942), p. 21a.
61 MO FR1315, *Death and the Supernatural* (1942), p. 21a–b.
62 MO FR1315, *Death and the Supernatural* (1942), p. 21b.
63 S. O. Rose, *Which People's War? National Identity and Citizenship in Wartime Britain 1939–1945* (Oxford: Oxford University Press, 2003); M. Francis, 'Tears, tantrums, and bared teeth: the emotional economy of three Conservative prime ministers 1951–1963', *Journal of British Studies*, 41:3 (July 2002), pp. 354–387, here 355.
64 A. Calder, *The People's War. Britain 1939–1945* (London: Jonathan Cape, 1971), p. 423; A. Aldgate and J. Richards, *Britain Can Take It: The British Cinema in the Second World War* (London: I. B. Tauris, 2nd edition, 2007), p. 3.
65 *The Way Ahead* (dir. C. Reed, 1944). The film was released in the United States as *The Immortal Battalion*. It had its royal premiere in London, in aid of the 1939 War Fund and the ATS Benevolent Fund, on 8 June 1944.
66 MO FR393, *Film 'Fade Out' Competition* (1940).

5

Dying
Death and destruction of the body in war

Introduction: the body at war

In her seminal work *The Body in Pain*, Elaine Scarry argues that 'the main purpose and outcome of war is injuring'; it is injuring and killing more of the enemy than the enemy are able to injure or kill that, she concludes, fundamentally separates warfare from other forms of human competition.[1] The aim of injuring and killing the enemy, imagined in modern, total war to include civilians alongside mobilised combatants, was certainly fully realised in the Second World War. People were killed by gunfire, by high explosive, by bayonet and sword, by fire, by asphyxiation, by crushing, by atomic weapons and by shrapnel. They drowned at sea, were blown out of the air, were murdered in death camps in Europe and in Japanese prison camps. They died of disease, of starvation, of neglect and of cold. The scale of the war, and the weaponry that combatant states had access to, meant that more died in the Second World War than in the Great War that had preceded it. In addition, the ratio of combatant to civilian death, which stood at approximately three to one during the first war, was reversed in the Second World War, in which civilians numbered approximately two-thirds of the global dead.[2]

Of the approximately 63 million dead left behind as the tide of war receded, about one-third of a million were British. The vast majority of the British dead had served in the army, and the majority of these died during and following the invasion of continental Europe, their numbers rising steeply after June 1944. Around 65,000 members of the Royal Air Force (RAF) died, most in the bombing campaign after 1943; bombs also killed over 60,000 British civilians. Many thousands also died while serving in the Royal Navy and the merchant navy.[3] These deaths, like most things in life, were shaped by class, age and gender. In the egalitarian 'people's war', death did not touch all members of the community alike. Most obviously, young men of military age accounted for the bulk of the British war dead. Because British civilians escaped the very worst effects of war, not being subject to the extended saturation bombing suffered by city dwellers in Germany and Japan nor (with the notable exception of the Channel Islands) to the rigours and demands of invasion and occupation, military deaths significantly outnumbered civilian in the British Isles, in contrast to the majority of other combatant nations.[4] Men were more likely than women to become victims of air raids, perhaps because they were more likely to be outside; of the 6,838 Civil Defence casualties listed by T. H. O'Brien in his official history of Civil Defence, 6,220 were male.[5] Working-class civilians were more likely to be killed than their middle- or upper-class counterparts: the majority of the high explosive and incendiaries dropped on Britain during the war fell on the densely populated districts of working-class housing that surrounded the docklands of London, Clydeside, Liverpool, Hull, Southampton, Portsmouth, Plymouth, Bristol and Belfast, and on the manufacturing centres of the Midlands, south Wales, northern England and western Scotland. In woefully unprepared Belfast, for example, at least 955 people were killed in just four air raids.[6] The upper classes, meanwhile, lost their sons in battle; 748 alumni of Eton died in the Second World War, 15 per cent of those from the school who served, three times the overall casualty rate among enlisted men of approximately 5 per cent. As Adrian Gregory has noted, the Angel of Death was as 'elitist between 1943 and 1945 as he had been in 1915 and 1916'; in 1940 and 1941, in contrast, he was more egalitarian, focusing his attentions on the slum dwellers of Britain's industrial cities.[7]

The focus of this chapter is on the nature of these deaths; on the impact of modern weaponry on the human body. Until the late twentieth century, bodies were largely understood by historians as 'timeless and static'.[8] In fact, they both act, and are acted upon, are subject to the historical forces that shape, aid, injure and destroy them. In wartime, human bodies gain new meanings and a new importance; they are regulated, trained and equipped for combat, and their governments attempt to harm and to protect them as a means of both winning battles and undermining or supporting 'morale'.[9] While bodies are bearers of symbols and meanings, they are also physical and material, 'actual living bodies of flesh and blood' that are shaped by and

Dying: death and destruction of the body in war

experienced in particular historical moments.[10] While more British people died as a result of the Great War than the Second World War, deaths in this conflict nonetheless impacted enormously on families and communities, leaving a legacy of emotional and often economic turmoil in their wake. As the novelist William Samson commented in his memoir of service in the Auxiliary Fire Service during the London Blitz, 'no disaster can be greater than the death or maiming of a single person'.[11] The family of twenty-two-year-old Alex Walker of Greenock, who had been posted 'missing' in Malaysia in 1942, had his death confirmed in 1946. Alex's father died, aged only fifty-one, the following year, and his younger sister spent the next fifty years trying to discover how her brother had died.[12] Alex's death reached down through the decades, as did the death of the novelist Storm Jameson's sister in an air raid on Reading; recalling her death nearly forty years later, Jameson commented that she still could not write about it calmly.[13] The impact of wartime deaths, and the labour of loss that these often entailed, was contained neither within the war years, nor by the culture of emotional restraint and emotional self-management that was explored in Chapter 2. This chapter focuses on some of the ways that modern warfare impacted on the human body.

The human body is at the heart of modern warfare. Bodies have to be trained and prepared for warfare; they have to be equipped and protected from modern weaponry; they have to be treated and reconstructed when injured, and they have to be buried or otherwise disposed of when life has left them. In total war, the bodies of its citizens become, to a greater or lesser extent, the property of the state. While 'totalitarian' states such as Nazi Germany and the Soviet Union may have been able to utilise the bodies of their citizens with relatively little restraint, the Battle of Stalingrad alone seeing between 1 million and 2 million casualties, social democracies such as Britain relied on consent as well as coercion to mobilise the bodily labour of its citizens, and to persuade them that the state would do its best to protect them, would provide medical care if they were injured and would care for their bodies after death.[14] The body was both the physical target of warfare, and a symbol of something more than the individual: the sacrificial body of the combatant killed in battle or the civilian killed from the air stood for more than the individual dead. Instead, these bodies were meant to symbolise both a shared determination to achieve victory, and the otherness of the enemy, prepared to kill and maim so many members of a united national community. As Chapter 6 will show, however, such attempts to attach meanings to the bodies of the war dead were not always successful. Protection of the body was also key: not only to try and ensure that trained combatants survived long enough to win battles, but also to reassure combatants and civilians alike that the state had their best interests at heart, recognising their value as individuals, not just as contributors to a total war effort, but as family members, friends and members of a community.

As such, medical services did their utmost to ensure the survival of those injured in wartime. Of course, militaries had long had medical branches: a medical officer, known as the regimental surgeon, had been attached to regiments of the British army since the seventeenth century, and the Royal Army Medical Corps was formally established at the end of the nineteenth century. The RAF had its own medical corps which ran mobile field hospitals, mobile dental units and casualty evacuation sections. The Royal Navy also had its own, long-established, medical corps, with each ship carrying its own surgeon or assistant surgeon, and senior physicians working on capital ships or in hospitals on land. The weapons of the Second World War, however, demanded that the civilian medical services also turn their attentions towards the impact of new forms of warfare on the civilian body, and following the creation of voluntary schemes and a register of doctors willing to attend the casualties of air raids, the Emergency Medical Service, which brought many hospitals under the control of the Ministry of Health for the first time, was created in 1939. Building on the experience of emergency medical care for battle casualties of the First World War, developing systems for the rapid evacuation of injured troops to base medical facilities, and utilising more recent innovations and discoveries such as blood transfusions and penicillin, both the military and civilian medical services saved many lives.[15] For many, however, the injuries they received were so traumatic that they could not be saved, despite the innovations in organisation and medical treatment of the war years.

Military death

In the British army, the military service to suffer the highest casualty and fatality numbers of the war, most of those who died did so as the result of bullet and shell wounds, the same weaponry that had killed soldiers so efficiently on the battlefields of the Great War. Indeed, an article in the *British Medical Journal* following the evacuation from Dunkirk commented on the similarity of battlefield wounds inflicted in 1940 with those suffered in the earlier conflict.[16] Illness, disease and infection also killed British combatants: 'desert sore' in North Africa, the term given to infected insect bites or wounds, could prove fatal, as could dysentery, malaria and other tropical diseases and infections among troops stationed in the Middle East, Africa and the Far East. Prisoners of war (POWs), particularly those who found themselves in Japanese camps in the jungles of the Far East, were vulnerable to these and other diseases, but also to the diseases of poor hygiene and malnutrition: beriberi, pellagra, typhus and cholera. Exact figures for the dead, whether through injury, illness or infection, are difficult to trace: the Central Statistical Office did not incorporate casualty figures into its monthly reports until 1943, and the War Office did not collect monthly casualty reports for the army until 1942.[17] The term casualty usually incorporated the dead, the injured and the missing, some of whom would later prove to be POWs. For the military, the term signified those whose labour could no longer be utilised; for their friends and family, it meant something quite different. *Fighting with Figures*, the statistical digest of the war that drew on the data of the Official History Civil Series, gives the figure of 144,079 killed in the army between September 1939 and August 1945, but notes that several thousand combatants were still officially listed as 'missing' in February 1946.[18] Civilian casualties of air raids were almost as difficult to account for: families sometimes took bodies for burial before they could be counted and formally identified; mortuaries lost details of identification, and in any case some bodies were unrecognisable and unidentifiable. It was not unusual for the mass graves of wartime to contain coffins holding multiple body parts rather than intact corpses, and for local authorities to have differing figures for the numbers interred in these graves. The difficulties inherent in constructing consistently accurate fatality figures, for civilians and combatants alike, at different points in the war should be borne in mind then when reading what follows.

The British army suffered its first significant casualties and fatalities in the late spring and early summer of 1940. Following the 'bore war' of September 1939 to May 1940, when casualties were overwhelmingly among the Royal and merchant navies, the army's first major losses were a result of the abortive Norwegian campaign of April to June and the retreat from France and Belgium of May–June. Over 3,500 British soldiers were killed during the Battle of France, the majority of whom were infantry troops.[19] While the evacuation from Dunkirk marked the end of a large-scale British presence in northwest Europe for four years, British soldiers were deployed elsewhere in Europe, fighting, and dying, in the Battle of Greece in 1940–1941 and the Italian campaign between 1943 and 1945. They also fought in East Africa between June 1940 and the surrender of Italian troops there in November 1941. While these battles, unlike Dunkirk, are largely peripheral to the British cultural memory of the war, they were nonetheless sites of death, injury and suffering: over 1,700 British, Australian and New Zealand troops died in the Battle of Crete, of whom approximately 1,000 were British.[20] Exact figures for battlefield casualties could be hard to substantiate, the often chaotic nature of battle combining with the destructive force of modern weaponry so that bodies could be difficult to find, identify and bury: in August 1942, the director of graves registration in the Middle East claimed that of approximately 20,000 Allied dead in the Middle East, North Africa and East Africa, only 1,000 to 2,000 had been formally identified and buried. The rest remained, at that point, unidentified and sometimes unburied, or interred in temporary graves close to the place of death.[21] The Imperial War Graves Commission cemeteries around El Alamein were expected to eventually hold 6,000 bodies.[22] At least 6,600 British, empire and dominion combatants died in the Burma campaign between 1941 and 1945.[23] Of the 61,000 British, Australian and Dutch prisoners who worked as slave labour on the infamous Thai–Burma railway, about 12,000 died.[24] It was in Europe, however, that British army fatalities were at their highest. Approximately 18,607 died in the fighting in Italy between September 1943 and May 1945, and almost 11,000 were killed in northwest Europe between June 1944 and Victory in Europe (VE) Day.[25] While overall British fatality figures remain small when compared to many other combatant nations, each and every one of these deaths would radiate out, entangling the family and friends of the original victim in a web of bereavement, loss and grief.

The weapons that killed these men in battle often left little of them to be buried. Amputation of limbs was common, as was evisceration and decapitation. Bearing witness to such deaths could live on vividly in memory for many years: one man, recalling his participation in the D-Day assault on Juno Beach, described a 'shattered assault craft' as 'a bloody mess [with] two bodies hanging from the side, where they had been blown by the force of the explosion'.[26] Alex Bowlby, who cathartically wrote and rewrote his memoirs of the Italian campaign between the 1940s and the 1960s as a means of 'paying a debt' to the dead of his

Dying: death and destruction of the body in war

battalion, recalled the moment when he found a companion ahead of him on a mountain path:

> Meredith's face looked into mine. His eyes were glazed in terror. His mouth was open. He was screaming ... It took a second or two to realise it would never come. Meredith was dead. Buried to the waist. The base plug of the bomb lay beside him. As I straightened up I saw his arms. They stuck up like a drowning man's. Avoiding them I shuffled on up the path.[27]

When Bowlby and his comrades returned to collect the body for burial, it had already begun to decompose. A paratrooper, depicting the aftermath of an attack on his brigade by low-flying aircraft in Normandy, recounted how

> I saw a leg lying in the middle of the path and I thought, by God, that's mine. Then I noticed it had a brown boot on. I didn't allow brown boots in my brigade and the only person who broke that rule was my friend Lieutenant Peters. I was lying on top of him. He was dead.

Only two of the group of forty-two were fit to continue after the attack, and he described taking morphine from the dead and leaving it with the injured, concluding 'that memory was as vivid today as it ever was. It was a ghastly sight'.[28]

The death of soldiers in tank regiments often held a particular horror for many of those who witnessed them. Trapped inside a tank that had been hit by artillery, itself full of fuel and explosive, the crew often burnt to death – a 'brew up' being army slang that could be used to describe a burning tank as well as a cup of tea.[29] Third-degree burns, as would have been suffered in the searing heat of a burning tank, not only can destroy all layers of skin and subcutaneous fat, but can also obliterate muscle and bone.[30] One man, recalling the battle of El Alamein some sixty years later, described the heat from burning tanks that was enough to throw trucks into the air and to lift the skin from his face.[31] Military memoirists often commented on the horrific nature of tank crews' deaths. In his record of service in North Africa, Henry Ritchie described 'tanks and vehicles with the bodies of men raw and bloody from violent death', while Alex Bowlby's memoir of the fighting in Italy portrayed the post-battle landscape at Monte Cassino where tanks 'lay around like burnt tins on a rubbish heap'.[32] Norman Lewis came upon a German tank in northern Italy, where a pool of fat 'quilted with brilliant flies of all descriptions and colours', was all that he could see of the remains of the crew.[33] Perhaps the most vivid descriptions of the aftermath of attacks on tanks and their crews were those recorded by Leslie Skinner, an army chaplain attached to the Sherwood Rangers Yeomanry, who fought in France and the Low Countries in 1944 and 1945. As chaplain, Skinner took responsibility for burying the dead and for communicating with their families. Skinner's diary for 4 August 1944 paints a vivid and visceral picture of the process of trying to retrieve bodies from 'brewed up' tanks:

> Only ash and burnt metal in Birkett's tank. ... Searched ash and found remains of pelvic bones. At other tank three bodies inside – partly burnt and firmly welded together. Managed with difficulty to identify Sergeant Campbell. Unable to remove bodies after a lengthy struggle – nasty business – sick.[34]

For many, the tank was also a tomb.

The unburied corpses that remained after battle, on the ground and in tanks, were able to make their presence known to the living. They were objects of both revulsion and fascination; a reminder that their fate could be shared, perhaps an enemy combatant, or a dead friend or comrade, but also sometimes a source of plunder, new boots, a watch, a revolver to take home as a souvenir. As Mary Louise Roberts has perceptively observed with regard to US troops, combatants' 'journals, memoirs and letters testify to a near obsession with the corpse'.[35] At least one man carried a camera into battle with him and collected photos of the dead, keeping them in a scrapbook only discovered by his children sixty years later, after his own death.[36] Indeed, the observation and sometimes the recording of the violently dead body, so rarely encountered in civilian life by the majority of these conscript soldiers, can be understood as one of the defining features of combat, a means by which men who had seen death in battle attempted to make claim to an experience that set them apart from others. This fascination, and desire to record the physical impact of war on the human body, was shared across different strata of the military. Ike Eisenhower, supreme commander of Allied forces in Europe, described how, after the fighting at the Falaise Gap in Normandy in August 1944, 'it was literally possible to walk for hundreds of yards, stepping on nothing but dead and decaying flesh'.[37] Alex Bowlby wrote again and again about his encounters

Dying: death and destruction of the body in war

with dead bodies, describing how he came upon corpses on the road to Rome:

> I walked along like one who knows 'a frightful fiend, Doth close behind him tread', dreading what I might see yet needing to see it. The unseen dead stuck in my throat. Two bodies puffed up like Michelin men broke the spell. I shot away from them, up a lane.[38]

Both men, despite differences in age, in nationality and in rank, give voice to a fascination with the corpse; a wish to bear witness to the aftermath of battle, to the impact of weaponry on the body and to the process of decomposition and decay which was as much a part of the mobile battlefields of the Second World War as it was of the Western Front trenches of the Great War.

Even when corpses were not visible, perhaps buried under rubble, or fused to the metal walls of a tank, their presence was often unmistakeable. Soldiers quickly came to recognise the smell of decomposition; as Alex Bowlby passed through the aftermath of the battle of Monte Cassino he noted how 'instinctively I realised I was smelling my own kind, not animals'. For Bowlby, the unseen presence of the dead was more terrifying than the sight of corpses: he remembered the smell as a 'protest' by the 'unseen, unconsecrated dead' who lay unburied among the debris of battle.[39] Walter Robson, a lance corporal with the Queen's Own Royal West Kent Regiment, who fought across North Africa and southern Europe, only to die of tuberculosis in Greece in 1945, also at Cassino, described how one man crept forward from the frontline each night to scatter Lysol over the putrefying bodies that lay across the battlefield.[40] Many military memoirists commented on the smell of the corpse. Norman Craig, in North Africa, wrote that tanks 'oozed the sickly sweet scent of scorched human flesh', while in Italy, Philip Brutton described 'the sickly sweet smell of putrefying bodies'.[41] Recalling the retreat from Burma with troops and civilian refugees after the Japanese invasion, Dr A. Desmond Stoker of the 57th Indian Field Ambulance wrote that 'so heavy a toll was disease, starvation and the country taking that we saw corpses every hundred yards or so of the journey and nowhere were we to be out of sight or smell of a dead body'.[42] Robson wrote to his wife that Cassino 'would always be remembered for the stench of death', explaining that the house in which he was billeted had the rough grave of a New Zealand soldier beneath the fallen staircase. Robson and his men cooked by the grave and left 'tea leaves on it and empty tins ... None of it is very sanitary and as the days wear on so the smell grows worse.'⁴³ Four years earlier, 'Gun Buster', the pseudonymous author of the popular book *Return Via Dunkirk*, had described his arrival at Dunkirk in terms of the overwhelming presence of death in the town, a presence that he largely sensed through the odour of corpses:

> A group of dead and dying soldiers on the path in front of us quickened our desire to quit the promenade ... down on the beach you immediately felt yourself surrounded by a deadly evil atmosphere. A horrible stench of blood and mutilated flesh pervaded the place ... Not a breath of air was blowing to dissipate the applying odour from the dead bodies that had been lying in the sand, in some cases for several days. We might have been walking through a slaughterhouse on a hot day ... It created the impression that death was hovering around, very near at hand.⁴⁴

The smell of death, of decomposing bodies, was transgressive; even when bodies were hidden or eyes were averted, their presence could be reluctantly sensed through their odour. Their smell affected the living combatants physically, emotionally and socially. For these soldiers, often living and dying in the presence of corpses, the seen and unseen bodies of other combatants were the bearers of multiple meanings. They served not only as reminders of their own potential death, but also sometimes as an inconvenience or an obstacle, as a source for the spoils of war, as a poignant reminder of mortality, as a reason for fear or revulsion and as comrades to whom they owed a duty of not only burial but remembrance.

In contrast, the deaths and the corpses of men in the RAF, in Fighter, Coastal and Bomber Command, were only rarely directly witnessed by their surviving comrades. These deaths were often the result of fire, when a plane was hit by artillery, either from another plane or anti-aircraft fire. Some airmen drowned when their planes crashed into the sea, and others died as the result of piercing injuries caused by shell, shrapnel and bullet. Still more died in training accidents, the RAF pilot Tim Vigors recalling that when two cadets were killed during training at RAF Cranwell just before the war, 'the grief of the bereaved parents around the graveside' brought home to him that 'death in the air' no longer 'belonged only in Biggles books'.⁴⁵ In the summer of 1940, 544 pilots died during the Battle of Britain, with many more dying in the Battle of France that preceded it, and in the years that followed.⁴⁶ The men of Bomber Command, which like Fighter Command included

Dying: death and destruction of the body in war

volunteers from the dominions and Poland, suffered some 55,500 casualties during the war, the majority dying on active service over Europe, but some 8,305 of whom were killed in training accidents.[47] In total, 69,606 men of the RAF were killed during the war.[48] A 1941 article in the *British Medical Journal* listed the most common injuries for airmen as fractures of the spine and legs, burns and gunshot wounds.[49] The list of injuries suffered by the crew of a Blenheim aircraft brought down over Wilhelmshaven on 4 September 1939 tells us much about the dangers of flying in combat. One man broke his neck and both thighs, dying in a German hospital; another drowned after breaking his right leg; and one survivor was recorded as having 'multiple injuries ... including broken lower jaw, concussion, wounds on neck and left cheek, tip of nose torn off'.[50] The exhumation reports returned by the RAF's Missing Research and Enquiry Service give a harrowing sense of the kinds of death these men sometimes suffered: when a grave said to contain four British airmen was opened it was found to contain intermingled body parts, the report stating simply that the men 'had disintegrated in the crash', while another exhumed body was noted as being 'badly smashed and burnt – skull smashed ... lower jaw missing, fingers and hand not found'.[51]

Exact causes of death were often unknown, especially when men were shot down or bailed out over enemy or occupied territory. Although Britain and Germany established a reciprocal system for reporting the death of air crew over enemy territory, with *Totenlisten*, or death lists, being sent regularly from Germany to the Casualty Department of the Air Ministry via the Red Cross, these rarely included detailed accounts of the manner of death. The Air Ministry's own records of air crew deaths, which included those in Fighter Command who were killed over home territory, and those who lost their lives in training accidents, or on take-off or landing, were equally vague. Cause of death was recorded under the categories of multiple injuries with fractures, multiple injuries with burns, fractured skull with other injuries, multiple missile wounds, generalised burns, drowning, carbon-monoxide poisoning. As Martin Francis noted in *The Flyer*, these classifications 'failed to do justice to the full repertoire of the grim reaper, which was as prolific as it was gruesome'.[52] If the *Totenlisten* and Air Ministry casualty reports give us little sense of the violent deaths faced by airmen, the operational reports and diaries for Bomber Command give us some idea of the scale of losses, if not of the exact manner of death or of the emotional impact of these deaths on both fellow air crews and the bereaved relatives. For example, on the night of 22/23 April 1944, Bomber Command carried out a heavy raid over Dusseldorf, an industrial city on the Rhine in western Germany. A total 596 aircraft took part in this attack: 323 Lancasters, 254 Halifaxes, and 19 Mosquitos. Of these, twenty-nine aircraft were lost – sixteen Halifaxes and thirteen Lancasters. Both types of aircraft carried seven crew members, so 203 men of Bomber Command lost their lives, or became POWs, that night. While this figure is small in comparison with the civilian casualties of the raid in Dusseldorf (between 883 and 1,286 dead), it was part of a war of attrition, with the survivors likely to be flying over the following nights as men completed a thirty-sortie 'tour' before a break.[53] A raid on Nuremburg the previous month had seen the heaviest losses of the war for Bomber Command, with sixty-four Lancasters and thirty-one Halifaxes being shot down by fighters and anti-aircraft fire from the ground.[54] Denis Hornsey gave voice to the sense of destiny that some men came to feel:

> If you live on the brink of death yourself, it is as if those who have gone have merely caught an earlier train to the same destination, and whatever that destination is, you will be sharing it soon, since you will almost certainly be catching the next one.[55]

Less poetically, the men of Bomber Command were well aware that their chances of suffering a violent death increased relentlessly with the number of operations on which they were engaged.

Flyers adopted a range of strategies to enable them to cope with the possibility of violent death. These included rituals, discussed in further detail in Chapter 4, to be enacted before take-off and lucky charms including photos, soft toys and items of women's clothing, to be carried with them on the flight. Given the heavy losses among flyers, it should not be surprising that superstition was widespread in all branches of the RAF; like the inhabitants of early modern England discussed by Keith Thomas in *Religion and the Decline of Magic*, the use of totems and rituals gave many of these men with relatively little control over their own fate a sense that they had some autonomy, some agency.[56] Some theories regarding survival gained widespread credence: George Aylmore, an Australian who had volunteered for service as a wireless operator in a Lancaster, remembered the belief that 'it was during the first five and the last five ops that you were likely to get the chop'.[57] Flying with a temporary member of the aircrew (a 'spare bod') was also believed to be bad luck among Bomber Command crews.[58] The coping

Dying: death and destruction of the body in war

mechanisms that these men were able to draw on were shaped by the complex emotional landscapes in which they lived. The men of Fighter Command usually flew alone and, at least in the early years of the war when prior flying experience was a distinct advantage, were more likely than the crews of Bomber Command to be both young and drawn from a social elite, bringing with them the culture of the public schools and elite universities. Schoolboy mischief and pranks, together with a culture of heavy drinking, were a part of life on the RAF bases where these men were stationed, Francis arguing persuasively that the prevalence of reckless and dangerous activities among flyers on the ground was an outlet for stress and tension and a means of managing fear and grief among men whose emotional culture gave them little opportunity to speak of these feelings to one another.[59] Geoffrey Wellum's memoir of Fighter Command recalls how, on a month's home leave, 'things weren't quite the same .... I found I was fidgety and unable to converse easily', disconcerted by the way his mother 'would look at me when she didn't think I'd notice'. On his return to his squadron and to active service, he was 'home again. The atmosphere in this place I understand. This is much better.' His first activity was to go to the bar.[60] A similar culture existed in Bomber Command bases where the more multi-national and less class-specific crews also indulged in reckless behaviour and heavy drinking. Flying as part of a team, giving voice to fears about death and injury could be seen by these men as something that undermined morale, and could perhaps bring bad luck in its wake. Miles Tripp, in his memoir *The Eighth Passenger*, recalled his friendship with a bomb aimer called Nicky, described as 'both horrified by the prospect of being killed and yet excited by the idea', and who urged Tripp to overtake on blind corners when riding pillion on his motorbike.[61] The recreational use of alcohol and of Benzedrine, distributed to ensure alertness on long overnight missions, also helped men to live with the fear of violent death, both their own and their colleagues'. The masculine, emotional culture of the RAF base, together with the omnipresent threat of violent death, made the expression of fear and grief difficult, and an emotional rectitude, at least around other men, tended to dominate.

Men in the Royal Navy and the merchant navy also spent the majority of their working lives in homosocial environments, with their own sets of rituals and culture, and were also faced with the threat of violent, sudden death as an aspect of their daily lives. The 'bore war' was never boring at sea. The very first vessel to be attacked was the SS *Athenia*, a liner bound for Montreal that was sunk about 200 miles into its voyage, just hours after the declaration of war on 3 September 1939. Ninety-three passengers and nineteen crew members were killed.[62] The first major British loss of the war was the sinking of the aircraft carrier HMS *Courageous*, with the deaths of over 500 men on board, by U-boat southwest of Ireland on 17 September 1939. When HMS *Royal Oak* was sunk in Scapa Flow on the night of 14/15 October 1939, over 800 men and boys lost their lives, many of them drowning in the dark, cold waters of the Orkney Isles. In all, almost 51,000 members of the Royal Navy and over 30,000 merchant mariners were killed between 1939 and 1945.[63] When enemy attacks did not claim lives, the sea still could. The diary of an able seaman serving on HMS *Glasgow* in the Atlantic recorded how, in December 1939, 'the captain of "A" turret was killed today, a wave swept him while on the fo'castle, against a fan, and a rib punctured his lung'.[64] Men drowned or died of their injuries in heavy seas, died of hypothermia or dehydration after their ships were sunk; they were killed by missiles, bombs and bullets, and burned to death or asphyxiated when they were caught in burning oil at sea, or in burning ships.

Conditions on the Arctic convoys, which took ammunition and other supplies into the Soviet Arctic ports of Archangel and Murmansk from 1941 onwards, were among the worst faced by sailors, because the freezing water temperatures reduced the chances of survival after a shipwreck, as did the heavy Arctic clothing these men wore, the weight of which dragged men down into the sea as it absorbed water.[65] The records of the medical care of survivors of shipwrecks in these convoys provide some sense of the ways that these men could die: 'grossly shocked, pupils widely dilated, limbs rigid, unconscious and stomach and lungs containing oil fuel'.[66] Men could sometimes be saved if they had not been in the icy water for too long, but survivors were rare. The official history of the medical services in wartime noted that there were fewer survivors of shipwrecks in the Arctic convoys than in warmer waters. It attributed this to the large number of ammunition ships in the convoys, which exploded when hit, leaving very few survivors, and to the speed with which these ships sank, meaning the injured often drowned before they could be rescued, and noted that

> Such injured and shocked casualties as did manage to escape did not survive many minutes in the very low temperature of the water. A number of ships reported that bodies, obviously badly injured, were seen floating in the sea.[67]

Dying: death and destruction of the body in war

Heat as well as cold could kill on the convoys. One naval veteran serving on HMS *Norfolk* recalled an attack on Convoy JW55B, by the German battleship the *Scharnhorst*. When a shell hit the gun turret he heard 'a terrible screaming; coming towards us was a Marine from X Turret, a ball of fire from head to toe'. So great was the man's agony that he attempted to throw himself over the guardrail into the Arctic Sea to extinguish the flames.[68]

Death at sea came to civilians travelling in the dangerous waters of the Atlantic and the Mediterranean as well as to the sailors of the Royal and merchant navies. The sinking of the SS *City of Benares*, carrying evacuee children, most of them travelling without parents, from Liverpool to Canada in September 1940 was the most infamous of these tragedies. The British government were quick to seize the propaganda opportunity offered by the sinking of what was termed 'an evacuee ship', and the deaths of almost eighty children, together with over 170 adults, many of whom were Indian merchant seamen, was seen as further proof of the inhumanity of Nazi Germany.[69] At least one survivor spoke of her ordeal in terms that were almost perfectly shaped by the culture of emotional reticence. Showing remarkable sangfroid, she had embarked on a second Atlantic convoy shortly after being rescued from the *Benares*. When passengers on this second ship were woken in the middle of the night by a loud noise, followed by the ship shuddering and the alarm being sounded, she reassured her fellow travellers as they gathered on deck in their life jackets,

> It's all right. The ship's not sinking ... I was in the *City of Benares* that went down, drowning all those children, a few days ago, so I know what it's like.

Her composure, however, was not quite total; she explained that she could not bear to hear a baby crying as 'it reminds her of the cries of those children who were drowned'.[70] In the aftermath of the sinking, the government scheme evacuating children to Canada and the United States was abandoned. If death had to come, then dying at home, among family and friends, was preferable to death at sea. The memoirs of Rear Admiral Kenelm Creighton, who was convoy commander when the SS *Avoceta* was torpedoed north of the Azores, gives some sense of what these deaths might have been like. Like the *Benares*, the *Avoceta* was attacked at night:

> There was complete pandemonium; the thunderous bangs and crashes of furniture and cargo being hurled about below decks all mingled with the

ghastly shrieks of the people waking to their deaths. As the bows went higher so did the shrieks. I clung to a stanchion feeling sick and helpless as I had to look on while the children were swept out into the darkness below by the torrent of water which roared through the smoking room.[71]

Just twelve of the eighty-eight passengers, and twenty-eight of the seventy-six crew, survived.

The Battle of the Atlantic began in the spring of 1941, as Royal Navy ships guarded merchant vessels transporting vital supplies of fuel, food and weapons across the Atlantic. Nicholas Monsarrat's 1951 novel *The Cruel Sea* probably contains the most vivid descriptions of death in the Atlantic convoys. Monsarrat had been a naval reservist who served on convoys during the war, and drew on his own wartime experiences in the novel. Describing the book as 'one of the best novels of the sea to come out of the last war', the reviewer in the *Times Literary Supplement* noted that 'the *Cruel Sea* is cruel indeed', and its vivid depictions of life and death at sea are both heartfelt and, at times, gruelling.[72] Monsarrat's flawed heroes – Ericson, a merchant seaman and naval reserve who captains the corvette HMS *Compass Rose*, and his sub-lieutenants Lockhart and Ferraby – accompany Atlantic convoys in the first four years of the war. When the *Compass Rose* picks up survivors from a torpedoed ship on one convoy, Lockhart provides medical care:

> He had set a broken leg, using part of a bench as a splint. He bound up other cuts and gashes, he did what he could for the man with the burnt arm, who was now insensible with pain: he watched, doing nothing with a curious hurt detachment, as a man who had drenched his intestines and perhaps his lungs with fuel oil slowly died.[73]

Describing the crew of the *Compass Rose* in the summer of 1941, a few months into the Battle of the Atlantic, Monsarrat writes, 'it was … no longer a shock to see the derelict humanity that was hoisted over the side after a ship went down; it was no longer moving to watch the dying and bury the dead'. By 1942, the Atlantic has become 'a corpse-ridden ocean' in which Ericson, going to rescue what he thinks are the survivors of a sinking, instead finds nine cadavers tied together, and wonders what it was like 'for the last man left alive, roped to his tail of eight dead ship-mates'.[74] When the *Compass Rose* is torpedoed later in the same year, Monsarrat describes life rafts in which the dead outnumbered the living, surrounded by 'a horrifying fringe of bobbing corpses, with their meaningless faces blank to the sky and their hands frozen to

Dying: death and destruction of the body in war

the ratlines'.[75] By the war's end, his surviving characters are hardened and distanced from the death they have witnessed, caused and fought to prevent, struggling to remember the names of the men they served with, and wondering whether there was a 'special kind of war-memory, showing mercy in fading quickly, drowning for ever under the weight of sorrow'.[76]

Civilian death

Approximately 60,595 civilians died as a result of enemy action during the war years. Of these, 29,890 were in Greater London, and 537 were recorded as 'unclassified', meaning that the destruction of their bodies was so great that age and sex, much less identity, could not be determined.[77] The first civilian to be killed by aerial bombardment in Britain was twenty-seven-year-old Orcadian James Isbister, killed as he tried to help neighbours when a German plane jettisoned its bombs after a raid on Scapa Flow on the 16 March 1940. Isbister was described rather unsympathetically by the medical superintendent of Kirkwall as being 'killed instantaneously' when he was 'caught at the door of his house while running inside, and got a bomb all to himself'.[78] Four sailors on board HMS *Norfolk*, the target of the attack, were also killed. Two of them were aged eighteen. Civilian deaths as a result of war activity were highly localised and concentrated: many areas of the country completely or almost completely avoided air raids. The Blitz on London between September 1940 and May 1941 killed and seriously injured over 80,000. More than 43,500 civilians were killed nationwide during this period.[79] These figures included almost 4,000 on Merseyside, approximately 568 killed in one night in Coventry on 14/15 November 1940, 1,230 in Bristol, approximately 1,200 in Hull and almost 1,000 in Belfast.[80] 'Tip and run' raids, when German aircraft dumped their bombs before heading back to the continent, the 'Baedeker raids' on Exeter, Bath, Norwich, Canterbury and York in 1942 and the 'Little Blitz' of January–April 1944 killed many thousands more, as did the numerous small raids throughout the war. Almost 9,000 were killed in V1 and V2 attacks on London and southeast England between June 1944 and March 1945.[81] Not all of the civilian dead were victims of air raids; war killed in other ways as well. Nights spent in cold, wet Anderson shelters were conducive to bronchitis and pneumonia, and the water tanks around London, used to store water for the fire brigade to use during air raids, proved fatally attractive to many children. More than 1,000 extra road deaths were attributed to the blackout in the first months of war.[82] Civilians died at sea, were torpedoed on ships evacuating them to North America, or from Singapore. They died of disease, of hunger and of mistreatment in internment camps in Southeast Asia. Thirty-eight young children were among the sixty-one fatalities when a USAAF B24 bomber crashed into their school in Freckleton, Lancashire in August 1944.[83] The majority, however, died as a result of air raids, killed by high explosive and by incendiary bombs.

These weapons could kill in a wide variety of ways. As discussed in Chapter 3, preparation for air raids had been extensive, if not always entirely effective, and in fact far greater fatality figures were anticipated than were experienced. The two Spanish doctors interviewed by the Air Raid Precautions (ARP) Department of the Home Office in 1939 reflected on their experience of air raids on Barcelona during the Spanish Civil War. The doctors estimated that about 17 per cent of the 10,000 overall air raid casualties had been dead on arrival at hospital. They found that 'mortality rates are highest when people are crushed in buildings' and that people in the open and close to sites where high explosive bombs hit city pavements were 'inevitably killed'. Of those Spanish victims who reached hospital alive, abdominal injuries caused the highest number of fatalities, many patients arriving 'with such extensive evisceration that it is useless to attempt to reconstruct the intestinal canal'. Head injuries were close behind, with 72 of 112 recorded cases dying.[84] Blast and crushing injuries are the most common types of injury caused by explosive weapons. Medical researchers divide blast injuries into four categories. The first are primary blast injuries which are caused by the immediate pressure wave released by the explosion. The gas-filled organs of the body – the lungs, the abdomen and the ears – are likely to rupture and haemorrhage as a result of this blast wave. Often, blast kills without leaving visible marks on its victims. William Samson described the aftermath of a bomb falling on Marble Arch subway, which had been filled with shelterers:

> When wardens and stretcher and rescue parties arrived they were faced with a terrible scene. The dead had been killed by blast – there was hardly a scratch on them, though in every case their clothes had been ripped off.[85]

The second category of blast injuries are penetrating and tearing wounds caused by flying missile and debris, such as the Spanish dead killed by fragments of cobbles and pavement tiles, and the young delivery boy in Brixton, found dying in the street after a raid in which 'half

Dying: death and destruction of the body in war

of his face was blown away'.[86] Blunt trauma caused by the same projectiles form the third category, and the fourth and final category of blast injury includes any other form of injury inflicted on the body by high explosive, including burns and psychological trauma.[87]

The use of high explosive against cities and towns meant that people also died of crush injuries when they were buried beneath the debris of a collapsed building or shelter. Crushed muscles release proteins as they break down, and this process can lead to confusion, vomiting, kidney failure and death. Renal failure could be a slow and painful death, and casualties who had been successfully rescued from the wreckage of buildings by the Heavy Rescue Squads trained to do this work sometimes died several days later in hospital. One medical report noted that 'even in patients well restored and safely past operation, death may occur unexpectedly within forty-eight hours'.[88] This phenomenon, in casualties who had appeared relatively unscathed by their ordeal, was observed by a warden in the heavily bombed city of Plymouth. He wrote,

> It has been found by experience that such casualties, when they have been trapped frequently complain of nothing more than stiffness of the crushed part. When ultimately released, their general appearance seems good, but in many cases, despite this apparent lack of serious injury, shock develops in a few hours and frequently death occurs a few days later. It is clear therefore that trapped persons on release, must be deemed serious casualties ... the reason why crushed casualties suffer in this way is that the kidneys become deranged and first aid treatment should be given by giving plenty of fluid to the casualty while the operation to effect release is going on.[89]

The suffering of many of those who survived being trapped in collapsed buildings, only to die in hospital, was often extreme. One forty-year-old woman from London

> was buried for 18 hours in a doubled-up position, sustaining severe bruising, a fracture of the pelvis, and injuries to the lungs, in which extensive haemorrhage was found .... She died about four hours after admission to hospital ... she told her name, age etc., described the bombing, said it had been a very horrible experience, wanted to know if she was going to die, and was anxious not to be a bother to the nurses and doctors.[90]

Dying quietly and politely, anxious not to 'be a bother', this woman exemplified the stoicism that had been urged on the British people in the interwar years.

The Air Raid Casualty Committee of the Medical Research Council collected data on air raid fatalities dying in British regional hospitals. Often people died from a combination of the different categories of blast injury, while others died of crush injuries and loss of blood after hours spent buried under debris. An analysis of causes of death among seventy-eight of these victims found that, unlike the Spanish doctors' report of 1939, which had found that abdominal injuries had the highest fatality rate, the majority, twenty-two, died of head injuries, twelve of chest injuries, nine of abdominal injuries, seven of fractures and five of shock. Of these, one fifty-five-year-old man was recorded as dying three weeks after his injuries, cause of death being given as 'skull fracture, due to large projectile. Large abscess of right frontal lobe rupturing into ventricle. Meningitis', while a thirteen-year-old girl who died eight days after admission suffered 'blast lung changes, fat embolism of lungs and brain'. As would be expected with blast, not all of those who died had visible injuries. An auxiliary fireman admitted to South Shields Infirmary with 'only slight superficial injuries' died two hours later of 'haemorrhage in lungs', a victim of blast.[91] Numerous studies of the injuries sustained in air raids were published in the medical press. Many of these supported the findings of the Spanish doctors interviewed in 1939. A report of cases of air raid injury received at London's Royal Free Hospital during the Blitz stated that of forty-three patients brought in, six had abdominal injuries and three had suffered injuries to the head:

> The abdominal injuries were all fatal. Two cases of evisceration were too bad for operation to be attempted. ... the three patients with severe head injuries had compound fracture with laceration of the brain; all died within a few hours.[92]

Other victims died of shock following wounds to their limbs from flying debris and from crushing. One twenty-two-year-old man had his case recorded in detail. He was described as having

> Compound ... fracture of upper end of left tibia and fibula with much destruction of tissue and the limb almost completely severed ... This patient was suffering from extreme shock and the pulse was imperceptible ... he ... died seven hours after the injury.[93]

At times, the multiple injuries suffered by air raid victims, together with the dirt and dust in which they were often coated, shocked even

Dying: death and destruction of the body in war

hardened medical practitioners. One doctor, working in a London hospital during the Blitz of 1940/1941, strove to convey the horrors that he faced to his colleagues:

> A sight which must be seen to be appreciated fully is the almost indescribably filthy condition of many who evidently had been clean and well clad. A patient is brought to the receiving ward with her clothes cut and torn to shreds, her hair singed, filled with dirt, and matted with blood and cement dust, her body and limbs covered with grit and oil, her face blackened, bruised and bleeding, her eyes, nose, lips and ears filled with dirt, her head bandaged and her limbs immobilised by improvised splints at the first-aid post. Truly it is not a picture easy to forget ... Their ages varied from an infant a few hours old, born and bombed on the same day, to a man aged 92.[94]

For this doctor, trained by profession, and also probably by social class and gender, to be reticent about the emotional impact such work could have, the nature of the injuries, and the number of those needing treatment, proved a potent challenge to a long-established professional culture of emotional distance.

Many, of course, died where they had been sheltering. As with combatants, the weaponry used frequently destroyed bodies, leaving body parts, rather than intact corpses, to be collected, identified if possible and buried. Rescue workers had the often repulsive task of collecting body parts after air raids. One man, recalling his service with the Heavy Rescue Squad in Lambeth, south London, remembered the aftermath of a direct hit on a garden Anderson shelter. He wrote,

> I could see what looked like treacle sliding down the wall ... During training I had instructed my men to treat the dead with reverence and respect, but I did not think we would have to shovel them up. Nor that this job had to be done with a stiff broom, a garden rake and shovel. We had to throw buckets of water up the wall to wash it down. The only tangible things were a man's hand, with a bent ring on a finger, a woman's foot in a shoe on a windowsill. In one corner of the garden was a bundle of something held together with a leather strap, as I disturbed it it fell to pieces, steaming, it was part of a man's torso. ... We gathered up six bags of bits and pieces; one pathetic little bundle, shapeless now, tied with lace and ribbon, had been a baby.[95]

The Civilian War Dead forms, distributed to mortuaries by local authorities as a means of both keeping records of the dead and the means of death, and to help with the identification of these dead, recorded injuries suffered as well as describing the corpse. All too often there was little left to describe. During the Blitz on Glasgow and Clydeside of March 1941, Yarrow's shipyard received a direct hit. The mortuary superintendent, whose job it was to complete the Civilian War Dead forms, scrupulously recorded not just the corpses, but the body parts he received in the aftermath. These included 'right hand', 'left foot', 'portion of body', 'parts of bodies absolutely unidentifiable', 'portions of trunk only', 'right leg and foot', 'portion of chest and ribs' and 'portion of foot'. These body parts were buried together at Lambshill Cemetery, Glasgow.[96] Similar records were kept in Hull. After the devastating air raid on the city of May 1941, the superintendent of Albert Avenue Mortuary, in the east of the city, listed among the remains he received a 'female scalp with brown hair', 'burnt remains', 'fingers and skin', 'portion of spine with foot' and 'nine ribs'.[97] A girl whose mother and sister were killed in a raid on Birmingham recalled trying to view the bodies, but 'the wardens quickly pushed me away and told me not any of them bodies were fit to be seen'.[98] Perhaps the closest the wartime press came to describing the impact of high explosive on the human body was in the journalist Hilde Marchant's account of the wax models following a raid on Madam Tussauds, the famous waxworks museum in central London. Marchant explained how

> Heads, arms, legs and torsos were strewn around the Hall of Tableau ... models were heaped on the floor in agonising and painful positions, some with their heads at the side. A workman was picking up the arms and legs and sorting them out in stacks of left and right, and putting all the heads together in a neat row.[99]

As William Samson noted, 'it was known that people did not necessarily die prettily, that wounding was not a neat and clean affair, and that there was being entered into A.R.P. logbooks a cruel, recurrent, most contemporary phrase: "Pieces of flesh"'.[100]

Conclusion

In wartime, members of combatant states generally find that they have less autonomy over their bodies than they do in times of peace. The body becomes subject to the wishes of the state's rulers in a way that differs from peacetime. In peacetime, bodies are still subject to regulation and to regimentation, disciplined to work, to fulfil particular social roles and to appear in ways acceptable to society. Movements like the various health, beauty and fitness organisations of interwar Britain trained bodies to become the bearers of good citizenry; through self-management, individuals could develop well-managed bodies that fitted not just the social criteria for attractiveness but also a range of political needs. These bodies could be successfully mobilised as efficient workers, as healthy parents and as physically strong participants in any future conflict.[101] As discussed in Chapter 2, this management of the body went hand in hand with the management of the emotions: bodily and emotional restraint were the twin markers of a virtuous citizenship. However, individuals did not have to participate: membership of organisations like the Sunshine League, while widely approved of, were not compulsory, and people still wept in public, particularly at nationally shared events such as the funeral of George V in 1936 and, as Thomas Dixon reminds us, in the cinema.[102] In wartime, the state's control of the body became more extensive and more visible. Rationing and austerity measures provided some control over food that could be consumed, and clothing that could be worn. Bodies struggled through the blackout, and wartime diet and labour meant they often changed their shape. Agency diminished as bodies became subject to the demands and the constraints of total war.

It was in the state's use of its citizens' bodies in combat and industry, however, that this loss of agency was felt most keenly. As Corinna Peniston-Bird has argued, 'in order for war to be waged effectively, the body of the individual was classified and reclassified according to the needs of the armed forces and the labour market, and by sex, age and physical fitness'.[103] Young men were subject to conscription from 1939 onwards, many of them effectively losing control of the fate of their own bodies as they underwent training, examination and, for many, participation in front-line combat. Young women retained slightly more autonomy. Although they too were subject to conscription from December 1941 onwards, service on anti-aircraft guns, the area of female service with the highest casualty rate, was by choice, rather than direction.[104] Civilians could choose to evacuate themselves and their families from the cities expected to be attacked, if wealth and circumstance allowed, and parents could make the difficult decision to send their children away from the immediate danger zones to live with strangers in the countryside, or with relatives overseas. Many however, stayed in the cities, and many were killed and injured in air raids. In wartime, the state's power over life and death, usually only seen in the use of the death penalty for those convicted of murder, extended in varying degrees to all of its citizens. While male combatants were to experience this loss of agency to its fullest extent, civilians too, dying in their homes, in the street and in air raid shelters, also lost much of the control that they had over their own bodies.

The bodies discussed in this chapter – bodies in pain, bodies mutilated and bodies dying and dead – clearly demonstrate the lack of autonomy that combatants and non-combatants have over their own bodies and their own lives in times of war, when the individual body becomes subject to the wartime body politic. Few would have chosen to die in this way. The overall willingness of the British people to accept the dangers that war brought, to 'carry on' despite these dangers, and to bear not only the loss of any degree of agency over the body, but also the threat to one's own life and the lives of loved ones, and the loss of these lives, was crucial to the sense of a shared war effort, and to the maintenance of wartime morale. The pain and death experienced by many was, at its heart, a physical, embodied experience, but it also existed and was experienced within a particular set of historical circumstances. War both increased the collective political value of bodies, seen in the need for healthy bodies in combat and in industry and in their eventual commemoration on memorials or in remembrance activities, but also decreased their individual value, as death and bereavement were forced on people as the cost of membership of the national body. The following chapter considers the value of the dead in wartime through the management of their corpses, and their burial, by the state and by loved ones.

Notes

1 E. Scarry, *The Body in Pain: The Making and Unmaking of the World* (Oxford: Oxford University Press, 1985), p. 63.
2 R. Bessel, 'Unnatural deaths', in R. Overy (ed.), *The Oxford Illustrated History of World War II* (Oxford: Oxford University Press, 2014), pp. 322–43, here 323.
3 Figures for the war dead are complex and contested. The figures cited here for Britain are taken from D. Todman, 'Death in Britain in the Second World War', *Institute of Historical Research*, unpublished paper (March 2010). Todman has conducted the most detailed investigation into British war death figures to date. For a summary, see D. Todman, *Britain's War: Into Battle, 1937–41* (London: Penguin, 2017), pp. 655–7.

Dying: death and destruction of the body in war

4 This study focuses on the British Isles, not the British Empire. If the deaths of civilians in Burma, India, Malaysia, Hong Kong and Singapore were included for example, the ratio of civilian to military death would vary significantly.
5 T. H. O'Brien, *Civil Defence: History of the Second World War* (London: HMSO, 1955), Appendix II, p. 678. These are casualties, not fatalities. O'Brien gives 2,379 as the number of Civil Defence fatalities, but does not break this down by gender.
6 Public Record Office of Northern Ireland (PRONI), CAB 3/A/60, *Air Raids on Belfast*, undated cutting from *Belfast News*.
7 A. Gregory, *The Silence of Memory: Armistice Day, 1919–1946* (Oxford: Berg, 1994), pp. 213–14.
8 L. Davidoff, *Worlds Between: Historical Perspectives on Gender and Class* (London: Polity, 1995), p. 229.
9 E. Newlands, *Civilians Into Soldier: War, the Body and British Army Recruits, 1939–45* (Manchester: Manchester University Press, 2014).
10 L. J. D. Wacquant, 'Pugs at work: bodily capital and bodily labour among professional boxers', *Body and Society*, 1:1 (1995), pp. 65–93, here 65.
11 W. Samson, *The Blitz: Westminster in War* (London: Faber & Faber, 1947), p. 33.
12 Maclean Museum, 'Alex Walker', BBC People's War website, www.bbc.co.uk/history/ww2peopleswar/stories/57/a5857257.shtml (accessed 5 May 2016).
13 S. Jameson, *Journey from the North. Volume 2* (London: Collins and Harvill, 1970), p. 132.
14 Catherine Merridale states that 80 per cent of the 34.5 million men and women mobilised in the Soviet Union's Great Patriotic War were dead, wounded or prisoners by 1945 – C. Merridale, *Night of Stone: Death and Memory in Russia* (London: Granta, 2000), pp. 273–4. For Germany, see N. Stargardt, *The German War: A Nation Under Arms, 1939–45* (London: Vintage, 2016). Stargardt gives the figure of 4.8 million soldiers and 300,000 Waffen SS dead at the war's end, p. 557.
15 On military medical services in wartime, see M. Harrison, *Medicine and Victory: British Military Medicine in the Second World War* (Oxford: Oxford University Press, 2004); for military and civilian services (including psychiatric), see A. S. MacNalty and W. F. Mellor (eds), *Medical Services in War: The Principal Medical Lessons of the Second World War* (London: HMSO, 1968).
16 H. Cairns, 'Treatment of head injuries in war', *British Medical Journal*, 1:4146 (22 June 1940), pp. 1029–30.
17 Todman, 'Death in Britain' (2010), p. 9.
18 Central Statistical Office, *Fighting with Figures: A Statistical Digest of the Second World War*, Table 3.8., 'Casualties suffered during the war by the

armed forces, auxiliary services and merchant navy' (London: HMSO, 1995), p. 43. Those still registered as missing in February 1946 were overwhelmingly members of Bomber Command who had been shot down over enemy or occupied territory and whose bodies had not been recovered. Some, such as Alex Walker, were POWs who had died in captivity.

19 D. French, *Raising Churchill's Army* (Oxford: Oxford University Press, 2002), p. 156.
20 J. R. M. Butler, *History of the Second World War. Volume II: The Mediterranean and Middle East* (London: HMSO, 1956), p. 147.
21 Cited in S. Spark, *The Treatment of the British Military Dead of the Second World War* (Unpublished PhD, University of Edinburgh, 2010), p. 70.
22 Spark, *Treatment of the British Military Dead*, p. 74.
23 L. Allen, *Burma: The Longest War, 1941–1945* (London: Phoenix Press, 2000. First published 1984), p. 638.
24 B. Moore, 'Prisoners of War', in J. Ferris and E. Mawdsley (eds), *The Cambridge History of the Second World War. Volume I: Fighting the War* (Cambridge: Cambridge University Press, 2015), pp. 664–89, here 684.
25 The National Archives, London (TNA), CAB 106/1207, *British and Allied Battle Casualties 1939–1946*.
26 Reg. A. Clarke, 'My D Day: with the royal engineers', BBC People's War website, www.bbc.co.uk/history/ww2peopleswar/stories/98/a1144298.shtml (accessed 12 May 2016).
27 A. Bowlby, *The Recollections of Rifleman Bowlby* (London: Leo Cooper, 1969), p. 185.
28 'D Day Veterans, James Hill's D Day. Third Parachute Brigade', BBC People's War website, www.bbc.co.uk/history/ww2peopleswar/stories/16/a2523016.shtml (accessed 12 May 2016).
29 Reverend L. Skinner, *The Man Who Worked on Sundays: The Personal War Diary 2 June 1944 to May 17 1945 of Reverend Leslie Skinner, RAChD, 8th (Independent) Armoured Brigade Attached to the Sherwood Rangers Yeomanry Regiment* (Privately printed, n.d.), p. 44.
30 Stockholm International Peace Research Unit, *Incendiary Weapons* (Cambridge, MA: MIT Press, 1973), p. 126.
31 Thomas Arthur Murray, 'Tom's story of El Alamein', BBC People's War website, www.bbc.co.uk/history/ww2peopleswar/stories/56/a2719956.shtml (accessed 12 May 2016).
32 H. Ritchie, *The Fusing of the Ploughshare: From East Anglia to Alamein: The Story of a Yeoman at War* (Ritchie: Dunmow, 1987), p. 208; Bowlby, *The Recollections of Rifleman Bowlby*, p. 20.
33 N. Lewis, *Naples '44*, cited in A. Allport, *Browned Off and Bloody Minded: The British Soldier Goes to War, 1939–1945* (New Haven, CT: Yale University Press, 2015), p. 247.
34 Skinner, *The Man Who Worked Sundays*, p. 44.

35 M. L. Roberts, 'Five ways to look at a corpse: the dead in Normandy 1944', forthcoming, *The Male Body of War* (2020).
36 Thanks to the member of my master's class in Cultural Memory at the University of Brighton who shared this scrapbook with me in 2013.
37 Cited in P. Fussell, *The Boy's Crusade: The American Infantry in Northwestern Europe, 1944–1945* (New York: Modern Library, 2003), p. 64
38 Bowlby, *Recollections of Rifleman Bowlby*, p. 42.
39 Bowlby, *Recollections of Rifleman Bowlby*, p. 20.
40 W. Robson, *Letters from a Soldier* (London: Faber & Faber, 1960), p. 102.
41 N. Craig, *The Broken Plume: A Platoon Commander's Story, 1940–1945* (London: The Imperial War Museum, 1982), p. 65; P. Brutton, *Ensign in Italy: A Platoon Commander's Story* (London: Leo Cooper, 1992), p. 31.
42 Cited in Harrison, *Medicine and Victory*, p. 193.
43 Robson, *Letters from a Soldier*, p. 102.
44 Gun Buster, *Return via Dunkirk*, p. 245.
45 T. Vigors, *Life's Too Short to Cry* (London: Grub Street, 2006), p. 75.
46 Royal Air Force History, www.raf.mod.uk/history/thebattleofbritain.cfm (accessed 8 May 2016).
47 M. Middlebrook and C. Everitt, *Bomber Command War Diaries: An Operational Reference Book* (London: Viking, 1985), p. 708; M. Francis, *The Flyer: British Culture and the Royal Air Force 1939–1945* (Oxford: Oxford University Press, 2008), p. 107.
48 Central Statistical Office, *Fighting with Figures*, Table 3.8, p. 43.
49 R. N. Houlding, 'Rehabilitation of injured air crews', *British Medical Journal*, 2:4212 (27 September 1941), pp. 429–33.
50 TNA, AIR 20/9305, *Air Ministry Report of RAF and Dominions Air Forces Missing Research and Enquiry Service 1944–1949*, 'Missing Memo number 8' (14 October 1939).
51 TNA, AIR 20/9305, *Air Ministry Report of RAF and Dominions Air Forces*, 'Search Methods'.
52 Francis, *The Flyer*, p. 108.
53 Middlebrook and Everitt, *Bomber Command War Diaries*, p. 291.
54 Middlebrook and Everitt, *Bomber Command War Diaries*, p. 278.
55 Flight Lieutenant Denis Hornsey, cited in M. Hastings, *Bomber Command* (London: Michael Joseph, 1979), p. 197.
56 K. Thomas, *Religion and the Decline of Magic: Studies in Popular Beliefs in Sixteenth and Seventeenth Century England* (Oxford: Oxford University Press, 1971).
57 George Aylmore, 'The good guts', BBC People's War website, www.bbc.co.uk/history/ww2peopleswar/stories/33/a2281033.shtml (accessed 12 May 2016).
58 RAFShropshireLad, 'My training and operational duties in the RAF', BBC People's War website, www.bbc.co.uk/history/ww2peopleswar/stories/41/a4292741.shtml (accessed 12 May 2016).

59 Francis, *The Flyer*, p. 118.
60 G. Wellum, *First Light* (London: Penguin, 2002), pp. 186–7.
61 M. Tripp, *The Eighth Passenger* (London: Heinemann, 1969), pp. 61–2.
62 D. Mitchell, 'The *Athenia*', BBC People's War website, www.bbc.co.uk/history/ww2peopleswar/stories/83/a2035883.shtml (accessed 12 May 2016).
63 *Fighting with Figures*, Table 3.8, p. 43.
64 Cited in G. Prysor, *Citizen Sailors: The Royal Navy in the Second World War* (Viking: London, 2011), p. 52.
65 HnWVSVActionDesk, 'Arctic convoys Part 3', BBC People's War website, www.bbc.co.uk/history/ww2peopleswar/stories/99/a7147299.shtml (accessed 12 May 2016).
66 Surgeon-Captain C. H. Joynt, 'The Royal Naval Medical Services', in MacNalty and Mellor (eds), *Medical Services in War* (1968), pp. 1–46, here 10.
67 Joynt in MacNalty and Mellor (eds), *Medical Services in War*, p. 9.
68 Terry Hulbert, 'Lady Luck Part 3: Battle of the North Cape 1943', BBC People's War website, www.bbc.co.uk/history/ww2peopleswar/stories/39/a2456039.shtml (accessed 12 May 2016).
69 'Rescue from the Atlantic', the *Times* (27 September 1940), p. 4.
70 W. Farr, 'We even danced in our life jackets', *Daily Mail* (8 October 1940), p. 2.
71 Cited in Prysor, *Citizen Sailors* (2011), p. 168.
72 A. S. F. Rippon, 'The Cruel Sea by Monsarrat, Nicholas', the *Times Literary Supplement*, 2590 (21 September 1951), p. 593.
73 N. Monsarrat, *The Cruel Sea* (London: Penguin, 2002. First published 1951), p. 121.
74 Monsarrat, *The Cruel Sea*, pp. 140, 259.
75 Monsarrat, *The Cruel Sea*, pp. 297–8.
76 Monsarrat, *The Cruel Sea*, p. 444.
77 Central Statistical Office, *Fighting with Figures*, p. ix.; A. S. MacNalty and Lieutenant-Colonel C. L. Dunn, 'The Emergency Medical Services', in MacNalty and Mellor (eds), *Medical Services in War*, pp. 273–310, here 306.
78 TNA, FD 1/5372, *Air Raid Precautions Department, Home Office*, 'Letter to Dr Bradford Hill from Ian H. McClure, Medical Superintendent Kirkwall, on recent air raid casualties Orkney' (16 March 1940). Later accounts of Isbister's death highlight his attempt to help neighbours when their house was hit.
79 J. Gardiner, *The Blitz: The British Under Attack* (London: Harper Press, 2010), p. 359.
80 PRONI, CAB 3/A/60, *Air Raids on Belfast*.
81 A. Calder, *The People's War: Britain, 1939–1945* (London: Jonathan Cape, 1969), p. 647.
82 Todman, *Britain's War*, p. 259.
83 'Aircraft crash on school', the *Times*, 24 August 1944, p. 2.

84 TNA, Medical Research Committee and Medical Research Council, FD 1/5372, *Air Raid Precautions Department, Home Office: Spanish Civil War Air Raid Casualties, 1939*, 'Medical Aspects of Air Raid Casualties in Barcelona' (25 March 1939).
85 Samson, *The Blitz*, pp. 43–4.
86 S. Rothwell, *Lambeth at War* (London: SE1 People's History Project, 1981), p. 20.
87 Thanks to Afxentis Afxentiou, who has conducted detailed research into different types of blast injury as part of his PhD on the impact and experience of drone warfare. A. Afxentiou, *The Politics and Ethics of Drone Bombing in its Historical Context*, unpublished PhD, University of Brighton (2018).
88 R. T. Grant and E. B. Reeve, 'Clinical observations on air raid casualties', *British Medical Journal*, 2:4209 (6 September 1941), pp. 329–32, here 332.
89 Plymouth and West Devon Record Office, *Civil Defence Preparations*, n.d., File Reference 854/4.
90 R. T. Grant and E. B. Reeve, 'Clinical observations on air raid casualties, *British Medical Journal*, 1:4208 (30 August 1941), pp. 293–7, here 294.
91 TNA, FD 1/6523, *Air Raid Casualties: Records of Post Mortem Examinations*, 'Analysis of causes of death in 78 air raid casualties'.
92 M. Ball and G. Quist, 'Some recent cases of air raid injury', *British Medical Journal*, 1:4181 (22 February 1941), pp. 273–5, here 274.
93 Ball and Quist, 'Some recent cases', *British Medical Journal*, pp. 273–4.
94 J. R. Lee, 'Experiences in the reception and treatment of air raid casualties, *British Medical Journal*, 1:4189 (19 April 1941), pp. 584–6, here 584.
95 Rothwell, *Lambeth at War*, p. 17.
96 The Mitchell Library, Glasgow, D/CD/7/2, *Register of Unidentified Dead*.
97 Hull History Centre, C TYC/1, *Register of Air Raid Casualties. 3 April to 7 November 1941*.
98 C. Chinn, *Brum Undaunted: Birmingham During the Blitz* (Birmingham: Birmingham Library Services, 1996), p. 128.
99 H. Marchant, *Women and Children Last: A Woman Reporter's Account of the Battle of Britain* (London: Victor Gollancz, 1941), pp. 82–3.
100 Samson, *The Blitz*, p. 38.
101 I. Zweiniger-Bargielowska, *Managing the Body: Health, Beauty and Fitness in Britain, 1880–1939* (Oxford: Oxford University Press, 2010).
102 T. Dixon, *Weeping Britannia: Portrait of a Nation in Tears* (Oxford: Oxford University Press, 2015), pp. 230–6.
103 C. Peniston-Bird, 'Classifying the body in the Second World War: British men in and out of uniform', *Body and Society*, 9:4 (2003), pp. 31–48, here 33.
104 By 1942, approximately 50 per cent of new recruits to the Auxiliary Territorial Service were choosing to work in air defence. L. Noakes, *Women in the British Army: War and the Gentle Sex 1908–1947* (Oxford: Routledge, 2008), p. 119.

6

Burying
The disposal of the war's dead

Introduction: the work of the dead

In *The Work of the Dead*, Thomas Laqueur traces the work that the dead have done in different times and places throughout history. In ancient Egypt and ancient China, the dead literally worked, as slaves, servants, concubines and prisoners were killed and buried with the rich and powerful so that they could continue to serve them in the afterlife.[1] The bodies of saints and holy people have worked hard as objects of veneration, their bodies preserved for display and worship, with an apparent lack of decomposition demonstrating their purity. The bodies of political leaders have done similar work. The embalmed body of Vladimir Lenin, displayed in the Lenin Mausoleum since his death in 1924, served first as a symbol of the Soviet project and now works as a tourist attraction in Red Square.[2] Despite his wish to be cremated, the body of Chairman Mao Zedong was set to do similar work in China, embalmed and placed in the Mausoleum of Mao Zedong in Tiananmen Square, Beijing, in 1977. Other bodies too have done political work: the exhumation, grand funeral and reburial of the body of the executed Hungarian leader Imre Nagy in Budapest in June 1989 acted as a focus for those who opposed the communist government, while the pomp and ceremony that surrounded the funeral and reburial of the corpse of the English Plantagenet King Richard III in Leicester Cathedral in England in 2015 helped to assert the claims of the British monarchy to a continued role in the life of the nation, at a time when political unity was felt to be under threat.[3] Bodies can thus serve both as symbols of the political order and as indicators of political rupture and historical change. This political work is also emotional: the body of the Unknown Warrior, returned to Britain and buried in Westminster Abbey on

Armistice Day 1920, acted both as an emblem of the value the British Empire attributed to the dead of war, but also as the focus for an outpouring of grief, when numerous women, whose sons and lovers were lost on the battlefields, claimed the body as their own.[4]

The bodies of the dead thus have value. They maintain an emotional value for the bereaved, for whom the rituals that surround the disposal of the corpse can be an important aspect of the grieving 'process' and a social indicator of both bereavement and the stages of mourning. They have a financial value, which in wartime was set by the state. And they also have a political value. In wartime, the bodies of the dead could continue to work for the nation, acting as signifiers of a shared national cause and as a unifying symbol of shared suffering, support and resolution. However, this political value depended not only on the careful management of the corpse by the state, but also on the ways in which the bereaved expressed emotions around the corpse, and found the state's treatment of the dead and of their grief to be appropriate. Elaine Scarry argues that the wartime corpse has a 'referential instability'; treated and represented appropriately, it can function as a symbol of a shared sacrifice and steadfastness, while in the hands of a wartime enemy it can become a potent symbol of triumph and humiliation.[5] Perhaps most dangerous for wartime unity is a perception that bodies are being treated without due reverence by the community that sent them to their deaths; in this case the dead, and the emotions of those who mourn them, can threaten the sense of shared aims and shared suffering between citizen and state that is so necessary to wartime union. Throughout history, the belief that the living have a duty to the dead, that they should treat their bodies in a manner that local custom and tradition dictates, has endured. While customs may differ and change across geographic and historical spaces, this belief seems to be constant, and in wartime the state has to demonstrate that it is treating the bodies of the dead appropriately. In its treatment of the bodies of dead civilians and combatants, the British state worked hard to try and ensure the stability of the wartime corpse. This work was more successful in some cases than in others.

This chapter explores the processes by which the state attempted to ensure this stability, and the ways that the bereaved responded to both the event of violent death in wartime, and to the state's treatment of the bodies of their loved ones. It begins by examining wartime attempts to attach a financial value to the dead; how much, if anything, should be paid in compensation to the bereaved, and what amount the state

Burying: the disposal of the war's dead

should contribute towards the burial or other disposal of the corpse. It continues by considering the practices of burial, in cases where this was possible, in the military services before discussing the treatment of the civilian dead in wartime. Violent death in wartime is one of the clearest ways in which the intimate world of family, love and friendship comes in contact with the structures, support and demands of the state. While the following chapter examines the emotional responses of the British people to wartime death in more detail, this chapter has at its centre a consideration of the relationship between the wartime individual and the wartime state as experienced through practices around the disposal of the dead.

Valuing the dead

On 26 September 1939, Mrs Mabel Perry, a Civil Defence volunteer in Plymouth, was badly injured when an ambulance she was travelling in overturned. She died of her injuries two days later. The following month, the Ministry of Pensions in Whitehall received a letter from its regional office in Plymouth, warning that the town clerk there was threatening to have questions asked in the House of Commons should the ministry refuse to help with the costs of the funeral, as Mrs Perry's widower was a naval rating, and her mother 'a poor widow'. The town clerk considered that if 'the woman is buried as a pauper ... the matter might give rise to grave public scandal'.[6] Perry's death, the first to occur among the volunteers of the new wartime Civil Defence Services, threw the ministry into confusion, and served to highlight the very new sort of war that Britain was engaged in, and the consequently larger number of those who could be considered to have died for their country. The financial value of militarised bodies was regulated by the Ministry of Pensions, which valued the dead according to their military rank in life: while the widow of a private soldier could claim £91.00 per year, the widows of captains and generals were entitled to £150.00 and £540.00, respectively.[7] To put these figures into their historical context, the average weekly earnings for men employed in manufacturing were 89s. per week in July 1940, rising to 124s. per week in July 1944 (approximately £234.00 per annum in 1940, and £312.00 in 1944).[8] While it had been assumed that the military burial practices developed in the Great War – with the service departments bearing responsibility for burying those who died in their service, the graves to be marked and maintained by the Imperial War Graves Commission (IWGC) and a grant up to a maximum of £7 10s. to be made available for the private burial of those who died after discharge from the armed forces – would continue, no provision had been made for the burial costs of either Civil Defence volunteers or other civilians dying as a result of war operations.[9] Civil servants were coming to realise that, in the age of aerial warfare, the bereaved whose loved ones had died as civilians might well feel that they had cause to expect both financial and practical help from the state with their burial.

As discussed in Chapter 3, in planning for the devastation that it was widely anticipated aerial warfare would bring, the secret Interdepartmental Burials (Civilians) Committee assumed that the chaos and destruction would be so great that most corpses would have to be buried or otherwise disposed of by the state.[10] An Air Raid Precautions (ARP) Sub-Committee, known informally as the Craig Committee, had already investigated compensation and grants towards funeral expenses for 'civilians in respect of death or injury caused by hostile air attack' in 1934.[11] This committee had concluded that no grants should be made for funeral expenses, as 'responsibility for interment will be undertaken by the state', and thus those who decided nonetheless to make their own burial arrangements would not be able to claim for any costs. It did, however, recommend that the system of pensions, already in existence for the dependants of combatants killed as a result of their military service, should be extended to the dependants of civilians killed by enemy action. The scale of compensation they developed was shaped by the 'domestic inequalities of wealth and power' of interwar Britain.[12] If an adult male was killed, his widow would receive between 10s. 6d. and 17s. 6d. per week, dependent on whether or not she had young children. If the mother was killed, her children would receive a flat rate of 10s. per week only if their father 'is incapable of work, had died or disappeared'.[13] In the new form of total war, which saw the militarisation of many aspects of domestic and civilian life in response to the threat of air raids, those killed as a result of military service were still valued, financially, as being of greater worth than the civilian dead.

However, the scale of actual air raids, and the consequently lower death rate than anticipated, together with the service of many thousands of civilians in Civil Defence, meant that the assumptions of the interwar period regarding the burial of the wartime civilian dead, and the financial value of their bodies, had to be revisited. Debate focused around the difference in value of those such as Civil Defence volunteers,

Burying: the disposal of the war's dead

who could be considered to have given their lives in service of the wartime nation, and other civilians killed as a result of enemy action. In the autumn of 1939, the Cunnison Committee, an interdepartmental committee composed of representatives of the Ministries of Housing and Local Government, Health and Pensions, whose Deputy Secretary, Sir Alex Cunnison, chaired the committee and gave it its name, met to discuss the tricky question of funeral grants and expenses for civilians killed as a result of enemy action, including Civil Defence workers. The committee quickly spotted an anomaly in existing provision: the Craig Report and Ministry of Health Circular 1779 of February 1939 had recommended that local authorities be able to claim from central government for the costs involved in mass burials, organised by the authority, after air raids.[14] However, there was no mechanism by which the relatives of the dead buried privately could be compensated, even though these might include Civil Defence volunteers killed while on duty. Both the Craig Report and Circular 1779 had presumed that the vast majority of burials under aerial bombardment would be undertaken by the local authority as mass burials, an assumption also made by the Cunnison Committee, which pointed out that 'it would be inequitable that the state should accept liability for the mass burial of persons killed outright in an air raid' while refusing any payment to those where there was no mass burial, or when victims died of their injuries at a later date.[15] On this basis, the committee recommended that funeral grants, not to exceed £7 10s. should be introduced for *all* victims of air raids, Civil Defence workers and civilians alike. However, the Treasury had other ideas. Writing to the committee in January 1940, the Treasury's War Expenditure Emergency Committee found itself in general agreement with the recommendation, but insisted that as the state could not bear the expense of burying all potential victims of air raids, the grant should be limited to Civil Defence workers killed on duty. Still believing that mass burials by local authorities would 'account for a very large percentage of the total deaths of the victims of air raids', the second meeting of the Cunnison Committee agreed with this proposal.[16]

By the summer of 1940, the Ministry of Pensions was having second thoughts. In a memo to the Treasury that recognised that the value attached to the dead was not only, or always, financial, the ministry imagined the case of 'a mother being called to the hospital to see a grievously injured child, and expressing the intention of herself carrying away the dead body in her arms', concluding that 'however much private burials were to be discouraged as an alternative to mass burial, some provision would be made to meet the special case'.[17] The Treasury, however, held firm, replying that while a grant could be made available towards the funeral expenses of Civil Defence volunteers 'who die as a result of war service injuries …. as regards civilians, we think that no expenses should be paid'.[18] When the Blitz started in September 1940, local authorities could claim for the cost of mass burials, and individual burials when they carried them out, while the families of Civil Defence volunteers could claim the £7 10s. funeral grant, thus matching that available to bury service personnel who died after discharge from the armed services. In 1944, the payment was increased to £10. While the families of those civilians killed in air raids, and buried privately, could not claim for funeral expenses, they could claim pensions; by the war's end, £2,752,000 was being paid in pensions related to death or injury as a result of enemy attacks on the home front.[19]

The British state thus attempted to balance the financial value it attached to a corpse with the political value such bodies held, and, to a lesser extent, their emotional value for those who mourned the war dead, with a desire to limit expenditure. These attempts, however, were not always successful. Four weeks after the Blitz on London had begun, a Mr C. H. A. Flashman, a driver with the London Auxiliary Ambulance Service, wrote to his commanders, to County Hall London and to the home secretary asking to be relieved of his service.[20] The reason for Flashman's disquiet was an article in the *Sunday Chronicle* claiming that

> Last week a number of Poplar A.R.P. workers were killed on duty. Those men died in the service of their country as surely as if they had been in the front line. They were taken to the cemetery in a lorry. They were buried in a common grave. No representative of the authorities graced the burial service … King George has instituted the George Cross for heroes such as these men were. Yet they were given only a lorry for a hearse.[21]

The letters which followed between the London Civil Defence Regional Head Quarters and the Home Office reveal much about both concerns that the corpses of Civil Defence volunteers be treated in the same manner as the military dead, and the perceived need to avoid any form of burial that carried the taint of the hated pauper's funeral. An internal memo within the Home Office questioned the veracity of the story, given 'the known sensitivity of the East End to the question of pauper funerals'.[22] A subsequent letter from the London Civil Defence Regional Head Quarters, however, suggested there was some truth in the article, noting that in Poplar 'those who are killed are certainly buried in a common grave', as those who were buried by the local authority as paupers would have been. In this case, however, burial in a communal grave was due to lack of space, rather than a desire to save money. No representatives of the local authority had attended the burial as 'the continuous and intensive raiding … made it impossible for them to leave the control room'.[23] No mention was made of the allegation that the bodies were taken to the cemetery in a lorry rather than a hearse. In this case the hurried funeral of Civil Defence workers, organised under Blitz conditions in the crowded East End of London, failed to attach the necessary political value to the bodies of the dead volunteers. Despite claims that Civil Defence service was the equivalent of military service, this burial appeared to be devoid of the value that had been attached to bodies of the military dead since the Great War.

When the financial value attached to a body by national and local authorities failed to accord with its political or emotional value, this was often expressed with reference to the image of the pauper's grave which sometimes overshadowed the public burial of the wartime civilian dead. This chapter will go on to examine the ways in which national and local authorities negotiated, and attempted to negate, the linkage of mass burials with the memory of the pauper's grave, not always successfully. In November 1940, four generations of one family were killed when a bomb hit their house during a christening party for baby Monica Mary, the youngest member of the family to die. In a front-page article titled 'Profiteers in Death', the *Daily Mirror* described how the baby, her parents and her grandparents were buried in one grave by Wembley Corporation. Her great-grandmother, who also died, was buried separately in her husband's grave in the same cemetery. Although the victims were buried together, with the child being placed in her mother's coffin, the authority charged surviving family members for separate funerals, with an extra 7s. added to the bill for the baby's burial, an addition that no doubt reminded many readers of the austere and carefully costed nature of local authority burials of the poor.[24] To ensure the 'referential stability' of the dead civilian victims of warfare, and to make certain that the 'work of the dead' benefited the wartime state by demonstrating the close ties between state, nation and people, these corpses had to be treated with reverence, their financial value matched by their political and emotional worth. This stability was imagined to be achieved through a careful matching of the treatment of the civilian corpse with those of the military, an equivalency that was seen to have failed in the treatment of Monica Mary's family. However, the treatment of the military dead itself often failed to match expectations, or follow the careful pre-war planning.

The military dead

At the outbreak of war, detailed plans were in place for the burial of the military dead. While these differed to some extent across the three military services, all were shaped by the aim that, first, as many of the dead as possible were identified, with details of both their death and their place of burial, where available and appropriate, shared with their next of kin; and secondly, that these next of kin should be confident that the corpses had been treated with all due reverence. The Royal Navy, the oldest of the three military services, continued its established practice of 'burying' corpses at sea wherever possible. When a man died on board ship, the funeral service concluded with his body, sewn into a weighted hammock and wrapped in the Union flag, being slipped over the side of the vessel into the sea. The dead man's personal effects were then auctioned among his shipmates and the proceeds sent to his family.[25] Bodies lost at sea, which washed up on beaches and coastlines, became the responsibility of the army. Those who were buried at sea, or whose bodies were lost, are commemorated on naval memorials, which also act as markers for shipping, at Chatham, Portsmouth and Plymouth in England. Memorials at Tower Hill, London and Liverpool commemorate the men of the merchant navy who died, and who have no known grave. Without such long-standing traditions to draw on, the army and the air force developed policies that both built on models established in the First World War, and attempted to meet the challenges to these models posed by the new forms of warfare seen in the Second. As many military records and memoirs show us, this was not always easily achieved.

The Directorate of War Graves and Enquiries, a department of the Adjutant General's Office, was responsible for overseeing and recording the burial of the army's dead after battle. As outlined in Chapter 3, this burial was envisaged as taking place in three stages. First, battlefield commanders were expected to provide men to bury the bodies close to where they fell. All possible attempts were to be made to identify the dead, and Army Form (AF) W 3314, recording the identity of the corpse and the exact place of burial, was to be completed before being sent back to headquarters. Once battle had moved on, Graves Registration

Burying: the disposal of the war's dead

Units (GRUs) had the job of formally establishing the place of burial; wherever possible, confirming the identity of the deceased; and, often, exhuming the corpse to move it to a larger 'concentrated' cemetery. Graves Concentration Units (GCUs) would reinter the dead in these cemeteries. The IWGC would oversee the eventual maintenance of the war cemeteries, as it had done since the Great War.[26]

Plans were carefully laid to try and ensure the identification of the dead. All men were expected to wear a two-part identification disc; after death, one half would be removed and the other half would be buried with the body. Men were also expected to keep their pay book, which included the details of next of kin, and a short will with them at all times. If these forms of identification were missing, burial parties were detailed to record the deceased's cap badge, shoulder title, equipment and date and place of death to make the naming of the dead possible.[27] The 1930 Field Service Regulations added new guidelines, including the measurement of individual graves, the distance between graves, the size of the temporary cross to be placed on the grave, the details of the dead to be recorded and the distance of any war cemetery from the nearest building. Chaplains were to minister to the dying and to officiate at funerals, and field staff were to discreetly choose suitable burial sites before battle, preferably ones that would not interfere with the existing landscape such as farmed land or roads. The men of the army, trained to act as a cohesive unit, were, it was envisaged, to be buried as individuals. Trench burial was not to be used, except when 'operational or other conditions preclude single burials'.[28] Military chaplains serving in Europe with Operation Overlord were reminded that while funerals close to the front line would often take place under rushed and sometimes dangerous conditions, with the bodies wrapped in blankets rather than encased in coffins, 'those you bury have made the supreme sacrifice', and should be treated with reverence.[29] The Royal Air Force (RAF) Manual, issued in 1932 and revised in 1934 and 1939, was based on the army's Field Service Regulations, with RAF personnel being responsible for the identification and burial of bodies, while the army's Directorate of Graves Registration and Enquiries dealt with the administrative burden of the dead. In these plans, discussed in committees, and written at desks, in peacetime, ease of identification of the dead, and the respectful treatment of their bodies, was to be paramount, even when burial took place under fire and in the midst of battle.

The efficiency with which the detailed regulations set out by the armed services for the burial and recording of the dead were followed varied greatly between theatres of war, campaigns and battles. The accurate identification and burial of dead airmen became much harder as the war went on, with more men losing their lives over enemy or occupied territory in Europe during the heavy bombing campaign waged by Bomber Command in the last three years of the war. For many, their final resting place was the sea. As this chapter will go on to discuss, the subsequent identification of bodies buried in Germany and occupied Europe was often fraught with difficulties. Identifying and recording the place of burial of the army's dead could also be problematic. In 1938, Fabian Ware, the founder and vice-chairman of the IWGC, had returned to the War Office to run the Directorate of Graves Registration and Enquiries. Ware established separate GRUs to work in the various theatres of war, the first formed in Aldershot in September 1939 to accompany the British Expeditionary Force. Ware often employed officers he had worked with during the Great War and since. He wrote to reassure Neville Chamberlain in 1939 that he could 'count on them to establish links of sympathy, confidence and affection with the relatives of the dead'.[30] Nonetheless, the efficiency with which the dead and their place of burial were identified and recorded varied greatly; in the chaos that was the retreat to Dunkirk in 1940, for instance, the GRUs attached to the British Expeditionary Force registered 552 graves from a total dead and missing of over 3,500.[31]

Men caught up in the retreat to Dunkirk convey some sense of the confusion that surrounded the evacuation of the British Army from France in the early summer of 1940. In *Third Class to Dunkirk*, the platoon commander Peter Hadley recalled both the 'wrecked vehicles' and the 'contorted shapes of their human victims that lay sprawled by the roadside'.[32] Anti-tank Gunner Harry Munn described burying the victims of an attack by the Luftwaffe, wrapping the corpses in white sheets; visiting the cemetery near Waterloo some years later he found only one of the graves was named, the others bearing the inscription 'Unknown Soldier of the Worcestershire Yeomanry'.[33] For those who reached Dunkirk, the turmoil in the town and on the beaches, packed with soldiers and civilian refugees, meant that few of those who died there were identified or buried promptly. Fred Barker, a member of the Royal Engineers who spent five days at Dunkirk during the evacuation, remembered watching men drown when they attempted to swim out to the boats waiting offshore, 'their pathetic waterlogged bodies lying face down in the water' while the almost continuous bombing and strafing of the beaches by the Luftwaffe left 'bodies everywhere'.[34]

Burying: the disposal of the war's dead

The chaos that had accompanied attempts to identify the dead and record the place of burial during the retreat continued when the survivors of the British Expeditionary Force returned to Britain in the early summer of 1940. Bombed and strafed as they collected soldiers from the beaches and returned across the channel, and again when they docked at Dover and other channel ports, the ships and small boats of the Dunkirk evacuation brought home the dead as well as the living. Approximately 200 of those who died during the evacuation were buried on their return in Dover, Ramsgate and Folkestone. In the summer of 1940, and especially in the days and weeks immediately following the fall of France, invasion was widely anticipated. Perhaps unsurprisingly, burial of the dead of Dunkirk was not high on the list of priorities for the army in the aftermath of the evacuation, and ninety-two of the corpses were buried, hurriedly, in a mass trench grave in Dover. Later that summer, when the threat of invasion had diminished, a conference was held between the IWGC, the Home Office and the War Office, to discuss whether the bodies buried so hurriedly at the Channel ports should be disinterred for burial by their families. Given an urgency by requests from several families for permission to remove bodies for private burial, the summary notes of the conference reveal the disparity between the language and symbolism of sacrifice and honour that surrounded the graves of the military dead, and the often squalid nature of their interment. Many of the bodies were hurriedly buried in shrouds, blankets or greatcoats, those in Dover placed in one long trench grave, meaning that 'the work of removal will be … if not impossible, in the highest degree repulsive'.[35] In August, the Home Office wrote to the Diocese of the Archbishop of Canterbury, which had supported the families in their attempts to remove the bodies, alerting them to the nature of the burials:

> bodies, to the number of about 200, were buried under active service conditions at the various ports of landing i.e. the great majority were buried in shrouds or blankets, not in coffins, and at Dover 92 bodies were buried in a single multiple grave … It will be obvious that where a large number of bodies have been buried in one grave the work of removal will in any case be difficult and repulsive, though not perhaps actually impossible, and there is likely to be difficulty in identifying a particular body or finding it without uncovering many more.[36]

The conference decided that 'the soldiers buried in the ports after the evacuation from Dunkirk must be regarded for all practical purposes as having fallen in action abroad'.[37] As with many of those buried during the Great War, the dead of Dunkirk who lay in Kent were interred by the state, resting beneath headstones which paid tribute to individual names when, beneath the ground, their bodies lay entangled, contained not within wooden coffins, but in shrouds, blankets or the coats in which they died.

Burial overseas could also be fraught with difficulty, and battle, climate and geographic conditions often made the clear rules set out for military burial in the Field Notes impossible. If bodies were not buried, or the place of burial was not recorded, soon after death, the work of the GRUs was extremely challenging. The official war diaries of the GRUs working in the Middle East and North Africa reveal the problems that the climate and geography of these regions caused for those tasked with identifying, disinterring and reburying the war dead in the concentrated cemeteries overseen by the IWGC. In North Africa, sandstorms could obliterate the original site of a grave, and wild animals could disturb and remove the grave's contents. Tanks and other vehicles could effectively destroy the burial site. Rapidly moving battle meant that in any case, bodies were left unburied. As a War Office memo of 1944 explained,

> In many cases no formation burial grounds were selected or made known to units, battlefields were not cleared, nor did many units bury their dead, as unburied dead are still being found in open positions. Even when burial was carried out, little attempt was made to collect bodies at all before interment, and in many cases no burial returns were made out or submitted.[38]

Walter Robson, a lance corporal with the Queen's Own Royal West Kent Regiment, wrote home from North Africa in 1943, describing the scattered nature of the graves left behind after battle, the widespread presence of the dead making the landscape itself – where 'the white rocks and stones can easily become skulls, especially when you come upon a lonely grave' – uncanny.[39] Sometimes the very presence of these bodies was imagined: cases occurred where the units opened up a marked grave only to find there was no body within it, usually when the dead recorded as being buried there had been killed in a tank or truck, 'leaving very little "remains" at the time of death'. In these cases, it was proposed, reburial in a concentrated cemetery could be achieved by removing some of the earth from the site or sites and reinterring it in a permanent cemetery.[40]

Burying: the disposal of the war's dead

At other times, the task of disinterring corpses for reburial was dangerous. Bodies were often buried in the large minefields that marked the mobile tank battles of North Africa. While minefields were identified and marked as far as possible, surrounded by barbed wire to keep both people and animals out, members of the GRUs often had to enter them to recover isolated corpses that had been buried close to where they fell. In June 1943, four members of a GRU were injured, one later dying of his wounds, when they were disinterring corpses for concentrated burial from a minefield at El Ruseiwat Ridge. When one member of the unit put 'his shovel under the shoulder of the body to raise it for searching', a mine close to its feet exploded.[41] The victim was himself buried in the large, concentrated cemetery at El Alamein, together with 7,341 others.[42]

In the Far East, the climate and geography posed other problems for GRUs. As with Dunkirk, the chaos of the retreat towards Singapore in 1941 and 1942 meant that there was little time for organised burials and registration of graves. The Field Service Regulations, which underpinned the treatment of the military war dead, were designed for military advances, not retreats. The first GRU was only formed in the Far East with the creation of the 11th Army in 1943, and as with the units operating in northwest Europe in 1944 and 1945, who had to identify and sometimes disinter the bodies of the dead of 1940, those operating in the Far East had to try and locate and identify 'the graves ... of previous campaigns during our withdrawal'. This was often difficult; the climate meant that decomposition occurred quickly, while bodies had often been left unburied, one man recalling some sixty years later that 'bodies were left in the jungle where they fell'.[43] The identification and concentration of graves had to be conducted quickly in the tropical climate as 'the rapid growth of jungle and monsoon conditions' meant that 'all such graves would be irretrievably lost at a very early stage'. Local wildlife, including large predators and white ants, also caused 'other difficulties that were not usually met with in European theatres'.[44]

Despite the difficult conditions that were often encountered in both the initial burial of the dead, and in their later disinterment and reburial in the larger, concentrated cemeteries that would be run by the IWGC, the majority of the military war dead were eventually identified, and are buried in named graves. During the Battle of Monte Cassino in 1944, it was often deemed too dangerous to venture on to the battlefield to collect and bury the dead. Instead, men were sent to bury, and wherever possible identify, the dead, once battle had ended. Infantryman Ken

Bond was one of these. Selected, with others from the Essex Regiment, by drawing lots, he remembered,

'I personally found two chappies from our own lot. They were just lying there all those months after, among many more, including Germans'.⁴⁵ At Tobruk, where the siege and subsequent fighting left 2,435 soldiers from across the empire dead, only 171 were unidentified.⁴⁶ At El Alamein, where many of the dead were killed by artillery and tank fire, making identification difficult, and where many of the original graves were isolated and widely spread across 1,000 kilometres of desert, 815 of the 7,240 soldiers buried there are unidentified.⁴⁷ Of the 4,144 imperial combatants buried at Bayeux, the largest of the Normandy concentrated cemeteries, 338 are unidentified.⁴⁸ When deaths occurred during a retreat, however, and bodies were left unburied, or buried hurriedly without the identity or exact place of death being recorded, later identification proved much more problematic. The most difficult circumstances were probably in Southeast Asia: the Rangoon memorial, at Taukkyan concentrated cemetery, names the almost 27,000 men of the Burma campaign who have no known grave, while a similar number are buried inside the cemetery; the Singapore memorial inside Kranji Commonwealth War Graves Commission (CWGC) cemetery records the names of the 24,000 troops who died during the campaigns in Malaysia or Burma, or subsequently while in captivity, and who have no known grave, while 3,692 identified dead have graves there.⁴⁹ The missing, and the emotional devastation often left in their wake, were not just a phenomenon of the First World War: in the Second, mobile, industrial warfare combined with climate and geography to ensure that many fields of battle could lay claim to the unknown body.

In his memoir of his time as regimental chaplain to the Sherwood Rangers Yeomanry Regiment, fighting in Western Europe in the aftermath of D-Day, the Reverend Leslie Skinner recounted not only the deaths of men in his regiment, but the challenging conditions in which the subsequent burials often took place. The regiment landed in Normandy on D-Day, 6 June 1944, and on 7 June Skinner was busy identifying a burial ground behind the beachhead while under rifle fire.⁵⁰ Skinner was unusual in the lengths that he went to in order to bury and, wherever possible, identify the corpses of those killed from his regiment. Despite the War Office's plans for the burial of the military dead, outlined in Chapter 3, many laid unburied in the battles that were fought across northwest Europe in 1944 and 1945. Many frontline

Burying: the disposal of the war's dead

soldiers believed that rear echelons would bury the dead, one man who fought with an Infantry unit stating that 'the job of men in a rifle company was to fight ... the dead were left where they fell'.[51] On 22 June, Skinner's diary recalled retrieving and burying the bodies of two men who had been killed a week previously. The task was deeply unpleasant: Skinner described the bodies, which he found lying in a ditch, as 'crawling'. He continued:

> Scrounged some blankets and started to tie them up. DWs officer went away to be sick and did not return until I had finished. DWs had dug graves for me and I read funeral service – then violently sick myself.[52]

The importance of Skinner's task, however, remained at the forefront of his mind, and his diary repeatedly tells of the 'awful business' of recovering, identifying and burying bodies after battle.[53] He was injured by shrapnel and sent home for a month to recover on 26 June. By that point the regiment had lost thirty-three men, with another sixty-six wounded and three posted as missing, a description Skinner claimed to hate as it was 'so distressing for families'.[54] Ensuring the identification and burial of bodies was central to Skinner's work as regimental chaplain; naming and placing the dead was an attempt both to give comfort to the bereaved, who would have a grave to visit when the conflict had moved on, and to safeguard their referential stability by ensuring that, through the care given to the dead, the political value that the military, as an arm of the state, placed on their service was visible. By identifying and burying these battlefield corpses, Skinner was both performing the duty of the living to the dead as understood in mid-twentieth-century Britain, ensuring that these dead could subsequently work as symbols of a national as well as an international will, and attempting to provide some solace to the bereaved.

It was the dead of the RAF, however, especially those who died while serving with Bomber Command in the area bombing of Germany between 1942 and 1945, whose identification and burial was to prove the most problematic. In July 1945, at the end of the war in Europe, the Casualty Branch of the Air Ministry estimated that approximately 31,000 air crew were still listed as 'missing'. Of these, it believed that around 24,000 were dead, with at least 1,000 bodies lost to the sea.[55] By the time the RAF set up Missing, Research and Enquiry Service (MRES) units to try to find and identify the bodies of the men of Bomber Command towards the end of 1945, the processes of decomposition combined with the violent manner of many of these deaths to make this an unusually difficult, and often unpleasant, task. In both Germany and occupied nations, bodies had usually been buried by local authorities. When aircraft crashed or were shot down over Germany or German-occupied countries, the German authorities compiled lists of the dead, *Totenlisten*, which were sent to Britain via the Red Cross, and which included deaths, injuries and places of burial where known.[56] Building on this knowledge, the MRES units working in Europe set out to try and locate the dead – a task that was easier in some areas of Europe than in others. While in Denmark MRES teams were gratified to find 'carefully preserved records of RAF crashes and burials' where 'local inhabitants had erected elaborate monuments over graves', those working in the Netherlands found that 'there was a special problem in this country arising from its flooded condition' and in Germany, 'the destruction in this area rendered search work very difficult'.[57]

Those working in Germany sometimes found the inhabitants, many of whom had suffered under nightly bombardment, to be 'generally unco-operative'. Local burghers had to be ordered to collate accounts of crashes and burials, and the subsequent exhumations, undertaken so that bodies could be concentrated into larger IWGC cemeteries, found that the details of over 50 per cent of those contained within these graves were wrong. The search teams used a range of techniques to try and identify the dead: infra-red photography to try and detect remaining markings and insignia on clothing; tooth charts, which recorded the airmen's fillings and extractions; and measurements of the thigh bone, which acted as a predictor of the overall height of the body. However, as some of the exhumation reports show, the violent deaths that these men often suffered meant there was little left to identify. For example, an exhumation report on bodies found in a communal grave in a cemetery in Ahlen recorded a body which was badly decomposed, with fingers, hands and teeth missing, the height impossible to estimate, and no identification disc, documents, letters or clothing remaining.[58] On at least one occasion the search teams turned to unconventional means to attempt identification. The team attempting to find the graves of the two crew members who died when their Mosquito crashed near Dusseldorf in 1945 called on the expertise of a psychiatrist to help the town's gravedigger recall where the two bodies were buried, after two attempts at exhumation had failed to recover them.[59]

On another occasion the search teams turned to the British press for help identifying a body. A corpse found in France was unidentifiable, the only clue to the identity of the dead airman being a small

Burying: the disposal of the war's dead

pocket case containing two photos of 'an attractive girl ... and a card on which was written an affectionate message to "Bob" from "Barb"'. In September 1945, the Air Ministry passed the photo and details to the press. The response was extraordinary:

> Barbara was recognised from Land's End to John O'Groats. She was a WAAF [Women's Auxiliary Air Force], a WREN [Women's Royal Naval Service (WRNS)], a dentist, a nurse ... Barbara was also a very bad girl, at present in a remand home, and the wife of a Baronet ... one writer sent us a photo of a girl he did not know but which he stated 'had fallen out of a library book at Hammersmith' thus presenting us with a second unknown.

Eventually Barbara was recognised as a nurse from Toronto, the fiancée of Canadian Flight Lieutenant Sergeant Bob Whitley. Barbara was sent the pocket case and its contents, while Bob was finally buried in a communal cemetery in Viroflay, near Versailles, one of seventy-four IWGC graves there.[60]

The formal announcement from the IWGC in October 1945 that, as after the Great War, the bodies of the empire's dead would remain in the country where they had fought and died, again caused some disquiet. Questions were asked in the House of Commons, Lieutenant-Colonel Thomas Moore, MP for Ayr, asking Jack Lawson, Secretary of State for War, whether the government was 'prepared to bring home the bodies of British soldiers buried abroad whose relatives wish to have them interred on British soil'.[61] The wording of the IWGC announcement demonstrates a keen awareness of the importance of ensuring that the bereaved across the empire felt certain that the bodies of their dead were being well cared for. Noting that it had given 'careful consideration' to the requests from 'relatives of members of his Majesty's forces buried overseas that their bodies should be brought back to their native countries', the IWGC had nonetheless concluded that final burial would take place overseas. The reasons given were two-fold. First, as in the Great War, private repatriation by those who could afford it would be unfair, and 'contrary to that equality of treatment' that drove IWGC policy. Secondly, although there were fewer war dead than in the aftermath of the Great War, repatriation would be a larger job as 'the graves are far more widely scattered and shipping facilities are practically non-existent'. Pragmatism thus intertwined with Ware's imperial beliefs and notions of a democracy in death, particularly important in the aftermath of the 'people's war'. Reassuring the bereaved that the cemeteries would be 'reverently tended' and 'honoured for all time', the IWGC sought to reassure its audience that it had learnt 'from intimate contacts with the relatives over the past 25 years that real consolation is derived from the knowledge that the last resting places of their dead are so honoured'.[62] Although the bodies became, to all intents and purposes, the property of the imperial state, the wording of the announcement, as much as the creation and maintenance of the war cemeteries, was designed to both guarantee equity of treatment across the empire, and to ensure that the bereaved felt that the private, emotional value the dead held for them was matched by the symbolic value they held for the state. As with the dead of the Great War, next of kin were invited to add a short personal inscription to the name, the military details, the age, the date of death and, usually, a religious symbol that were inscribed by the IWGC.[63]

The identification of bodies and the place of burial was important to the bereaved. Letters sent to Squadron Leader Reverend G. H. Martin by the relatives of men 'lost' while serving with Bomber Command in 1944 and 1945 express time and time again the overwhelming anxiety felt by those whose loved ones had been posted missing, and their desperate desire for information.[64] A Mass Observation respondent described how a friend of hers 'wishes she could die' after her husband was reported missing in Malaya, but that she had to 'keep on, for the children's sake'.[65] After the fighting in North and East Africa in 1942, the War Office released a press statement explaining how difficult it was proving to quickly identify bodies in response to a 'growing expectation among Britons that news be provided of their missing and dead relatives'.[66] When this information was not available, or when there was a fear that bodies were not being treated with due reverence, it was difficult to match the emotional value the dead held for the bereaved with a sense that they were equally valued by the state. The burial of bodies, when identified, in war graves within Germany often caused particular anguish, one woman writing to the *Times* in 1946 about a friend who was 'in great distress' because her son's final grave was to be in Germany:

> She and her relatives have appealed for a reversal of this decision … parsimony on the part of Government is responsible. It is unbearable that those who mourn the loss of their heroic dead should have their hearts wrung by the thought that England allows them to lie in enemy territory.[67]

Burying: the disposal of the war's dead

Writing in a similar tone to the *Daily Telegraph*, Margery Swanwick explained that 'I myself lost a son and a nephew, both killed in Germany, and it is with the utmost distaste that I contemplate visiting their graves in a country, and among inhabitants, with whom we have so recently been at war.'[68] The decision to maintain IWGC cemeteries within German borders was unpopular, the bereaved perhaps fearing that the graves would not be treated with the respect often shown to those in formerly occupied countries.[69] Some 33,511 British, imperial and Allied combatants are buried in IWGC graves and cemeteries within Germany.[70]

Wherever their bodies lay, those who would have been the nameless dead of preceding centuries were given names and, wherever possible, burial places in the total wars of Britain's twentieth century. Men such as Leslie Skinner, serving in Europe in 1944 and 1945, went to extraordinary lengths to try and ensure that this was the case, and GRUs and MRUs, together with the IWGC, worked to identify bodies and to provide and maintain permanent cemeteries in the aftermath of battle. In these attempts to achieve a referential stability for the war's dead, and to provide some consolation for the bereaved, the burials policy of the wartime state was both a product and an extension of the desire to democratically name the dead that had begun to take shape in the nineteenth century.[71] While the naming of the military dead had a precedent in the memorials and cemeteries of the Great War, the new technologies of conflict meant that these now had to be extended for the first time to the civilian dead of warfare. This chapter now turns to examine burial practice in Britain as aerial warfare began to claim its civilian victims.

The civilian dead

The new forms that death could take in wartime were brought home to the small town of Petworth, West Sussex on the morning of 29 September 1942. A lone bomber dropped three bombs on the town, one hitting Petworth Boys' School during the mid-morning break. Thirty-two people, including twenty-eight schoolboys and their headmaster, were killed. The impact of an event like this on a small, close-knit community can only be imagined: according to the *Daily Mirror*, 'from one road alone, out of a dozen or so boys who left for school in the morning, only four returned home'.[72] The child victims were buried together in a trench grave, with Canadian soldiers, who had helped to dig out the bodies of the dead and injured from the rubble of the school, accompanying the funeral cortege, their trucks carrying the small coffins to the church and on to the graveyard. The bishop of Chichester conducted the funeral, and the cortege paused next to the town's war memorial for local civic and military dignitaries to pay their respects. This carefully choreographed funeral and burial illustrates the ways in which death in wartime, and wartime practices of burial and commemoration, interwove the administrative and the intimate, the public world of the state and civic society with the private world of grief and bereavement. Even in such a carefully managed funeral, composed in a manner designed to emphasise both the value the state placed on the dead schoolboys and, through the involvement of the Canadian servicemen, the wider community of the imperial and Allied war effort, the importance of personal relationships and family traditions remained strong.[73] Writing years later, a Canadian soldier recalled seeing an elderly man place a coin on one of the coffins.[74] He was a grandfather of the dead boy, and the coin was the pocket money he gave him each week; the gift was a final act of familial intimacy symbolising the relationship between grandfather and grandson and demonstrating that, for the grandfather, the relationship continued after the boy's death.

The burial of the civilian dead killed in air raids between 1939 and 1945 proved to be one of the most contentious aspects of the growth of the state during the Second World War.[75] State and civic involvement in the burial of the dead was, of course, not new. While the Great War had seen the state organise the burial of the military dead of war, pauper burials, 'on the parish', of those who could not be buried by friends or family, had long been a feature of British society. Rather than signifying the 'exclusion from the social body' suffered by the poor buried in pauper's graves, it was hoped that the civilian dead of the Second World War, whom the interwar state had assumed would be buried in communal graves by local authorities, would signify a collective will and a collective identity, continuing to work politically long after their material bodies had ceased to exist.[76] However, for this to be the case, collective funerals of civilian victims of war would need to overcome the stigma which such funerals, and interment in 'common' graves, had long held for many. As Julie-Marie Strange has argued, antipathy to the pauper funeral in the nineteenth and early twentieth centuries was motivated less by the 'shame associated with material hardship' than by 'the anonymity of the grave, the inability to claim ownership of the dead and the denial of mourning rites' that pauper burial could entail.[77]

Burying: the disposal of the war's dead

The numbers of those buried privately are often striking. In two of the poorest communities in Britain, Shoreditch in the East End of London and Clydeside in Scotland, the majority of the civilian war dead were claimed for burial at private expense.[78] Of course, it would have been in communities such as these that the shadow of the pauper funeral loomed largest, perhaps making it less likely that the state's preferred meaning of collective funerals – that they mirrored the 'honourable' burial of combatants by the nation – was locally accepted. The wartime government certainly did their utmost, short of an actual ban, to dissuade the bereaved from holding individual funerals. Although funeral directors had been classified as a reserved occupation towards the end of the First World War, those aged thirty and younger were called up in the Second. When the undertaking firm Smith of Southwark requested exemption from military service of two of its workers (the sons of the director) towards the end of the Blitz on London in April 1941, the official response was both scathing and illustrative of attitudes within Whitehall regarding private burial:

> Smith's description of his son as his chief assistant and most efficient coffin maker is accepted. We can not, however, regard the making of coffins as vital ... in time of war there can be no doubt that the making of coffins is not work for which any man should be kept out of the army ... the younger Smith, who is not yet in the army ... is described amongst other things as a funeral engraver. I suppose this means that he engraves brass plates for coffins, surely a completely futile job in time of war. In another of the long letters which Smith has sent us he complains that it has been necessary to request mourners to assist in the bearing of coffins to the graveside. In time of war there can be no reason for keeping men away from National Service to act as bearers ... the root of the difficulty in the undertaking trade is the encouragement which is being given by undertakers, and probably by burial authorities, who are interested in the fees available, to the extravagant practice of burial in single private graves.[79]

This 'extravagant practice' of burial in single graves, however, continued throughout the war, despite the restrictions placed on funeral practice by the government. Petrol and wood rationing meant that fewer cars could participate in funeral processions, and that coffins became smaller and lighter. The Lancashire town of Bolton introduced a minimum speed of fifteen miles per hour for funeral processions, to eliminate the practice of mourners walking in front of vehicles, while in Hampshire, Southampton City Council proposed that copper coffin handles be reduced from four to two. Funeral corteges were encouraged to take the most direct route to the cemetery or crematorium, and mourners to meet the funeral at the church, rather than follow it through the streets.[80] These new practices of course shaped the burial of those dying of illness, accident or old age as much as those who were victims of the war. However, despite these restrictions, private burial, by family or friends, remained the principal means of 'disposing of the dead' during the Second World War.

For some, however, private burial was not an option. When bombardment was especially heavy, disrupting essential services and communication, and when large numbers from the same community were killed together in one raid, the collective burial of victims by the local authority was a more widespread practice. At times, usually when there was a particularly strong sense of community among the bereaved, and when official commemorative and funerary practice was understood to be both appropriate and respectful, a referential stability was achieved: the civilian dead were able to do the 'work' of signifying a national unity and a shared identity. When these elements were not in place, however, the collective burial of civilian air raid victims was haunted by memories of the pauper's grave, and the dead threatened the stability of the wartime nation, in particular the willingness of people to suffer both the dangers of life beneath the bombs, and the collective burial of private individuals by the wartime state.

The collective funerals and burial of the majority of the civilian victims of the air raid on Coventry in November 1940 appears to have largely avoided the stigma associated with the common graves of pauper funerals, despite 422 of the 568 dead being buried in layers three deep in long trench graves in the city's London Road cemetery. The dead were buried in two mass funerals, held on 20 and 25 November, the first funeral being filmed by British Pathé, which contrasted the ferocity of the attack with the stoicism of the community under bombardment, urging young men to join the RAF to defend other civilians from a similar fate and 'avenge this awful catastrophe'.[81] Although the term 'common grave' was associated with the pauper's burial place, and the War Office had warned against using these words in 1940 precisely because of this association, the graves in Coventry were nonetheless widely described in the media as 'common' graves.[82] The description of the funeral in the *Times* recorded the bodies being placed in a 'common grave' and Tom Harrisson, observing the funeral for Mass Observation, used the same terminology in his report for the BBC European News, stating that 'they buried the dead of Coventry yesterday, in a common grave. The whole town mourned for these dead, most of them women and children, all of them citizens and civilians.'[83] National and regional newspapers, including the *Daily Record*, the *Scotsman* and the *Dundee Courier*, also termed the burials as being in a 'common grave'.[84] The bishop of Coventry led the funeral service over the graveside, which included a Catholic ceremony alongside Anglican burial rites and Free Church prayers. The funeral was attended by soldiers, sailors, airmen, firemen and ambulance workers together with civilians and representatives from the city and the voluntary services.[85] Inter-church and involving civilian and military, the bereaved and city officials, the mass funeral in Coventry built on the sense of a community of suffering and the shared experience of heavy bombardment which dominated the small industrial town, emphasising the shared sense of loss and successfully disguising the underlying reasons for the mass burial: concerns that repeated individual funerals would have a detrimental impact on morale and the difficulties experienced by many of the bereaved in identifying the bodies of their loved ones. The small city was in chaos in the days following the raid, and existing arrangements for the storage and identification of bodies were swiftly overwhelmed. One man, who had been a rescue worker in Coventry, recalled fifty years later how they used a stretch of ground to store dead bodies during the night between 'two big green tarpaulins, one to lay the bodies on, the other to lay over them'.[86] The two mass funerals that accompanied the burials successfully disguised these circumstances, functioning instead as symbols not only of a shared grief, but of a shared sense of purpose, constructing, through their use of ritual, the presence of civic and military dignitaries, and the national and international coverage of, and sympathy for, the devastated city – a form of 'fictive kinship' that linked the individual bereaved with both the civic and the national.[87]

The widespread recognition of the suffering in Coventry, and the promise to erect memorials to the victims of the raids over the trench graves, may also have helped the two mass burials to achieve the referential stability that was sought. The coverage of the first funeral in the *Birmingham Post* exemplified the state's wish that the burial of civilian dead by a local authority be 'no less honourable than the burial of a soldier by the military' and that for this to be realised such funerals should be 'as far removed as possible in atmosphere from "poor law" burial'.[88] The *Birmingham Post* softened the brutal picture of 'unvarnished coffins … ranged three deep' in 'one large grave' with a claim that the 'citizens of Coventry' so buried 'died with all the honour of those who fell in the front-line trenches in the world's battle for liberty and freedom'. Ray Daniell, the London correspondent of the *New York Times*, covered both the raid and the funeral for his North American audience, remarking on both the stoicism of the mourners and the unusual nature of this wartime funeral:

> Only one woman in that long line broke down and wept and had to be supported by friends. Others bore their grief silently and inwardly in the traditional British fashion. That was the end. There was no singing, no music, nothing to alleviate the stark ugliness of what was more like a soldiers' burial in the field of battle than anything else.[89]

The victims thus became symbols not only of the city, ensuring that 'the name and fame of Coventry shall never die', but of a commitment to victory, and a willingness to suffer and die, more widely shared.[90] Although those buried individually by families, and those buried at the second mass funeral, received far less attention in the media than those buried in and mourning at this first collective funeral, the recognition of Coventry's suffering, seen for most outside the city in the coverage of this burial, seems to have helped to stabilise the meaning of these corpses.[91] The dead of Coventry, dying as civilians but buried like soldiers, thus continued to work for the war effort through both the means of their death and of their burial.

As seen in Petworth and in the sinking of the *City of Benares*, the bodies of children killed in enemy attacks could work especially hard as symbols both of a united national and imperial community and of the brutality of an enemy 'other', willing to destroy the lives of innocents in pursuit of victory. When Sandhurst Road School in southeast London was hit by a lone bomber during the lunch break on 20 January 1943, thirty-eight pupils and six teachers were killed. The youngest children killed were aged five; the oldest, fifteen. Thirty-one of the child victims and one teacher were buried together in a trench grave at Hither Green cemetery a week later. As with Coventry, a decision was taken to publicise the tragedy and to allow the press to publish details of the funeral and mass burial. The young age of the victims brought about an outpouring of compassion from around the country, and among the many 'In Sympathy' messages published in the local newspaper, the *Kentish Mercury*, were condolences from the National Union of Women Teachers, the Women's Co-operative Guild, civil defence organisations and educational authorities and the city of Cardiff.[92] Bereaved parents were accompanied on the funeral procession from the church to the cemetery by air raid wardens, and the funeral address was given by the bishop of Southwark, who described the children as 'martyrs' and urged his congregation to work to ensure that 'never again shall this curse of war fall upon the world'.[93] Empathetic and sympathetic responses across place and time were made visible through the presence of a wreath from the American Embassy, which had arranged for US soldiers to visit the bombed school, and another wreath from teachers and pupils at Upper North Street School, Poplar, where eighteen children had died in a 1917 air raid.[94] Yet the age of these victims meant that they were unstable symbols of national unity and a collective will to victory. The overwhelming grief of bereaved parents constantly threatened to break through the carefully managed funerary and burial rites; a grief made visible in the *Daily Herald*'s coverage of the funeral:

> They listened to the Bishop of Southwark's words of comfort, but they were words that could not console. They listened to music that could not solace. In that church they had only the memory of Jim fidgeting in his Sunday suit, of Mary beside that pillar.[95]

While the decision to bury the majority of the child victims in one grave, and the presence at the graveside of air raid wardens and local dignitaries, can be understood as an attempt to both honour the dead and imbue them with a collective identity and a collective meaning, the anguish of the bereaved remained profoundly personal.

In Belfast and in Clydebank, just west of Glasgow, the mass burial of the dead following heavy air raids in 1941 largely failed to convey a sense of unity and shared determination. In these instances, the political value attributed to the dead through the collective management and burial of their bodies failed to accord with their emotional value for the bereaved. While a discontent with these mass burials may, in part, have been driven by the local and national identities, and a sense of distance from, and lack of identification with, faraway metropolitan London, this explanation alone does not account for the failure of these burials to act as symbols of collectivity and stoicism.[96] Like Coventry, both Belfast and Clydebank were small municipalities, made up of tightly knit working-class communities, though both were divided by religious and (in Belfast) political allegiance. Both suffered badly under intensive bombardment in 1941: Clydebank was devastated in March 1941, and Belfast suffered its worst raid in April of the same year. Unlike Coventry, however, their suffering was not recognised on the wider stage – Clydebank was referred to in the press as 'a town in Western Scotland', and while Belfast was named in much of the coverage of the raid in the British press, it received nothing like the attention paid to Coventry.[97] Both Clydebank and Belfast had inadequate shelters in place for their populations, and both struggled to reinstate civic authority and organisation in the aftermath of their Blitzes. In the chaos and confusion that followed the bombing, many of those whose homes had been destroyed or damaged, and who were fearful of further raids, chose to leave and take shelter in nearby towns or countryside. The absence of family members who could identify the victims, and the scale of the destruction and the numbers of dead and injured, meant that Civil Defence and mortuary services were overwhelmed, leaving many bodies unidentified and awaiting burial in mass graves. In these circumstances, the desire that local authorities bury civilians with honour and dignity was to prove deeply problematic.

The Easter Tuesday raid on Belfast, the heaviest that the city suffered during the war, left almost 750 dead, and provision for storing the bodies at the city's hospitals and mortuaries was 'utterly overwhelmed'.[98] Preparation for air raids had been inadequate in Northern Ireland, as the provincial government at Stormont had complacently assumed that its position to the west of the British Isles meant it was unlikely to be bombed. Recruitment to Civil Defence organisations was poor, and Belfast, which had a large quantity of badly maintained terraced housing, lacked sufficient air raid shelters, as the high water table in the city made excavation difficult, and shelters were only available for approximately 15 per cent of the population.[99] By April 1941, the city's mortuaries could only hold some 200 bodies.[100] Following the devastating air raid on the city on the night of 15/16 April, the official mortuaries were quickly overwhelmed, and bodies were sent to other public buildings including the Falls Road Baths where Joseph McCann, an air raid warden in west Belfast, recalled volunteers struggling to carry 'a large, heavy, awkwardly shaped parcel. It bore a tag, which read: "believed to be a mother and five children."'[101] After three days, approximately 250 people, just under one third of those killed, had not been identified. These bodies were taken in coffins to St George's Market in the city centre and prepared for viewing by those still searching for the missing. Nurses and city officials were stationed inside the market to accompany those viewing the bodies, and when a body was identified, and a private funeral requested, the word 'private' was written in chalk on the coffin lid.[102] Emma Duffin was one of the nurses on duty at St George's

Market, and she described how, during her time as a hospital nurse during the Great War 'death had, to a certain extent been ... made decent'. Here, however, 'it was grotesque, repulsive, horrible. With tangled hair, staring eyes, clutching hands, contorted limbs, their grey-green faces covered with dust, they lay bundled into the coffins, half shrouded in rugs or blankets or an occasional sheet, still wearing their dirty torn garments.'[103] Of those whose corpses were taken to St George's Market, 151 were identified, and ninety-two of these were taken for private burial by families.[104]

The mass funerals of the Belfast victims took place on 21 April; 163 were buried in 153 coffins in mass graves; those who could be identified as Catholic were buried at Milltown cemetery in the west of the city, and the remainder at the City Cemetery. The coffins were taken from St George's Market to the cemeteries on military lorries after funeral rites had been conducted inside the market by a Rabbi and representatives of the Catholic, Presbyterian and Church of Ireland clergy. Coverage of the funeral and burial in the *Northern Whig and Belfast Post* emphasised the shared sorrow of the city in its description of women who knelt 'in the thronged streets near the market and prayed as the procession passed' and the housewives who 'stood at their doorsteps in silent sympathy'. A photograph published alongside this article showed nurses marching in the funeral cortege, accompanied by white-helmeted Civil Defence workers. Like Coventry, Belfast was also visited by royalty, in this case the Duke and Duchess of Gloucester, who toured the bombed areas but did not attend either of the burials, while Lady Carson wrote to the prime minister of Northern Ireland from her home in England to convey her sympathy.[105]

Of the 163 who were buried by the Belfast authorities on 21 April, 104 were unidentified and fifty-nine identified, demonstrating once again that, for many, the traditions of private funerary practice were preferable to the promise of 'honourable' burial by the state.[106] In the chaotic aftermath of the Easter Tuesday bombing raid, the referential stability sought by the state through mass burials was not achievable. Distant from London, poor, divided, unprepared for an air raid of this magnitude and hampered by a complacent and unprepared Stormont government, many of the inhabitants of Belfast saw interment in a common grave as redolent of pauper burial rather than the military burial of combatants. Alongside its 21 April 1941 description of demolition squads uncovering bodies as they worked, the *Northern Whig* recorded the 'many funerals' which passed through the city during the weekend following the raid, at which 'onlookers – friends and strangers alike – wept bitterly as they passed'.[107] Morale, a nebulous subject that government agencies spent large amounts of time trying to assess, was low in Belfast after the air raid.[108] John Simpson, an RAF pilot stationed in Ulster during 1941, wrote disparagingly during May that 'the people in Belfast were badly shaken by the bombing and have been very Irish about it'.[109] Many left Belfast after the Blitz, some to stay in nearby towns, while thousands of others trekked out of the city to sleep at night, returning every morning.[110] According to a letter published in the *Northern Whig* which unfavourably compared the people of Belfast to those of 'London, Liverpool, Glasgow, Birmingham, Manchester, Bristol and Coventry', those leaving the city included air raid wardens, leaving one post with eight wardens out of an original twenty.[111] In an already divided city such as Belfast, struggling with the aftermath of aerial bombardment, the war dead buried in collective graves struggled to do the work of symbolising togetherness and determination.

Clydebank in western Scotland was bombed on 13 and 14 March 1941. A small industrial town just to the west of Glasgow, which was attacked at the same time, Clydebank suffered not only a large loss of life proportionate to its population, but also large-scale destruction of property and a collapse in the town's infrastructure in the immediate aftermath of the raids. Many residents left the town for the rural areas nearby, fleeing not only expected further attacks but a lack of food, shelter and clean water. A senior officer of the Royal Engineers, reporting fifty-eight hours after the final raid, noted disapprovingly that 'civil authority … still appeared to have no co-ordinated plan of work'.[112] Like Belfast, Clydebank was unprepared for an attack on this scale, and the town was put under further strain by the concurrent attacks on Glasgow, which meant its large, urban neighbour was unable to send the level of help that might otherwise have been expected. In the chaos that followed the bombing, identification of the dead for burial by their families proved difficult. The emergency mortuary, which had been established at the greyhound stadium, had been destroyed, and as bodies were removed from the debris by rescue and demolition squads they were taken to improvised mortuaries at a church hall and a school. When a Mr MacRobbie of the Department of Health for Scotland arrived from Edinburgh to help the Mortuary Services on 16 March, he was told that the town's stock of Civilian War Dead forms, which recorded the details of the deceased and aided later identification, had been destroyed. No arrangements had been made to photograph the dead to help identification, and there was a shortage of coffins, gravediggers, pall bearers and Union flags to lay over the bodies. In these circumstances, MacRobbie and the Clydebank officials agreed, 'mass burial of the unclaimed bodies was the only practicable method'.[113]

While plans were laid for the burial of the unclaimed bodies at Dalnotter Cemetery, attempts at identification continued. MacRobbie sent for mortuary staff from Edinburgh, who began the process of washing the dead before police officers took take photos for subsequent possible identification. The scene was chaotic. Mortuary workers worked alongside undertakers who were preparing identified bodies for burial and with ARP workers who 'found the task distressing'. At some sites, bodies had to be prepared out of doors. Meanwhile, there was a constant stream of relatives attempting to identify the dead. In one case, identification happened just before the body was transferred to the cemetery for burial:

> At about 4.30 p.m. it was reported that a father was seeking the body of a three-year-old child ... I arranged for him to see the bodies of, I think, four children not yet loaded. Not one of these was, however, that he sought and there remained only for examination one body which had been loaded on to the first van ... it was clear that mass burial would be distasteful to him and, in particular, to his wife. I therefore had to detach one of the staff to retrieve the body from the first van and produce it for inspection. This proved to be the body that the caller was after.[114]

At least one of the temporary mortuaries, the Janetta Street school, was also a first aid post. Anne Fielding, visiting the post with her mother, remembered looking in the school windows: 'I remember freezing inside. I saw my first dead body – no, I saw many dead bodies and parts of dead bodies.'[115] By 17 March there were some sixty-six unclaimed bodies at St James' Church hall, forty-eight unidentified and eighteen identified but unclaimed for private burial, which the ever resourceful MacRobbie, having acquired shrouds and gravediggers from Glasgow and Union flags from the navy, arranged to be buried in Dalnottar Cemetery that afternoon. Watched by a small group of dignitaries, including the Secretary of State for Scotland, Protestant and Catholic clergymen conducted a funeral service while the shrouded bodies were placed in a trench grave. The following day, a smaller number of bodies from the other temporary mortuaries were added to the grave.[116]

Disquiet about the burials, and rumours about the number of dead, started almost immediately. In the confusion of post-raid Clydebank, the funeral was recorded as 'not to be kept secret' but it was also 'not to be publicised'.[117] Coverage of the burial in the *Daily Record* was headlined 'The nameless dead' and described how 'unknown victims of the Nazi onslaught on a Clydeside town were buried yesterday in a common grave'.[118] Sir Stephen Bilsland, the Civil Defence district commissioner, complained about the lack of bearers at the burial, about the availability of only two men in the trench to receive the bodies and about delays in leaving the mortuary and the burials.[119] A week later, James Reid, the Unionist member of Parliament (MP) for Glasgow Hillhead and the Scottish solicitor general, wrote to the Secretary of State for Scotland to complain that the actual numbers of dead in Clydebank was being suppressed. Reid claimed 'the real figures are about 1,200 dead for the whole area', and that the perception that the authorities were lying about this was 'incredibly bad for morale'.[120] At the beginning of April, John McGovern, MP for Glasgow Shuttleton, raised the issue of casualty figures in the House of Commons. Claiming that there was 'great resentment in the Clydeside area', McGovern highlighted the sense in the region that their suffering was being ignored by the national government; a belief felt profoundly in Clydebank. Herbert Morrison passed the blame for this back to local government, reminding him that any casualty figures published by the Home Office were provided by the regional authorities.[121] The lack of infrastructure following the heavy air raid, and the lack of faith in both the casualty figures and regional and national government, meant that the casualty numbers were still being contested in the local press a year later, when the *Sunday Post* claimed 1,200 had died in Clydebank.[122] In such circumstances, it should not be surprising that few of those who had been able to identify their own dead were willing to allow the state to bury them.

In both Belfast and Clydebank, unlike Coventry, the majority of those buried in mass graves were unidentified. The same was true of other regional cities that suffered heavy losses in air raids. Liverpool, which was heavily raided throughout the winter and spring of 1940–1941, buried the 554 victims of the May raid in Anfield cemetery on 13 May 1941. Of these, 373 were unidentified – fewer, according to the *Liverpool Daily Post*, 'than was first expected'.[123] One hundred and thirty-four of the 660 victims of the bombing of Sheffield were buried in a mass grave in City Road cemetery.[124] Of the 1,174 who died as a result of the bombing of Plymouth in 1940–1941, 397 were buried together in Efford cemetery, next to the communal grave of the children and nurses killed together when a hospital was hit in March 1941, the nurses 'still with their little charges in death'.[125] In these, and many other instances, the private identities of the dead, their familial and personal relationships and the emotions and memories that were left in their wake, meant that private burial was usually the preferred option among those mourning the civilian casualties of war.

Conclusion

In order for the war's dead, both military and civilian, to successfully act as symbols of a united nation and a shared national will to victory, their burial by the British state had to provide the bereaved with a sense that the dead were being honoured, and treated with reverence. However, as well as having a symbolic value, the dead were also material objects; corpses that had to be managed and disposed of, often in the chaos of battle or the turmoil that followed heavy air raids. For the military dead, traditions of bodily disposal already existed: burial at sea, or eventual interment in one of the IWGC cemeteries, or an individual grave marked by the IWGC, that were scattered across the globe. When there were no bodies to be buried, the memorial traditions of the Great War were utilised to name the dead and provide a site at which their service could be acknowledged by the state and local community, and at which the bereaved could mourn.

But the burial and commemoration of the dead had to do more than simply represent them as members of a united community who had died for nation or empire; for them to successfully conduct political work of such high value to the wartime state, their treatment also had to address the emotional needs of the bereaved. While the existence of established modes of burial and commemoration within the military meant this could often, but by no means always, be achieved for the combatant dead, it was much harder to realise for the civilian dead of air raids. In the disorder and distress of post-raid towns and cities, where the disposal of corpses was made urgent by the needs of both hygiene and morale, the bereaved could struggle to feel that their loved ones were being treated with respect and reverence by the agencies of the state. When there was a clear collective identity shared between the dead and the bereaved, as seen in the burials of school children and teachers in Petworth and Sandhurst Road, and children and nurses in Plymouth, collective burial could seem appropriate: together in life, they were together in death, and mourned both individually and as a group. In Coventry, where the decision was taken to publicise the raid and its impact on the town, collective burial again appealed to many, as international recognition of the suffering in the town imparted a sense that the dead were recognised and remembered, burial in a collective, rather than individual, grave perhaps ensuring the individual's place in this wider remembrance. In other instances, like Belfast and Clydebank, where morale was low and there was a lack of trust in both local and national government, the collective grave of wartime retained the markers of the pauper's grave. In such cases, the referential stability and emotional consolation that were sought through the burial and remembrance practices was harder to come by. The next chapter goes on to consider the wider experience of bereavement, and the feeling and management of grief, in wartime Britain.

Notes

1 T. Laqueur, *The Work of the Dead: A Cultural History of Mortal Remains* (Princeton, NJ: Princeton University Press, 2015), p. 81.
2 See A. Yurchak, 'Bodies of Lenin: the hidden science of Communist sovereignty', *Representations*, 129:1 (2015), pp. 116–57.
3 'Hungarian who led '56 revolt is buried as a hero', the *New York Times*, 17 June 1989; 'Britain mourns a monster', the *Guardian*, 26 March 2015. For a wide-ranging discussion of the role of dead bodies in post-Socialist Europe, see K. Verdery, *The Political Lives of Dead Bodies: Reburial and Post Socialist Change* (New York: Columbia University Press, 1999).
4 J. Bourke, *Dismembering the Male: Men's Bodies, Britain and the Great War* (London: Reaktion Books, 1996).
5 E. Scarry, *The Body in Pain* (New York: Oxford University Press, 1985), pp. 116–17.
6 The National Archives (TNA), Housing and Local Government (HLG) 7/436, *Volunteers Killed and Civilians Dying as Result of Enemy Action*, Letter from the Regional Office of the Ministry of Pensions to the Ministry (12 October 1939).
7 Cited in E. Newlands, *Civilians into Soldiers: War, the Body and British Army Recruits, 1939–45* (Manchester: Manchester University Press, 2014), p. 172.
8 Central Statistical Office, *Fighting with Figures: A Statistical Digest of the Second World War* (London: HMSO, 1995), Table 12.3, 'Average weekly earnings in manufacturing and other certain industries', p. 236. Over the same period, the cost of living rose (most swiftly between 1939 and 1941, after which price controls and rationing were extended), and longer hours were worked.
9 TNA, HLG 7/436, *Volunteers Killed and Civilians Dying*, 'Memo: funeral expenses: civilians'.

Burying: the disposal of the war's dead

10 TNA, Home Office (HO), 45/18142, *War. Burial of the Dead Killed in Air Raids*, 'Disposal of the dead' (1936).
11 TNA, HO 45/18136, *War. Burial of the Dead*, 'Committee of Imperial Defence ARP Sub-Committee: scheme for the payment of compensation to civilians in respect of death or injury caused by hostile air attacks' (1934).
12 S. Pederson, 'Gender, welfare and citizenship in Britain during the Great War', *The American Historical* Review, 95:4 (1990), pp. 983–1006, here 1006.
13 TNA, HO 45/18136 (1934).
14 TNA, HLG 7/761, *Civilian War Dead Bible*, Ministry of Health Circular 1779 'Civilian deaths due to war operations' (28 February 1939).
15 TNA, HLG 7/436, *Volunteers Killed and Civilians Dying*, Cunnison Committee (25 October 1939).
16 TNA, HLG 7/436, *Volunteers Killed and Civilians Dying*, Cunnison Committee (13 February 1940).
17 TNA, HLG 7/436, *Volunteers Killed and Civilians Dying*, Letter from Ministry of Pensions to Treasury (18 April 1940).
18 TNA, HLG 7/436, *Volunteers Killed and Civilians Dying*, Letter from Treasury to Ministry of Pensions (3 June 1940).
19 Central Statistical Office, *Fighting with Figures*, Table 2.10, 'War pensions, grants and allowances', p. 24.
20 TNA, HO 186/376, *Blitz Casualties/Burial of Casualties*, Letter marked 'To Miss Waller, T.S.5' (29 September 1940).
21 'The test', *Sunday Chronicle*, 29 September 1940.
22 TNA, HO 186/376, *Blitz Casualties*, 'Home Office internal memorandum', undated.
23 TNA, HO 186/376, *Blitz Casualties*, 'Letter from London Civil Defence Region Head Quarters to Home Office' (8 October 1940).
24 'Profiteers in death', *Daily Mirror*, 3 December 1940, p. 1.
25 G. Prysor, *Citizen Sailors: The Royal Navy in the Second World War* (Penguin: London, 2011), pp. 139–40.
26 For a full overview of the management of the British military dead of the army and air force in Europe and Africa, see Seamus Spark, *The Treatment of the British Military War Dead of the Second World War* (University of Edinburgh, unpublished PhD, 2009).
27 TNA, War Office (WO) 171/3926, *Graves Registration and Enquiries. Allied Expeditionary Force North West Europe. War Diaries 1945*, 'Notes for Divisional Burial Officers' (February 1945).
28 TNA, WO 171/3926, *Graves Registration*, 'Notes for Divisional Burial Officers'.
29 TNA, WO 171/4474, *Chaplains, Allied Expeditionary Force North West Europe. War Diaries 1945*, 'New edition of routine orders. Chaplains' (February 1945).

30   Letter from Ware to Chamberlain (9 September 1939), cited in Spark, *Treatment of the British Military Dead*, p. 56.
31   Altogether, approximately 3,500 British soldiers were killed between 10 May and 22 June 1940. D. French, *Raising Churchill's Army* (Oxford: Oxford University Press, 2002), p. 156.
32   P. Hadley, *Third Class to Dunkirk* (London: Hollis and Carter, 1994), p. 134.
33   P. Hunt, 'Rearguard at Dunkirk', BBC People's War website, www.bbc.co.uk/history/ww2peopleswar/stories/68/a2349768.shtml (accessed 17 March 2016).
34   Warwickshire Libraries and Trading Standards, 'Five Days at Dunkirk', BBC People's War website, www.bbc.co.uk/history/ww2peopleswar/stories/32/a4198232.shtml (accessed 17 March 2016).
35   TNA, HO 45/21922, *Civilian War Dead Burials, 1947*, Summary of conference (16 July 1940).
36   TNA, HO 45/21922, *Civilian War Dead Burials*, Letter to principal registrar, Diocese of Canterbury (1 August 1940).
37   TNA, HO 45/21922, *Civilian War Dead Burials*, Summary of conference (16 July 1940).
38   Cited in Spark, *The Treatment of the British Military Dead*, pp. 95–6.
39   W. Robson, *Letters from a Soldier* (London: Faber & Faber, 1960), p. 29.
40   TNA, WO 169/13802, *British Forces, Middle East War Diaries. Graves Registration and Enquiries 1943*. 'Report on general position of Middle East Graves Registration Service' (19 June 1943).
41   Commonwealth War Graves Commission website, TNA, WO 169/13802, 'Accident, mines. Preliminary report' (4 June 1943).
42   www.cwgc.org/find-a-cemetery/cemetery/2019000/EL%20ALAMEIN%20WAR%20CEMETERY (accessed 6 April 2016).
43   Thanet Libraries, 'Burma and Malaysia', BBC People's War website, www.bbc.co.uk/history/ww2peopleswar/stories/56/a2636156.shtml (accessed 9 April 2016).
44   TNA, WO 203/909, *Graves Registration South East Asia. Command*, 'Summary of the start and expansion of the Graves Registration Service in South East Asia. Command report' (June 1945).
45   Cited in Spark, *Treatment of the British War Dead*, pp. 28–9.
46   Commonwealth War Graves Commission website, Tobruk cemetery www.cwgc.org/find-a-cemetery/cemetery/2020400/TOBRUK%20WAR%20CEMETERY (accessed 9 April 2016). These figures include a number of Polish, Czech and Greek combatants.
47   Commonwealth War Graves Commission website, www.cwgc.org/find-a-cemetery/cemetery/2019000/EL%20ALAMEIN%20WAR%20CEMETERY (accessed 9 April 2016).
48   Commonwealth War Graves Commission website, Bayeux cemetery, www.cwgc.org/find-a-cemetery/cemetery/2033300/BAYEUX%20WAR%20CEMETERY (accessed 9 April 2016).

Burying: the disposal of the war's dead

49 Commonwealth War Graves Commission website, Kranji cemetery, www.cwgc.org/find-a-cemetery/cemetery/2004200/KRANJI%20WAR%20CEMETERY (accessed 9 April 2016).

50 Skinner, L., *The Man Who Worked on Sundays: The Personal War Diary June 2nd 1944 to May 17th 1945 of Reverend Leslie Skinner, RAChD 8th (Independent) Armoured Brigade, Attached to the Sherwood Rangers Yeomanry Unit* (privately printed for the author by Plus Printing, n.d.), p. 16.

51 Spark, *The Treatment of the British Military Dead*, p. 30.

52 Skinner, *The Man Who Worked on Sundays*, p. 26.

53 Skinner, *The Man Who Worked on Sundays*, p. 45.

54 Skinner, *The Man Who Worked on Sundays*, pp. 31, 27.

55 Figures cited in Spark, *Treatment of the British Military Dead*, p. 183.

56 TNA, Air Ministry (AIR) 20/9305, *Air Ministry Report of RAF and Dominions Air Forces Missing Research and Enquiry Service 1944–1949*. According to this report, little was done to record deaths and burials by Japan or Italy. Foreword.

57 TNA, AIR 20/9305, *Air Ministry Report*, p. 23.

58 TNA, AIR 20/9305, *Air Ministry Report*, p. 57.

59 TNA, AIR 20/9305, *Air Ministry Report*, p. 133.

60 TNA, AIR 20/9305, *Air Ministry Report*, p. 137.

61 *Hansard*, House of Commons (HoC), 5:414, 'War graves', Thomas Moore, col. 1848 (23 October 1945).

62 'War dead not being brought home', the *Times*, 4 October 1945, p. 6.

63 Some of these inscriptions are discussed in Chapter 8.

64 Imperial War Museum (IWM), Department of Documents, 93/48/1, *Papers of Squadron Leader G. H. Martin*. This correspondence is discussed in Chapter 7.

65 Mass Observation (MO), Diarist 5277 (May 1942).

66 The *Guardian* (7 March 1942). Cited in Spark, *Treatment of the British Military Dead*, p. 67.

67 Letters, the *Times*, 5 December 1946, p. 5.

68 The *Daily Telegraph*, 10 December 1946. Cited in Spark, *Treatment of the British Military Dead*, p. 143.

69 See, for example, the detailed description of the care of Allied graves in the Cher region of central France in 'French remembrance of fallen airmen', the *Times*, 9 November 1945, p. 4. The newspaper's Paris correspondent noted that 'it will be a solace to those at home to know that the graves are cared for with reverence, and the dead are held in abiding remembrance'.

70 Commonwealth War Graves Commission website, Germany, www.cwgc.org/find/find-cemeteries-and-memorials/results?country=Germany&secondwar=true&tab=cemeteries&pageSize=50&casualtypagenumber=1 (accessed 17 January 2019).

71 See Laqueur, *The Work of the Dead*, pp. 388–412. During the Boer War, the British government had considered, but eventually rejected, erecting memorial cairns over the mass graves of the dead. It did provide small iron crosses to mark the graves of those 6,000 dead who were not privately commemorated. Laqueur, p. 458.
72 '12, dragged pal from bombed school', the *Daily Mirror*, 1 October 1942, p. 5.
73 For a suggestive discussion of the relationship of empire to formations of British identity in wartime, see M. Francis, 'Foreword', in W. Ugolini and J. Pattinson (eds), *Fighting for Britain? Negotiating Identities in Britain During the Second World War* (Edinburgh: Peter Lang, 2015), pp. ix-xv.
74 The *Petworth Society Magazine*, no. 81 (September 1995).
75 For an overview of the development of policy, see J. Rugg, 'Managing civilian war deaths due to war operations': Yorkshire experiences during World War II', *Twentieth Century British History*, 15:2 (2004), pp. 152–73.
76 T. Laqueur, 'Bodies, death and pauper funerals', *Representations*, no. 1 (1983), pp. 109–31, here 109.
77 J. M. Strange, *Death, Grief and Poverty in Britain, 1870–1914* (Cambridge: Cambridge University Press, 2005), p. 132. It should be noted that Strange convincingly contests the often oversimplified dichotomy between the 'shaming' pauper's funeral and a 'respectable' burial.
78 Hackney Archives (HA), S/A/27, *Burial Records of Civil Defence Personnel and Civilians, 1945–1950*; Mitchell Library (MLG), D/CD/9/16, *Air Raids, Casualties*. These sources state that of the 964 killed in air raids on Shoreditch, ninety were buried in two common graves, and in Clydebank 173 unidentified bodies were buried by the local authority after approximately 448 were killed in two raids.
79 TNA, HLG 7/761, *Civilian War Dead Bible* (16 April 1941).
80 B. Parsons, 'The management of civilian funerals in the Second World War', *British Institute of Funeral Directors Journal*, no. 3 (2011), pp. 48–54.
81 *The Tragedy of Coventry*, British Pathé (1940).
82 TNA, HO 45/21922, *Civilian War Dead Burials*, War Office Reply to Minutes of Meeting Concerning Exhumation of Bodies (19 July 1940).
83 'Common grave for Coventry's dead', the *Times*, 20 November 1940, p. 4; MO File Report (FR), *Coventry* (November 1940).
84 'Coventry mourns', *Daily Record*, 21 November 1940, p. 1; 'First mass funeral', the *Scotsman*, 21 November 1940, p. 6; '172 buried in one grave', the *Dundee Courier*, 21 November 1940, p. 2.
85 The king and queen visited Coventry three days after the raid, and this visit also seems to have strengthened morale, which had been seriously shaken by the intensity of the raid and the scale of damage. See Coventry City Archives (CCA), 1456, *Reminiscences*.
86 CCA 1456/22, Ted Cross.

Burying: the disposal of the war's dead

87 On fictive kinships, see J. Winter, *Sites of Memory, Sites of Mourning: The Great War in European Cultural History* (Cambridge: Cambridge University Press, 1995), p. 30.
88 'Air raid victims funeral', *Birmingham Post*, 21 November 1940, p. 3.
89 'Coventry dead laid in one grave; air raid siren is their requiem', *New York Times*, 21 November 1940, p. 3.
90 'City's tribute to its dead', *Birmingham Post*, 21 November 1940, p. 3.
91 The only reference to individual burials in Coventry in the national and international press that I have seen is the *New York Times* coverage, which notes the 'many newly made graves' in London Road cemetery 'where were buried other victims of last Thursday's raid whose relatives preferred private burial'. *New York Times*, 21 November 1940, p. 3.
92 London Metropolitan Archive (LMA), File LCC/EO/War/03/028, *Damage and Casualties at Sandhurst Road School, Catford*, cuttings from the *Kentish Mercury*, 27 January 1943, n.p.
93 'Bombed school dead buried', the *Times*, (28 January 1943, p. 2.
94 'The martyred children', the *Dundee Courier*, 28 January 1943, p. 3.
95 'The bombed children', the *Daily Herald*, 18 January 1943, p. 3.
96 For essays discussing the 'four nations' approach to Britain in the Second World War, see Ugolini and Pattinson (eds), *Fighting for Britain*.
97 A sense that the suffering of regional towns and cities in air raids was not widely recognised, and that London's Blitz dominated the popular imagination, was common to many of the blitzed areas of Britain.
98 Accurate numbers of casualties are difficult to determine, but the report of the Medical Civil Defence Services claim that 745 were killed in the raid of 15 and 16 April. Public Record Office of Northern Ireland (PRONI), CAB 3/A/58, *Civil Defence Medical Folder no. 13*, p. 7; B. Barton, *The Blitz: Belfast in the War Years* (Belfast: Blackstaff Books, 1989) p. 146.
99 PRONI, CAB 3/A/69, *Draft Typescript of History of Civil Defence in Northern Ireland to 1939*; J. W. Blake, *Northern Ireland in the Second World War* (Belfast: HMSO, 1956), p. 218.
100 Barton, *The Blitz*, p. 14.
101 Cited in Barton, *The Blitz*, p. 147.
102 PRONI, MPS2/3/99, *Deaths Due to War Operations. Lists of Dead Identified at St George's Market*, 'Fatal air raid casualties: mass identification parade'.
103 PRONI, D2109/20, *Diary of Miss Emma Duffin, while Serving as VAD Commandant at Stranmillis General Hospital*.
104 PRONI, MPS2/3/99, 'Dead at St George's Market. Summary' (26 April 1941).
105 'Belfast's unknown raid victims buried', the *Northern Whig and Belfast Post*, 22 April 1941, p. 4.
106 PRONI, MPS2/3/99, 'Dead at St George's Market' (26 April 1941).

107 'Belfast's "business as usual" motto', the *Northern Whig and Belfast Post*, 21 April 1941, p. 3.
108 On civilian morale, see Daniel Ussishkin, *Morale: A Modern British History* (Oxford: Oxford University Press, 2017), pp. 97–103.
109 H. Bolitho, *Finest of the Few: The Story of Battle of Britain Fighter Pilot John Simpson* (Stroud: Amberley Publishing, 2012) p. 44, first published as H. Bolitho, *Combat Report: The Story of a Fighter Pilot* (London: B. T. Batsford, 1943).
110 PRONI, CAB 3/A/68A, *Notebook on Raids*.
111 'Letters', the *Northern Whig and Belfast Post*, 22 April 1941, p. 2.
112 Clydebank Archive Centre, 941.37, *Clyde Air Raid Papers: Volume One*.
113 National Records of Scotland (NRS), HH 50/92, *Report by Mr MacRobbie, Department of Health, Edinburgh, on his Assistance to Mortuary Services in Clydebank 20–21 March 1941*.
114 NRS HH 50/92, *Report by Mr MacRobbie*.
115 A. Fielding, 'The Blitz and beyond', in Clydebank Life Story Group, *Remembering Clydebank in Wartime* (Clydebank: Clydebank Life Story Group, 1999), p. 26.
116 NRS HH 50/92, *Report by Mr MacRobbie*.
117 NRS HH 50/92, *Report by Mr MacRobbie*.
118 'The nameless dead', *Daily Record*, 18 March 1941, p. 2.
119 NRS, HH 50/92 *Report by Mr MacRobbie*.
120 NRS, HH 50/98, *Letters, Reports and Cuttings about Raids*, Letter from James Reid (25 March 1941).
121 *Hansard*, HoC, 370, 1 April 1941, col. 856. For further coverage of this debate, see J. Macleod, *River of Fire: The Clydebank Blitz* (Edinburgh: Birllin, 2010), pp. 245–7.
122 'Clydebank remembers', *Sunday Post*, 15 March 1942, p. 2.
123 'Our unknown warriors. City's homage to air raid victims', the *Liverpool Daily Post*, 14 May 1941, p. 1.
124 'The day the Luftwaffe bombed Sheffield', the *Yorkshire Post*, 11 December 2015, www.yorkshirepost.co.uk/our-region/south-yorkshire/sheffield/sheffield-blitz-the-day-the-luftwaffe-bombed-the-city-1-7618271 (accessed 15 May 2016).
125 'One grave for raids victims', the *Western Morning News*, 28 March 1941, p. 2.

7

Grieving
Bereavement, grief and the emotional labour of wartime

Introduction: an airman's letter

In June 1940, soon after the fall of France and the evacuation of Dunkirk, and at the start of what was to become known as the Battle of Britain, the *Times* published, posthumously, an airman's letter to his mother. The anonymous letter was not published on the letters page but given a column of its own, introduced with an editorial that quoted the dead man's station commander. Describing the letter as 'perhaps the most amazing one I have ever read', the officer stated that he had published it in the hope that 'its contents may bring comfort to other mothers'. In the letter the airman, a pilot with Bomber Command, cautioned his mother to accept his death stoically, as she would 'disappoint me if you do not at least try to accept the facts dispassionately'. He went on to warn her that 'you must not grieve for me' as the war had enabled him to find his calling and to be a part of something greater than his individual self. Her 'sacrifice', he continued, 'is as great as mine,' as 'the home front will still have to stand united for years after the war is won'.[1]

In death, the author, later revealed as twenty-three-year-old Vivian Rosewarne, a Canadian pilot who had grown up in Essex, came to represent a shared international determination in the face of a powerful enemy. The newspaper's editorial claimed Rosewarne as a symbol of imperial unity, stating that his words showed how the empire 'was built by sacrifice; it holds the present and future of peace, justice and freedom for all', concluding 'could our enemies ponder it, they must learn something at last of the faith which they have chosen to challenge'.[2] The letter struck a chord both in a nation grieving for those lost at Dunkirk while nervously anticipating invasion, and further afield. The *Times* received requests for the letter to be reprinted, and it was published as a pamphlet that, by the end of 1940, had sold more than 500,000 copies in Britain, across the empire and in the United States.[3] In 1941, filmmakers Michael Powell and Emeric Pressburger made a short film based on Rosewarne's letter for MGM, narrated by John Gielgud.

Similar letters, exhorting those on the home front not to grieve for their dead, were published later in the war. In December 1941 the *Times* published 'Another airman's letter', this time written by an officer of the Fleet Air Arm. The author 'desired to put his parents' minds at rest' by assuring them that 'I believe in these things for which I have joined in the fight. I believe in them with all of my being.' Drawing on religious imagery he reassured them that he had not died, but had simply changed from one state of being to another as 'flesh and blood has undergone a conversion, and been able to add something to the spirit'.[4] In these texts, parental grief is understood as counterproductive, working to undermine the willing sacrifice of the soldier son, whose martyrdom can only be worthwhile if it is matched not just by his parents' emotional self-control, but by a disavowal of grief. Grief is seen as out of place both in a nation fighting a total war, but also in the private realm of the family, where we might expect grief to be expressed.

These letters, and their popularity, should be understood as part of a wider attempt to manage and strengthen morale during a long and costly total war.[5] The maintenance of morale was understood as crucial to the war effort as it underpinned social cohesion and a willingness to undergo the rigours and sacrifices demanded by war and vital to eventual victory. Concern about civilian morale had emerged in the late 1930s, when it largely focused around responses to air raids, and led to plans being laid for specialist psychiatric hospitals, termed 'neurosis centres', on the outskirts of major cities and conurbations.[6] Despite the evidence that morale had generally held up well among civilian populations subjected to air raids in Spain and China, it was expected that psychiatric would outnumber physical casualties by three to one.[7] Although these expected psychiatric casualties failed to materialise, government interest in morale continued.

Mass Observation (MO) was employed by the Ministry of Information to submit weekly reports on morale, the early results of which were summarised in *War Begins at Home* in 1940. Drawing on responses to directives by their national panel of volunteers, and on observations of daily life and particular topics by a small group of paid observers, Tom Harrisson and Charles Madge emphasised that they were trying to 'visualise and analyse some of the early evidence

Grieving: bereavement, grief and the emotional labour of wartime

about the war and its affects in terms of mass behaviour and mentality'.[8] Much of this work and analysis, and much of the concern about morale as a whole, focused on people's emotional responses to the conflict. MO described the outbreak of war as 'an emotional occasion', one young woman recording 'the funny feeling inside me' when she heard Chamberlain's announcement on 3 September, while another vividly described the physical symptoms of anxiety: 'we could eat no breakfast hardly and just waited with sweating palms and despair for 11 o'clock'. When war was declared, this same woman 'leant against [her] husband and went quite dead for a minute or two'.[9] The *Daily Mail* reassured its readers that 'the calm, impressive tones of our Prime Minister ... spoke for the spirit of this people', while in his speech to Britain and the empire that evening, King George VI urged emotional restraint, asking that people remain 'calm, firm and united in this time of trial'.[10] Anne Temple, the *Daily Mail*'s agony aunt, and thus one of the 'everyday experts' identified by Claire Langhamer as emergent managers and mediators of 'everyday emotions', had a 'special message' for her female readers: 'in quietness and confidence shall be your strength'. Anxiety and fear, she suggested, could be silenced by war work as 'you rest the mind when the body is kept invigorated by work' and 'the moment you do nothing the mind is apt to fill up with worry'.[11] Emotions then were a resource to be mobilised for the war effort.

How people feel in war matters. As Chapter 2 discussed, advocates of popular psychology in the late 1930s had taught that emotions should be the subject of self-reflection in order that they could be understood and managed by the individual, who would then be able to both benefit personally from this self-knowledge, and contribute effectively to the wider community. The reaction of a member of the Auxiliary Territorial Service who 'threw herself on the floor of the hut, screaming and trying to dig a hole in the floor with her hands' when a V1 rocket fell close to her anti-aircraft battery in east London, may well have been an understandable response to a large explosion, but it did little to help the work of the battery in its attempted defence of the city.[12] If people could learn to recognise and manage their emotional responses, not only would they feel more in control of their lives, they would also be contributing to the war effort, through their increased ability to carry out their daily duties, but also because they would be 'setting an example' to others by remaining externally calm and focused.

Emotions, however, were not always easy to manage, either by the individual or by the wartime state that wanted to organise and control them. And no emotion was more unruly, or less manageable, than grief. Grief, when successfully mobilised, presented as unifying, and as evidence of a brutal enemy that needed to be defeated, could be an extremely powerful force, empathy with and sympathy for the bereaved acting to bind people together around common war aims. Press coverage of the communal burial of victims of the Coventry air raid of November 1940, discussed in the previous chapter, did just this, provoking a national and a transnational outpouring of sympathy for the dead and bereaved of the town, and acting as a visceral symbol of a Nazi brutality that had to be defeated. However, when grief could not be framed and utilised in a manner that made it usable, it had the power to disrupt narratives of togetherness, commonality and a shared commitment to war aims. The distress and the grief of those bereaved that did not serve to emphasise the enemy's brutality, or that refused incorporation into a wartime narrative in other ways, could destabilise both the bereaved, and the wider collective of wartime. In the emotional economy of Britain in the Second World War, grief had a high social and cultural value when it was expressed in a manner that strengthened wartime resolve and collectivity, but was of no value at all when it threatened or undermined these notions.

The philosopher Judith Butler has argued that grief is one of the most disruptive and transformative of emotions, as in its destruction of relationships, it can also injure and dislocate a sense of self as, after all, 'who am I without you?'[13] The loss of loved ones can bring with it a destabilisation of selfhood and a sense of alienation from what is known and established, with the bereaved feeling anger, shame and guilt as well as despair, loneliness and sorrow.[14] As Inge Del Rosario has explained, 'grief transforms. Grief changes you as few other experiences can … it strikes deep, unsettling, breaking apart, shattering what was once stable and secure.'[15] Such feelings, however, are not always easily expressed, and when they are articulated, verbally, physically or in material culture, these articulations are always socially and culturally mediated. In wartime Britain many worked hard to police and contain the expression of grief, and when it did become visible, to make it work for the nation. Emotions like grief then are liminal, existing within and constituting the boundary between the internal and the external, the subjective and social, the political and personal.

This understanding of emotions has an extra dimension when we think of grief, which can be understood as transformative, as being about the passage from one state of being to another. The work of grief,

Grieving: bereavement, grief and the emotional labour of wartime

what Joy Damousi has aptly termed 'the labour of loss', is hard, in part because of its transformative nature.[16] Bereavement can be profoundly unsettling, but it can also be transitional as the life and the identity of the bereaved are altered by the death of someone close, and the subsequent changes in a relationship which had been constitutive of an individual's subjectivity. The ferocity of grief, its ability to unsettle and change both relationships and subjectivities, can be especially apparent in wartime, when sudden, mass bereavement is experienced. It is also during war that this destructiveness can be especially damaging to the wider community, society and nation, as it threatens cohesiveness, stability and morale. As such, it had to be carefully managed and rigorously policed, by the wartime state, within cultural texts and by bereaved individuals and those around them. This chapter turns first to examine the management of grief in wartime Britain before going on to consider what happened when grief could not be so managed, and could not be put to work for the nation.

Policing grief

At the outbreak of war, a culture of restraint dominated the British emotional economy. While this was always mediated through differences of region, of class and of gender, the British were nonetheless accustomed to social structures and cultural texts that advised them to practice self-control. As discussed in Chapter 2, the interwar years had seen the practices of self-reflection and emotional management disseminated through a range of different sites and cultural texts. As war moved ever closer, the need to police the expression of feelings that could be detrimental to morale became more and more important. Grief, with its ability to destabilise both the self and the wider community, was subject to rigorous policing.

This policing took place at a number of levels: the state and cultural texts endeavoured to formulate the parameters within which grief could be expressed, and the language with which it could be articulated, while individuals practised self-management, often attempting to rigorously control both the manner in which they demonstrated their distress, and the spaces in which they did so. The ability of grief to disrupt and undermine wartime morale was recognised well before the war began. In the planning for wartime funerals that took place in the 1930s, special attention was paid to the relationship between violent death in war, public morale and bereaved relatives. A conference held in 1936 and attended by representatives of the Ministry of Health, the Home Office and the Registrar General noted that the rapid collection of bodies after air raids was vital 'on grounds of public morale and public sentiment, and from the viewpoint of bereaved relatives'.[17] By 1940, the Home Office felt that 'in some cases a multiplicity of funerals may be undesirable', as the repeated procession of funeral cortèges through the streets, and the visibility of the bereaved and grieving would be bad for morale.[18] The careful management of the interment of the civilian dead was accompanied by attempts to ensure that the bereaved felt that their dead had been honoured in the same way that combatants were, and the Imperial War Graves Commission (IWGC), which managed the graves of the military dead, was given a charter in January 1941 to collect and memorialise the names of the civilian dead, while a royal message of sympathy was sent to the relatives of all those killed in air raids. Fabian Ware of the IWGC was keen to emphasise the commonalities between the civilian and combatant dead, suggesting to the dean of Westminster Abbey that a record of the civilian dead be placed in the abbey's Warrior Chapel, where 'adjacency and companionship with the Unknown Soldier would, I think, give a right inspiration'.[19] This honouring of the civilian dead by agencies of the state gained wide approval. Letters from bereaved relatives to the IWGC, and forwarded to the War Office in support of their campaign to commemorate civilians, suggest that, at least for some, the memorialisation of those killed in air raids served the same purpose as the memorialisation of the dead of the Great War, the recognition of loss perhaps serving to partially alleviate the pain of grief, and a sense that civilian loss of life was of less value to the state than that of the military. For example, a Mr Hawksley of Hull wrote,

> May I express most grateful thanks for the kindliness ... especially as this is the first recognition I have so far received of my terrible loss. It makes one happier to think that we are not merely nonentities, or shall I say, a number that can be rubbed out and forgotten.[20]

This acknowledgement of individual loss was as vital for civilians as it was for combatants; if grief was not to be transformed into anger, resentment or opposition to war, then the state had to demonstrate both its respect for the dead and its appreciation of the sacrifice of the bereaved.

Much of the official recognition of the dead and of the grief of the bereaved took place at a local level. When Bristol, in the southwest of

Grieving: bereavement, grief and the emotional labour of wartime

England, was heavily bombed during the winter of 1940–1941, the city authorities worked to try and ensure that official recognition of the victims of these raids alleviated some of the pain of loss for the bereaved. In 1942, the mayor's office published *Bristol Under Blitz*, a short book designed to act as both a permanent record of 'the ordeal suffered by the people of Bristol at the hands of the Nazis' and a collective memorial to the lives, buildings and communities that were destroyed.[21] As in most other cities hit by air raids, many of the dead were buried in communal graves. However, in Bristol these collective interments took place in the early morning, away from the public eye but attended by relatives, city officials and religious leaders:

> Many raid victims were laid to rest in large communal graves in Greenbank cemetery, where after each major raid during those winter months a funeral service was held at the graveside, usually in the early morning mist. Civilians and civil defence workers who had fallen victim to the Nazi bombings were placed to rest side by side amidst the expressions of a silent sympathy, more expressive than the spoken word. Father, mother, child, brother, sister, in one great family, accompanied by the Lord Mayor and members of the civil defence organisations gathered there on the brink of the collective tomb in one great company of sorrow.[22]

These collective burials were shaped by contesting desires and concerns: a concern about the impact on morale of repeated interments in common graves, leading to the early morning ritual, countered by a desire to express sympathy for the bereaved.

The address given by the bishop of Bristol at one of these services illustrates the desire to mark and recognise both the dead and the loss of the bereaved. Stating that 'those who have lost their lives in these air raids have died upon the battlefield even as the soldier', the bishop equated their deaths with those of combatants, claiming 'those [who] have died have lost their lives for their country'. The shared sacrifice articulated here was accompanied, he reassured the bereaved, by 'the sympathy of your fellow citizens in this hour of sorrow and trouble'.[23] This was echoed in a declaration issued by the city council on 11 December 1940, which directly addressed the bereaved, making a claim for solidarity with them in its statement that 'side by side with you we mourn your loss and share your sorrow'.[24] Similarly, the mayor's office wrote to offer sympathy to the relatives of those killed in the city's air raids, its statement that 'our hearts and minds mingle with yours in sympathetic regard' attempting to both shape a collective response to bereavement and claim an emotional connection with the bereaved.²⁵ The political import of wartime emotions is clear here: the hope that this sympathy would alleviate the potential of grief to destabilise wartime resolution and collective morale was perhaps especially important in Bristol. In its reports for the Ministry of Information on Bristol during 1940–1941, MO found that the people of the city were more depressed, more nervous and more defeatist than the inhabitants of other provincial blitzed cities. Noting that 'the damage in Bristol is considerably less … than in Coventry and Southampton', the report nonetheless concluded that 'there is more depression in Bristol than in any other city studied', with 'quite open defeatism' and 'less laughter and cheerfulness in Bristol than in Southampton or other places'.²⁶ While grief was not the only factor seen to be undermining morale in Bristol, which suffered from cold, damp and overcrowded shelters, repeated heavy raids and bitterly cold weather during the winter of 1940–1941, emotional management was still crucial to morale, and containing the grief of the bereaved, through early morning funerals and official reassurance that their loss was recognised and sympathised with, was critically important.

In other cases, the desire to extend sympathy to the bereaved was outweighed by a perceived need to contain and restrain public expressions of grief. When 173 people died in an accident at Bethnal Green Underground station, still under construction but being used as a shelter, in March 1943, the conditions in which they died were believed to be so potentially detrimental to public morale that the findings of a government enquiry into the accident were largely kept secret.²⁷ The enquiry, led by the London magistrate Laurence Rivers Dunne, found that there were structural issues with the shelter, including a lack of handrail, steep and slippery steps and dim lighting in the stairwell where people were killed and injured, crushed after one woman lost her footing. However, the main cause of the disaster was 'a number of people hurrying forward to enter the shelter at a particularly unfortunate place and time', a conclusion that was interpreted by Home Secretary Herbert Morrison as 'a number of people losing their self control at a particularly unfortunate place and time'.²⁸ This was a subtle but important difference. It was Morrison's reading of events – the disaster was caused by panic and loss of self-control, rather than by a poorly maintained shelter entrance – that led to the decision not to release Dunne's report until 1945, when it was read in its entirety to the House of Commons. Although the disaster was widely covered in newspapers at the time, the *Daily Mail* for example describing how victims were 'crushed and suffocated in a struggling mass', government fears that 'public references to the psychological causes of the disaster would ... be likely to assist the enemy' meant that there was little subsequent public discussion of the accident until the war ended.[29] In combination with an emotional economy that valued stoicism and restraint, the lack of a public dialogue about the disaster led to the silencing of expressions of grief, or anger, in the more private sphere. Survivors and the bereaved recalled many years later that 'their families never spoke about it', while one female doctor who treated the survivors remembered that 'we were sworn to secrecy ... they said we mustn't tell anybody what happened'.[30] A lack of public recognition of the accident, combined with existing emotional cultures of restraint, meant that expressions of loss, in this case perceived as especially damaging to wider morale, remained largely unspoken.

The grief of the relatives of dead combatants, in contrast, could be recognised, but had to be harnessed to the aims of the wartime state. Anger at the means of death, or a belief that the corpse was not being treated with due respect, had to be avoided at all costs. The War Office went to great lengths to try and ensure that the bodies of those killed on the battlefield were buried in identifiable graves, and that the next of kin were reassured that the graves would be cared for. At times this backfired. The IWGC sent a pamphlet to the next of kin of the military dead, designed to provide comfort to the bereaved by explaining that, as in the aftermath of the Great War, they would care for the empire's dead in cemeteries that were 'universally recognised as places of beauty', graves marked by headstones 'symbolising equality of sacrifice'.[31] At times, however, this pamphlet, delivered by the War Office to the next of kin of the dead of both the army and the Royal Air Force (RAF), arrived before any formal notification of death. Isabel Blades, whose brother had been reported missing in October 1941, received one of these pamphlets in 1942. She wrote to the Air Ministry to complain that 'I think your use of the term "bereavement" very misplaced.' She continued,

> The nation is asked to have faith. Well, we have that faith. Faith is our own conviction that Robert will come back to us when this war is over, and I think that it is a very terrible thing to even contemplate the erection of a cross or memorial to any man who, unless you have very definite news to the contrary, may be a prisoner of war... my mother, who is 66, has had about as much as she can stand at the moment.[32]

Lady Ampthill of the Red Cross wrote to Ware in May 1942 to complain that the parents of a man who had been reported killed by German authorities following the St Nazaire Raid, but whose comrades believed was a prisoner of war, had also received the pamphlet, and had been 'terribly upset'. Meanwhile, the Air Commodore RAF HQ Gibraltar wrote to ask the IWGC to cease sending the pamphlet 'about burials and headstones' to the next of kin of RAF personnel who died while serving in Gibraltar, as 'RAF burials here now take place at sea'.[33] When next of kin continued to hope that 'missing' would eventually mean 'prisoner', and when the dead were lost or buried at sea, attempts at comfort and consolation such as this could instead prove destabilising and emotionally devastating.

Attempts were made close to the field of battle to ensure that the treatment of the dead was perceived as appropriate, and that battlefield and unit morale was not undermined by a disorderly grief. As discussed in Chapter 6, chaplains attached to fighting units were expected to oversee the identification and interment of the dead, to ensure that corpses were buried with 'full reverence' and to communicate this to the bereaved.[34] Working in the frontline of battle, military chaplains in northwest Europe after D-Day were reminded that 'those you bury have made the supreme sacrifice' and that when interring Jewish, Hindu and Muslim combatants, care should be taken to follow their burial traditions.[35] Such care was not always possible: one chaplain attached to the 46th Division fighting in northern Italy recorded how 'the men are very critical of the temporary expedients which conditions force upon us at times', such as bodies left unburied for days, and the sites of isolated burials being lost.[36]

Avoiding the disruptive influence of grief on the comrades of the dead was important; Leslie Skinner, chaplain to the Sherwood Rangers, recalled many instances when he had buried the dead in order that their friends be spared the sight of their corpses. Skinner also reflected on the importance, and the difficulty, of writing to relatives. He wrote to the families of the dead and missing of his regiment, reflecting that 'finding time to write these letters ... possibly casting one's mind back to a battle scene of some weeks ago ... was a continuing problem to us all'. He was concerned not to pass on information that might further distress families:

> Hardest of all was the impossibility of giving complete detail. Having dealt with the remains of a body blown to pieces either in the tank or

Grieving: bereavement, grief and the emotional labour of wartime

on a minefield, it was possible truthfully to say that their boy had died instantly without suffering. If they wrote back – as some did – wanting to know how I could be sure that he had not suffered, replying was not easy.

Personal possessions created another problem: when they had been burnt or otherwise injured in battle, their return risked further distress by indicating how their owner might have died. Some families wrote to say that they wished possessions like rings or watches had been buried with the deceased; at other times 'the parcel never reached them. Transport trucks were hit and ships were sunk.'[37] The desire to avoid further distressing the bereaved was based, in large part, on a sympathy or sometimes an empathy with their suffering; but it was also political, driven in part by a need to contain the more disruptive elements of grief.

The bodies that Skinner cared for were buried close to where they fell, the management of their graves attempting to follow the patterns established at the outset of the war discussed in the previous chapter. When servicemen and women died during training or in accidents, their bodies could be claimed for burial by the family. The Air Ministry issued careful instructions for those involved in managing these deaths. Letters of sympathy were always sent, and station commanders were urged to ensure that these were written and signed by the commanding officer of the deceased, as 'these may be of a very personal or sympathetic nature'. Care had to be taken, however, over descriptions of the cause of death:

> Because of the extremely harrowing and harmful effects such details frequently cause a dead person's relatives, all reference to the possibility of death being due to burning or to the body being badly mutilated should be most carefully avoided ... In cases of burning it should be explained, whenever possible, that death took place before the fire occurred, or that, in the case of mutilation, death must have been instantaneous.

Likewise, any reference to an 'error of judgement' had to be avoided in these letters, as 'use of the term may prevent a [next of kin] from showing the letter around and detract very considerably from any satisfaction given by its possession'. As viewing a mutilated body was also likely to cause distress, officers were urged to dissuade relatives from this, suggesting that they explain the only reason for a denial was to spare the feelings of *other* relatives, 'the remains of whose deceased might not be in a fit state for inspection'. When funerals were held by the family, the guidelines stipulated that the coffin, covered by a Union flag, should under no circumstances be transported on an open truck, and that an officer should try to attend. The politics of emotion, and their importance in the case of bereaved relatives, was seen as vitally important. One paragraph in the guidelines made the links between morale and grief explicit:

> It should be borne in mind by those responsible for the conduct of RAF funerals, that the avoidance of giving the relatives of the deceased any cause for grievance is of great importance. Every effort to consider their feelings should be made, remembering that persons subject to the shock of grief are particularly sensitive to small things. This policy has a marked effect on public morale, the maintenance of which necessarily plays a large part in public policy.[38]

In the midst of total war, emotions, together with other vital aspects of the wartime state, had to be carefully managed.

While the state attempted to regulate the expression of grief and the experience of bereavement through careful management of the war's dead, cultural texts provided informal guidance on how grief could be managed and, if appropriate, articulated. A common trope running through many of these wartime texts was that grief could be managed best, would be less painful, if it could be subjugated to a commitment to common war aims, and put to work for the war effort. Magazines were a rich source of information for women preparing themselves for the impact of total war on their private, intimate lives. Leonora Eyles, the agony aunt for the popular magazine *Woman's Own*, advised readers who had lost a husband or children and who subsequently struggled with feelings of disorientation, that this was essentially their own failing, as they needed to look outwards and, rather than dwell on the past, use their grief as a way of reaching out to and supporting others, as if they offered their 'services to those in need, to the poor, you will soon find that you have more friends than you know what to do with, and that everyone wants you'.[39] A story published in the same magazine at the height of the Blitz, 'The Frozen Heart' by Vera Wynn-Griffiths, told of a bereaved mother who recovered from her loss by taking in two orphaned evacuees, whom she and her husband subsequently adopt, both allowing her to recover from her grief through the act of mothering, and helping the wider wartime community.[40] Advice like this was consistent throughout the war years. Writing in the *Daily Mail* in 1943, Anne Temple advised a bereaved wife that she would find comfort

Grieving: bereavement, grief and the emotional labour of wartime

in looking outwards and thus receiving the compassion of the 'warm hearted, loving, tender, sympathetic' people of her community.[41] In each of these pieces, the destabilising and transformative effect of grief on the self is alleviated through the reintegration of the bereaved in to the national community of wartime.

The popular film *Millions Like Us* (1943) told the story of Celia, a reluctant conscript to a munitions factory, who found satisfaction through her integration in to the factory community, itself imagined as a microcosm of a wartime state (largely) unified across divisions of class, nation and region, and through her romantic involvement with Scottish RAF recruit Fred Blake. Soon after they marry, Fred is killed, and a devastated Celia returns to work, finding consolation in the regionally, nationally and socially diverse collective of the wartime factory, the penultimate scene showing her emotional shift from a lonely grief to a unified determination, as the women next to her in the factory canteen encourage her to join in with communal singing.[42] Likewise, when Chief Petty Officer Hardy receives the news of the death of his wife and mother in the Plymouth Blitz in the film *In Which We Serve* (1942), his anguish is acknowledged, but is quickly assuaged by his participation in the communal life of HMS *Torrin*.[43] In these texts, the isolation of grief was eased by the community of the wartime nation. If, as Langhamer has argued, love offered 'an antidote to the brutality of war, acting as social cement', then grief, its wartime companion, had to be carefully managed, with stoicism and restraint acting to contain and moderate its disruptive potential, and integration into the collective of wartime serving as an antidote to loss.[44]

Novels too provided their readers with narratives in which the bereaved sublimated their anguish in both their own commitment to the war effort and in recognition that this very commitment meant that the loved one's death had not been in vain. In Eileen Marsh's 1942 novel, *We Lived in London*, 'Ma', the working-class matriarch at the heart of the novel, redirects her grief at the loss in air raids of her daughter Irene, daughter-in-law and grandchildren towards helping her surviving daughter-in-law with her new baby.[45] Edith Pargeter's 1942 novel, *She Goes to War*, tells the story of Caroline Saxon, a gossip columnist who finds the fulfilment missing from her previous career when she joins the Women's Royal Naval Service (WRNS). Written in epistolary form to an older man, wounded in the Great War, Pargeter's novel narrates Saxon's engagement to Tom Lyddon, an idealistic soldier who had previously fought in Spain. *She Goes to War* is more critical of the wartime state than many other texts, particularly of the ways that inequalities of social class were translated into inequalities of shelter provision, noting that while 'an influential family ... had a beautiful deep shelter made under their house ... the people in little houses along the side streets' had to make do with surface, Anderson or Morrison shelters. When Tom is killed in the Battle of Crete, her response is stoical; although she is already a member of the wartime community through her membership of the WRNS, she commits herself to the socialist principles for which he fought and died:

> It will not be over when we march through Berlin. It ends only when we have cut away from our own national body all the inequalities and exploitations ... that enfeeble it now ... they have called me to war. Well, let them be satisfied. I am at war.[46]

The transformative qualities of both love and grief are put to work here in an explicitly socialist vision of the people's war; a war fought not in defence of the status quo, but for a new, postwar, society. Grief here is disruptive, but of the status quo, not of the individual.

Grief was also written as transformative in two films that were released shortly after the war's end, a period both of reconstruction and relief, but also one that continued to demand stoicism as Britain struggled with the economic aftermath of war and individuals came to recognise that the 'missing' would, all too often, never return. In *The Way to the Stars*, released in 1945 and based on Terence Rattigan's 1941 play *Flarepath*, grief is acknowledged yet contained, restrained by the over-arching narrative of willing sacrifice in much the same way as the letters to bereaved mothers with which this chapter opened. Telling the story of an air force base and its nearby village over a number of years, the narrative at the heart of the film is the relationship between the hotel manager Toddy; her husband, RAF Squadron Leader David Archdale; his best friend Peter, also a pilot; and the US Army Air Forces pilot Johnny Hollis. Both Peter and Johnny die selfless deaths, Peter on a mission over France and Johnny when he deliberately crashes his plane rather than bailing out and risking it crashing into the village when a landing goes wrong.[47] The poem 'For Johnny', written by John Pudney in 1941, is used multiple times in the film, signifying both the willingness of those who die in war to give their lives, and the resultant denial of the grief of the bereaved. In the film the poem is written by David, and read by Toddy and Peter after his death; it ends with

Grieving: bereavement, grief and the emotional labour of wartime

Toddy looking at the night sky while bombers fly overhead and a voiceover reads,

> Do not despair
> For Johnny-head-in-air
> He sleeps as sound
> As Johnny underground
>
> Fetch out no shroud
> For Johnny-in-the-clouds
> And keep your tears
> For him in after years
>
> Better by far
> For Johnny-the-bright-star
> To keep your head
> And see his children fed[48]

A postponement of grief is urged in this poem, together with a gendered stoicism. Bereaved wives and mothers, it suggests, could best memorialise their husbands by caring for their children.

The Powell and Pressburger fantasy *A Matter of Life and Death*, released in 1946, and premiered at the Royal Command Performance that year, begins with the story of Squadron Leader Peter Carter, played by David Niven. As Carter pilots his damaged Lancaster bomber over the Channel, the crew having bailed out, he speaks to June, an American radio operator, reciting the poetry of Andrew Marvell. As June listens to him prepare for a selfless death the two fall in love. Carter jumps from the plane without a parachute but miraculously cheats death and is washed up on a beach, alive, where he meets June. Love, it seems, has defeated death, and grief is not contained, but denied. For the many who had lived for years with the slight hope encompassed in the term 'missing', this story of miraculous survival must have been seductive. Women like the twenty-six-year-old neighbour of an MO observer, whose immediate response to a telegram stating that her husband, a member of a bomber squadron, was missing, was to deny the possibility of death because 'he was home only last Wednesday', must have wished for such a possibility.[49] Put on trial by 'the immortals' for escaping death, Peter is spared when June steps forward to take his place, offering to selflessly give her life so that he can carry on living. Dr Reeves, Peter's defending lawyer, triumphantly declares that 'nothing is stronger than the law in the universe, but on earth, nothing is stronger than love'.⁵⁰ Selfless love, and a willingness to sacrifice oneself for the loved one, once again, overcomes death. At the war's end, many must have wished fervently that love *could* conquer death.

When death was confirmed, the bereaved were urged to face it stoically, and even cheerfully, remembering that they were not alone in their loss. While most of the cultural texts that policed grief focused on the bereaved female figure, women being long imagined as less stoical, and more volubly emotional than men, some representations of bereaved men also circulated. Like Chief Petty Officer Hardy of *In Which We Serve*, these men are able to place the needs of the wartime community above their own anguish. The response of 'Dad' in the novel *We Lived in London*, remarking after hearing that his daughter-in-law and grandchildren had been killed in the Blitz that 'there's more households wiped out than that one' before going on duty as an air raid warden, was exemplary in its placing of the common good above individual grief.⁵¹ When the couple's daughter Irene is killed in the large air raid on the city of London in December 1940, her boyfriend, who had been falsely claiming medical leave from the army, channels his grief in a highly gendered manner, explaining his return to battle by declaring that

> Each Jerry I kill I'll say Ireen, and the last thing he'll hear will be her name ... I'll take no prisoners, and I'll stick 'em in the guts so they'll die slow. And they'll go to hell hearing her name.⁵²

The family in the short story 'Pa was Always Whistling', published in *Woman's Own* just after the war's end in November 1945, did not initially manage to respond to the death of their son in Asia with positivity: 'the first few days we were so stunned and grieved over Jamie we went around in a daze'. The grief of the family was represented through the father, usually cheerful, who stops whistling until the family receive a letter from Jamie's nurse, who tells them that he died knowing his father's optimism would sustain the family. After reading this, he starts to whistle again.⁵³ Peter, the friend and comrade of David Archdale in *The Way to the Stars*, also amends his first response to David's death, which had been to break off his romance with Iris for fear of bereaving her, proposing to her instead in a move that embraced both the statistical chances of death for those in Bomber Command, and the need to nonetheless continue with living.⁵⁴ Bereaved men in these texts embodied and articulated the 'qualities of emotional restraint and understatement which supposedly constituted the British national character'.⁵⁵

Grieving: bereavement, grief and the emotional labour of wartime

These qualities, in the cultural representations of wartime, were represented as innate to masculinity, crossing the boundaries of social class and military and civilian status.

Women were understood as being less reliably restrained in their response to bereavement.[56] While men, particularly of the upper and middle classes, had long been expected to demonstrate stoicism, the codes of emotional behaviour identified with late Victorian and Edwardian masculinity were urged upon women and the working class in the first decades of the twentieth century. As women entered into full citizenship they were expected to emulate the emotional restraint associated with men, such restraint being connected with reason and resolve. Characters as diverse as the middle-class and middle-aged Toddy in *The Way to the Stars*, the young Celia in *Millions Like Us* and the working-class matriarch 'Ma' of *We Lived in London* all manage to successfully contain the disruptive potential of grief through a combination of dedication to the war effort, absorption into the wartime community and a desire not to 'let down' the sacrifice of others by allowing their sorrow to overcome them. In June 1940, at the height of the invasion fear that followed the fall of France, the weekly magazine *Woman* suggested that women might be particularly well placed to support one another in their anxiety and grief. In response to a letter from a reader asking what she should say to a neighbour who had lost her son, but was nonetheless 'very brave, carrying on with her war work', the magazine's agony aunt stated,

> The magnitude of the sacrifice which our men are making on the battlefront will stiffen the resolution of their women at home. Every woman will ask herself 'Am I taking my share in the war effort?'[57]

While the war at this point demanded physical labour and potential physical sacrifice from men, women were expected to undertake emotional labour, supporting one another and bearing their grief bravely as they continued with their daily lives. This selfless response to grief is epitomised by the character of Ellen in Arnold Wareing's short story 'Next of Kin'. Ellen works for the Casualty Branch of the War Office, receiving details of deaths and sending telegrams to the next of kin. One afternoon she discovers that the love of her life, married to her 'more vivacious' friend Sylvia, has been killed. Her response is exemplary:

> She glanced quickly aside to see if any of the other girls had noticed her distress … no one had noticed … she could be hurt, but keep her hurt to

herself. She was self-controlled now. A deep grief had come to her but she was not weeping.

Ellen decides, selflessly, to deliver the news to his wife in person, and is rewarded by discovering that the dead man had always loved her best of all.[58] In the emotional economy of wartime, difficult and demanding emotional labour not only had to be undertaken, it had to look like no effort at all.

One way of reading sources such as these is to consider their historical contingency: did the prevalence of texts urging emotional restraint indicate a lack thereof in everyday life? Were stories like 'Next of Kin' an indication not of a widely shared emotional economy of self-control and selflessness but of an anxiety about a perceived lack of fortitude among the citizens of wartime Britain? Had the emergence of the 'psychological subject' focused on the interior self, on feelings and emotions, created an emotional economy which enabled the successful recognition and hence management of disruptive emotions, or conversely brought into being a new type of citizen whose self-interest and focus on the interior life was antithetical to the selflessness demanded by wartime?[59] As Langhamer has argued, Second World War Britain was a key moment for the reshaping of the relationship between concepts of duty and self-fulfilment.[60] The wartime citizen was motivated not simply by patriotism, but often by a desire for a better, more rewarding life, at both the individual and the national level. By turning to personal or observational accounts of grief, we can begin to consider the ways in which people negotiated with the emotional experts advising restraint, and the cultural texts representing this as an ideal response to wartime bereavement.

The bereaved

The stoicism and restraint attributed to many fictional figures was emulated in acts of self-policing by many of the wartime bereaved. Taught to be self-reflective, and to manage their emotions, the people of wartime Britain lived within and negotiated with an emotional economy that valued the careful management of grief. For some of the bereaved the cultural scripts, and the advice on self-management, restraint and self-reflexivity that circulated, provided a model that they could draw on; for others, the experience and communication of grief was less straightforward.

Grieving: bereavement, grief and the emotional labour of wartime

The value attributed to stoicism within the emotional economy of wartime shaped the experience of loss, providing both a language for its articulation, and a way of understanding and managing the disruptive emotion of grief. One MO diarist, writing in August 1942, noted the response of her friend to the news that her son was missing in Libya: 'I thought she would be upset badly, but found that ... she could yet say "and of course we must take it as others have had to if the news is bad."'[61] When the dead and the missing had been members of a wartime community, particularly a military unit, the bereaved often sought to draw comfort from contact with other members of that community, both comrades and friends of the dead, and from their relatives. Indeed such groups, with their particular affective bonds, based on shared experience and forms of emotional expression, might be understood as – in Barbara Rosenwein's much deployed term – 'emotional communities', claims to membership of which could provide a measure of consolation for the bereaved.[62] Squadron Leader Reverend G. H. Martin, who was chaplain to a Pathfinder squadron based at Oakington, just outside Cambridge, wrote to the next of kin of those squadron members who were posted as missing or killed in action. Many of those who wrote to Martin asked for details of the next of kin of the airplane's crew, often also posted as lost or missing. A mother wrote from Carlisle to ask for the addresses of those who were lost with her son, and the wife of a missing man wrote from Sheffield that 'whatever may have happened, they will have given a good account of themselves, as I know from my husband that they were all experienced, and always have had the greatest faith in one another'.[63] These bereaved understood the often close-knit bomber crews to be emotional communities, and the probability that all members of the crew shared the same destiny perhaps provided them with some measure of consolation, and a reminder that they were not alone in their anxiety and grief, as their loved ones were not alone in their fate.

Others also demonstrated emotional restraint when faced with the sudden losses that were so typical of wartime. The architectural author A. S. G. Butler chronicled his work surveying Blitz-damaged buildings in London in the book *Recording Ruin*, published in 1942. Butler described his feelings under bombardment in physical terms: 'I've got worms in my head with all the noise and my legs won't quite walk', setting this within the wider context of emotional reticence in his comment that wearing Civil Defence badges of rank was 'the same as displaying emotion, and is therefore not done'. In April 1941, Butler was visiting a block of mansion flats in Chelsea that had been hit, when he met a 'nicely dressed lady' who

> called to me and asked if I had been into numbers 58 or 59 … number 58 was hers but she had lent it to her niece who was there when it happened – she was afraid – or with friends in the flat below. Did I think there was any hope? So I sat down beside her on the bit of stonework and looking up at the piled up rocks of concrete, steel girders, broken doors and baths all upside-down I said 'no my dear' and she said 'thank you'. And that was all.[64]

Of course, the inhabitant of a Chelsea mansion block might be expected, much like her fictional counterpart Mrs Miniver, to carefully manage the public expression of her emotions, but attempts at self-restraint like this were recorded by a range of people, in multiple wartime spaces.[65] In letters written to his wife, James Driscoll, a working-class man from east London who was a registered conscientious objector serving in Normandy with the Royal Army Medical Corps, recorded his response to the news that his brother's plane had been lost near Malta. The brothers had been close, sharing a bed until the author's marriage, and he described his loss as 'an awful helpless agony'. Driscoll was careful to hide his grief from those around him, recounting how, when he received the news, he 'had to go and hide myself and sob', reminding himself that 'I must pull myself out of it for there is work to be done'.[66] Both self-reflective, noting and explaining his grief, and self-managing in his attempts to contain his potentially disruptive emotions, Driscoll's letters demonstrate how the emotional economy of wartime Britain could enable each of those suffering the disruptions of bereavement to continue to function as a useful member of the wartime community.

The author Naomi Mitchison, living in Carradale in Kintyre, Scotland, and writing for MO, provided the organisation with a detailed observation of the impact and management of grief, and the ways in which its expression was shaped by social class, gender, religious belief and local custom, when a neighbour's son was killed during the Clydeside Blitz in March 1941. The raids on Clydeside, which initially felt very distant to those in Carradale, who first learnt of their severity when newspapers failed to arrive, killed many hundreds on the nights of 13 and 14 March, including Jim, the seventeen-year-old son of her friends and neighbours on Kintyre, Peter and Ellen McKinven. Mitchison, who had her own experiences of parental loss, recorded the impact of Jim's death on the wider community as well as on his parents, describing a committee meeting where 'everyone seemed pretty gloomy' and visiting friends who 'took me in, weeping'.[67] Jim's family travelled to Glasgow to find his body, helping with the difficult job of digging through the rubble to try and retrieve it. As 'laird', Mitchison felt it was her duty to support the family, so she undertook the journey to Glasgow on 19 March, six days after the first raid. Usually writing detailed daily entries in her diary, she begins her entry for 19–21 March 'These days have been extremely moving, and I find it hard to write about them; it was impossible to do so at the time.' Mitchison recorded both the uncertainty that beset families when bodies were unaccounted for after air raids, the hard physical labour sometimes undertaken in searching and the ways in which stress and grief were felt in the body as well as the mind. Ellen, the missing boy's mother, was 'collapsed, and drinking some medicine with a lot of bromide in it, which was having no good effect on her stomach'. Mitchison drew on her own experiences of maternal grief, telling her 'what I have suffered myself in similar ways and how I have dealt with it; to give her a sense of moral security and strength'.[68] When Peter returned from digging for his son's body, she offered the comforts of religious and secular belief, reassuring him that he and his son would be together after death, and that Jim had been happy in Glasgow. In the intimate space of a Glasgow family home (belonging to close relatives of the parents), an emotional community of suffering and solace was created; Mitchison mobilised her own experience of grief in an attempt to offer comfort to Ellen, and her position as leader in the local community to offer reassurance and certainty to the father. Within the home, as much as in the public sphere, expressions of grief were shaped by social class and gender.

When Jim's body was found Ellen collapsed, screaming that 'Jim had laid in pain all these days'. Again, Mitchison sought to reassure her, 'explaining that he would be excited and full of a sense of adventure and then there would be a bang like an explosion of light inside his eyes, and then he would be free of pain and free of the body, able to be in the hills that he loved again, and with her, part of the life of the eager young Highlander'.[69] The comforts offered by Christianity, so often articulated in the Great War, and visible again in many of the letters from the families of missing and dead airmen to the Reverend G. H. Martin, are less evident here. Mitchison's vision of a life after death resurrected the dead son in the land of his birth, rather than a distant heaven. Nonetheless, the bereaved family wanted to keep the traditional burial rituals, as when Mitchison suggested cremation, they refused, Ellen stating that 'she wanted to lie by him herself when her time came'.[70] Mitchison and the family accompanied Jim's coffin on the boat back to Kintyre, where 'Peter and Ellen adjured one another to be brave'. In an echo of the claims to consolation through integration in the wartime community found in many cultural texts, Mitchison suggested to the bereaved couple that they sell their tea room on Kintyre and run a canteen in a blitzed town, a suggestion she claims they agreed to eagerly.

Following local custom in Kintyre, Ellen did not attend the funeral, which was a male-only ceremony. The return to the Highlands continued the mixture of spiritual belief with formal religious practice, and of restraint with local, gendered traditions around the expression of grief. Driving to the village with Mitchison, Ellen found some consolation in stoicism, asking 'I am being brave aren't I? This is how Jim would have wanted me to be?' While the funeral went on elsewhere, they drove past the hills of Arran and 'she said, "he's there, isn't he"', repeating Mitchison's earlier vision of Jim's presence after death in the landscape of his home. However, when she returned home the self-control that she had tried so hard to maintain with Mitchison broke down, as

> A wailing crowd of sisters in mourning burst into the passage and all over her. She began to cry; they were all crying … They all began to cry over me too … saying the most frightful things about poor wee Jim being too good for this world, he's happier where he is, all the personal things which I'd managed to get her away from in my concept of immortality … and Ellen threw back her head and keened and howled and began calling for her wee boy (original emphasis).

This display of Highland mourning dismayed Mitchison, who came from the wealthy, liberal Haldane family of Edinburgh, and she sought to 'get Ellen steady before Peter came back' from the funeral. The outpouring of grief that had so perturbed Mitchison was highly gendered, a local version of the female 'labour of loss' identified by Damousi.[71] On his return from the funeral, Peter 'came straight to me and said "I nearly broke down but not quite. I was brave."'[72] Mitchison's position as laird, and her social class, overrode the gendered conventions of grief on Kintyre, and her diaries express an aversion to its (female) vocal expression, and a preference for restraint and stoicism. What they do not record is the extent to which Ellen and Peter found comfort in their local rituals, or in the less expressive emotional economy of the wider nation that so valued self-control. Moving between the intimate and the public, between gendered traditions of Highland mourning and the realities of death on blitzed Clydeside, they attempted to fit their expression of emotion to the different contexts in which they found themselves.

However, although female grief was both more visible and more policed than male grief, many men also struggled to articulate their personal loss in a manner that was valued within the dominant emotional economy. In *Recording Ruin*, Butler recounted visiting a friend, a Mr Fleming, one evening, only to discover that his wife had been killed and his daughter seriously injured in a raid the previous week.[73] Fleming was struggling to continue with his usual routine, trying to cook his evening meal, but unable to find the kitchen essentials that his wife would have dealt with. The absence of his wife and daughter are thus felt through Fleming's inability to carry out his daily routine – burning bacon, unable to locate the tea caddy – but also through these very attempts to 'carry on'. Eventually the two men sat down to talk, and Fleming's composure, such as it was, finally broke:

> Then he stopped and I saw he was looking at an old photo of his wife which was hanging by the fire. He gave a short gasp and sat quite still, just staring in the fading light.[74]

Fleming's emotional struggle, his attempt to come to terms with the death of his wife and injury of his daughter, come to the fore in this description, in the 'short gasp' and ensuing silence, demonstrating how absence of expression, and silence, can effectively communicate an emotion, even when the expression of feeling is circumscribed by the dominant emotional economy. Attempts to 'carry on' in the face of overwhelming loss could entail as much emotional labour for men as for women, the proscription of expressive grief acting to shape the response to bereavement of both genders in the realm of personal, intimate relationships as well as in the more public sphere.

For some, the emotional communities to which they belonged acted to shape the ways that they articulated grief. Men in the armed forces were members of particular emotional communities, ones that, while they often differed from one another in terms of regimental traditions and cultures, shared an emotional style that valued the restraint, good humour and selflessness that Sonya Rose has associated with the 'temperate male' of the wartime nation.[75] Such men, however, came from a range of other emotional communities – families, the workplace, schoolroom or university – and they had to negotiate between the emotional demands and styles of these different communities. Writing was a means by which many men attempted to do this, both keeping diaries that recorded their experiences of participation in warfare, and writing letters to family and friends at home. Walter Robson, fighting his way up through Italy in 1944, wrote regularly to his wife at home in Britain. In July, he wrote to tell her of the death of a mutual friend:

> This won't be a very cheerful letter. Percy Ross was killed yesterday ... I've been trying to write to Hilda but I can't poor kid. I keep thinking about her. Percy didn't know much about it. There wasn't a sound. A cloud of dust, a choking smell and a ringing in my ears. I expected to see them scramble clear but there was young Percy, and young Tony Konstantinou, the Cypriot, and two others lying still on one side, two more dead on the other ... it was as bad as [Monte] Cassino.[76]

For Robson, the letter acted as a link between his home life and his military life, providing space for a personal reflection on wartime loss for which there was rarely time on active service. Writing of his service in northwest Europe following D-Day, Stanley Whitehouse recalled that 'a platoon is like a large family', yet expressive grief for members of this 'family' could be disruptive of group cohesion, acting to remind others of their own, possible, fate.[77] Death could be unsettling, both for the individual reminded of his own mortality, but also for group morale and cohesion. Writing in 1944 of his experiences of fighting in France in 1940, Peter Hadley affected a nonchalance and humour very much in tune with the emotional style of Rose's 'temperate masculinity'. When his platoon came under fire however, and members were killed, this tone faltered, as he described one man's serious injuries and a 'dusty and unrecognisable figure whose face already had the pallor of death'.[78] The emotional style of the militarised man could be hard to maintain in the face of death, grief, and fear.[79] For others, like the novelist George MacDonald Fraser, recollecting the deaths of two members of his unit in Burma, the restraint and stoicism expected of the militarised man provided a useful coping mechanism:

> There was no outward show of sorrow, no reminiscences or eulogies, no Hollywood heart-searchings or phoney philosophy ... It was not callousness or indifference or lack of feeling for two comrades who had been alive that morning and who were now just names for the war memorial: it was just that there was nothing to be said ... Better and healthier to forget about it, and look to tomorrow.[80]

Grieving: bereavement, grief and the emotional labour of wartime

For some of these men, however, grief was simply delayed, not denied.[81]

Military groups like Hadley's platoon and MacDonald Fraser's unit were 'imagined' families, brought together as a cohesive unit that could withstand the multiple demands of warfare. Domestic families too were expected to support one another through the experience of bereavement, a support that was often offered via the medium of letters that bridged the separations of wartime. When the SS *City of Benares* was torpedoed taking child evacuees to Canada in September 1940, nine-year-old Beryl Myatt of Hillingdon in Middlesex was one of the seventy-seven child victims.[82] News of the sinking reached the British press on 23 September, shortly after Beryl's parents, Emma (Emmie) and Tom Myatt, had written to Beryl and the relatives who would be caring for her in Canada, expecting that she had 'enjoyed your voyage on the boat across the wide Atlantic ocean, and your long journey on the train to Winnipeg', ending the letter with kisses that lined the bottom of the page.[83] Subsequent letters from friends and family, written to Emmie and Tom after the fate of the ship became known, provide a window on to the means by which one family attempted to support one another through bereavement, across a significant geographical distance. While many of the children who died came from London and Middlesex, travelling as part of an evacuee group organised by the Children's Overseas Reception Board, Emmie's extended family lived in Newcastle-under-Lyme and Stoke-on-Trent in Staffordshire, and so, in addition to the potential empathy of other bereaved families nearby, Emmie and Tom received the support of their family by letter. The formalities of a consolatory language shaped much of what was written. Emmie's parents' first letter, written on 23 September, began 'we do tender to you both our deepest heartfelt sympathy in your sad bereavement', and the following month an aunt wrote 'our thoughts are with you'. A Mrs Isaac wrote on 24 September that she 'could find no words that would express my feelings for you both in your great loss and sorrow', going on to advise them 'not to grieve too much for her' but to 'think of her happy days' as 'it will lighten your burden'. Such formal, restrained language appears to have often been used to open letters, enabling the authors to express difficult and complex emotions in a manner that was widely recognised, and valued in the emotional economy of wartime Britain.

The consolations of religious belief, and belief in an afterlife, were also widely expressed in these letters. At times, this sat comfortably within the established rituals and beliefs of the Christian church. An aunt and uncle wrote to reassure them that Beryl was 'safe in the arms of Jesus', while Emmie's parents organised a memorial service for Beryl in their local church. Mrs General Carpenter of the Salvation Army wrote to express her hope that 'our loving Lord and saviour ... may also be with you and bless you in your sore bereavement'. However, as seen in Mitchison's account of grief in the Scottish Highlands, the concept of life after death was not confined to the traditional Christian heaven. Another relative, 'Dollie', described her visit to a spiritualist who told her that Beryl was now called Rosemary (for remembrance), and had a 'wreath of forget-me-nots around her hair', while Emmie's sister Doreen wrote that 'I thought I saw her with father, she was leaning against him. There was a beautiful light behind them. Remember Dad loved her and the ways he talked about her.' At times the anguish of loss broke through the formalities of consolation and the reassurances of eternal life: a letter from Emmie's mother which began by urging her to 'bear up' and remember that some parents had lost several children ended with the cry 'Emmie she was my baby.' This empathetic connection with the bereaved parents can be seen as an attempt to share their grief, and thus to alleviate the isolation and disorientation that can accompany it; a reassurance that the bereaved are not alone.

Without a body to bury, and a graveside to visit, Beryl's parents had to look elsewhere in their attempts to materially mark her death and to ensure that she was remembered. They donated 10s. to a children's home in memory of Beryl in 1940, and again on the anniversary of her death in 1941. Their request that the Children's Overseas Reception Board arrange for a wreath to be dropped into the ocean at the spot where the SS *City of Benares* sank was less successful, a letter explaining that this could not be arranged as 'ships rarely follow the same path' suggested that instead 'you will have to try and think of the whole sea as poor little Beryl's grave'. Included in the file of letters and newspaper clippings donated to the Imperial War Museum are photos of Beryl, her school certificates, her ration book, her birthday cards and her Mickey Mouse Club Card from the Hillingdon Odeon. These traces of a life cut short at nine years old, and the donation of these traces to a public archive speak to us of both a parental desire to keep the material reminders of a lost child, and of a desire to ensure that she was remembered in the public, as much as the private, sphere.[84]

Some of the wartime bereaved kept diaries, where they reflected on their loss, and on others' responses to this loss. As discussed in Chapter 2, diary writing had grown in popularity in the interwar years, providing one of the sites in which individuals could work on the self. Writing

Grieving: bereavement, grief and the emotional labour of wartime

a wartime diary could be one aspect of the emotional labour that loss and grief entailed; a means of examining and managing feeling, and of beginning to compose the ways these feelings would be articulated. The language in which the grief and shock of sudden death was recorded in diaries was shaped by a wide variety of factors. For example, men in the military, when they were able to keep diaries, could use these spaces to express their shock at the death of a friend and comrade, but also to reflect on what such a death might mean for them. In the midst of the fighting at Monte Cassino in 1944, Ron Goldstein recorded the death of a man in his unit, killed by a mortar blast: 'when the news filtered back to us we were all shocked … it worried us deeply with its implication that if Geoff could be killed, so could we'.[85] At other times, the ideal of reticence and understatement shaped diary entries as much as more public utterances. Four days after arriving in France in August 1944, Doug Mayman's tank regiment suffered its first fatalities. With an understatement that pervades much of the writing in his combat diaries, he wrote 'not a very pleasant first day in action. I wonder whose turn it will be next?'[86] Leslie Skinner's diary shows how he had to control his feelings while serving as chaplain to the Sherwood Rangers in northwest Europe. The poet Keith Douglas, a member of the regiment, was killed soon after the Normandy landings, on 9 June 1944, and Skinner buried him, describing in his diary how 'being quite alone and reading the brief Order of Service over the grave affected me deeply'. By January 1945 the regiment had crossed the border from the Netherlands to northwest Germany, and Skinner held a regimental memorial service. He stated that 'we were all painfully aware how many of our friends had gone since the last service, and equally aware that the next list might include any of us'. Such services were a brief moment of reflection and remembrance for men in battle, as Skinner wrote, 'I did not normally speak on such a theme as death, and the Christian belief in life after death.'[87] For some militarised men, diaries were a small space in which they could record feelings which, publicly expressed, could undermine morale. For others, the carefully patrolled parameters of emotional expression shaped their most private responses to death. As the following chapter will show, military memoirs, written long after the immediacy of battle, were sometimes more likely than diaries written in the midst of fighting to invite reflections on death and grief.

Diaries could provide a space for reflections on grief that the author felt they had to contain elsewhere. Audrey Deacon was a member of the WRNS when her husband, Terry, died in hospital after an accident in training, on 5 June 1944, one day before the D-Day landings. In the immediate aftermath of his death, she wrote of her feelings of shock and loss:

> Everybody has been very kind, but it doesn't help. I just don't know how to start again ... absolutely everything was bound up with him.

A combination of the sense of isolation that can be a part of grief, and the knowledge that the D-Day landings had begun meant that Audrey returned to work on the evening of 6 June, writing in her diary that 'I feel I must go back on duty this evening'. Following the advice found in cultural scripts, Audrey sought some relief through her work, commenting that 'it settles my problem ... by giving me an excuse not to face it'. She turned down the leave that was offered as 'I wouldn't know what to do with it', but work did not offer the distraction that she hoped: by 8 June, her diary recorded that 'I can't remember things very well, I have very little physical energy' and on 11 June, a national day of prayer, she described feeling 'cut off from everything during the past few days'. Audrey continued working but confided in her diary on 19 July that 'I have been very depressed and bored with things in general', and over a year later, on 25 September 1945, she concluded 'for 15 months I have lived absolutely without any aim of purpose ... effectively I have just not existed'. Despite returning to work almost immediately, Audrey found little consolation in her membership of the wartime community, neither in her role as a member of the WRNS nor in the 'letters from a good many people' that she received.[88] The silences in this diary, the record of attempts to suppress or avoid grieving, and the depression and isolation that accompanied this, speak powerfully of the private struggles of many to manage their grief.

In contrast Nella Last's diary, written for MO, was eloquent in its depiction of the emotional impact of wartime death, acting, in William Reddy's phrase, as an emotional refuge in which Last could express the feelings that remained largely unvoiced in her domestic and social life.[89] When Last heard of the death of a young neighbour in an air raid, she wrote that 'I'm not a fainting woman, but I felt for one second that I'd melt and pour out of my clothes', illustrating the physical impact of shock and grief. This internal, individual response though is balanced by her observation that the death of this young woman shows that 'we are all, indeed, in the fighting line'. When a close friend of her son was killed, Last described the difficulty of comforting her child, as 'words are only hollow and brittle things'. Last was a mother of two sons, one of whom was serving in the army, and her diary expresses the anxiety that she shared with other parents, and the empathy she felt towards those bereaved: 'I think of the millions of bereaved parents and wives, and my heart ticks with the futility, the waste'. Writing for MO allowed Last to express her concern with the losses of war, and the pain that this caused to individuals and families across national borders, declaring angrily that 'not all this big talk of next year and the next will stop our lads dying uselessly'. While Last worked for the war effort, as an active volunteer in her local Woman's Voluntary Service and at a Red Cross shop, her diary narrates the gap between the public and the private, between the strategy and politics of war, and its impact on individual lives.[90]

Storm Jameson's *The Journal of Mary Hervey Russell*, presented as a fictitious journal, in fact drew on much of Jameson's own diary, recounting her thoughts and experiences between 1938 and 1943, when Jameson's younger sister Dorothy was killed in an air raid.[91] Intimate and impressionistic, the *Journal* captures the shock of sudden death, and the denial that Elizabeth Kübler Ross famously identified as the first stage of grief.[92] The entry for 24 February 1943, recording Dorothy's death, begins with a refusal: 'It is not true that, two weeks ago, an air raid killed my young sister ... it is not true that she is dead.'[93] Guilt, which the sociologist Tony Walter has argued is often associated with the death of a sibling, followed: 'Why, God, take one so filled with the future? You could have taken me and that column of the past that I am becoming.'[94] Dorothy died while working as a volunteer in a Reading canteen, but her death as an active member of the nation at war offered Jameson little consolation. Instead, it is the destructive nature of grief and her disjointed emotional response to her sister's death that is chronicled here, Jameson noting that 'I have to remind myself of what has happened. There is not a nerve in my body that consents to it.'[95] Like Deacon and Last, Jameson expressed her grief in the pages of her journal, describing its disorientating effects in her reflection that 'I have sometimes wondered whether I am, as they say, all there. Am I?'[96] The pages of Jameson's journal provided a space for her to record the confusion, guilt and isolation that accompanied bereavement, feelings that had little space in the public culture of wartime.

Conclusion

Wartime grief was rigorously policed. This policing was informed in part by the pre-existing shift in the emotional economy of Britain, which saw stoicism and reticence valorised above an emotional expressiveness, but also by the need to maintain morale, to not undermine the collective effort and sacrifice that the war demanded. Cultural texts worked hard to delimit both the spaces within which grief could be articulated, seen and heard, and the ways that this grief could be expressed. While the wartime experience of bereavement was acknowledged, visible in a wide range of texts, its expression was contained within a fairly narrow range of responses. The bereaved could communicate their grief, but in order for this most unruly of emotions not to damage morale, it had to be accompanied by other expressions of feeling. These could include pride in the dead, a commitment to the aims for which they died, a denunciation of the enemy as barbarous and a valorisation of the wartime collective. A culture of emotional restraint shaped the representation of grief in wartime texts, containing it within parameters that could be useful in the ongoing work of maintaining wartime morale.

Gender, social class, religious belief and prevailing local custom also acted to shape and contain expressions of grief in wartime Britain. Women in particular were counselled to exercise self-restraint, while an emphasis in numerous cultural texts on the stoicism demonstrated by working-class communities under bombardment undoubtedly helped to control the expression of emotions in a social group long seen, like women, as more likely than the middle class, and men, to express their feelings in an uncontrolled manner. As Naomi Mitchison's diary shows, local custom, and religious belief, were also powerful determinants of the ways that the bereaved could, or could not, give voice to their experiences. Members of military units worked hard to put their shock or grief at the loss of comrades and friends to one side, conscious that grief could both effect their own actions, and also disrupt and undermine the work of the collective. The labour of loss was thus shaped by collective social identities within the nation-state, as well as by the wartime demands of this state.

The bereaved also policed themselves, trying to manage the ways they expressed their grief in public spaces. Drawing on the culture of emotional self-management that developed between the wars, the bereaved of wartime Britain often worked hard to ensure that the most destructive elements of grief were hidden, recorded in diary entries perhaps, or communicated to those to whom they were closest, but largely invisible to others. While private spaces of expression, like diaries, sometimes acted as an emotional refuge in which the bereaved could express their sense of loss and dislocation, at other times they followed the pattern of emotional restraint seen in the public sphere. Again and again, however, the disruptive nature of grief becomes visible: in the tears of James Driscoll and the screams of Ellen McKinven, in the 'short gasp' of Mr Fleming and in the nervous rebellion of Storm Jameson. These records of wartime grief remind us that emotions are experienced, felt within and expressed through the body as well as through language. While bodies were killed and destroyed in war, bodies also responded to the shock of death and to subsequent grief. The people of Second World War Britain experienced grief within an emotional economy that valued restraint and stoicism, and while this helped some to manage their grief, the physical, written and verbal expressions of grief recorded by others tell us of the multiple ways in which the disruptive experience of bereavement could threaten both self-composure, and the composure of the national body in wartime.

Notes

1. 'An airman's letter', the *Times*, 18 June 1940, p. 7.
2. 'Per Ardua ad Astra', the *Times*, 18 June 1940, p. 7.
3. S. Crook, The Powell and Pressburger Pages, www.powell-pressburger.org/Reviews/41_Airmans/Letter2.html (accessed 14 April 2017).
4. 'Another airman's letter', the *Times*, 9 December 1941, p. 7.
5. Morale is notoriously difficult to define. For thoughtful discussions of morale in the context of twentieth-century Britain, see B. Beaven and J. Griffiths, 'The blitz, civilian morale and the city: mass-observation and working class culture in Britain 1940–41', *Urban History*, 26:1 (1999), pp. 71–88; D. Ussishkin, *Morale: A Modern British History* (New York: Oxford University Press, 2017).
6. E. Jones, R. Wooleden, B. Durodie and S. Wessely, 'Civilian morale during the Second World War: responses to air raids re-examined', *Social History of Medicine*, 17:3 (2004), pp. 463–79.
7. B. Dibley and M. Kelly, 'Morale and Mass Observation: governing the affective atmosphere on the home front', *Museum and Society*, 13:1 (2015), p. 24.
8. T. Harrisson and C. Madge, *War Begins at Home* (London: Chatto and Windus, 1940), p. 24.
9. Harrisson and Madge, *War Begins at Home*, p. 39.
10. 'War', *Daily Mail*, 4 September 1939, p. 6; 'The King to his peoples', the *Times*, 4 September 1939, p. 8.
11. 'In quietness and confidence', *Daily Mail*, 4 September 1939, p. 6; C. Langhamer, *The English in Love: The Intimate Story of an Emotional Revolution* (Oxford: Oxford University Press, 2013).

12 Imperial War Museum (IWM), Department of Documents (DD), 95/27/1, B. Holbrook, *No Medals For Us*, p. 76.
13 J. Butler, *Precarious Life: The Powers of Mourning and Violence* (London: Verso, 2004), p. 22.
14 See E. Kübler-Ross, *On Death and Dying: What the Dying Have to Teach Doctors, Nurses, the Clergy and their own Families* (London: Tavistock Publications, 1970).
15 I. Del Rosario, 'A journey into grief', *Journal of Religion and Health*, 43:1 (2004), p. 19.
16 J. Damousi, *The Labour of Loss: Mourning, Memory and Wartime Bereavement in Australia* (Cambridge: Cambridge University Press, 1999).
17 The National Archives, London (TNA), Home Office (HO), 45/18142, *War. Burial of the Dead Killed in Air Raids*, 'Conference on the Burial of Those Killed in Air Raids' (29 October 1936).
18 TNA, Housing and Local Government (HLG), 7/761 *Civilian War Dead Bible*, 'Circular 2192, Deaths Due to War Operations' (1 November 1940).
19 Commonwealth War Graves Commission (CWGC) Archives, CWGC/1/2/D/10/3, *Section 13: Civilian War Dead*, 'Letter from Ware to the dean of Westminster Abbey' (22 January 1942).
20 TNA, War Office (WO), 32/9850, *Imperial War Graves Commission Commemoration of Civilians Killed in Air Raids*, 'Civilian war dead: extracts from letters' (1942).
21 Alderman T. H. Underdown, *Bristol Under Blitz: The Record of an Ancient City and Her People During the Battle of Britain 1940–1941* (Bristol: Lord Mayor's Office, 1942), p. 5.
22 Underdown, *Bristol Under Blitz*, p. 13.
23 Underdown, *Bristol Under Blitz*, p. 14.
24 'Tribute to gallant dead', *Western Daily Press and Bristol Mirror*, 11 December 1940, p. 5.
25 Bristol City Archives, LM/C/X18/8, *Lord Mayor's Office, Correspondence: Relating to Air Raids, Sympathy Letters, and Casualties*.
26 Mass Observation (MO), File Report (FR) 529, *Report on the Aftermath of Town Blitzes* (19 December 1940), pp. 1–2.
27 TNA, Cabinet Papers (CAB), 66/35/37, *Tube Shelter Inquiry* (3 April 1943).
28 TNA, CAB 66/35/37, *Tube Shelter Inquiry*, pp. 7, 1.
29 '60 children died in shelter disaster', *Daily Mail*, 5 March 1943, p. 1.
30 T. Butler (ed.), *The 1943 Bethnal Green Tube Shelter Disaster: An Oral History* (London: University of East London, 2015), pp. 55, 59.
31 CWGC, CWGC/1/1/A/416, *Present War Graves. Proposed Commission Circular, The Care and Marking of War Graves Pamphlet* (1942 edition).
32 CWGC, CWGC/1/1/A/416, *Present War Graves*, Letter from Isabel Blades to Air Ministry (n.d.).

33 CWGC, CWGC/1/1/A/416, *Present War Graves*, Letter from Lady Ampthill to Fabian Ware (13 May 1942); Memorandum from Air Commodore RAF HQ Gibraltar to IWGC (10 November 1942).
34 TNA, WO 171/4474, *Chaplains. Allied Expeditionary Force North West Europe. War Diaries. Lines of Communication. New Edition of Routine Orders*. Chaplains (February 1945).
35 TNA, WO171/4474, *Chaplains. Allied Expeditionary Force North West Europe. New Edition of Routine Orders*. Chaplains (February 1945).
36 M. Snape, *The Royal Army Chaplains Department, 1796–1953: Clergy Under Fire* (Woodbridge: Boydell & Brewer, 2008), p. 302.
37 L. Skinner, *The Man Who Worked on Sundays: The Personal War Diary June 2nd 1944 to May 17th 1945 of Revd Leslie Skinner RAChD, 8th (Independent) Armoured Brigade Attached to the Sherwood Rangers Yeomanry Regiment* (printed for the author by Plus Printing, n.d.), pp. 27, 33, 44.
38 IWM, DD, *Air Ministry: Casualty Procedure in War* (Air Publication 1922, 2nd edition, 1942), p. 16, 23, 27.
39 L. Eyles, 'Problem of the moment', *Woman's Own* (6 January 1940), p. 30.
40 V. Wynn Griffiths, 'The frozen heart', *Woman's Own* (27 January 1940), pp. 14–16.
41 A. Temple, 'Human casebook', *Daily Mail*, 30 November 1943, p. 2.
42 *Millions Like Us* (dir. S. Gilliat and F. Launder, 1943).
43 *In Which We Serve* (dir. N. Coward and D. Lean, 1942).
44 Langhamer, *The English in Love*, p. 28.
45 E. Marsh, *We Lived in London* (London: Lutterworth Press, 1942).
46 E. Pargeter, *She Goes to War* (London: Heinemann, 1942) pp. 155, 312. Pargeter was also known by her *non de plume* Ellis Peters, under which name she published the popular 'Brother Cadfael' medieval-detective book series.
47 *The Way to the Stars* (dir. A. Asquith, 1945).
48 J. Pudney, *Selected Poems* (London: John Lane The Bodley Head, 1946), p. 18.
49 MO, Diarist 5447 (September 1943).
50 *A Matter of Life and Death* (dir. M. Powell and E. Pressburger, 1946).
51 Marsh, *We Lived in London*, p. 138.
52 Marsh, *We Lived in London*, p. 191.
53 T. Freeman, 'Pa was always whistling', *Woman's Own* (23 November 1945), pp. 5–9.
54 *The Way to the Stars*.
55 M. Francis, *The Flyer: British Culture and the Royal Air Force, 1939–1945* (Oxford: Oxford University Press, 2008), p. 120.
56 See P. Jalland, *Death in War and Peace: A History of Loss and Grief in England, 1914–1970* (Oxford: Oxford University Press, 2010), pp. 159–66 for an account of one woman's attempts to manage her grief in wartime.

57 'Woman to woman', *Woman* (22 June 1940), p. 30.
58 A. Wareing, 'Next of kin', *Woman's Own* (20 January 1940), pp. 8–11.
59 M. Thomson, *Psychological Subjects: Identity, Culture and Health in Twentieth-Century Britain* (Oxford: Oxford University Press, 2006).
60 Langhamer, *The English in Love*.
61 MO, Diarist 5446 (August 1942).
62 B. Rosenwein, *Emotional Communities in the Early Middle Ages* (Ithaca, NY: Cornell University Press, 2007).
63 IWM, Department of Documents (DD), 93/48/1, *Papers of Squadron Leader Reverend G. H. Martin*, Letters from next of kin of missing personnel (6 May 1944).
64 A. S. G. Butler, *Recording Ruin* (London: Constable and Company, 1942), pp. 51, 27, 60.
65 I refer here to the Mrs Miniver of Jan Struther's 1930s column in the *Times*, who lived with her family in a west London apartment, though she shared with her film version an unwavering commitment to emotional restraint. For a discussion of Struther's columns, see A. Light, *Forever England: Femininity, Literature and Conservatism Between the Wars* (Abingdon: Routledge, 1991) pp. 113–55.
66 IWM, DD, 16877, *Private papers of J. Driscoll: Transcript of Wartime Letters to Wife*.
67 MO, Diarist 5378 (15 March, 1941), p. 254. Mitchison's son, Geoffrey, had died of meningitis in 1927, and her daughter, Clemency, had died shortly after her birth in 1940.
68 MO, Diarist 5378 (19–21 March), p. 261.
69 MO, Diarist 5378 (19–21 March), p. 263.
70 MO, Diarist 5378 (19–21 March), p. 264.
71 Damousi, *Labour of Loss*.
72 MO, Diarist 5378 (19–21 March), p. 267.
73 Mary Fleming was killed in the heavy air raid of 16/17 April 1941, which was largely targeted on central and southern London. The raid was so ferocious that it was known for some time afterwards simply as 'the Wednesday'.
74 Butler, *Recording Ruin*, p. 77.
75 S. O. Rose, *Which People's War? National Identity and Citizenship in Wartime Britain, 1939–1945* (Oxford: Oxford University Press, 2003), p. 195.
76 W. Robson, *Letters From a Soldier* (London: Faber & Faber, 1960), p. 117.
77 S. Whitehouse and G. B. Bennett, *Fear is the Foe: A Footslogger from Normandy to the Rhine* (London: Robert Hale, 1995), p. 48.
78 P. Hadley, *Third Class to Dunkirk: A Worm's Eye View of the BEF, 1940* (London: Hollis & Carter, 1944), p. 72.
79 On British military cultures and masculinity during the war, see A. Allport, *Browned Off and Bloody-Minded: The British Soldier Goes to War*,

1939–1945 (New Haven, CT: Yale University Press, 2015); J. Crang, *The British Army and the People's War* (Manchester: Manchester University Press, 2000); M. Francis, *The Flyer: British Culture and the Royal Air Force, 1939–1945* (Oxford: Oxford University Press, 2008); E. Newlands, *Civilians into Soldiers: War, the Body and British Army Recruits, 1939–45* (Manchester: Manchester University Press, 2014); G. Prysor, *Citizen Sailors: The Royal Navy in the Second World War* (London: Viking, 2011); G. Sheffield, 'The shadow of the Somme: the influence of the First World War on British soldiers' perceptions and behavior in the Second World War', in P. Addison and A. Calder (eds), *Time to Kill: The Soldier's Experience of War in the West, 1939–1945* (London: Pimlico, 1997).

80 G. MacDonald Fraser, *Quartered Safe Out Here: A Recollection of the War in Burma* (London: Harvill, 1996), pp. 88–9.

81 See, for example, A. Bowlby, *Recollections of Rifleman Bowlby* (London: Leo Cooper, 1969).

82 Of the ninety child evacuees, seventy were 'lost at sea', together with 122 members of the *City of Benares* crew and fifty-one adult passengers. I Kikuchi, 'The story of child evacuee Beryl Myatt and the sinking of the SS *City of Benares*', Imperial War Museum website, www.iwm.org.uk/history/the-story-of-child-evacuee-beryl-myatt-and-the-sinking-of-the-ss-city-of-benares (accessed 15 June 2017). The sinking ended the overseas evacuation scheme.

83 IWM, DD 05/56/1, *Miss Beryl Myatt* (letter dated 21 September 1940).

84 All previous quotes are from IWM, DD 05/56/1, *Miss Beryl Myatt*. Beryl is also commemorated in the IWGC record of the civilian dead.

85 R. Goldstein, 'Monte Cassino, March to May 1944', BBC People's War website, www.bbc.co.uk/history/ww2peopleswar/stories/16/a2293616.shtml (accessed 12 June 2017).

86 D. Mayman, *Led Soldiers: The Second World War Diaries of a Royal Hussar* (Bedfordshire: Authors Online, 2008), p. 116.

87 Skinner, n.d., pp. 18, 118.

88 IWM, DD 89/17/1, *The Second World War Diaries of Mrs A. D. Deacon, MBE*.

89 W. Reddy, *The Navigation of Feeling: A Framework for the History of Emotions* (New York: Cambridge University Press, 2001), p. 77.

90 N. Last, *Nella Last's War: A Mother's Diary 1939–1945*, ed. Richard Broad and Suzie Fleming (Bristol: Falling Wall Press, 1981), pp. 145, 197, 225, 209.

91 S. Jameson, *The Journal of Mary Hervey Russell* (London: Macmillan, 1945). Much of the writing on her sister's death was reproduced in Jameson's autobiography, *Journey from the North: Volume Two* (London: Collins & Harvey, 1970).

92 Kübler Ross, *On Death and Dying*.

93 Jameson, *The Journal of Mary Hervey Russell*, p. 236.
94 T. Walter, *On Bereavement: The Culture of Grief* (Maidenhead: Open University Press, 1999), p. 87; Jameson, *The Journal of Mary Hervey Russell*, p. 237.
95 Jameson, *The Journal of Mary Hervey Russell*, p. 237.
96 Jameson, *The Journal of Mary Hervey Russell*, p. 238.

8

Remembering

Remembering and commemorating the dead of war

Introduction: thank you for coming back to me

In November 1945, just months after Japan's surrender had brought almost six years of conflict to an end, Celia Johnson made the nation cry. Her performance as the desiring, despairing, yet ultimately self-denying Laura Jesson in David Lean's *Brief Encounter* was at the heart of a film which, according to Mass Observation (MO), did more than any other film of the period to bring its audience to tears.[1] Why did this film, described by the *Times*' film reviewer as 'lacking in dramatic force and imaginative range', so stir the emotions of its audience?[2] Lean's film, scripted by Noel Coward and based on his 1936 play *Still Lives*, tells the story of Laura's brief encounter with Dr Alec Harvey at Milford railway station buffet. Over the course of a few weeks they fall in love and consider – and reject – both consummation and elopement, the film ending with Laura's return to husband Fred, suburban home and children, and Alec's departure for South Africa. It is also about much more than this, however, both its narrative and its reception giving us a window on to the emotional economy of the immediate postwar period. Through the emotional intensity of Johnson's performance, and the yearning and longing that her face exhibits in the many close-ups of Lean's cinematography, it also provides a sense of the effort needed to maintain emotional equilibrium in the aftermath of war.

Brief Encounter is both a narrative that in its focus on the suburban, the middle class, the everyday and the feminine, is determinedly about 'the ordinary', a term shown by Claire Langhamer to have exceptional ideological weight in the postwar period, but which also speaks of the emotional work needed for, and the emotional cost of, the maintenance of the everyday and the ordinary amidst and immediately after the disruptions of wartime.³ In *Brief Encounter* the weight of this emotional labour falls on Laura, and is expressed, largely without words, by Johnson. As Kent Puckett argues, the film has a complex relationship with temporality: based on Coward's 1936 play, it is both set within a world that would have been recognisably pre-war to its audience, with its abundant food and Johnson's pleasure in consumption, but it is also a film expressly about the war. The war is present, Puckett contends, not only in the background figures of soldiers, but also in the cinematography's use of light and dark, and of sound, to convey emotional extremes, and the ability of the external world to disrupt personal equilibrium.⁴ Like *The Way to the Stars* and *A Matter of Life and Death*, discussed in Chapter 7, it was made at the tail-end of the war, and released in the war's immediate aftermath. The film can be read as a war film, the disruption of the romance between Laura and Alec acting as a metaphor for the disordering experience of war, while Laura's return to the domestic stands for the difficult and complex transition to peacetime. It spoke to its audience about the disruptions of the past six years, and in Laura's 'return' to her family and Fred's closing lines, 'You've been a long way away … thank you for coming back to me', it gave voice to a desire for a return to the everyday, and to the ordinariness of a peacetime, domestic life. However, it is also ambiguous about this return: Laura does not appear especially contented, or relieved, at her decision to remain within the family home with 'sweet, dull Fred'; in the course of the film she may have decided to put duty before desire, retreating to her companionate marriage in the face of her disruptive longing for Alec, but she is still mourning the relationship that she could have had, and the loss of the man she loves. *Brief Encounter*, then, is a film about war, about romance and reconstruction, but it is also a film about grief, about individual desire and responsibilities to the collective, and about living with loss.⁵

By 1945, Celia Johnson had already played two roles that placed her at the heart of representations of a mid-century, middle-class English female sensibility, one that was particularly suited to the rigours of war. In the characters of Alix Kinross in *In Which We Serve* (1942) and Ethel Gibbons in *This Happy Breed* (1944), she played wives and mothers who both successfully put the needs of family and nation before their own feelings, but who, through her performance, also showed the emotional labour that such success demanded.⁶ Johnson, then, was recognisable as a figure who embodied the desirable affective response to the demands of wartime. As Stephen Brooke has argued, Johnson's face, and particularly her large, expressive eyes, 'became central to the representation of a particular kind of mid-twentieth century English emotional sensibility', through her ability to show the 'tension between emotional expression and emotional restraint' that was at the heart of this sensibility.[7] In *Brief Encounter*, Johnson demonstrates the cost of this tension almost wordlessly, showing the emotional labour involved in containing the turmoil that lay just beneath the surface of her apparently controlled exterior. Johnson's capacity for showing the very place where interior affect became outwardly expressed or restrained no doubt spoke to the immediate postwar audience as much as it spoke to earlier audiences experiencing the rigours and demands of total war. While much analysis of *Brief Encounter* has focused on the multiple ways that the film reflects the war's disruption of gender roles, and the difficulties of rebuilding both these and romantic relationships in its aftermath, Johnson's unspoken, repressed grief over her loss of Alec would also have resonated with those who had experienced their own loss, and who were struggling to manage their feelings in the emotional economy of mid-century Britain.[8]

In her analysis of 1940s literature, literary historian Gill Plain has traced the contours of grief, and the management of this emotion, through postwar British culture.[9] Plain shows that, like *Brief Encounter*, many of these texts reject a clear temporal division between wartime and peacetime, exposing instead the complex and multiple ways in which the impact of conflict breaks out of the chronological parameters of the war's political beginnings and ends. War does not, in social, cultural and affective terms, end with an armistice, and the war leaked into the postwar in numerous, often unsettling, ways. In Elizabeth Bowen's *The Heat of the Day* (1948) for example, the multiple disruptions of war are embodied in the character of Louie, her very sense of self uncertain and fluid, shaped by the loss of her parents in an air raid and the absence, and later death, of her husband on service overseas. This instability and uncertainty is eventually resolved, at the war's end, by motherhood, as she reimagines herself to be the widowed mother of a child she resolves to raise as the son of a heroic husband.[10] As Plain shows, however, it is poetry rather than prose that most self-consciously addresses the issue of bereavement and grief, following much of the poetry of the Great War in producing a 'poetics of grief'.[11] The popularity of this poetry, seen in the sales of Dylan Thomas's *Death and Entrances* (1946) in the immediate postwar period, demonstrates the existence of an audience that wanted to reflect on, and grapple with, the extraordinary experiences and challenges of wartime.¹² Outside texts like these however, we have to pay attention to what is unsaid, to the gaps and absences that, shaped by the dominant emotional economy of restraint and self-discipline, themselves mirrored the gaps and absences in streets, households and lives in the aftermath of war.

This chapter considers the emotional and memorial afterlife of the war, thinking about the multiple ways in which the war's dead were remembered, memorialised and grieved for in the immediate postwar period. Following the archaeologist Sarah Tarlow, it considers remembrance of the dead at the national, local and personal level, and reflects on the relationship between the attempted reconstruction of empire, and remembrance practice.¹³ However, it reverses Tarlow's ordering of these sites of remembrance, and of grief, following Jay Winter in his assertion that the bereaved individual stands at the heart of mourning practice.¹⁴

Postwar bereavement

While the war leaked into the postwar, outlines of the postwar could also be seen during the war years. Seen in political, economic and physical plans for reconstruction, it was also present in the pre-emptive management of grief and bereavement. In 1946, the paper company Basildon Bond ran a competition to find the best soldier's letter of the war. The competition was won by a 'last letter' from the front. On the eve of the Battle of Arnhem in September 1944, twenty-two-year-old Ivor Rowbery, a private in the South Staffordshire Regiment, wrote to his mother, at home in the West Midlands. This was to be Rowbery's last letter, as he was killed in battle, and he spent much of it urging his mother not to grieve. He wrote,

> I am not afraid to die and am perfectly willing to do so, if by my doing so you benefit in any way whatsoever. If you do not then my sacrifice is all in vain. Have you benefitted Mom, or have you cried and worried yourself sick? I fear it is the latter. Don't you see Mom, that it is doing me no good, and that in addition you are undoing all the good work I have tried to do.¹⁵

While maternal grief can be put to particularly effective political work, it is understood here as pointless and as selfish, as working against the collective aims of the war, the 'good work' that the son has died for, and thus as undermining the very justification for his sacrifice. In his attempt to shape the grief of those mourning his death, Rowbery was not alone. Major Lionel Wigram, who had founded the army's first battle school in 1941, was killed fighting in Italy in 1944, when he was thirty-seven years old. Before his death he wrote to his wife, and informed her of his (gendered) hopes for their children:

> [Y]ou must be economical ... as a lot of my income can't be earned if I'm not there to earn it. You should have at least £2000 pa to live on which – after all – isn't too bad is it? I want Anthony to be a lawyer and businessman. I want Michael to follow whatever line he fancies – I think he might take to writing or being a Don. I'm sure he'll be studious. Dena of course will marry very young .... We've had a lot of fun together and I have no regrets.[16]

Wigram's last letter differs from Rowbery's in that there is no mention of the war, of war aims or of sacrifice. Instead, the focus is entirely on the personal and the familial. It is like Rowbery's, however, in its disavowal of grief. While Rowbery urges his mother not to grieve, Wigram reminds his wife of the 'fun' that they have had, and his lack of regret, again positioning her (imagined) grief as inward looking, selfish in the face of his selflessness and focus on others, even as he contemplates his own death. While both letters were no doubt intended to provide comfort, and by so doing can be seen as recognising the distress that would be caused by their deaths, in their privileging of the practical and the stoical as desirable responses, they anticipate the emotional economy in which the work of grief was undertaken in the postwar period.

In *Death, Grief and Mourning in Contemporary Britain*, his classic study of grief and bereavement in the twentieth century, anthropologist Geoffrey Gorer argued that the move away from the formal rituals which had provided social markers of bereavement, and a framework through which the bereaved were expected to process in the mid-Victorian period, had left people at a loss. For Gorer, grief became privatised in much the same way as death, which was increasingly taking place in hospital, away from the everyday lives of friends and family. Grief, Gorer argued, had become an embarrassment, something that had to be controlled in public lest it upset the equilibrium of others, leaving the bereaved 'without adequate guidance as to how to treat death and bereavement, and without social help in living through and coming to terms with ... grief and mourning'.[17] The emotional economy of the interwar period, and the stoicism demanded of people during the years of total war had bequeathed to postwar Britain a culture that gave little space to explicit, public expressions of grief. This was strengthened in the immediate postwar period by a popular culture that, perhaps appealing to a people exhausted by years of total war, often reflected a desire to turn away from war, and to focus instead on the pleasures and demands of peacetime. The bereaved were often more isolated than the bereaved of the Great War: while they numbered in the hundreds of thousands, overall losses were approximately one-third of those in the earlier conflict, and the fictive kinships that Jay Winter has identified as key agents of remembrance were perhaps harder to find for many.[18] The stoicism and restraint that had shaped the expression of grief during the war continued to do so in the postwar world.

Alex Bowlby, who served with the infantry in the Italian campaign, struggled to compose a narrative of his wartime experiences. Eventually completing his memoirs in the late 1960s, Bowlby recounted how he had attempted to write of his time in the military six or seven times between 1947 and 1954. Nothing came of any of these attempts. Bowlby's struggle to compose was also an emotional and psychic struggle: in 1955 he had a 'breakdown'. He wrote,

> I tried another draft. The dialogue came back. I saw the words in my head just as they had been spoken. As I scribbled them down I thought of the dead. I owed them so much. I was writing a book for them … and at the same time I was trying to forget the dead, to get shot of them. You can't grieve forever. You can't bottle it up either … I was still earthed with grief. On November 5 1957 it exploded. I walked the six miles from Swiss Cottage to Notting Hill gate crying the whole way.[19]

Riven by guilt at his survival when so many of his friends and comrades had been killed in the battles of the Gothic Line in 1944, and struggling with his inability to either forget or to express his feelings about his wartime experiences, Bowlby found both narrative and psychic composure impossible. First coined by Graham Dawson, the term composure refers to the doubled work of remembering; of creating 'stories' of the past that the individual self can live with. Such stories have to be composed in a narrative sense, drawing on and making sense within a wider cultural memory of the event or period being remembered, but also have to be psychologically composed, creating a story that enables the individual to maintain their emotional and psychic equilibrium in the present.[20] In his inability to compose such a narrative in a postwar world that first, had little space for memories of the war, and then by the 1950s represented the male military experience in a largely (though never entirely) heroic light, or to find a means of making peace with his past in a manner that enabled him to live with it, Bowlby's postwar struggles illustrate Michael Roper's argument that some experiences 'seem to elude containment in narrative, and ... may thus not be capable of achieving composure for the narrator'.[21]

Bowlby finally managed to compose his memoirs in the 1960s, after his 'breakdown', and in an emotional economy that was beginning to move towards the more expressive and reflective model, 'embracing emotion and individual desire' associated with the 'permissive society'.[22] His memories of military service in Italy are permeated with death: as discussed in Chapter 4, Bowlby lived close to the corpses both of his comrades and of the enemy, and they both repelled and fascinated him, as did the finality of death. After burying a fellow infantryman who was killed by a landmine in a remote mountain area, Bowlby recalled thinking that no one would ever visit this grave, concluding 'if I'm killed, let it be near a town so that I'll be remembered'.[23] Remembrance of the dead was important to Bowlby. The book was dedicated to 'the memories of Corporals Hardy and Brandon, Gothic Line, 1944', and he hoped that 'the dead would live on in the book' and that through this process of ensuring remembrance, he could thus be rid of the guilt he felt for surviving.[24] In the epilogue, Bowlby described a cathartic visit to the military cemetery outside Arrezzo, where many of the men he had served with were buried. While rejecting what he termed the '"they shall grow old not as we that are left grow old" approach to those killed in war', he found an unexpected sense of tranquillity being among the dead, reflecting that 'they gave their lives and God gave them joy. It's here, all around me.'[25] Through the act of writing his memoirs, and thus memorialising the dead on paper, and then by visiting their graves, Bowlby finally found something of the peace that he wished for and was eventually able to ascribe to his dead friends and comrades.

Others also found the emotional economy of postwar Britain a difficult environment in which to come to terms with their loss. In 1990, Thames Television interviewed a number of veterans of the Second World War for a documentary about the London Blitz of 1940–1941. Some had vigorous and assured 'composed' narratives that they were able to draw on, one man fluently arguing that 'the war itself and the Blitz were watersheds in the lives of people of my generation ... something that would never be forgotten as a remarkable, astonishing time', but questions about the immediate impact of the Blitz sometimes revealed ongoing difficulties in telling war stories, particularly those that involved personal loss.[26] One woman described the air raid that injured her and killed all of her immediate family:

> My mother died, my baby sister died, my younger sister died, my father died. I had two aunts that died and an uncle. The seven were buried on the same day ... I didn't go to the funeral.

When she was asked about the immediate aftermath of their deaths her composure, such as it was, broke down:

> I think I knew almost immediately because I came home from hospital and, er, when I got to the home and there were milk bottles outside I just knew no one had come home.

While describing being sent to the outskirts of London to recover, and becoming distressed by local people who viewed the Blitz 'like a spectacle', she became upset and the interview was halted.[27] Such equanimity as she had in the recounting of this story was fragile, disrupted by the questions of the interviewer.[28] Composure – both psychic and narrative – continued to elude her.

At times, the trauma of sudden bereavement combined with the emotional economy of restraint and rectitude to make some deaths, literally, unspeakable in the postwar world. When the east coast city of Hull was bombed in March 1941, the neighbouring Taylor and Owens families of 6th Avenue were devastated. In a moving interview in 2017 for a BBC television documentary on the bombing of Hull, two sisters, children during the war, recalled the death of their baby brother Pete in that air raid. While describing the bomb's impact, their older sister's injury and their own entrapment under the rubble of the house, they were able to vividly and clearly describe the confusion and destruction of the direct hit on their house. When they came to talk of Peter's death, however, once again the composure previously on display broke down:

> That's what he was, under the bed, so ... and he's still ... yeah. I think he was on the draining board in Mrs Anson's back kitchen. I think that's where they'd laid him, and then we never saw him any more. Never spoke about it any more, Peter, our Mum or Dad's or ....
> Didn't know where he's gone did we?
> No. I think this is the first time we've ever spoken about it in depth [cries] .... the fire ... It's all come out and I'm pleased.

Moving between the past and present tense, and between the moment of the bomb falling and the immediate and longer aftermath, the story of their baby brother's death, and their confusion as small children when this was never spoken of, the interview showed the difficulty some suffered in coming to terms with wartime loss and bereavement in the aftermath of war. The neighbouring family, the Taylors, lost three children to the same bomb. Janet Taylor, born nine years later in 1950, was not told about her siblings for some twenty years:

> I was brought up in that house, never knowing what happened, never knowing about the war, never talking about the war, because my father would not allow us to talk about it. You didn't talk about things like that in the house. You don't need to know about it. You don't talk about it .... It was like they never existed.[29]

The silence in her household, while extreme, reflected something of the wider emotional economy, where there was little space for outwardly expressed grief, even while the dead of war were beginning to be memorialised.

The cultural scripts available for the bereaved at the end of the war overwhelmingly suggested that the kind of overpowering, disruptive grief no doubt felt by the Owens and Taylor families should be contained within the private sphere, and be prevented from spilling out and unsettling a country that was in the throes of reconstruction. While grief was not denied, the bereaved were expected to contain and control their emotions. The best-selling novelist Leonora Eyles, agony aunt for *Woman's Own*, published a letter from a young woman who was 'unable to forget' her uncle, killed in the war. Her grandmother would not let his room be used, keeping it as a form of shrine, and the woman wrote that 'I can't help feeling miserable, as if life isn't worth living'. Writing in the immediate aftermath of war, Eyles replied,

> [I]f everyone who has lost a relative in this war let it affect them as it does you, life could not go on could it? Try to see that love should be creative; let this love for a relative make you kinder to others who have lost dear ones. Beg your Granny to use your Uncle's room for some useful purpose. I am sure that if the dead know what we are doing they must be very distressed if we let our love for them spoil our lives.[30]

As with the dead of the war, grief was to be put to work in the postwar period. Eyles' advice was to draw on the experience of grief to become more empathetic to the suffering of others, and to make use of his old room; to look forward to the postwar world rather than back to the losses of the war. Like Rowbery's letter to his mother of 1944, grief is positioned here as letting down the dead, pathologised rather than seen as a normal response to bereavement.

The cases discussed here, of the bereaved struggling to find a space in which to 'come to terms' with their loss in a postwar society keen to look forward rather than back, demonstrate the difficulty some encountered in giving voice to grief when the cultural scripts available emphasised restraint as the foundation of a shared emotional economy. In other instances, existing traditions, sites and words did allow the grieving to mark their bereavement, and conduct the hard emotional labour of grief. At both a local and a national level, postwar society found some spaces for remembrance, which make visible the ways in which grief did, sometimes, become visible in the public sphere.

Communal remembrance

In his work on the aftermath of the Great War in Europe, Jay Winter argues that the bereaved came to form a 'fictive kinship', both with one another and with those who sought to aid them in their loss.[31] War memorials provided a site at which these affective bonds were made visible and, as places where 'people grieved, both individually and collectively', could both reinforce these affective kinships, and make them, and the grief which informed them, visible to the wider community.[32] In the aftermath of the Second World War, the meaning of these sites was often different; as time elapsed following the losses of the Great War, they appeared, to many, to be an appropriate means of commemorating and marking the deaths of the earlier conflict but not that of the casualties of the more recent war. As this chapter will go on to discuss, the last months of the Second World War saw a national debate about the physical form that memorialisation should take, but at the same time, and in the war's aftermath, other local and communal sites provided a means through which the dead could be marked and the bereaved could articulate their loss.

Winter has argued that the fictive kinships formed in the aftermath of war produce forms of remembrance that

> occupy a space between individual memory and the national theatre of collective memory choreographed by social and economic leaders. They flourish at a point between the isolated individual and the anonymous state; a juncture almost certainly closer to the individual than the state.[33]

Remembering: remembering and commemorating the dead of war

The *In Memoriam* notices in both local and national newspapers occupy exactly this space, acting as a site where the war's dead could be remembered, and where the mourning of the bereaved could be communicated. As sociologist Tony Walter has noted, they illuminate the double-layered nature of grieving within what he terms the 'reserved' grief culture of England, Scotland and Protestant – though not Catholic – Ulster.[34] *In Memoriam* notices, for Walter, function to both let the community know that an individual or a group are mourning, but at the same time demonstrate that they are successfully controlling their grief, expressing it through the (usually) traditionally worded notice in a newspaper.[35] In addition, they provide a similar social function to that associated by Winter with memorials to the Great War: they remind the community who had been bereaved, and thus who might need social, emotional and economic support. *In Memoriam* notices differ from death notices, also often placed in newspapers. While the primary function of a death notice is to inform the wider community of an individual's passing and often of the time and place of a funeral service, an *In Memoriam* acts both as a form of memorialisation, and as a reminder of ongoing loss.

In the aftermath of war such notices often specified the military service undertaken by the dead. They thus acted as a reminder of individual sacrifice for the common good; the *Times* separated *In Memoriam* notices for those who had died on active service from notices marking the anniversaries of civilian and peacetime deaths. These notices often emphasised the collective nature of this sacrifice, perhaps as a means for the bereaved to feel an affective kinship with others, much as the missing airmen's relatives, who wrote to Squadron Leader Reverend G. H. Martin asking for details of other members of the same aircrew in the aftermath of an aeroplane going missing in action, searched for some consolation in collectivity.[36] In one such notice, published on 8 May 1946, the first anniversary of Victory in Europe (VE) Day, Betty Greenwood remembered her husband Alfred, a navigator with 44 Squadron, Bomber Command, but also 'his very gallant comrades'. The wife of Captain Myles A. Blomfeld of the Royal Navy, killed while commanding HMS *Viva II*, also remembered 'the Officers and Men who gave their lives with him'. Such notices formed part of a community of wartime bereavement that stretched back to the Great War, the same column containing three memorial notices for men of the Monmouthshire Regiment who had died in action at Ypres on 8 May 1915.[37]

In Memoriam notices tell us something of the ways in which the expression of bereavement, and of grief, was shaped by social class, by region and by gender. Those published in the *Times* often made use of classical references, demonstrating the education and social class of both the deceased and of the bereaved, binding them together in a community with those reading the newspaper. Violet Duke, remembering her son Sir Charles Thomas Hewitt Mappin, who had been shot down over Germany while serving as an air gunner with the 75th (New Zealand) Squadron of the Royal Air Force (RAF) in 1941, used the motto of the Mappin family, '*Cor Forte Calcar Non Requient*' (a strong heart needs no spur), in her *In Memoriam* notice on the fifth anniversary of his death in 1946.[38] The memorial notice for John Miller Bliss, a member of the RAF Volunteer Reserve, who died over Germany in 1943, combined the motto of the RAF, '*Per Ardua Ad Astra*' (through adversity to the stars), with more personal sentiments:

> Think not he had too short a day
> Who knew the dawn but not decay.[39]

Such consolatory sentiments were common, echoing Binyon's 1914 poem, 'For the Fallen', read at memorial services in Britain and at memorial sites overseas since the end of the Great War. An assertion of life after death, and of the reunion of the dead with the living, was also used in an attempt at consolation. The *In Memoriam* notice for James Erskine Cumming, of Eton and Corpus Christi College, Cambridge, published on 8 August 1946, the fifth anniversary of his death, asserted,

> He is not dead. He could not die, so young he was and gay
> So gallant and so brave a soul could never pass away
> And though I cannot see his face I know he walks with me
> In immortality.[40]

Likewise, the family of 'our beloved Sandy, Lieutenant H. Gordon' wrote

> And you will speed us onwards with a cheer
> And wave beyond the stars that all is well.[41]

Classical references and traditional language provided social elites with a class-specific means of communicating their grief, and of memorialising the war's dead in the immediate postwar years. Yet, while such language provided a recognised script for the articulation of loss, it was not always enough. Remembering his 'dear son ... Lieutenant Robert Charles Diserens (Bobby)', his father combined a statement of worthwhile sacrifice – 'he gave his life for his country' – with a statement of its personal cost: 'So greatly loved, so sadly missed.'[42] A week earlier, the parents of Geoffrey Walker, killed in North Africa in 1943, marked the anniversary of his birth, not his death, with the words

> To greater safety than we could provide he turned, and from our arms withdrew, not knowing, that upon the day you died, death came to us, my son, but not to you.[43]

Here the denial of death, so central to Christian belief, while asserted, provides no comfort to the bereaved, who emphasise instead their feeling, their sense that their own lives ended on the day that their son died. The repeated appeals, in 1945, 1947 and 1948, for information by the parents of twenty-three-year-old Geoffrey Maxton, an RAF flight lieutenant who had been reported missing on operations in the Mediterranean in 1942, remind us that for some families of the missing, even the somewhat uncertain consolations of the *In Memoriam* notice remained unobtainable after the war's end.[44]

While the special status given to military deaths in the *Times* acted to sharpen the divide, weakened by a war that saw over 60,000 British civilians killed, between combatant and civilian, some local acts of remembrance and memorialisation emphasised individual and collective civilian sacrifice. The industrial town of Coventry, decimated in the air raid of November 1940, remembered its civilian dead on a memorial erected over the shared graves of many of the victims in London Road cemetery. The bereaved took to the pages of the local newspaper, the *Coventry Evening Telegraph*, to remember their dead. In the years immediately following the war, the paper dedicated pages to the memorialisation of the dead of the air raid on its anniversary, and many made use of this to make their loss public, and to try and ensure that their loved ones were remembered by the wider community. These individual acts of remembrance were framed by an editorial, which in 1946 reminded readers that 'this is Coventry's day of remembrance and rededication', a day when 'the people of Coventry will be drawn closer together in purpose and understanding'. Six years on, the editorial contended 'time has healed much of the anguish ... today our thoughts are of the future'.[45] In 1947, the front page showed the mayor of Coventry laying a large white floral cross on the mass grave at London Road cemetery, and the anniversary was used each year as a means of raising donations to rebuild the city's cathedral.[46] The city built on its identity as a civic victim of war in its official 'bond of friendship' with besieged Stalingrad in 1944 and through twinning with the German cities of Kiel (1947) and Dresden (1956), both devastated by Allied bombing. Individual and family remembrance of the dead within the newspaper pages, however, showed that they did not just serve as a collective symbol of civic identity, but as loved and missed individuals.

Many of the individual memorial notices drew on established forms for the public expression of bereavement, using a stylised language to make a private remembrance public. For example, the passage

> The years are swiftly passing
> But still we don't forget
> For in the hearts that loved you
> The memories linger yet

was chosen by two families to express their loss in 1946. The classical references so visible in the *Times* were largely absent from the notices published in industrial Coventry. The idea of heaven, and eventual reunion, provided some consolation for the family who believed their father was 'watching from his heavenly home on high', but perhaps less for those who 'would give the world to say "hello Dad" the same old way'. Some made the Air Raid Precautions service of the dead explicit, such distinction perhaps performing the same function as the differentiation of military and civilian deaths seen in the *Times*. For example, Albert Bawden, a special constable killed in the air raid, was 'a dear son who gave his all', dying as a combatant and remembered and 'dearly loved' by his parents, who recalled 'the great surrender made'.[47] Remembrance through the medium of *In Memoriam* notices on 14 November became part of a wider set of memorial traditions for many, with church and memorial services being held, and the same names, and often the same sentiments, being published year after year. By the tenth anniversary of the raid in 1950, while the newspaper's editorial argued that remembrance of the city's losses was a means of 'looking forward' to 'measure the magnitude of the task that has been given to our generation', the individually bereaved continued to look back, mourning their dead through the *In Memoriam* column, using the same language to express their loss that they had for the past decade.[48] In these annually repeated lists of the dead, an emotional community of the city's bereaved was

Remembering: remembering and commemorating the dead of war

formed on the pages of the newspaper through the use of a ritualised language and a shared date for remembrance.

Individual remembrance of the dead was also incorporated into the Imperial War Graves Commission (IWGC) cemeteries that were built in the aftermath of war to both inter and commemorate the empire's dead. When war broke out in 1939, the IWGC had only recently completed the construction of all of its cemeteries and memorials for the dead of the Great War. At the end of the Second World War, it had to bury and commemorate approximately 581,000 of the empire's dead.[49] As discussed in Chapter 6, in September 1945 the commission formally announced that the imperial governments had agreed that the war's dead would not be repatriated but would, instead, be buried close to where they had fallen. While some of the dead were interred in cemeteries that had been built originally for the victims of the Great War, such as privates Martin Flaherty and John Linley, both killed in May 1940 and buried with the bodies of 107 combatant dead of the Great War in Grootebeek British Cemetery in West Flanders, and others were buried in communal civic or religious cemeteries with IWGC headstones, the majority of the empire's military dead were interred in new cemeteries, or commemorated on new memorials to the missing.[50] By the 1950s, the commission had constructed 559 new cemeteries and built thirty-six new memorials.[51] Of the fifty-two new cemeteries in France, almost half were in Normandy, and the largest, Bayeux, contained the graves of 4,256 casualties of the Allied offensive of 1944, 338 of whom were unidentified. The Bayeux memorial alone commemorates over 1,800 of the missing.[52]

As in the years following the Great War, many original sites of burial close to battlefields were 'concentrated' in new, larger cemeteries. On the first anniversary of VE Day, the *Times* described how in southern Holland, 'bodies from the pathetic, lonely single graves by the roadside and in corners of fields and gardens are being gathered together in the larger cemeteries'.[53] Less poetically, the IWGC's inspector in Asia reported that in Ceylon, the three military cemeteries that existed in 1946 were to be 'concentrated' into two military cemeteries, in Kandy and Trincomalee, where, respectively, 203 and 366 of the war's dead were buried. Seven municipal cemeteries held the bodies of several hundred others.[54] In the immediate aftermath of the war, travel restrictions meant that it was often difficult for next of kin to visit the graves of loved ones: in April 1945, Churchill had announced that the government would not be supporting such visits.[55] The inability of many to visit war graves – to tend to them and thus to care for the dead – evidently caused suffering. In response to multiple requests, the War Office announced that it could not place wreaths on individual graves, and in 1948 questions were asked in Parliament about the case of Mrs Rosier, whose son Edwin was buried in the Sangro River Cemetery, Italy.[56] Mrs Rosier had requested that the IWGC send a photograph of her son's grave, and was unhappy that the photograph of a wooden cross sent in 1946 had not been followed by a photograph of the permanent headstone. Emmanuel Shinwell, then Secretary of State for War, explained that it 'has not yet been possible for the Commission to replace the wooden cross with a permanent headstone' but that they had forwarded the details of a local photographer who Mrs Rosier could pay to take a photograph once the headstone was in place. The foreign exchange restrictions in place, however, meant that it was impossible for Mrs Rosier, and presumably others like her, to obtain currency to pay for such services.[57] Although the government eventually agreed to provide free passage for next of kin visiting war graves in Europe, and the British Legion and regimental and corps associations helped to organise such visits, the graves of those buried further afield in Africa, the Middle East and Asia were in many cases simply too far away for the bereaved to visit. When visits to cemeteries were possible, their often incomplete state in the years immediately following the war could cause misery, one man writing to the *Times* in September 1946 to complain that his sister-in-law's attempt to visit her husband's grave in Nijmegen, the Netherlands, a cemetery that had not yet been handed to the IWGC by the Army Graves Service, had left her 'considerably distressed'.[58] In such circumstances, it has to be hoped that the IWGC's reassuring description of the cemeteries it was building as 'universally recognised as places of beauty' provided at least some of the comfort that was intended.[59]

These cemeteries were both sites of collective, imperial remembrance, and of the communication of personal loss. Headstones, with the exception of those marking Allied or enemy graves, were uniform, and each cemetery contained a Cross of Sacrifice and a Stone of Remembrance. As in the aftermath of the Great War, the bereaved were invited to submit a short personal inscription that would follow the listing of name, rank, awards, service number, unit, regiment and date of death that was inscribed on headstones, where known, by the IWGC. Some chose to use a language that was already associated with military sacrifice: 'At the going down of the sun and in the morning we will remember you', and 'he will not grow old as they that are left grow old.

Remembering: remembering and commemorating the dead of war

He sleeps with the brave', both adapted from Lawrence Binyon's 1914 poem 'For the Fallen', read each year at Armistice Day ceremonies, was inscribed on the headstones of many of those buried at Bayeux cemetery in Normandy, France and Kohima cemetery in India. Like many others, the next of kin of Private Dennis Lord, also buried at Bayeux, chose a verse from Rupert Brooke's 1914 'The Soldier': 'There is some corner of a foreign field that is forever England.'[60] Adaptations of 'For your tomorrow, we gave our today', from John Edmunds' 1918 epitaph, were popular at Kohima, where the epitaph also appears on the cemetery's memorial to the 2nd Infantry Division. Together with versions of a verse from the New Testament that was often found on war memorials – 'Greater love hath no man than this, that a man lay down his life for his friend' (John, 15:13), inscribed on at least sixty-seven headstones at Bayeux, and another twenty-five at Kohima – inscriptions that referenced the Great War acted both to reassure the bereaved that their loved ones had died for a higher purpose, and to remind visitors to the cemeteries of their sacrifice.[61]

Other inscriptions speak less of consolation that could be found in a narrative of military sacrifice, and more of the pain and grief of the bereaved mourning lives cut short by war. Some headstones record the distress that could be caused by burial overseas in hard-to-reach graves. The next of kin of Robert Pointer, buried at Kohima, inscribed 'Far away he lies, greatly beloved by all. He gave that we might have' on his headstone, combining a recognition of the distance between the dead and the bereaved with an assertion of sacrifice, while Alfred Hawkins, also buried in Kohima, was 'So far away, but also in our hearts.'[62] Corporal William Robinson's grave in Bayeux records his family's anguish at his burial overseas: 'A foreign grave is a painful thing where loving hands no flowers can bring', and for the parents of Edgar Loader, killed on D-Day and also buried at Bayeux, he was 'So very far away darling son, but always in our thoughts, Mum and Dad'.[63] Despite efforts to reassure the bereaved that the dead 'rest in surroundings of tranquil beauty', with 'graves held in honour' and 'devoted care given to the British dead of both wars by local populations', the inability of some of the bereaved to tend to graves themselves continued to bring pain to many.[64]

Family and civilian identities took precedence over the military in many of the inscriptions. Family relationships were often commemorated. In Bayeux, Frances Ryce is 'Fondly remembered by his loving wife and wee son Frankie', while Robert Toomer is commemorated as 'A smiling face so true, fondly remembered by your mam, dad and family'.[65] In faraway Kohima, the wife of Leonard Thake remembered 'My beloved husband who gave happiness to everyone around and was beloved by all', and Eric Mackenzie was 'A much loved son and brother, a valued friend of many. Never forgotten'.[66] In these inscriptions the military identity of the deceased is invisible, a counter to their burial under an IWGC headstone, in a military cemetery. It is the civilian identity, and civilian relationships, the individual rather than the collective, that are being commemorated. In some cases, the epitaphs read as messages to the dead: Frank Crawford's headstone in Bayeux tells him that 'You were taken but baby Frances came to take your place', and in Kohima Leslie Lewis is reassured that 'As long as life and memory last I will always remember you. Dad'.[67] For some of the bereaved, however, the consolations of collective remembrance by the imperial state, burial with their friends and colleagues and the opportunity to write a personal epitaph seem to have provided little in the way of comfort. The headstone of Thomas McGowan, buried at Kohima, reminds us of the emotional impact of grief in its recording of 'A lonely home, and empty heart, something missing everywhere', while in Bayeux the wife of Henry Clark recorded 'The parting hard, the shock severe, to part with one so dear'.[68] Individual loss shaped the personal inscriptions on headstones in multiple ways, recording family relationships, military sacrifice and the pain of grief.

Local identity also often shaped remembrance forms, and the language used to remember the dead. While the *In Memoriam* notices and IWGC headstone inscriptions made the individual and familial experience of bereavement, and grief, visible in the public sphere, some public forms of individual remembrance were produced by the local community rather than agencies of the state or bereaved individuals and families. When the small mining village of Cwmparc in the Rhondda Valley, south Wales, was hit by an air raid in April 1941, twenty-seven people were killed, including three evacuee children. A memorial service was held at Cwmparc library in 1948, and a memorial, in the form of an illuminated clock, was unveiled. The village also published its own *In Memoriam* leaflet, not only naming the dead but recording something of their lives; a form of brief, collective obituary. The descriptions of the dead tell us of lives lost, but also of the community that mourned them, and the ways that gender, occupation and age shaped the ways in which they were remembered in the village. Several of the dead were miners, employed in the Parc Pit that the village was built around. Tom Williams was remembered as a 'typical middle aged collier, always bluff, hearty and jocular', while David T. Pierce was described as 'a miner, with a whimsical sense of humour, whose drolleries made him always a "good companion"'. Pierce was a veteran of the Great War who died 'like a true soldier, cheerfully encouraging his comrades "under fire"'. Female victims were recalled for their domestic and maternal attributes: Cissie Williams was 'young, married and radiantly happy', and Annie Mary Williams was 'a widow, serene in her daily comings and goings. She died erect and standing knee deep in debris, holding a dead evacuee child in her arms, and smiling like a guardian angel.' Cissie Williams was pregnant when she was killed, at 'the portals of woman's sacred temple of Motherhood', while for Annie Pearce motherhood was 'a sacred shrine'. The shared privations of life in the mining communities of south Wales were imprinted in some of the descriptions. Margaret Ferguson was described as a housewife 'industrious and thrifty', and Annie Pearce 'valiantly overrode circumstances to rear proudly sons and daughters'. The dead of Cwmparc were both members of a close-knit community, their lives shaped by the collective economic hardships of the coal mining Rhondda, the emotional and cultural economies of the south Wales valleys, and the political and religious formations and loyalties of the region, but they were also remembered as individual members of this community, with their own experiences and character traits. The publication of the *In Memoriam* leaflet, dedicated to 'our fellow villagers who fell victim to the murderous fury of Nazi war planes', showed a desire not only to re-inscribe the village's dead into the local community, but also to remember the dead in terms of individual agency in the face of random and impersonal wartime death.[69]

Local acts of remembrance such as the Cwmparc leaflet were among a range of local practices and memorial forms that grew up in the post-war period to mark the civilian dead who did not fall within the compass of pre-existing memorial practice. Cities like Liverpool, Plymouth and Coventry, which had seen repeated bombing raids and many hundreds, sometimes thousands, of civilian deaths, raised the funds for memorials to the dead, such as the memorial unveiled at Anfield cemetery in Liverpool in May 1951, marking the communal grave of the 554 victims of the city's Blitz of May 1941. In 1948, the government had announced a limited amount of funding to local authorities who wished to erect memorials over both the mass graves of air raid victims, and the individual graves of those buried by the local authority. While authorities could claim £8 per person for mass graves, and £11 for the permanent marking of individual graves, no money was made available to the majority of those bereaved through air raids, who had preferred to bury their loved ones privately. Following the memorial traditions established by the IWGC, the marking of publicly funded graves was imagined as being 'simple ... without elaborate sculpture or architectural features'. 'For example', the Home Office suggested, 'the marking might well take the traditional form of a low border in stone with a headpiece or memorial displaying a suitable non-denominational inscription and the names of those buried, the ground within the border being either paved or planted with grass or flowering shrubs.'[70] Collective, publicly funded memorialisation of the civilian dead, however, did not always convey the hoped for level of consolation. When the Reverend E. H. Moir was injured, and his wife killed, in a V1 rocket attack on their London suburb in 1944, she was buried in a communal grave while he recovered in hospital. While recuperating, he had agreed to his wife's burial in the same manner 'as our soldiers who died on the front line'. However, writing to the Home Office in 1947, he now wanted her body disinterred for a private burial in his family plot. Moir had been dismayed to discover that his wife's body had been placed in a grave with other victims of the raid. He made a clear link between mass interment and the shame that he associated with a pauper's burial, describing his distress when he discovered that 'my wife had been buried in a common grave with other coffins piled on top, as paupers might be'. Moir concluded that the treatment of his wife's corpse showed that 'the National pledge, so solemnly given, has been broken'.[71] For Moir, his wife's burial and memorialisation by the state, far from providing a measure of consolation and a permanent marker of membership of the emotional community of wartime Britain, instead provoked further suffering.

Moir's wife, and other victims of air raids who had been buried privately, were not only remembered at their place of burial. Since 1941 the IWGC had been collecting and collating lists of the civilian war dead, sent to them by the Registrar General's Office and by local authorities. As discussed in Chapter 7, Fabian Ware had long argued that the commission should be commemorating the civilian dead alongside those who died on military service, and by 1942 had agreed that a list of the civilian dead would be placed in Westminster Abbey. Home Secretary Herbert Morrison argued that a ceremonial listing of civilian casualties during the war was premature, and it was not until November 1945 that the list of the civilian dead was placed next to the Warrior's Chapel in Westminster Abbey, forming a 'roll of honour' of those who 'endured the agonies of war without aspiring to its glories'.[72] The names of these war dead were also recorded in a published roll of honour, eventually running to seven volumes when they were finally completed in 1958.[73] Pages from the rolls of honour and books of remembrance of local casualties were also displayed in civic centres and town halls. East Ham, in heavily bombed east London, unveiled its own book of remembrance of the borough's dead in May 1950, placing it on a vestibule in the lobby of the town hall, with a dedication by the bishop of nearby Chelmsford. The list included the 458 civilian casualties and eleven council employees who were victims of the Blitz, listed alongside the 254 from the borough who had died on military service. In its naming of the civilian and military dead, all of whom were listed as having 'made the supreme sacrifice', East Ham's communal memorialisation both demonstrated the nature of this new type of total war, and represented these deaths as equivalent, extending the notion of a sacrificial wartime death from military to civilian, and placing these deaths at the heart of a borough, and a nation, reconstructing itself as a new, more egalitarian, community.[74]

Memorialisation such as this, however, should not be confused with the expression of grief. While the experience of grief was often ongoing, shaping the lives of the bereaved in numerous ways, these public and civic acts of remembrance tended to be focused around specific sites, and particular dates, for example *In Memoriam* notices often commemorating the date of a particular air raid. Rituals of remembrance for the civilian dead tended to follow remembrance patterns established in the interwar years to commemorate the dead of the Great War: memorials, often over mass graves, acts of remembrance once a year at the memorial, local rolls of honour and books of remembrance that could be consulted in civic spaces, and memorial notices in local and sometimes national newspapers were the most common forms and practices of public remembrance. The emotional communities that were formed through such practices only become publicly visible at these specific sites and moments, and as the nation worked to reconstruct civic life in the aftermath of war, the conflict's dead were increasingly contained, on the public stage, in particular geographic and temporal spaces.

National remembrance

As the war came to an end, one commemorative space where it was expected that the war's dead would be remembered was in the ceremonies of remembrance that had been established in the aftermath of the Great War. The Armistice Day ceremonies, focused on the Cenotaph in Whitehall but enacted at local memorials throughout the country and the empire, which had been such an important date in the calendar of the interwar years, had been abandoned in 1939 for the duration of the second conflict. At the war's end, the Home Office began to consider the introduction of some form of memorial day, suitable to commemorate 'two national deliverances and the fallen of both the wars'.[75] As 11 November 1945 fell on a Sunday, this was chosen as the most appropriate date to mark the dead of both wars. While Remembrance Sunday had been marked in the 1930s, it was subordinate to Armistice Day in the national calendar; from 1945 it replaced it. The Home Office were keen to ensure a sense of continuity in remembrance practice from the interwar years, searching out the numbers of attendees, the music played and the order of service from Armistice Day ceremonies. However, the number of civilian and civil defence deaths meant that the Home Secretary would now lay a wreath in memory of Civil Defence workers, and the field of remembrance outside Westminster Abbey included crosses and poppies dedicated to the civilian dead, alongside the military.

Women, once again, enacted much of what Joy Damousi has termed 'the labour of loss'.[76] Women's role in the ceremony, as the public face of wartime loss and grief, was reflected on in the press the following day. The leader in the *Daily Mail* placed their presence centre stage:

> When they have forgotten all else that happened during the national service of remembrance at the Cenotaph yesterday, many will still remember that long procession of black clad women that moved slowly through the dense crowds in Whitehall, with the blood red poppies of sacrifice in their hands ... the old and the young side by side had come together in a sisterhood of sorrow.[77]

For the *Daily Mail*, these women represented the timelessness of wartime sacrifice – a grieving, embodied link between the losses of the Great War, and the losses of the war just ended, their participation in the ceremonies of remembrance demonstrating the recognition and sympathy of both state and civil society. For some of the bereaved however, the reintroduction of the ceremony of remembrance was of no comfort. One woman, whose son had died in a bombing raid over Germany, wrote to Clement Attlee in 1945 to oppose the reestablishment of the interwar traditions, including the two-minute silence that lay at the heart of the ceremony. She wrote angrily that this 'mechanical two minute silence' was a 'hypocrisy' designed to limit and contain the expression of her grief and that of others like her for whom 'life has been completely silent for the past two years'.[78] For some of the bereaved, state ceremonies and public acts of remembrance were just empty vessels that did nothing to alleviate their personal grief.

While thousands did attend the remembrance ceremony in 1945, many were unwilling to simply repeat the wider memorial processes associated with the dead of the Great War. In the aftermath of that conflict, public spaces in cities, towns and villages, as well as workplaces, transport junctions, schools and churches, were given over to the physical remembrance of the war's dead. War memorials, paid for by public subscription, were erected around the country, listing the names of the local dead whose bodies were usually buried close to where they fell, or had never been recovered from the battlefield, and these both formed the focus of local Armistice Day ceremonies and acted as a means of reminding people in the community who had been bereaved, and thus might be in need of emotional and sometimes economic support. Although a small number of memorials to the dead of the Great War took the form of memorial halls or housing for veterans, most memorials existed purely to memorialise, to place the names of the dead back in the heart of their communities, and by thus naming, to build a link between the sacrifices of the war, the communities present and a shared future. Visible across Britain, they were the most apparent material legacy of the Great War within national boundaries. As a key part of that war's legacy, they were perceived by some as an unsuitable means of memorialising the dead of a war that killed civilians alongside combatants, and which was understood by many as being fought for a new kind of society. As the war moved towards its closing stages, debates concerning reconstruction, memorialisation and the nature of modern warfare came together in a discussion of how best to commemorate the dead of the 'people's war'.

In April 1944, the Royal Society of Arts convened a conference to consider the most fitting means to memorialise the dead of the war. Opened by Lord Chatfield, attendees included those who might be expected to have a professional interest in memorials, such as the dean of Westminster, and Sir Fabian Ware of the IWGC, who were joined by, among others, Sir Noel Curtis Bennett, chairman of the National Playing Fields Association, and Richard St Barbe Baker, founder of 'Men of the Trees', present to urge the extension of open spaces.[79] The published summary of the conference reveals much about the mood of the time and is worth quoting at length:

> [Military] men and women are, in the main, determined to break away from the purely monumental memorials which appeared all over the country after the last war in the form of statues or groups of statues, ornate drinking fountains, clock towers and obelisks. The trend seems to be more towards a more practical type of memorial which will benefit the families and descendants of those who have lost their lives in the war. Many possibilities suggest themselves: community centres, youth clubs, village halls, the preservation of tracts of land, public parks or gardens of remembrance, hospitals and convalescent homes, and component parts of these such as mobile x-ray units, laboratories and clinics, schools and school equipment and playing fields etc.[80]

In this statement, memorialisation, war aims and reconstruction are neatly folded into one another and set against the monuments to the dead erected after the Great War. Utility was linked to remembrance in proposals for living memorials which would both commemorate the dead and ensure that the war's aims, which they were understood to have died for, would be met.

In February 1945, the House of Lords debated war memorials. Opened by Lord Chatfield, chair of the War Memorials Advisory Council which had been established following the Royal Society of Arts's 1944 conference, the debate considered the recommendations made in the council's first publication, *War Memorials: A Survey Made by a Committee of the Royal Society of Arts*.[81] In this debate, Bishop George Bell, the bishop of Chichester, and Cosmo Lang, archbishop of Canterbury, emphasised both the 'sacred' nature of memorials and the suitability of places of worship as sites for these.[82] Archbishop Lang argued that, far from the aims of the living memorial movement, which emphasised the creation of memorials that were of use to the living as the best means of memorialising the dead, 'we have to consider not what we would most wish for the living but what we owe to the dead'. Lang's conception of the function of memorials firmly emphasised commemoration and remembrance, and he stressed that 'the association of the war memorial visibly and permanently with those whom we desire to commemorate ought to be a guiding principle'.[83] Bell agreed, claiming that 'the church … has a natural relation to the memorials of the fallen', and that 'village halls, community centres and child welfare clinics are all most desirable in themselves but I think that they are to be deprecated as war memorials'.[84] Writing in *Canterbury Diocesan Notes* in March 1946, Lang's successor Geoffrey Fisher echoed these statements, urging his congregation to place memorials in churches and churchyards as 'the surroundings help the memorial, while commemorating the sacrifice of the fallen, to speak a spiritual message of Christian duty and hope'. He also perhaps reacted to the popularity of the living memorial in his acknowledgement that 'it is sometimes possible to provide a memorial which also serves a social purpose', though he concluded that 'it is my own feeling that … a memorial should be itself and nothing more'.[85] These representatives of the established church were not alone in urging caution regarding the collapsing together of memorialisation and reconstruction, but they were in a minority.[86]

The relationship of the church to memorial practice was most apparent when the issue of preserving bombed churches as war memorials was discussed in 1944. The *Architectural Review* had published a special article in January 1944 suggesting that ruined churches would make particularly fitting memorials, as they would both act as a physical reminder of the nature of mid-twentieth century warfare, and, because of their established role as places of worship, they could provide quiet sites for contemplation and remembrance in the midst of busy cities. The dean of St Paul's, W. R. Matthews, provided a foreword, in which he argued that 'the danger we must guard against is that of being too exclusively "practical and utilitarian"'. The article itself combined issues of reconstruction and memorialisation, suggesting that the preservation of a small number of ruined churches would provide space for 'worship' and 'meditation', 'recreation' and 'amenity', but would also be fitting memorials to 'those who gave their lives in the long nights of air raids'.[87] Churches, as physical symbols of the devastation inflicted on parts of urban Britain in the war, were imagined here as uniquely fitting memorials to the particular experience of that war and, crucially, as memorials which combined commemoration with more utilitarian and reflective functions. Coventry Cathedral, badly damaged in the bombing of the city in 1940, and redesigned following an architectural competition in 1951, united memorialisation with religious function, acting as both a site of remembrance for the city (memorial services for the dead had taken place in the ruins of the cathedral every November since 1940), and a symbol of rebirth and reconstruction. The rebuilt cathedral, designed by Basil Spence and incorporating the ruins of the old cathedral with Spence's modernist design, had at its core the concept of resurrection, an idea that was at the heart of Christian theology, as well as enshrined in plans for the reconstruction of both bombed cities and postwar society. Functioning as a memorial to the dead, and as a modern building designed to meet the needs of the modern city growing up around it, Coventry Cathedral was designed as a site of remembrance and reflection, and at the same time a functioning place of worship, in tune with, and of service to, postwar society.[88]

Debates about the role of ruined churches as war memorials largely took place in elite sites of discussion: the letter pages of the *Times*, professional publications, the House of Lords and the Royal Academy of Arts. However, others who had lived through the war also had opinions about how best to memorialise and commemorate the dead, recorded in responses to an MO directive on war memorials in 1944, and in plans for local war memorials sent to the War Memorials Advisory Council by local authorities, organisations and individuals.

The majority of those who replied to the MO directive of July–August 1944, asking 'what are your views on the form which memorials to the dead of this war should take?', favoured useful, utilitarian memorials, that had some function outside of a memorial one. One of the most frequently advocated memorial forms among Mass Observers was the preservation of open countryside for the use and enjoyment of the people. A thirty-six-year-old man wrote to suggest that 'large tracts of open country ... given to the people to enjoy' would be a fitting memorial, a twenty-three-year-old member of the Royal Signal Corps wanted 'the provision of national parks', while a forty-two-year-old chemist demanded 'a national policy of opening up the mountains for the people'.[89] Likewise, the War Memorials Advisory Council emphasised the use of land for memorial purposes in their advice to authorities and organisations planning memorials. They advised that 'in the restfulness and beauty of land developed as a memorial many districts will find the answer to their problems', as this form of memorial would 'make the minimum demand upon materials likely for some time to be in short supply'.[90] Land was thus seen as both an appropriate and a practical response to the desire for some form of memorialisation; combining a 'restfulness and beauty' seen as a counter to and reward for enduring the hardships and disruptions of wartime, with a pragmatic approach to resources, and the preservation of the land for which the dead had been fighting with access to that land for their survivors. The Land Fund, established by Hugh Dalton in 1946 to purchase land as a memorial to the dead of both wars and described by Dalton in his budget speech of that year as 'a war memorial ... which is better than any work of art in bronze or stone', was possibly the most substantial memorial project after the war, using funds to purchase land and buildings which were then donated to a range of charities for public use.[91] By 1952, twenty-seven properties and estates had been acquired by the fund, and were being utilised by the National Trust, the Youth Hostels Association and other charitable bodies.[92]

Parks and recreation grounds were also favoured by Mass Observers and correspondents to the War Memorials Advisory Council. Gardens of remembrance in bombed churches were a popular suggestion among the MO panellists, as were playing fields and playgrounds. Houses, hospitals, scholarships and improved school facilities were all also regularly suggested by panellists. The belief that memorials should benefit the children of the dead was widely shared, with a thirty-eight-year-old civil servant claiming that 'the best memorial is to try to realise the ideals for which we sacrificed the dead and give their children a better world to live in'.[93] This principle informed some local reconstruction policies; Alderman Scoulding, justice of the peace for West Ham, argued,

> I am opposed to putting up granite memorials. I am in favour of slum clearance and open spaces for our children and the children of the men who made the supreme sacrifice.[94]

The argument developed here, that memorials should benefit the living not just alongside the memorialisation of the dead, but as a means of doing so, was frequently expressed, demonstrating the widespread and popular interest in reconstruction that existed in the mid-1940s. As Lord Winster argued in the House of Lords debate on war memorials in 1945, 'the best and finest memorial we can erect to the men who have died in this war is to ensure good treatment of the men who come back and good treatment of their dependents'.[95] Mass Observers agreed. A sixty-one-year-old housewife suggested that 'a small home for an old couple … who may have lost their breadwinner' would be a fitting memorial, while a member of the Women's Auxiliary Air Force argued that, as 'these men died so that we might live, it seems reasonable to spend money on the living rather than the dead'.[96] Among the many letters to the War Memorials Advisory Council asking for guidance regarding intended war memorials was one from Cheriton and District Citizen's Union in Devon, declaring that public opinion in the district demanded that 'no more stone slabs should be erected as war memorials' and they therefore intended to use a memorial fund to build a 'larger public meeting centre'. In East Sussex, Crowborough and Jarvis Brook District Council produced a pamphlet arguing that a memorial community hall would 'hallow the cherished memories of those who gave their lives and at the same time serve in the social and cultural advancement of those who inherit the country'.[97] The *Leicester Mercury* reported that Coalville Rugby Football Club was planning to commemorate the eight members of the football club who lost their lives in the war by building a new, memorial, rugby ground.[98] Pendock Parish Council in Worcestershire decided to raise funds for memorial cottages close to the village church, and a war memorial village, offering homes to disabled veterans and their families, was built at Allenton, Derby.[99] In all of these plans and suggestions, the belief that the dead had sacrificed their lives to ensure a more equitable society underpinned the idea of 'useful' memorials, memorials that were not just utilitarian but were the material embodiment of a widely shared set of war aims.

While some defended the memorial forms that had been created in the aftermath of the Great War, arguing that 'the fundamental reason for erecting war memorials is to commemorate those who gave their lives for their country', not to provide opportunities for 'sports or children's playgrounds', these voices were in the minority.[100] For most of those who participated in these debates, in the aftermath of a war which many believed had been fought for a different, more egalitarian future, memorialisation went hand in hand with the creation of this new society. In this vision of the future, the war's victims had died to build the new Jerusalem.

In the immediate postwar period, the memorials to the Great War were understood by many to not only be out of step with the times, but also to have failed in what many had come to understand to be their function by the 1930s: warning against future wars by memorialising the multiple dead in public spaces.[101] One MO panellist, a Great War veteran who described himself as a 'pacifist' and a 'cripple', called for 'real homes for heroes ... to be built this time and not just talked about', while the War Memorials Advisory Council condemned the 'mere standardised products of commerce' that they felt formed the majority of Great War memorials.[102] Nella Last eloquently explained why she was 'one who hates dead, lifeless, sterile, dull' memorials. She wrote of the Barrow-in-Furness memorial, 'how I hated it. I knew so many of the lads and men whose names were on it, warm, vital laughing people – no connection with the lifeless cold thing which commemorated them.' Like many of her contemporaries, Last wanted to see 'living memorials', favouring 'putting the living first' and preferring 'an avenue of trees, a social club, a playing field' over the 'spate of cenotaphs, wayside crosses, bronze plaques etc. as the last war'.[103] The linkage expressed here, between memories of the dead as living, thinking, feeling people, and the sense that these memories were best embodied in the creation of memorials that could improve the lives of those still living, seems to have been widespread, and informed the move towards 'living memorials' in the immediate postwar period. War memorials are not simply a material manifestation of grief for, and remembrance of, the war dead; instead they stand at the nexus between the personal and the political, embodying feeling but also acting to strengthen the relationship between the individual and the nation-state. If, as Sarah Tarlow has argued, we can read the emotional economy of a period through its memorials, then postwar Britain was reluctant to enshrine its grief in memorial forms associated with the Great War, preferring instead to memorialise them, and perhaps find some consolation, through the fulfilment of widely shared war aims.[104]

Conclusion

Of course, the debates about how to memorialise the war's dead coincided with the lengthy period of austerity endured by Britain in the immediate aftermath of war. In common with many reconstruction schemes, the economic climate meant that relatively few of the plans for 'living memorials' would be realised. Both large and small projects were cancelled. East Grinstead Borough Council in East Sussex cancelled advanced plans for playing fields, a community centre, memorial garden and housing in 1946, while plans for a new national memorial, to be situated in central London, collapsed owing to a lack of public support and funding.[105] The addition of names and dates to existing memorials, alongside the creation of memorial books of the dead became the most common form of memorial.

While the war's dead often lived on in the memories of many of the bereaved, enshrined in the texture and routines of everyday life, with photos on mantelpieces and other heirlooms carrying memories and meanings that were personal to those living with loss, there was little space for them in the wider, public world. Public remembrance and commemoration of the war's dead was largely contained within particular dates and spaces. Loss, however, was everywhere. This loss, though, was rarely directly addressed in the cultural texts of the postwar period. Instead, films like *Brief Encounter*, and novels like *The Heat of the Day*, discussed in the introduction to this chapter, together with texts that, on the surface, seemed to have little to say about grief for the war's dead – such as Evelyn Waugh's eulogy to upper-class life *Brideshead Revisited*, Terence Rattigan's *The Winslow Boy* and Michael Balcon's 1948 film *Scott of the Antarctic* – can all be seen as texts that filtered reflections on wartime loss through a range of other narratives.[106] The bereaved of postwar Britain had to find ways to remember, grieve for and live with their dead in a world that wanted to contain them within set times and spaces. The messy, destabilising and sometimes destructive feeling of grief was no more allowed to disrupt the postwar than it was wartime; a society that was reconstructing itself, looking forward, had little space to look back and mourn the dead of war.

Notes

1. Mass Observation (MO), Directive (August 1950). See T. Dixon, *Weeping Britannia* (Oxford: Oxford University Press, 2015) for a detailed discussion of the MO responses.
2. 'Brief Encounter', the *Times*, 22 November 1945, p. 6.
3. C. Langhamer, 'Who the hell are ordinary people?', Royal Historical Society Lecture (London, 2017).
4. K. Puckett, *War Pictures: Cinema, History and Violence in Britain, 1939–1945* (New York: Fordham University Press, 2017), pp. 136–89.
5. Puckett, *War Pictures*, p. 182.
6. Like *Brief Encounter*, *This Happy Breed* was scripted by Coward and based on his play of the same name, while *In Which We Serve* was also scripted by Coward and directed by Lean.
7. S. Brooke, *Celia Johnson By Bill Brandt*, unpublished paper, North American Conference on British Studies (Montreal, 2012).
8. See R. Dyer, *Brief Encounter* (London: Bloomsbury, 2015); A. Lant, *Blackout: Reinventing Women for Wartime British Cinema* (Princeton, NJ: Princeton University Press, 1991).
9. G. Plain, *Literature of the 1940s: War, Postwar and 'Peace'* (Edinburgh: Edinburgh University Press, 2013).
10. E. Bowen, *The Heat of the Day* (London: Jonathan Cape, 1948).
11. Plain, *Literature of the 1940s*, p. 196.
12. The first edition of Thomas's *Death and Entrances* sold out within a month.
13. S. Tarlow, 'An archaeology of remembering: death, bereavement and the First World War', *Cambridge Archaeological Journal*, 7:1 (1997), pp. 105–21, here 121.

14 J. Winter, *Sites of Memory, Sites of Mourning: The Great War in European Cultural History* (Cambridge: Cambridge University Press, 1995).
15 'Heroes of Arnhem', *Tatler and Bystander* (18 September 1946), p. 356.
16 L. Wigram, cited in S. Price, *If You're Reading This: Last Letters from the Front Line* (London: Frontline Books, 2011), p. 189.
17 G. Gorer, *Death, Grief and Mourning in Contemporary Britain* (London: Cresset, 1965), p. 110.
18 J. Winter, 'Forms of kinship and remembrance in the aftermath of the Great War', in J. Winter and E. Sivan (eds), *War and Remembrance in the Twentieth Century* (Cambridge: Cambridge University Press, 1999), pp. 40–60.
19 A. Bowlby, *The Recollections of Rifleman Bowlby* (London: Leo Cooper, 1969), p. 222.
20 G. Dawson, *Soldier Heroes: British Adventure, Empire and the Imagining of Masculinities* (London: Routledge, 1994).
21 M. Roper, 'Re-remembering the soldier hero: the psychic and social construction of memory in personal narratives of the Great War', *History Workshop Journal*, 50 (2000), pp. 181–204, here 184.
22 M. Thomson, *Psychological Subjects: Identity, Culture and Health in Twentieth Century Britain* (Oxford: Oxford University Press, 2006), p. 251.
23 Bowlby, *Recollections*, p. 189.
24 Bowlby, *Recollections*, Frontispiece and p. 226.
25 Bowlby, *Recollections*, pp. 227–8.
26 Imperial War Museum (IWM), Department of Documents (DD) 67/262/1, *Transcripts of Interviews Made by Thames Television for a Documentary about London During the Blitz* (1990).
27 IWM, DD 67/262/1.
28 On the work involved in achieving composure, and the risks posed to this in the oral history interview, see P. Summerfield, *Histories of the Self: Personal Narratives and Historical Practice* (London: Routledge, 2019), pp. 209–10.
29 *The Bombs That Changed Britain, Episode 2: Hull*, Wall to Wall Productions, BBC (December 2017).
30 L. Eyles, 'Life and you', *Woman's Own* (24 August 1945), p. 22.
31 J. Winter, 'Forms of kinship and remembrance in the aftermath of the Great War'.
32 Winter, *Sites of Memory, Sites of Mourning*, p. 79.
33 Winter, 'Forms of kinship and remembrance in the aftermath of the Great War', p. 41.
34 T. Walter, *On Bereavement: The Culture of Grief* (Maidenhead: Open University Press, 1999), p. 140. Walter does not discuss Welsh cultures of grief or bereavement practices.
35 Walter, *On Bereavement*, p. 144.

36   IWM, DD 93/48/1, *Papers of Squadron Leader Reverend G. H. Martin*.
37   The *Times*, 8 May 1946, p. 1.
38   The *Times*, 9 November 1946, p. 1.
39   The *Times*, 18 November 1946, p. 1.
40   The *Times*, 8 May 1946, p. 1.
41   The *Times*, 18 November 1946, p. 1.
42   The *Times*, 18 November 1946, p. 1.
43   The *Times*, 11 November 1946, p. 1.
44   The *Times*, 12 November 1945, p. 1; 11 November 1947, p. 1; 11 November 1948, p. 1. Maxton is commemorated with 2,294 others on the Malta Memorial to airmen who lost their lives over the Mediterranean, and who have no known grave.
45   *Coventry Evening Telegraph*, 14 November 1946, p. 6.
46   *Coventry Evening Telegraph*, 14 November 1947, p. 1.
47   All from *Coventry Evening Telegraph*, 14 November 1946, p. 6.
48   *Coventry Evening Telegraph*, 14 November 1950, p. 6.
49   Commonwealth War Graves Commission (CWGC), 'Second World War', www.cwgc.org/history-and-archives/second-world-war (accessed 19 February 2019).
50   CWGC website, Grootebeek British Cemetery, West Flanders, Belgium, www.cwgc.org/find-a-cemetery/cemetery/2023723/grootebeek-british-cemetery/ (accessed 19 February 2019).
51   Longworth, *The Unending Vigil*, p. 206.
52   CWGC website, Bayeux cemetery, www.cwgc.org/find-a-cemetery/cemetery/2033300/bayeux-war-cemetery/ (accessed 20 April 2019).
53   'War graves in Holland', the *Times*, 8 May 1946, p. 5.
54   Commonwealth War Graves Commission Archives (CWGC), Add/1/5/15, *Notes on the Organisation of the Work of the Commission in India and Burma*, 'Letter from Graves Registration HQ' (21 January 1946).
55   *Hansard*, House of Commons (HoC), 5:409, 'War graves: relatives visits', Winston Churchill, col. 1672 (10 April 1945).
56   CWGC, CWGC/1/2/A/417, *The Care and Marking of War Graves Pamphlet*.
57   *Hansard* (HoC), 5:457, 'War graves', Emmanuel Shinwell, col. 656 (2 November 1948).
58   'A cemetery in Holland', the *Times*, 20 September 1946, p. 8.
59   CWGC, CWGC/1/1/A/416, 'Present war graves – proposed commission circular', *The Care and Marking of War Graves Pamphlet* (February 1942).
60   Dennis Lord, Kings's Own Yorkshire Light Infantry, Plot XV.C.19, CWGC Military Cemetery, Bayeux, France.
61   CWGC Military Cemetery, Bayeux, France and CWGC War Cemetery, Kohima, India; 'When you go home tell them of us and say, for your tomorrow we gave our today' is also the motto of the Burma Star Association.

Remembering: remembering and commemorating the dead of war

62 Robert Pointer, Royal Norfolk Regiment, Plot 3.D.21 and Alfred Hawkins, Royal Welch Fusiliers, Plot 5.E.8, both buried at CWGC War Cemetery, Kohima, India.
63 William Robinson, South Staffordshire Regiment, Plot XXIII.D.3 and Edgar Loader, Hampshire Regiment, Plot X.D.26, both CWGC Military Cemetery, Bayeux.
64 'How sleep the brave', the *Times*, 16 April 1945, p. 5.
65 Frances Ryce, Royal Engineers, Plot II.C.3 and Robert Toomer, Royal Warwickshire Regiment, Plot XXII.B.9, both CWGC Military Cemetery, Bayeux.
66 Leonard Thake, Royal Artillery, Plot 8.G.15 and Eric Mackenzie, Royal Berkshire Regiment, Plot 7.G.4, both CWGC War Cemetery, Kohima.
67 Frank Crawford, Royal Army Service Corps, Plot XI.C.1, CWGC Military Cemetery, Bayeux, and Leslie Lewis, Worcestershire Regiment, Plot 5.B.14, CWGC War Cemetery, Kohima.
68 Thomas McGowan, Manchester Regiment, Plot 9.B.4, CWGC War Cemetery, Kohima, and Henry Clark, Argyll and Sutherland Highlanders, Plot XV.M.14, CWGC Military Cemetery, Bayeux. Thanks to Max Dutton at the CWGC for sharing his records of the personal inscriptions at Bayeux and Kohima.
69 Glamorgan County Archives, D/DX/641/1, *In Memoriam Leaflet*.
70 The National Archives (TNA), Home Office (HO) 45/21922, *Civilian War Dead Burials*, 'Civilian war dead: marking of graves. questions to be considered' (March 1948).
71 TNA, HO 45/21922, *Civilian War Dead Burials*, Memo (23 May 1947). This case is also discussed in J. Rugg, 'Managing civilian war deaths due to war operations: Yorkshire experiences during World War Two, *Twentieth Century British History*, 15:2 (2004), pp. 152–73.
72 'A civilian roll of honour', the *Times*, 23 December 1942, p. 5.
73 CWGC, CWGC/1/2/D/10/3, *Civilian War Dead*.
74 Newham Local History and Archive Centre, *East Ham Book of Remembrance*.
75 TNA, HO 45/20277/891772/25, *Armistice Day Arrangements 1945*, 'Notes for Armistice Day Interdepartmental Conference' (2 October 1945).
76 J. Damousi, *The Labour of Loss: Mourning, Memory and Wartime Bereavement in Australia* (Cambridge: Cambridge University Press, 1999).
77 'Widows of two wars walk together to the Cenotaph', *Daily Mail*, 12 November 1945, p. 3.
78 TNA, HO 45/20277/891772/25, 'Letter from Mrs Harrison to Mr Attlee' (24 October 1945).
79 'Memorials to war's fallen', the *Times*, 28 April 1944, p. 2.
80 Royal Society of Arts (RSA) Archive, War Memorial Advisory Committee (WMAC) PR/GE/117/10/3, *Conference on War Memorials* (27 April 1944).

81 *War Memorial: A Survey made by a Committee of the Royal Society of Arts* (London: Royal Society of Arts, 1945).
82 Hansard, House of Lords Debates (HoL), 5:134, 'War memorials', Bishop Bell, cols 142, 143 (14 February 1945).
83 Hansard, HoL, 5:134, Lord Lang of Lambeth, col. 1038 (14 February 1945). On the living memorial movement, see A. M. Shanken, 'Planning memory: living memorials in the United States during World War II', *The Art Bulletin*, 84:1 (2002), pp. 130–47.
84 Hansard, HoL, 5:134, Bishop Bell, cols 1045, 1043 (14 February 1945).
85 RSA Archive, PR/GE/117/10/6, *Canterbury Diocesan Notes* (March 1946).
86 For more on the Church of England and memorialisation, see P. Webster, 'Beauty, utility and Christian civilisation: war memorials and the Church of England, 1940–47', *Forum for Modern Language Studies*, 44:2 (2008), pp. 199–211.
87 'Save us our ruins', *Architectural Review* (1944), pp. 13–14.
88 On the redesign of the cathedral, and its meanings in the postwar period, see L. Campbell, 'Towards a new cathedral: the competition for Coventry Cathedral, 1950–51', *Architectural History*, 35 (1992), pp. 208–34.
89 MO, Directive (July–August 1944), Respondents A2684, C3052, G2751.
90 RSA Archive, WMAC File PR/GE/117/10/1, *War Memorials Advisory Committee Overview*.
91 Hansard, HoC, Series 5, Vol. 421, 'Financial Statement', Hugh Dalton, col. 1840 (9 April 1946).
92 Hansard, HoC, Series 5, Vol. 503, 'National Land Fund', John Boyd Carpenter, col. 2310 (17 July 1952).
93 MO, Directive (July–August 1944), Respondent D1066.
94 RSA Archive, WMAC File PR/GE/117/10/3, *The Undertakers' Journal*, n.d.
95 Hansard, HoL, 5:134, Lord Winster, col. 1026 (14 February 1945).
96 MO, Directive (July–August 1944), Respondents H3405, L1657.
97 RSA Archive, WMAC File, PR/GE/117/10/6, *Advice Requests: Correspondents C-E*, 'Letter from Cheriton and District Citizen's Union' (15 April 1946), Crowborough and Jarvis Brook fundraising pamphlet, *We Will Remember Them! War Memorial Hall*, n.d.
98 The *Leicester Mercury*, 16 May 1946.
99 RSA Archive, WMAC File, PR/GE/117/10/9, *Advice Requests: Correspondents M-P*, 'Letter from Vicar of Pendock Church' (2 March 1946); *War Memorial Homes Opened*, British Pathé (1952).
100 RSA Archives, WMAC PR/GE/117/10/3, 'Letter from the Office of Maintenance Commander, HM Dockyards, Chatham' (24 October 1944).
101 On the politics of Armistice Day in the interwar years, see A. Gregory, *The Silence of Memory: Armistice Day, 1919–1946* (Oxford: Berg, 1994); L.

Noakes, 'A broken silence? Mass Observation, Armistice Day and "everyday life" in Britain, 1937–41', *Journal of European Studies*, 45:4 (2015) pp. 331–46.
102   MO, Directive (July–August 1944), Panellist B2703; RSA Archive, WMAC File PR/GE/117/10/1, *WMAC Overview*.
103   MO, Directive (July–August 1944), Respondent N1061.
104   Tarlow, 'An archaeology of remembering'.
105   RSA Archive, WMAC File PR/GE/117/10/7, *Advice Requests, Correspondents F–H*, 'Letter from L. Osman' (8 April 1946); 'Letter from C. Attlee to Chatfield' (29 January 1948).
106   Thanks to Gill Plain for discussion of these examples.

Conclusion
The personal and the political

On 7 July 1945, the day of the General Election, the Labour-supporting *Daily Mirror* urged its readers to remember the dead when they went to cast their vote. The paper's front page reproduced Philip Zec's cartoon, first published on Victory in Europe (VE) Day in May 1945, showing an injured soldier climbing away from a scene of battlefield devastation, with the corpses of combatants scattered across and around the ruins of a farmhouse. The cartoon spoke directly to the newspaper's readers: the exhausted-looking soldier offered up a wreath festooned with the words 'victory and peace in Europe', while the text beneath the image read 'here you are, don't lose it again'. The accompanying editorial made the message of the cartoon even clearer, reminding readers that they were not only voting for themselves, but for those who had died to create a different kind of postwar world. Readers were told that it was their duty to vote for 'the men that fought and died that their homeland and yours might live'. Looking back to the years following the Great War, the editorial argued that the promised 'land "fit for heroes" did not come into existence. The dole did. Short lived prosperity gave way to long, tragic years of poverty and unemployment.' This, it stipulated, could not be allowed to happen again. If it did, the living would be breaking trust with the dead. While urging its readers to 'let no one turn your gaze to the past', thus dismissing Conservative claims that Churchill should be allowed to 'finish the job', it argued that a vote for the Labour Party meant a 'march forward into new and happier times'. By voting Labour, readers would be following the path set out by the dead of the war: 'The call of the men who have gone comes to you. Pay heed to it. Vote for them.'[1] As in the campaign for 'living memorials', discussed in the previous chapter, the continued presence of the war's dead was seen here as being assured through the winning of the principles for which, it was argued, they had died. Conservative, or Liberal, victims of the war had no place in this vision of wartime sacrifice, and nor did civilians: it was the combatant dead alone who had died for the 'new Jerusalem' promised by Attlee's Labour Party.

The *Daily Mirror* editorial, published in the interval between victory in Europe and the final conclusion of the war in Asia, but nonetheless explicitly looking forward to the postwar period, was one of the few public sites where both the postwar was imagined and the war's dead became visible. Outside discussion around living war memorials, reconstruction left little time for looking back at the war years, and it is debatable whether a society exhausted by the multiple demands of war wanted to dedicate time or space to its immediate contemplation. In other ways, however, the war bled over into the postwar. Traditional modern British historical demarcations – the First World War, the interwar period, the Second World War and the postwar – clearly do not hold when we look at Britain's twentieth century through the lenses of social, cultural and emotional history. While the social, the cultural and the emotional were shaped by their historical circumstances, they also refused to be contained by political chronologies. The Second World War may have ended in political and military terms with the surrender of Imperial Japan on 15 August 1945, but it lived on in individual lives, in changed communities and in shared cultures. Although the war's dead may not have been visible in the same way that they were after the Great War, when the creation of Armistice Day and the erection of new war memorials meant that they occupied a visible cultural and geographic space, grief and loss were present, and these feelings and their management continued to shape the lives of individuals, families and communities for many years after 1945.

Zec's cartoon, and the accompanying editorial, serve to bring the three main arguments of this book together. First, in its mobilisation of the war's dead for political ends, it reminds us of the importance to the wartime nation and state of the dead, and of the ways that the bereaved expressed their emotions in the aftermath of loss. In planning for the management of the war's dead, both military and civilian, in the interwar period, and through its evolving response to the interment of casualties and to their eventual commemoration, the actions of the British state show how important emotions were in the 'people's war'. The people had to undertake emotional labour, and were expected to express their feelings through historically specific emotional styles, but the state also had to work hard to ensure that 'the people' felt that their loss was recognised, and their sacrifice properly valued. In an increasingly democratic age, feelings had a public, political value as never before.

Secondly, it shows the ways that the war's dead were put to work, here representing the electoral promises of the Labour Party, and the political beliefs expressed in the *Daily Mirror* editorial. They sacrificed their lives, readers are reminded, not only to win the war, but to win the peace, securing a new political settlement that would ensure the 'new and happier times' that were promised. Throughout the war the dead had worked in various ways for the nation: the civilian dead of Coventry for example, had served both as symbols of a shared determination born out of terrible loss, and as recruiting tools, the British Pathé film *The Tragedy of Coventry* urging its viewers to 'join the noble breed of flying men' to avenge the 'unholy massacre'.[2] Likewise, the children who died at Sandhurst Road School in 1943 were 'martyrs', whose deaths worked to emphasise the barbarity of the enemy, and thus the justness of the Allied cause.[3] Eric Baume, in his description of soldiers' graves at Nijmegen, showed how the combatant dead could work for their living comrades, signifying determination, sacrifice and war aims shared across nations, and between combatant and civilian.[4] While the dead did not always work in this way – their bodies, and the grief of the bereaved, often refusing to be corralled into such unifying narratives – the political and emotional power of the war's dead meant they could be uniquely effective symbols of unity and determination.

Finally, it speaks to us of the emotional economy of wartime Britain. This was an economy in which loss was recognised and death was visible, but it was also an economy that valued attempts by the bereaved to keep their grief largely private, and to recognise in public at least, that they were one of many, and that their loss, and their management of feelings about this loss, was for the greater, collective good. While expressive grief could be made to work for the wartime nation in particular conditions, such as the mass funerals of air raid victims in Coventry, or in Hilde Marchant's vivid descriptions of maternal loss and community solace when children were the primary victims, in most other circumstances vocally and physically expressive grief had little value in the emotional economy of wartime. By the end of the war, over 260,000 members of the British armed forces, and over 60,000 British civilians, had been killed as a direct result of the war.[5] In Britain, as elsewhere, a postwar world of peace and prosperity was promised as the reward for these losses.

Of course, the postwar period refused to settle into a world of peace and prosperity in numerous ways. Even as the peace treaties were being signed to mark the end of the Second World War, the Cold War was beginning, heralding a new age of uncertainty, lived under the threat of nuclear annihilation. Britain, which had entered the war as one of the world's great powers, ended it bankrupt and in debt to a newly powerful United States. The old empires, which had been the source of British and French power, were entering their final days, independence movements in India and elsewhere seizing the opportunities offered by the instability of the war years.[6] Occupied and occupying nations in Europe, North Africa and Asia struggled to rebuild social and political bonds while millions of refugees travelled across the world, trying to return to old homes, or to rebuild their lives in new ones.

In this new and uncertain world, people's feelings mattered at least as much as they had done during the war years. International instability meant that the management, and the self-management, of feeling, remained vital. By the war's end, people were accustomed to expressing their thoughts on, and relationship with, national and international affairs, in terms of the personal, the subjective and the emotional.[7] While, as Hera Cook has argued, the war years saw 'British people, of all social classes valorising emotional restraint and endurance', this should not be confused with the repression of feeling, or an with absence of introspection.[8] Instead, in a process that began well before the war, building on the growing interest in the new 'science' of psychology, and in particular through its practical uses, as discussed in the pages of magazines, newspaper advice columns and popular psychology publications, people learnt to examine, reflect on and manage their emotions.

This management of emotion, and especially the public expression of emotions such as grief, anger, fear and anxiety, that had, it was feared, the potential to undermine morale, served the wartime nation well. While all nations engaged in war, especially total war, urge stoicism on their citizens, the British had well-established styles of emotional restraint and control to draw on. Although this was not uniform, and was shaped by local, gendered and classed emotional cultures, it was nonetheless widely shared across the nation, part of an emotional economy in which the expression, or control, of feeling had a recognised social, cultural and political value. In the writing of any 'emotional history', we must take care not to assume that the emotional economy that the people of the past lived within, and the emotional styles that they

Conclusion

utilised, often very different from our own, were always imposed and constraining. Instead, we need to recognise the agency of those that we study, and to remember that for many, keeping their feelings private may have been both desirable and preferable to demands to articulate and to share these often disruptive and destabilising emotions. Talking is not always the route to recovery.[9] For the people of mid-century Britain, schooled as they were in both self-reflection and self-restraint, privacy may have been experienced by many as a comfort, and while some may have suffered from an inability to share their innermost feelings and to thus gain sympathy or empathy, others would have found consolation in the expectation that they should demonstrate composure in public.

War is disruptive in multiple and complex ways, and death, grief and bereavement are among the most disruptive aspects of conflict, not only destroying lives and relationships, but acting to destabilise a sense of self among the bereaved. Because of this, wartime nations, especially democratic nations such as Britain, that rely on consent as much as coercion, work hard to create a stability around death, based in large part on an understanding that the wartime nation values the sacrifice of the bereaved. Studies of memorialisation and commemoration in the aftermath of war have shown us, across multiple nations and periods, the ways in which nation-states attempt to ensure stability through the management of the war dead and those that they leave behind. What these studies are less adept at showing us, are the ways that the bereaved experienced grief, and attempted to manage their bereavement. While we can never fully comprehend the multiple ways that war impacts on, and is understood by, historical actors, we can at least try to understand the circumstances in which these experiences are felt and articulated. Writing a history of death, grief and bereavement in Second World War Britain is, inevitably and in part, to write a history of silence, of absence and of social and cultural elision – and to understand how loud these silences can be.

Notes

1 The *Daily Mirror*, 5 July 1945, p. 1.
2 *The Tragedy of Coventry*, British Pathé (1940).
3 'Bombed school dead buried', the *Times*, 28 January, 1943, p. 2.
4 E. Baume, *Five Graves at Nijmegen* (London: The Westminster Press, 1945).
5 The Central Statistical Office, *Fighting with Figures: A Statistical Digest of the Second World War* (London: HMSO, 1995) pp. viii–ix.

6 On this, see Y. Khan, *The Raj at War: A People's History of India's Second World War* (London: The Bodley Head, 2015); A. Jackson, Y. Khan and G. Singh (eds), *An Imperial World at War: The British Empire, 1939–45* (London: Taylor & Francis, 2015).
7 On emotional citizenship in postwar Britain, see C. Langhamer, 'Astray in a dark forest: the emotional politics of reconstruction Britain', in C, Langhamer, L. Noakes and C. Siebrecht (eds), *Total War: An Emotional History* (Oxford: Oxford University Press, 2019).
8 H. Cook, 'From controlling emotion to expressing feelings in mid-twentieth-century England', *Journal of Social History*, 47:3 (2014), pp. 627–46, here 628.
9 See for example, L. Robinson, 'Soldiers' stories of the Falklands War: recomposing trauma in memory', *Contemporary British History*, 25:4 (2011), pp. 569–89, here 579.

Bibliography

Primary Sources

Archives

Bristol City Archives

42206/1, *Air Raid Casualties, 1940–42*
44949/1/11, *Records of the East Bristol History Group*
LM/C/X18/8, *Lord Mayor's Office, Correspondence: Relating to Air Raids, Sympathy Letters, and Casualties*

Clydebank Local History Centre

File No. 941.37, *Clyde Air Raid Papers*, Volume 1

Commonwealth War Graves Commission Archives

CWGC/1/1/A/416, *Present War Graves. Proposed Commission Circular*
CWGC/1/2/A/417, *The Care and Marking of War Graves Pamphlet*
CWGC/1/2/D/3/24, *Civilian War Dead*
CWGC/1/2/D/10/3, *Section 13. Civilian War Dead*
CWGC Add/1/5/15, *Notes on the Organisation of the Work of the Commission in India and Burma*

Coventry City Archive

CCA/1456, *Reminiscences*
CCB/1/30/4, *City of Coventry Blitz Commemoration Book*
CCB/8/1/9/2, *Coventry Archives Education Service: The City Under Fire*
CCE/8/1/1/42. *Letters on Coventry Blitz*

Bibliography

Glamorgan County Archives

D/DX/641/1, *In Memoriam Leaflet*

Hackney Archives

S/A/27, *Burial Records of Civil Defence Personnel and Civilians*, 1945–50

Hull History Centre

C TYC/1, *Register of Air Raid Casualties*, 3 April–7 November 1941

The Imperial War Museum, London

Air Ministry, *Casualty Procedure in War* (Air Publication 1922, 2nd edition, 1942)
Department of Documents, 05/56/1, *Miss Beryl Myatt*
Department of Documents, 89/17/1, *The Wartime Diaries of Mrs A. D. Deacon, MBE*
Department of Documents, 93/48/1, *Papers of Squadron Leader G. H. Martin*
Department of Documents, 95/27/1, B. Holbrook, *No Medals For Us*
Department of Documents, 67/262/1, *Transcripts of Interviews Made by Thames Television for a Documentary about London During the Blitz*
Department of Documents, 16877, *Private Papers of J. Driscoll*

London Metropolitan Archive

LCC/EO/War/03/028, *Damage and Casualties at Sandhurst Road School, Catford*

The Mass Observation Archive

File Reports
FR44, *Astrology*, March 1940
FR393, *Film 'Fade Out' Competition*, September 1940
FR495, *Coventry*, November 1940
FR529, *Report on the Aftermath of Town Blitzes*, December 1940
FR569, *Airmen*, February 1941
FR693, *Paddington Church Count*, May 1941
FR769, *Mass Astrology*, July 1941
FR812, *Mass Astrology*, August 1941
FR975, *Report on Superstition*, November 1941
FR1315, *Death and the Supernatural*, June 1942

Bibliography

Day Surveys:
Armistice Day, November 1937
Armistice Day, November 1938
Munich, September 1938

Diaries
Diarist 5110
Diarist 5227, May 1942
Diarist 5378, March 1941
Diarist 5446, August 1942

Directives
January 1939
May 1944
July–August 1944
August 1950

Topic Collection
Religion, 1937–1950

Worktown Collection
Armistice Day 27/A, November 1937

The Mitchell Library, Glasgow

D/CD/1, *Air Raid Casualties, March 1941–January 1942*
D/CD/2, *ARP Memoranda, Circulars to and From Ministry of Home Security*
D/CD/4, *Emergency Mortuary Service*
D/CD/7/2, *Register of Identified Dead*
D/CD/7/3, *Register of Unidentified Dead*
D/CD/9/16, *Air Raids, Casualties*

Newham Archive and Local Studies Library at Stratford

East Ham Book of Remembrance

The National Archives, London

AIR 2/1267, *Chief of the Air Staff*
AIR 20/9305, *Air Ministry Report of RAF and Dominions Air Forces Missing Research and Enquiry Service 1944–1949*
CAB 66/35/37, *Tube Shelter Inquiry. Report by Mr Dunne*
CAB 106/1207, *British and Allied Battle Casualties 1939–1946*
FD 1/5372, *Air Raid Precautions Department, Home Office*
FD 1/6523, *Air Raid Casualties: Records of Post Mortem Examinations*

Bibliography

HLG 7/436, *Volunteers Killed and Civilians Dying as Result of Enemy Action*
HLG 7/761, *Civilian War Dead Bible*
HLG 120/1464, *Physical Training and Recreation Act, 1937*
HO 45/18136, *Committee of Imperial Defence Sub-Committee*
HO 45/18142, *War. Burial of the Dead Killed in Air Raids*
HO 45/20277/891772/25, *Armistice Day Arrangements 1945*
HO 45/21922, *Civilian War Dead Burials*
HO 45/25600, *Disaster at an Air Raid Shelter in East London. Position of Coroner Under the Defence Regulations*
HO 186/376, *Blitz Casualties/Burial of Casualties*
HO 186/629, *Blitz Casualties, Identification of*
HO 186/637, *Supplementary 'Blitz' Papers: Casualties, Analysis of Injuries*
HO 186/886, *Publicity. Rumour Regarding Air Raid Damage and Consideration of Counter Measures*
HO 186/1225, *General File: Dead Persons, Burial of*
HO 186/2550, *Dead Persons: Register of Deaths and Graves of 1. Civil Defence Volunteers and 2. Civilian Populations. National War Memorial Policy*
HO 186/2628, *Dead Persons Part 2: Proposals for Marking and Maintenance of Civilian Graves*
HO 207/22, *ARP London Region. Records of Civilians Killed by Enemy Action for Imperial War Graves Commission*
MH 76/9, *Air Raid Casualties. Removal and Certification of the Dead*
MH 96/165, *Welsh Board of Health. Treatment of Air Raid Casualties. Conferences of Medical Practitioners*
WO 32/9850, *Imperial War Graves Commission Commemoration of Civilians Killed in Air Raids*
WO 169/13802, *British Forces, Middle East War Diaries. Graves Registration and Enquiries 1943*
WO 171/3926, *Graves Registration and Enquiries. Allied Expeditionary Force North West Europe. War Diaries 1945*
WO 171/4474, *Chaplains. Allied Expeditionary Force North West Europe. War Diaries. Lines of Communication. Chaplains 1945*
WO 203/909, *Graves Registration South East Asia. Command. October 1943*
WO 219/1370, *Funerals, Burials and Reports, General*

The National Records of Scotland, Edinburgh

HH 50/2, *Reports on Air Raids on Southern Areas, Clydeside*
HH 50/3, *Reports on Air Raids on Clydebank. Department of Health for Scotland: The Clydebank Air Raids of March 13–15 1941*
HH 50/91, *Heavy Air Attacks Clydeside. General*
HH 50/98, *Casualties in Western District 13–15 March 1941*

Bibliography

HH 50/99, *Regional HQ Report on Clydeside Raids of 13/14 and 14/15 March 1941*
HH 50/103, *Air Raids Clydeside 5/6, 6/7 May 1941*
HH 50/126, *Burial of Civilian War Dead*
HH 50/127, *Burial of the Dead in Wartime. Questions Arising from D.P. Circular No. 2.*

The Public Record Office of Northern Ireland

CAB 3/A/58, *Civil Defence Medical Folder no. 13*
CAB 3/A/60, *Air Raids on Belfast*
CAB 3/A/62, *Civil Defence: Miscellaneous*
CAB 3/A/68 A and B, *Report on Belfast Air Raids*
CAB 3/A/69, *Draft Typescript of History of Civil Defence in Northern Ireland to 1939*
D2109/20, *Diary of Miss Emma Duffin, while Serving as VAD Commandant at Stranmillis General Hospital*
MPS2/3/99, *Deaths Due to War Operations. Lists of Dead Identified at St George's Market*

Plymouth and West Devon Record Office

FR 1562/2/16, *Circulars Relating to Civilian War Deaths*
FR 1714/1/2, *Plymouth Air Raid Casualties, 21 March–23 April 1941.*
FR 1495/54, *Plymouth Emergency Committee Minutes*
FR 854.4, *Civil Defence Preparations*

The Royal Society of Arts Archive

Papers of the War Memorials Advisory Committee:
PR/GE/117/10/1, *War Memorials Advisory Committee Overview*
PR/GE/117/10/3, *Conference on War Memorials,* 27 April 1944
PR/GE/117/10/6, *Canterbury Diocesan Notes,* March 1946
PR/GE/117/10/1–9, *Advice Requests,* 1944–1948

The Wolfson Centre, Library of Birmingham

MS 794/2, *Air Raid Diary with Notes of Attacks on Birmingham and with Special Attention to Area Controlled by Warden's Post B/7/A*
MS 1881/1, M. Ashby, *Record of Some Air Raids on Birmingham*
MS 1611/B/11/4, *Transcripts, Acocks Green*

Bibliography

Hansard Parliamentary Debates

House of Commons Debate, Series 5, Volume 270, 1932
House of Commons Debate, Series 5, Volume 295, 1934
House of Commons Debate, Series 5, Volume 232, 1937
House of Commons Debate, Series 5, Volume 409, 1945
House of Commons Debate, Series 5, Volume 414, 1945
House of Commons Debate, Series 5, Volume 421, 1946
House of Commons Debate, Series 5, Volume 457, 1948
House of Commons Debate, Series 5, Volume 503, 1952
House of Lords Debate, Series 5, Volume 134, 1945

Films

The Ghost Goes West, dir. R. Clair, 1935
National Day of Prayer, British Pathé, May 1940
The Tragedy of Coventry, British Pathé, 1940
In Which We Serve, dir. N. Coward and D. Lean, 1943
Millions Like Us, dir. S. Gilliat and F. Launder, 1943
The Way Ahead, dir. C. Reed, 1944
A Matter of Life and Death, dir. M. Powell and E. Pressburger, 1945
Brief Encounter, dir. D. Lean, 1945
The Way to the Stars, dir. A. Asquith, 1945
War Memorial Homes Opened, British Pathé, 1952

Magazines and Periodicals

British Medical Journal
The *Fortnightly Review*
The *Lancet*
Nash's Pall Mall Magazine
The *Petworth Society magazine*
Practical Psychology
Tatler and Bystander
The *Times Literary Supplement*
Woman
Woman's Own
You: The Popular Psychology Magazine

Newspapers

The *Birmingham Mail*
The *Birmingham Post*

Bibliography

The *Brighton Herald*
Coventry Evening Telegraph
The *Daily Express*
The *Daily Herald*
The *Daily Mail*
The *Daily Mirror*
The *Daily Record*
The *Dundee Courier*
Dundee Evening Telegraph
Glasgow Evening Times
Glasgow Herald
The *Leicester Mercury*
Liverpool Daily Post
The *Manchester Guardian*
The *New York Times*
The *News Chronicle*
The *Northern Whig and Belfast Post*
Portsmouth Evening News
The *Scotsman*
Sunday Pictorial
The *Sunday Post*
The *Times*
Western Daily Press and Bristol Mirror
The *Western Morning News*
Yorkshire Post

Memoirs

Bolitho, H., *Finest of the Few: The Story of Battle of Britain Fighter Pilot John Simpson* (Stroud: Amberley Publishing, 2012), [First published as H. Bolitho, *Combat Report: The Story of a Fighter Pilot* (London: B. T. Batsford, 1943]
Bowlby, A., *The Recollections of Rifleman Bowlby* (London: Leo Cooper, 1969)
Brutton, P., *Ensign in Italy: A Platoon Commander's Story* (London: Leo Cooper, 1992)
Butler, A. S. G., *Recording Ruin* (London: Constable and Company, 1942)
Cane, C., *Peace, War and Wigging In* (York: Courtney Publishers, 2013)
Craig, N., *The Broken Plume: A Platoon Commander's Story, 1940–1945* (London: The Imperial War Museum, 1982)
Dickens, M., *An Open Book* (London: Heinemann, 1978)
Dixon, B., *Raiders Overhead: The Record of a London Warden* (London: Lindsay Drummond, 1943)
Douglas, K., *Alamein to Zem Zem* (London: Editions Poetry, 1946)

Bibliography

Hadley, P., *Third Class to Dunkirk: A Worm's Eye View of the BEF*, 1940 (London: Hollis & Carter, 1944)
Jameson, S., *Journey from the North. Volume 2* (London: Collins and Harvill, 1970)
MacDonald Fraser, G., *All Quartered Safe Out Here: A Recollection of the War in Burma* (London: Harvill, 1996)
Mayman, D., *Led Soldiers: The Second World War Diaries of a Royal Hussar* (Bedfordshire: Authors Online, 2008)
Ritchie, H., *The Fusing of the Ploughshare: From East Anglia to Alamein: The Story of a Yeoman at War* (Ritchie: Dunmow, 1987)
Robson, W., *Letters From a Soldier* (London: Faber & Faber, 1960)
Samson, W., *The Blitz: Westminster in War* (London: Faber & Faber, 1947)
Skinner, L., *The Man Who Worked on Sundays: The Personal War Diary June 2nd 1944 to May 17th 1945 of Revd Leslie Skinner RAChD, 8th (Independent) Armoured Brigade Attached to the Sherwood Rangers Yeomanry Regiment* (printed for the author by Plus Printing, n.d.)
Tripp, M., *The Eighth Passenger* (London: Heinemann, 1969)
Vigors, T., *Life's Too Short to Cry* (London: Grub Street, 2006)
Wellum, G., *First Light* (London: Penguin, 2002)
Whitehouse, S. and G. B. Bennett, *Fear is the Foe: A Footslogger from Normandy to the Rhine* (London: Robert Hale, 1995)

Novels and Short Stories

Bowen, E., *The Demon Lover and Other Stories* (London: Jonathan Cape, 1945)
Bowen, E., *The Heat of the Day* (London: Jonathan Cape, 1948)
Buster, G., *Return via Dunkirk* (London: Hodder and Stoughton, 1940)
Jameson, S., *The Journal of Mary Hervey Russell* (London: Macmillan, 1945)
Llewelyn, J. R., *How Green was My Valley* (London: Michael Joseph, 1939)
Marsh, E., *We Lived in London* (London: Lutterworth Press, 1942)
Miles, *The Gas War of 1940* (London: Eric Partridge at the Scolatis Press, 1931)
Monsarrat, N., *The Cruel Sea* (London: Penguin, 2002. First published 1951)
Pargeter, E., *She Goes to War* (London: Heinemann, 1942)
Stokes, S., *Air-Gods' Parade* (London: Arthur Barron, 1935)

Pamphlets

Baume, E., *Five Graves at Nijmegen* (London: The Westminster Press, 1945)
Labour Party, *ARP: Labour's Policy* (London: Labour Party, 1939)
Wintringham, T., *Air Raid Warning* (London: Communist Party of Great Britain Leaflets, 1937)

Bibliography

Television

The Bombs That Changed Britain, Episode 2: Hull, Wall to Wall Productions, BBC (December 2017)

Secondary Sources

Articles

n.a., 'A brief history of cremation: the Manchester experience', *Manchester Genealogist*, 37:2 (2001)

Beaven, B. and J. Griffiths, 'The blitz, civilian morale and the city: Mass Observation and working-class culture in Britain, 1940–41', *Urban History*, 26:1 (1999)

Beaven, B. and J. Griffiths, 'Creating the exemplary citizen: the changing notion of citizenship in Britain, 1870–1939', *Contemporary British History*, 22:2 (2008)

Bessel, R., 'Hatred after war: emotion and the postwar history of East Germany', *History and Memory*, 17 (2005)

Bloch, M., 'Reflections of a historian on the false news of the war' (1921), trans. J. P. Holoka, *Michigan War Studies Review*, 51 (2013)

Campbell, L., 'Towards a new cathedral: the competition for Coventry Cathedral, 1950–51', *Architectural History*, 35 (1992)

Clark, J. C. D. 'Secularization and modernization: the failure of a grand narrative', *The Historical Journal*, 55:1 (2012)

Conway, R., 'Making the mill girl modern? Beauty, industry and the popular newspaper in 1930s England', *Twentieth Century British History*, 24:4 (2013)

Cook, H., 'From controlling emotion to expressing feelings in mid-twentieth century England', *Journal of Social History*, 47:3 (2014)

Das, S., 'Indian sepoy experience in Europe, 1914–18: archive, language and feeling', *Twentieth Century British History*, 25:3 (2014)

Del Rosario, I., 'A journey into grief', *Journal of Religion and Health*, 43:1 (2004)

Devereux, S., 'Famine in the 20th Century', *I.D.S. Working Paper* (Brighton: Institute of Development Studies, 2000)

Dibley, B. and R. Kelly, 'Morale and Mass Observation: governing the affective atmosphere on the home front', *Museum and Society*, 13:1 (2015)

Eley, G., 'Finding the "people's war": film, British collective memories and World War II', *The American Historical Review*, 103:3 (2001)

Featherstone, S., 'The mill girl and the cheeky chappie: British popular culture and mass entertainment in the thirties', *Critical Survey*, 15:2 (2003)

Field, S., '*Puzzled People* revisited: religious believing and belonging in wartime Britain, 1939–45', *Twentieth Century British History*, 19:4 (2008)

Francis, M., 'The domestication of the male? Recent research on nineteenth and twentieth century masculinity', *The Historical Journal*, 45:3 (2002)

Francis, M., 'Tears, tantrums and bared teeth: the emotional economy of three Conservative prime ministers 1951–1963', *Journal of British Studies*, 41:3 (2002)

Gammerl, B., 'Emotional styles – concepts and challenges', *Rethinking History: The Journal of Theory and Practice*, 16:2 (2012)

Grant, M., 'Historicising citizenship in postwar Britain', *The Historical Journal*, 59:4 (2016)

Hazelgrove, J., 'Spiritualism after the Great War', *Twentieth Century British History*, 10:4 (1999)

Jones, E., 'The psychology of killing: the combat experience of British soldiers during the First World War', *Journal of Contemporary History*, 41:2 (2006)

Jones, E., R. Wooleden, B. Durodie and S. Wessely, 'Civilian morale during the Second World War: responses to air raids – re-examined', *Social History of Medicine*, 17:3 (2004)

Julius Matthews, J., '"They had such a lot of fun": the Women's League of Health and Beauty between the wars', *History Workshop Journal*, 30 (Autumn 1990)

Kounine, L., 'Emotions, mind and body on trial: a cross-cultural perspective', *Journal of Social History*, 51:3 (2017)

Langhamer, C., 'Love, selfhood and authenticity in post-war Britain', *Cultural and Social History*, 9:2 (2012)

Laqueur, T., 'Bodies, death and pauper funerals', *Representations*, 1 (2003)

Lomas, J., '"So I married again": letters from British widows of the First and Second World Wars', *History Workshop Journal*, 38 (1994)

McCarthy, H., 'Parties, voluntary associations and democratic politics in interwar Britain', *Historical Journal*, 50:4 (2007)

McCarthy, H., 'Whose democracy? Histories of British political culture between the wars', *Historical Journal*, 55:1 (2012)

Meisel, J. R., 'Air raid shelter policy and its critics in Britain before the Second World War', *Twentieth Century British History*, 5:3 (1994)

Moran, J., 'Private lives, public histories: the diary in twentieth century Britain', *Journal of British Studies*, 54 (2015)

Morley, J., 'The memory of the Great War and morale during Britain's phoney war', *The Historical Journal* (online, Cambridge University Press, 27 March 2019).

Mort, F., 'Love in a cold climate: letters, public opinion and monarchy in the 1936 abdication crisis', *Twentieth Century British History*, 25:1 (2014)

Noakes, L., '"Serve to Save"': gender, citizenship and civil defence in Britain, 1937–41', *Journal of Contemporary History*, 47:4 (2012)

Noakes, L., 'A broken silence: Mass Observation, Armistice Day and "everyday life" in Britain, 1937–1941', *Journal of European Studies*, 45:4 (2015)

Noakes, L., 'Gender, grief and bereavement in Second World War Britain', *Journal of War and Culture Studies*, 8:1 (2015)

Noakes, L., '"My husband is interested in war generally": gender, family history and the emotional legacies of total war', *Women's History Review*, 27:4 (2018)

Bibliography

Parsons, B., 'The management of civilian funerals in the Second World War', *British Institute of Funeral Directors Journal*, 3 (2011)

Pearsall, C., 'Burying the Duke: Victorian mourning and the funeral of the Duke of Wellington', *Victorian Literature and Culture*, 27:2 (1999)

Pederson, S., 'Gender, welfare and citizenship in Britain during the Great War', *The American Historical Review*, 95:4 (1990)

Peniston-Bird, C., 'Classifying the body in the Second World War: British men in and out of uniform', *Body and Society*, 9:4 (2003)

Robinson, L., 'Soldiers' stories of the Falklands War: recomposing trauma in memory', *Contemporary British History*, 24:4 (2011)

Roper, M., 'Re-remembering the soldier-hero: the psychic, and social construction of memory in personal narratives of the Great War', *History Workshop Journal*, 50 (2000)

Roper, M., 'Between manliness and masculinity: the "war generation" and the psychology of fear in Britain, 1914–1950', *Journal of British Studies*, 44:2 (2005)

Rosenwein, B., 'Worrying about emotions in history', *The American Historical Review*, 107:3 (2002)

Rugg, J., 'Managing civilian deaths due to war operations: Yorkshire experiences during World War Two', *Twentieth Century British History*, 15:2 (2004)

Rugg, J., 'Consolation, individuation and consumption: towards a theory of cyclicality in English funeral practice', *Cultural and Social History*, 15:1 (2018)

Satia, P., 'The defence of inhumanity: air control and the British idea of Arabia', *The American Historical Review*, 111:1 (2006)

Scheer, M., 'Are emotions a kind of practice (and is that what makes them have a history)? A Bourdieuian approach to understanding emotion', *History and Theory*, 51 (2012)

Shanken, A. M., 'Planning memory: living memorials in the United States during World War II', *The Art Bulletin*, 84:1 (2002)

Stearns, P. N. and C. Z. Stearns, 'Emotionology: clarifying the history of emotions and emotional standards', *The American Historical Review*, 90:4 (1985)

Strange, J. M., 'Only a pauper whom nobody owns: reassessing the pauper grave circa 1880–1914', *Past and Present*, 178 (2003)

Summerfield, P., 'War, film, memory: some reflections on war films and the social configuration of memory in Britain in the 1940s and 1950s', *Journal of War and Culture Studies*, 1:1 (2008)

Tanner, A., 'The Spanish Lady comes to London: the influenza pandemic 1918–1919', *The London Journal*, 27:2 (2002)

Tarlow, S., 'An archaeology of remembering: death, bereavement and the First World War', *Cambridge Archaeological Journal*, 7:1 (1997)

Twells, A., '"Went into raptures": reading emotion in the ordinary wartime diary, 1941–1946', *Women's History Review*, 25:1 (2016)

Bibliography

Wacquant, L. J. D., 'Pugs at work: bodily capital and bodily labour among professional boxers', *Body and Society*, 1:1 (1995)

Webster, P., 'Beauty, utility and Christian civilisation: war memorials and the Church of England, 1940–47', *Forum for Modern Language Studies*, 44:2 (2008)

Williamson, P. 'National days of prayer: the churches, the state and public worship in Britain, 1899–1957', *English Historical Review*, CXXVIII:351 (2013)

Yurchak, A., 'Bodies of Lenin: the hidden science of Communist sovereignty', *Representations*, 129:1 (2015)

Books

Addison, P. and A. Calder (eds), *Time to Kill: The Soldier's Experience of War in the West, 1939–1945* (London: Pimlico, 1997)

Ahmed, S., *The Cultural Politics of Emotion* (London: Routledge, 2012. First published Edinburgh: Edinburgh University Press, 2004)

Aldgate, A. and J. Richards, *Britain Can Take It: The British Cinema in the Second World War* (London: I. B. Tauris, 2nd edition, 2007)

Allen, L., *Burma. The Longest War, 1941–1945* (London: Phoenix Press, 2000. First published 1984)

Allport, A., *Browned Off and Bloody Minded: The British Soldier Goes to War, 1939–1945* (New Haven, CT: Yale University Press, 2015)

Anderson, J., *War, Disability and Rehabilitation in Britain: Soul of a Nation* (Manchester: Manchester University Press, 2011)

Ariès, P., *The Hour of Our Death*, trans. H. Weaver (New York: Alfred A. Knopf, 1981)

Barton, B., *The Blitz: Belfast in the War Years* (Belfast: Blackstaff Books, 1989)

Bennet, G. H. and R. Bennet, *Survivors: British Merchant Seamen in the Second World War* (London: Hambledon Continuum, 1999)

Bessel, R., 'Unnatural deaths', in R. Overy (ed.), *The Oxford Illustrated History of World War II* (Oxford: Oxford University Press, 2014)

Bessel, R., 'Death and Survival in the Second World War', in M. Geyer and A. Tooze (eds), *The Cambridge History of the Second World War. Volume 3, Total War: Economy, Society and Culture* (Cambridge: Cambridge University Press, 2015)

Bingham, A., *Gender, Modernity and the Popular Press in Interwar Britain* (Oxford: Clarendon Press, 2004)

Blake, J. W., *Northern Ireland in the Second World War* (Belfast: HMSO, 1956)

Bourke, J., *Dismembering the Male: Men's Bodies, Britain and the Great War* (London: Reaktion Books, 1996)

Bourke, J., *An Intimate History of Killing. Face to Face Killing in Twentieth-Century Warfare* (London: Granta, 1999)

Bourke, J., *Fear: A Cultural History* (London: Virago, 2005)

Bibliography

Bourke, J., 'Foreword', in C. Langhamer, L. Noakes and C. Siebrecht (eds) *Total War: An Emotional History* (Oxford: Oxford University Press, 2019)

Boyd, K., 'Knowing your place: The tension of manliness in boys' story papers, 1918-1939', in M. Roper and J. Tosh (eds), *Manful Assertions* (London: Routledge, 1991)

Brown, C., *Religion and Society in Scotland Since 1707* (Edinburgh: Edinburgh University Press, 1997)

Brown, C., *The Death of Christian Britain: Understanding Secularism 1800-2000* (London: Routledge, 2001)

Butler, J., *Precarious Life: The Powers of Mourning and Violence* (London: Verso, 2004)

Butler, J. R. M., *History of the Second World War. Volume II: The Mediterranean and Middle East* (London: HMSO, 1956)

Butler, T. (ed.), *The 1943 Bethnal Green Tube Shelter Disaster: An Oral History* (London: University of East London, 2015)

Calder, A., *The People's War: Britain 1939-1945* (London: Jonathan Cape, 1971)

Cannadine, D., 'War and death, grief and mourning in modern Britain', in J. Whaley (ed.), *Mirrors of Mortality: Studies in the Social History of Death* (London: Europa, 1981)

Carden-Coyne, A., *The Politics of Wounds: Military Patients and Medical Power in the First World War* (Oxford: Oxford University Press, 2015)

Ceadel, M., 'Popular fiction and the next war, 1918-39', in F. Gloversmith (ed.), *Class, Culture and Social Change: A New View of the 1930s* (Brighton: Harvester Press, 1980)

Central Statistical Office, *Fighting with Figures: A Statistical Digest of the Second World War* (London: HMSO , 1995)

Chinn, C., *Brum Undaunted: Birmingham During the Blitz* (Birmingham: Birmingham Library Services, 1996)

Clydebank Life Story Group, *Remembering Clydebank in Wartime* (Clydebank: Clydebank Life Story Group, 1999)

Confino, A., P. Betts and D. Schumann (eds), *Between Mass Death and Individual Loss: The Place of the Dead in Twentieth-Century Germany* (New York: Berghahn, 2008)

Connelly, M., *We Can Take It! Britain and the Memory of the Second World War* (Harlow: Pearson, 2004)

Connelly, M. and S. Goebel, *Ypres* (Oxford: Oxford University Press, 2018)

Crang, J., *The British Army and the People's War, 1939-1945* (Manchester: Manchester University Press, 2000)

Damousi, J., *The Labour of Loss: Mourning, Memory and Wartime Bereavement in Australia* (Cambridge: Cambridge University Press, 1999)

Davidoff, L., *Worlds Between: Historical Perspectives on Gender and Class* (London: Polity, 1995)

Bibliography

Davis Biddle, T., 'Anglo-American strategic bombing, 1940–1945', in J. Ferris and E. Mawdsley (eds), *The Cambridge History of the Second World War. Volume 1, Fighting the War* (Cambridge: Cambridge University Press, 2015)

Dawson, G., *Soldier Heroes: British Adventure, Empire and the Imagining of Masculinities* (London: Routledge, 1994)

Dixon, T., *Weeping Britannia: Portrait of a Nation in Tears* (Oxford: Oxford University Press, 2015),

Dollimore, J., *Death, Desire and Loss in Western Culture* (New York: Routledge, 1998)

Douhet, G., *The Command of the Air* (1921), trans. D. Ferrari (London: Faber & Faber, 1943)

Dowding, H., *Many Mansions* (London: Rider & Co., 1943)

Dowding, H., *Lychgate* (London: Rider, 1945)

Dyer, R., *Brief Encounter* (London: Bloomsbury, 2015)

Edgerton, D., *Warfare State: Britain 1920–1970* (Cambridge: Cambridge University Press, 2006)

Febvre, L., 'Sensibility and history: how to reconstitute the emotional life of the past,' (1941), in P. Burke (ed.), *A New Kind of History: From the Writings of Febvre* (London: Harper & Row, 1973)

Francis, M., *The Flyer: British Culture and the Royal Air Force, 1939–1945* (Oxford: Oxford University Press, 2008)

Francis, M., 'Foreword', in W. Ugolini and J. Pattinson (eds), *Fighting for Britain? Negotiating Identities in Britain During the Second World War* (Edinburgh: Peter Lang, 2015)

Frevert, U., *Emotions in History – Lost and Found* (Budapest: Central European University Press, 2011)

Furneaux, H., *Military Men of Feeling: Emotion, Touch and Masculinity in the Crimean War* (Oxford: Oxford University Press, 2016)

Fussell, P., *The Boy's Crusade: The American Infantry in Northwestern Europe, 1944–1945* (New York: Modern Library, 2003)

Gardner, J., *The Blitz: The British Under Attack* (London: Harper Press, 2010)

Gerwarth, R., 'The continuum of violence' in J. Winter (ed.), *The Cambridge History of the First World War. Volume 2, The State* (Cambridge: Cambridge University Press, 2014)

Gibson, J. (ed.), *The Complete Poems of Thomas Hardy* (London: Macmillan, 1976)

Giles, J., *The Parlour and the Suburb: Domestic Identities, Class, Femininity and Modernity* (Oxford: Berg, 2004)

Gilpin Faust, G., *This Republic of Suffering: Death and the American Civil War* (New York: Alfred A. Knopf, 2008)

Gilroy, P., *Postcolonial Melancholia* (London: Routledge, 2004)

Glennerster, H., J. Hills, D. Piachaud and J. Webb, *One Hundred Years of Poverty and Policy* (York: Joseph Rowntree Foundation, 2004)

Bibliography

Gorer, G., *Death, Grief and Mourning in Contemporary Britain* (London: Cresset Press, 1965)

Grayzel, S. R., *Women's Identities at War: Gender, Motherhood and Politics in Britain and France during the First World War* (Chapel Hill, NC: University of North Carolina Press, 1999)

Grayzel, S. R., *At Home and Under Fire: Air Raids and Culture in Britain from the Great War to the Blitz* (Cambridge: Cambridge University Press, 2012)

Grayzel, S. R., '"Macabre and Hilarious": The emotional life of the civilian gas mask in France during and after the First World War', in C. Langhamer, L. Noakes and C. Siebrecht (eds), *Total War: An Emotional History* (Oxford: Oxford University Press, 2019)

Gregor, W., *Notes on the Folklore of the North-East of Scotland* (London: The Folklore Society, 1881)

Gregory, A., *The Silence of Memory: Armistice Day, 1914–1946* (Oxford: Berg, 1994)

Gregory, A., *The Last Great War: British Society and the First World War* (Cambridge: Cambridge University Press, 2008)

Haldane, J. B. S., *ARP* (London: Victor Gollancz, 1938)

Harrison, M., *Medicine and Victory: British Military Medicine in the Second World War* (Oxford: Oxford University Press, 2004)

Hastings, M., *Bomber Command* (London: Michael Joseph, 1979)

Hazelgrove, J., *Spiritualism and British Society Between the Wars* (Manchester: Manchester University Press, 2000)

Hinton, J., *The Mass Observers: A History, 1937–1949* (Oxford: Oxford University Press, 2013)

Holman, B., *The Next War in the Air* (Basingstoke: Ashgate, 2014)

Honigsbaum, M., *Living with Enza: The Forgotten Story of Britain and the Great Flu Pandemic of 1918* (London: Macmillan, 2009)

Howkins, A., *The Death of Rural England: A Social History of the Countryside Since 1900* (London: Routledge, 2003)

Hufton, O., *The Poor of Eighteenth Century France, 1750–1789* (Oxford: Clarendon Press, 1974)

Jackson, A., Y. Khan and G. Singh (eds), *An Imperial World at War: The British Empire, 1939–45* (London: Taylor & Francis, 2015)

Jalland, P., *Death in the Victorian Family* (Oxford: Oxford University Press, 1996)

Jalland, P., *Death in War and Peace: A History of Loss and Grief in England, 1914–1970* (Oxford: Oxford University Press, 2010)

Johnson, N., 'The overshadowed killer: influenza in Britain in 1918–19', in H. Phillips and D. Killingray (eds), *The Spanish Influenza Pandemic of 1918–19: New Perspectives* (Routledge: London, 2003)

Khan, Y., *The Raj at War: A People's History of India's Second World War* (London: The Bodley Head, 2015)

Bibliography

Kübler-Ross, E., *On Death and Dying: What the Dying Have to Teach Doctors, Nurses, the Clergy and their Own Families* (London: Tavistock Publications, 1970)

Langdon-Davies, J., *Air Raid: The Technique of Silent Approach High Explosive Panic* (London: George Routledge, 1938)

Langhamer, C., *The English in Love: The Intimate History of an Emotional Revolution* (Oxford: Oxford University Press, 2013)

Lant, A., *Blackout: Reinventing Women for Wartime British Cinema* (Princeton, NJ: Princeton University Press, 1991)

Laqueur, T., *The Work of the Dead: A Cultural History of Mortal Remains* (Princeton, NJ: Princeton University Press, 2015)

Last, N., *Nella Last's War: A Mother's Diary 1939–1945*, ed. Richard Broad and Suzie Fleming (Bristol: Falling Wall Press, 1981)

Light, A., *Forever England: Femininity, Literature and Conservatism Between the Wars* (London: Routledge, 1991)

Lodge, O., *Raymond, or Life and Death* (London: Metheun & Co., 1916)

Loez, A., 'Tears in the trenches: a history of emotions and the experience of war', in J. Macleod and P. Purseigle (eds), *Uncovered Fields: Perspectives in First World War Studies* (Leiden: Brill, 2004)

Longworth, P., *The Unending Vigil. The History of the Commonwealth War Graves Commission* (Barnsley: Pen & Sword Books, 2010. First published 1967)

Loughran, T., *Shell Shock and Medical Culture in First World War Britain* (Cambridge: Cambridge University Press, 2017)

McKibbin, R., *Classes and Cultures: England, 1918–1951* (Oxford: Oxford University Press, 2001)

Macleod, J., *River of Fire: The Clydebank Blitz* (Edinburgh: Birllin, 2010)

MacNulty, A. S. and W. Franklin Mellor (eds), *Medical Services in War: The Principal Medical Lessons of the Second World War* (London: HMSO, 1968)

Madge, C. and T. Harrisson, *Mass Observation* (London: Frederick Muller, 1937)

Madge, C. and T. Harrisson, *War Begins at Home* (London: Chatto & Windus, 1940)

Marchant, H., *Women and Children Last: A Woman Reporter's Account of the Battle of Britain* (London: Victor Gollancz, 1941)

Mass Observation, *First Year's Work, 1937–38* (London: Lindsay Drummond, 1938)

Mass Observation, *Puzzled People: A Study in Popular Attitudes to Religion, Ethics, Progress and Politics in a London Borough* (London: Victor Gollancz, 1947)

Mayhew, E., *Wounded: The Long Journey Home from the Great War* (London: The Bodley Head, 2013)

Merridale, C., *Night of Stone: Death and Memory in Russia* (London: Granta, 2000)

Bibliography

Middlebrook, D., *Her Husband: Hughes and Plath – A Marriage* (London: Viking, 2003)

Middlebrook, M. and C. Everitt, *Bomber Command War Diaries: An Operational Reference Book* (London: Viking, 1985)

Moore, B., 'Prisoners of war', in J. Ferris and E. Mawdsley (eds), *The Cambridge History of the Second World War. Volume 1, Fighting the War* (Cambridge: Cambridge University Press, 2015)

Murray, W. and A. R. Millet (eds), *Military Innovation in the Interwar Period* (Cambridge: Cambridge University Press, 1996)

Newlands, E., *Civilians Into Soldiers: War, the Body and British Army Recruits, 1939–45* (Manchester: Manchester University Press, 2014)

Newlands, E., 'Man, lunatic or corpse? Fear, wounding and death in the British Army, 1939–45', in L. Robb and J. Pattinson (eds), *Men, Masculinities and Male Culture in the Second World War* (Basingstoke: Palgrave, 2018)

Noakes, L., *Women in the British Army: War and the Gentle Sex 1907–1948* (Oxford: Routledge, 2008)

Noakes, L. and J. Pattinson (eds), *British Cultural Memory and the Second World* War (London: Bloomsbury, 2014)

O'Brien, T. H., *Civil Defence: History of the Second World War* (London: HMSO, 1955)

Omissi, D., *Air Power and Imperial Control: The Royal Air Force, 1919–1939* (Manchester: Manchester University Press, 1990)

Overy, R., *The Morbid Age: Britain and the Crisis of Civilisation, 1919–1939* (London: Penguin, 2009)

Overy, R., *The Bombing War: Europe 1939–1945* (London: Allen Lane, 2013)

Paris, M., *Warrior Nation: Images of War in British Popular Culture, 1850–2000* (London: Reaktion Books, 2000)

Parker, S., *Faith on the Home Front: Aspects of Church Life and Popular Religion in Birmingham, 1939–1945* (Oxford: Peter Lang, 2006)

Parr, H., 'Representations of grief and the Falklands War', in L. Åhäll and T. Gregory (eds), *Emotions, Politics, War* (Abingdon: Routledge, 2015)

Patalano, A., 'Feigning grand strategy: Japan, 1937–1945' in J. Ferris and E. Mawdsley (eds), *The Cambridge History of the Second World War. Volume 1, Fighting the War* (Cambridge: Cambridge University Press, 2015)

Plain, G., *Literature of the 1940s: War, Postwar and 'Peace'* (Edinburgh: Edinburgh University Press, 2013)

Plamper, J. 'Soldiers and emotion in early twentieth-century Russian military psychology', in J. Plamper and B. Lazier (eds), *Fear: Across the Disciplines* (Pittsburgh, PA: University of Pittsburgh Press, 2012)

Price, S., *If You're Reading This: Last Letters from the Front Line* (London: Frontline Books, 2011)

Priestley, J. B., *English Journey* (London: Victor Gollancz, 1934)

Bibliography

Prost, A., 'The dead', in J. Winter (ed.), *The Cambridge History of the First World War. Volume 3, Civil Society* (Cambridge: Cambridge University Press, 2014)

Prysor, G., *Citizen Sailors. The Royal Navy in the Second World War* (London: Viking, 2011)

Puckett, K., *War Pictures: Cinema, History and Violence in Britain, 1939–1945* (New York: Fordham University Press, 2017)

Pudney, J., *Selected Poems* (London: John Lane The Bodley Head, 1946)

Rasmussen, A., 'The Spanish Flu', in J. Winter (ed.), *The Cambridge History of the First World War. Volume 3, Civil Society* (Cambridge: Cambridge University Press, 2012)

Reddy, W., *The Invisible Code* (Berkeley, CA: University of California Press, 1997)

Reddy, W., *The Navigation of Feeling: A Framework for the History of Emotions* (New York: Cambridge University Press, 2001)

Richards, J., *The Age of the Dream Palace: Cinema and Society in 1930s Britain* (London: I. B. Tauris, 1984)

Roper, M., *The Secret Battle: Emotional Survival in the Great War* (Manchester: Manchester University Press, 2010)

Rose, N., 'Assembling the modern self', in R. Porter (ed.), *Rewriting the Self: Histories from the Renaissance to the Present* (London: Routledge, 1997)

Rose, S. O., *Which People's War? National Identity and Citizenship in Wartime Britain 1939–1945* (Oxford: Oxford University Press, 2003)

Rosenwein, B. H., *Generations of Feeling: A History of Emotions, 600–1700* (Cambridge: Cambridge University Press, 2016)

Rothwell, S., *Lambeth at War* (London: SE1 People's History Project, 1981)

Scarry, E., *The Body in Pain: The Making and Unmaking of the World* (Oxford: Oxford University Press, 1985)

Sebag-Montefiore, H., *Dunkirk: Fight to the Last Man* (London: Penguin, 2007)

Sedgwick, J., *Popular Film Going in 1930s Britain: A Choice of Pleasures* (Exeter: Exeter University Press, 2000)

Shapira, M., *The War Inside: Psychoanalysis, Total War, and the Making of the Democratic Self in Postwar Britain* (Cambridge: Cambridge University Press, 2013)

Shephard, B., *A War of Nerves: Soldiers and Psychiatrists, 1914–1994* (London: Jonathan Cape, 2000)

Snape, M., *God and the British Soldier: Religion and the British Army in the First and Second World Wars* (Abingdon: Routledge, 2005)

Snape, M., *The Royal Army Chaplains Department, 1796–1953: Clergy Under Fire* (Woodbridge: Boydell & Brewer, 2008)

Snape, M. and S. Parker, 'keeping faith and coping: belief, popular religiosity and the British people', in J. Bourne, P. Liddle and I. Whitehead (eds), *The Great World War 1914–45. 2. Who Won? Who Lost?* (London: Harper Collins, 2001)

Bibliography

Stargardt, N., *The German War. A Nation Under Arms, 1939-45* (London: Vintage, 2016)

Stockholm International Peace Research Unit, *Incendiary Weapons* (Cambridge, MA: MIT Press, 1973)

Stone, D., 'Memory wars in the "new Europe"', in D. Stone (ed.), *The Oxford Handbook of Postwar European History* (Oxford: Oxford University Press, 2012)

Strange, J. M., *Death, Grief and Poverty in Britain 1870-1914* (Cambridge: Cambridge University Press, 2009)

Summerfield, P., *Histories of the Self: Personal Narratives and Historical Practice* (London: Routledge, 2019)

Süss, D., *Death From the Skies: How the British and Germans Survived Bombing in World War II*, trans. L. Sharp and J. Noakes (Oxford: Oxford University Press, 2014)

Taylor, D., *Last Dawn: The Royal Oak Tragedy at Scapa Flow* (Argyll: Argyll Publishing, 2008)

Thomas, K., *Religion and the Decline of Magic: Studies in Popular Beliefs in Sixteenth and Seventeenth Century England* (Oxford: Oxford University Press, 1971)

Thomson, M., *Psychological Subjects: Identity, Culture and Health in Twentieth Century Britain* (Oxford: Oxford University Press, 2006)

Todman, D., *Britain's War: Into Battle 1937-1941* (London: Penguin, 2016)

Underdown, T. H., *Bristol Under Blitz:. The Record of an Ancient City and Her People During the Battle of Britain 1940-1941* (Bristol: Lord Mayor's Office, 1942)

Ussishkin, D., *Morale: A Modern British History* (Oxford: Oxford University Press, 2017)

Verdery, K., *The Political Lives of Dead Bodies: Reburial and Post Socialist Change* (New York: Columbia University Press, 1999)

Walter, T., *On Bereavement: The Culture of Grief* (Berkshire: Open University Press, 1999)

Whaley, J., 'Introduction', in J. Whaley (ed.), *Mirrors of Mortality: Studies in the Social History of Death* (London: Europa, 1981)

White, J., *Zeppelin Nights: London in the First World War* (London: The Bodley Head, 2014)

Winter, J., *Sites of Memory, Sites of Mourning: The Great War in European Cultural History* (Cambridge: Cambridge University Press, 1995)

Winter, J., 'Forms of kinship and remembrance in the aftermath of the Great War', in Winter, J. and E. Sivan (eds), *War and Remembrance in the Twentieth Century* (Cambridge: Cambridge University Press, 1999)

Zeigler, P., *London at War, 1939-1945* (London: Pimlico, 2002)

Zweiniger-Bargielowska, I., *Managing the Body: Beauty, Health and Fitness in Britain, 1880-1939* (Oxford: Oxford University Press, 2010)

Bibliography

Internet Sources

BBC Archive, www.bbc.co.uk/archive/
BBC People's War website, www.bbc.co.uk/history/ww2peopleswar/
British Pathé, www.britishpathé.com/
Commonwealth War Graves Commission, www.cwgc.org
S. Crook, The Powell and Pressburger Pages, www.powell-pressburger.org/
HMS Dunedin Society, http://www.hmsdunedin.co.uk/
Imperial War Museum, www.iwm.org.uk/
Royal Air Force History, https://www.raf.mod.uk/what-we-do/our-history/
The Yorkshire Post, www.yorkshirepost.co.uk/

Unpublished Papers

Brooke, S., 'Celia Johnson by Bill Brandt', unpublished paper, *North American Conference on British Studies* (Montreal, 2012)

King, L. 'The food cupboard door was a family archive: families and their archives in Britain, c. 1918–50', *European Social Science History Conference* (Valencia, 2016)

Langhamer, C., 'Who the hell are ordinary people?', *Royal Historical Society Lecture* (London, 2017)

Roberts, M. L., 'Five ways to look at a corpse: the military dead in Normandy, 1944', in *The Male Body of War* (forthcoming, 2020)

Todman, D., 'Death in Britain in the Second World War', unpublished paper, *Institute of Historical Research* (London: 2010)

Unpublished PhD Theses

Afxentiou, A., 'The politics and ethics of drone bombing in its historical context' (University of Brighton, 2018)

Lomas, J., 'War widows in British society' (University of Staffordshire, 1997)

Spark, S., 'The treatment of the British military dead of the Second World War' (University of Edinburgh, 2010)

Index

Ahmed, Sara 11, 15n.37
Air Raid Precautions (A.R.P.)
    85–7, 92, 93, 142, 146, 158, 160, 183
Allport, Alan 4, 16n.2, 17n.22, 97n.44, 150n.33, 226n.79
Armistice Day 3, 23, 30, 37, 46, 50–1, 67, 83–4, 156, 245, 250–1, 266
astrology 48, 102, 108–10, 119
Attlee, Clement 77, 250, 266

Baldwin, Stanley 77–8, 79
Barcelona, bombing of 83, 87, 91, 142
Baume, Eric 21–2, 41n.1, 267, 269n.4
Belfast, Blitz 179–82, 184, 186
Bethnal Green, shelter disaster 16n.10, 200, 224n.30
Birmingham, Blitz 146
Bourke, Joanna 18n.36, 19n.49, 42n.40, 69n.14, 186n.4
Bowen, Elizabeth 114, 122nn.50, 51, 231, 258n.10
Bowlby, Alex 130–1, 132–3, 234–5
Brief Encounter 229–31, 258
Bristol, Blitz 126, 141
    funerals 199
    morale 4, 200
    Prayer Service 103

Britain, Battle of 94, 112, 134, 193

Chamberlain, Neville 56, 93, 101, 164, 195
Churchill, Winston 78–9, 243, 265
City of Benares, sinking of 139, 178, 217–18
Clydebank, Blitz 3, 179, 180, 182–6
Coventry, Blitz 3, 141, 176–85, 200
    Cathedral 253–4
    In Memoriam notices 241, 242
    Crucifixion, vision of (1944) 104–6
The Cruel Sea (1951) 140
Cwmparc, air raid 246–7

Damousi, Joy 19n.49, 197, 214, 224n.16, 226n.71, 250, 261n.76
D-Day 118, 130, 168, 202, 216, 220, 245
Douglas, Keith, death of 219
    ZemZem to Alamein 4, 16n.7
Dowding, Hugh 112–14, 120
Dunkirk, retreat to and evacuation from 1, 104, 128, 129, 130, 134, 164–6, 193

El Alamein, Battle of 131
    Cemetery 130, 167, 168
Eton, military casualties 126

Index

Francis, Martin 71nn.56, 59, 96n.24, 108, 117, 122n.33, 123n.63, 135, 137, 151nn.47, 52, 152n.59, 190n.73, 225n.55, 227n.79

Gas Mask Sunday 64, 66, 68, 84
ghosts 114
Glasgow, Blitz 146, 182, 213
   influenza 39
   Necropolis 25
Grayzel, Susan 42nn.29, 42, 43n.46, 72n.91, 96n.28
Guernica, bombing of 81, 82, 83

HMS *Thetis*, loss of 67

Imperial War Graves Commission (IWGC), cemeteries 8, 36, 45, 89, 185, 243–6
   civilian dead 198, 248
   establishment of 35
   role in Second World War 91, 157, 163, 164–7, 171–3, 201–2
influenza epidemic (1918–19) 6, 10, 38–40
In Which We Serve (1942) 118, 205, 208, 230

Jalland, Patricia 12, 15, 19n.41, 19n.48, 24, 27, 33, 41nn.5, 6, 7, 13, 42nn.31, 32, 33, 39, 43n.61, 68n.7, 72n.98, 122n.41, 225n.56

Kingston-upon-Hull, Blitz 103, 126, 141, 146, 198, 236–7

Langdon-Davies, John 82
Langhamer, Claire 10, 18nn.34, 36, 72n.91, 195, 205, 210, 223n.11, 225n.44, 226n.60, 229, 258n.3, 270n.7

Laqueur, Thomas 15, 17n.26, 19n.44, 22, 25, 41nn.2, 4, 10, 11, 43n.44, 95n.59, 98nn.61, 67, 155, 186n.1, 190nn.71, 76
Last, Nella 220, 227n.90, 256
London
   air raid planning 79, 87, 88, 89, 90
   Blitz and other air raids 6, 94, 103, 104, 107, 114, 126, 135, 141, 144, 145, 146, 160–1, 178, 200, 211–12, 236, 249
   influenza pandemic 39–40

Marchant, Hilde 146, 153n.99, 267
Marsh, Eileen 205
   see also We Lived in London
Mass Observation 4, 9, 60–1, 83–4, 102, 104, 105–6, 107, 111, 114–17, 172, 176, 194–5, 229, 254–5, 256–7
A Matter of Life and Death (1946) 207, 230
Merseyside, Blitz 3, 40, 126, 141, 182, 184, 247
Millions Like Us (1943) 118, 205, 209
Mitchison, Naomi 212–15, 222
Monsarrat, Nicholas 140, 152nn.72, 73, 74, 75, 76
   see also The Cruel Sea
Monte Cassino, Battle of 131, 133, 167, 216, 219
morale 3, 7–9, 32, 75, 77, 82, 86, 87, 94, 115, 117, 118, 119, 126, 137, 177, 182, 184, 185, 186, 194–204, 219, 222

national days of prayer 104, 220

Petworth Boys School, bombing of and funeral 173–4, 178, 185
Plymouth, Blitz 126, 143, 184, 205, 247
Pudney, John, *For Johnny* (1941) 206

Index

Remembrance Sunday 250–1

Sandhurst Road School, bombing of and funeral 178–9, 185, 267
Singapore 103, 142, 167, 168
Skinner, Leslie 132, 150nn.29, 34, 168–9, 173, 189nn.50, 51, 52, 53, 54, 202–3, 219, 225n.37, 227n.87
Social Insurance and Allied Services Report (1942) 2
spiritualism 28, 48–50, 102, 111–12, 119, 120
Strange, Julie-Marie 25, 26, 41nn.9, 12, 15, 42nn.17, 18, 34, 35, 98n.61, 174, 190n.77
superstition 15, 48, 102–8, 110, 118, 119, 136

Todman, Daniel 16n.11, 148n.3, 149n.7

Ware, Fabian 34, 91, 164, 198, 248, 251
The Way Ahead (1944) 118
The Way To The Stars (1945) 206, 208, 209, 230
We Lived in London 205, 208, 209
Winter, Jay 15, 19n.45, 38, 43n.49, 49, 69n.16, 191n.87, 232, 234, 259nn.14, 18, 31, 32, 33

EU authorised representative for GPSR:
Easy Access System Europe, Mustamäe tee 50,
10621 Tallinn, Estonia
gpsr.requests@easproject.com

www.ingramcontent.com/pod-product-compliance
Lightning Source LLC
Chambersburg PA
CBHW070818250426
43672CB00031B/2795